J. F. C. FULLER: MILITARY THINKER

J. F. C. Fuller:
Military Thinker

Brian Holden Reid

St. Martin's Press   New York

All rights reserved. For information, write:
Scholarly & Reference Division,
St. Martin's Press, Inc., 175 Fifth Avenue, New York, NY 10010

First published in the United States of America in 1987

Printed in Hong Kong

ISBN 0–312–00828–7

Library of Congress Cataloging-in-Publication Data
Reid, Brian Holden.
J. F. C. Fuller.
Bibliography: p.
Includes index.
1. Fuller, J. F. C. (John Frederick Charles),
1878–1966.   2. Military art and science—Great Britain—
History—20th century.   3. Tank warfare—History.
I. Title.
U43.G7R45 1987   355'.0092'4   87–9819
ISBN 0–312–00828–7

For my parents

Contents

Preface

This book is an interpretative study of the military writings of Major General J. F. C. Fuller. Fuller has fascinated me since I was a schoolboy and I spent many hours while an undergraduate reading his books when I should have been concentrating on worthy treatises on the eighteenth-century Enlightenment or medieval constitutional history. I became impressed then with the idea that Fuller had been unfairly neglected and that a book needed to be written about his military thought to redress the balance. To some degree the pages that follow are the fruit of my undergraduate labours but anybody acquainted with the field of British military thought will be aware that a revival of interest in Fuller was already underway before I began serious research. Fuller now has a biography worthy of him with Major General A. J. Trythall's *'Boney' Fuller: The Intellectual General* (London, 1977) and other historians have added their contributions to our specialized knowledge of various aspects of his career.

Nonetheless, there still remained room for a detailed analysis of Fuller's ideas rather than his career, including only sufficient biographical information to provide the essential background. I have unashamedly fashioned my book after Brian Bond's *Liddell Hart: A Study of his Military Thought* (London, 1977), which in my opinion is a model of how such a study should be written. Newcomers to the subject would be best advised to read General Trythall's biography first; but I have never believed that historians should write for one another; instead they should reach out for the largest possible audience. After I had given my first paper at a postgraduate seminar I received a salutary reminder of this need. Present was an elderly American academic, specializing in contemporary nuclear strategy, who had no knowledge of British history. Having spent years reflecting on the subtleties involved in 'conceptualizing' the algebra of mutual deterrence, non-proliferation and megadeath, he found the problems of the 1930s difficult to cope with. 'Who *is* this guy, Fuller?' he suddenly asked as soon as I stopped speaking. This kind of question usually comes as quite a shock to the youthful researcher, who takes for granted the importance of his subject and hence that knowledge of it is commensurately widespread. Throughout this book I have tried to keep the needs of the non-specialist reader in mind, but this has not been easy given the limits of space and detailed descriptions of background events have not been possible. At any rate, if the non-specialist reader has been sufficiently stimulated to turn to Fuller's own books then my labours have been worthwhile. Certainly the reader will find that the effort is well rewarded.

Captain Sir Basil Liddell Hart, Fuller's fellow military pundit and friend, dedicated his *Memoirs* 'to all who helped', and a study such as this which perforce operates at a high level of generalization, is dependent more than most on the advice, guidance and specialist knowledge of others. In this I have been most fortunate. I was lucky in being among the very last scholars to work at States House, Medmenham, and enjoy the hospitality and stimulating conversation of Lady Liddell Hart. Like many scholars before me, I am deeply grateful to Lady Liddell Hart for numerous kindnesses and much encouragement: she is indeed the hostess who taught scholars. I was also singularly fortunate in enjoying the hospitality of the late Sir Oswald Mosley, who discussed Fuller with me on several occasions at his enchanting home outside Paris. It was a cause of deep regret to me that he did not live to see completed a project in which he took such a lively interest. To Lady Mosley I am indebted for permission to quote from their conversation and several of their letters. Two of Fuller's surviving friends, Mrs Alison Starr and Colonel R. Macleod were most generous with their time and hospitality in attending to my enquiries. Brigadier I. M. Stewart strained his memory to recall for me his days as a GSO 3 at Tank Corps HQ in 1917–18. Miss Jean Overton Fuller went to a great deal of trouble to provide me with her impressions of Fuller in old age. I have also discussed or corresponded about Fuller with Adrian Liddell Hart (Fuller's godson), Professor Lewis Mumford, Mr Anthony Powell, Lady Tuker, Lieutenant General Sir Ian Jacob and the late General Sir Richard O'Connor.

I have unashamedly culled ideas and advice from Major Kenneth Macksey, Dr Howard Bailes, Dr John Ferris, Dr David French, Mr Keith Simpson and Dr Hew Strachan. Professor William Gutteridge and Dr David Carlton have been the source of a great deal of encouragement; so has Professor Peter J. Parish, who kindly invited me to give papers on issues raised by my research at a number of seminars. To Dr John White I owe a

special debt, as it was he who initially encouraged me to undertake
postgraduate research when the auspices were far from favourable.
Times do not change, but this book, for better or worse, is the result
of his ceaseless efforts on my behalf. To Professor Marcus Cunliffe,
I am indebted for his patient guidance of my studies in the
American Civil War, and much else besides. I am grateful also to
Professor Jay Luvaas and Professor Robert Skidelsky for sage
advice. I have also enjoyed the support and encouragement of Mr
A. J. P. Taylor and his wife, Dr Eva Haraszti, though they may be
unaware just how much I have appreciated this. To all my friends
I am deeply grateful for their help over a number of years; though
they may not recall the occasion, I hope they approve of the
result.

Eight papers based on my research were delivered at various
times to the Military History Seminar, the Seminar on Modern
British History and the Seminar on the History of the United
States of America, Institute of Historical Research, University of
London, and the Staff Seminar at the Polytechnic of North
London. The appreciative reception which my ideas received on
these occasions was most encouraging. During the course of my
research I have been treated kindly by the Staffs of the Public
Record Office, the British Library and the Imperial War Museum.
More particularly, I would single out, Mr Edward Skipworth of the
Special Collections Department, Archibald Stevens Alexander
Library, Rutgers University, New Jersey, and Miss Patricia
Methven, College Archivist at the Liddell Hart Centre for Military
Archives, King's College, London; Miss Methven's predecessors,
Miss Julia Sheppard, Mrs Elizabeth Bennett and the former
assistant archivist, Mrs Bridget Malcolm, have all played a positive
part in the enterprise, as did Miss Joanna Connell, who before her
retirement as Departmental Secretary, was always available with
her enormous knowledge of College procedures, to smooth my
path.

I have benefited too from the comments of Professor Sir Michael
Howard and Mr Richard Ogorkiewicz, both international
authorities in their respective fields. Of all my intellectual debts
by far the greatest are to my friends and colleagues, Professor
Brian Bond and Dr Michael Dockrill. Brian Bond's sound common sense punctured my more fanciful notions and tempered a
tendency to take novel ideas perhaps more seriously than some of
them deserved. He has also provided, over the years, a model for

all military historians in his scrupulous and humane scholarship and vast reading. Dr Dockrill has been a steadfast friend over many years, and sometimes a valiant partner in adversity. He has made many wise comments on earlier versions of the typescript with a keen eye for stylistic infelicities and a prudent desire to temper a certain Fuller-like dogmatism that occasionally overtakes me.

As a former Editor of the RUSI *Journal* writing about a Chesney Gold Medallist, it is a great pleasure to thank all the past and present staff of the RUSI who made it such an agreeable place to work, and especially the former Chairman, Sir Clive Rose, from whose many kindnesses I have benefited, and the Director, Group Captain David Bolton, who has continually encouraged me to write and whose unstinting support and wise advice I greatly value. Brigadier Shelford Bidwell has illuminated many a military conundrum with his great learning so lightly worn and his sardonic wit, gently telling me to get the thing finished.

Nearer to home, I am especially beholden to a number of friends, Mr Robin Kershaw, Dr William S. Lee, Mr Michael Pearson and Mr Robert M. Read, who went out of their way to help me during the last frantic scramble. Mr Kevin Drury has steered me through life's pitfalls, ensuring that I am where I should be and that I have not forgotten my head: this book is as much his as mine. My sister, Mrs Linda Fleet, has always been ready to offer help, advice and sustenance. Mrs Sylvia Smither, with her customary zeal and diligence, and no little kidness, coped admirably with the typing of a rather haphazardly organized typescript. It can be safely said that this book would not have been completed without the unflinching support of my parents who have sustained me through so many vicissitudes with wise and earnest counsel and their incomparable generosity. Finally, as I have received so much help from so many quarters, it remains for me to conclude with what I once regarded as a tiresome convention but now realize is the most important statement in any author's preface, that I alone am responsible for those imperfections that remain.

BRIAN HOLDEN REID

Department of War Studies
King's College, London

Acknowledgements

It is pleasing to acknowledge the following who have graciously granted permission to reproduce copyright material. Alison Starr and her literary heirs for permission to quote from the books of Major General J. F. C. Fuller; Lady Liddell Hart for permission to quote from the books of Captain Sir Basil Liddell Hart. To the Controller of Her Majesty's Stationary Office for permission to quote from Crown Copyright material in the Public Record Office; David Higham Associates Ltd, for permission to quote from Fuller's letters to Captain Sir Basil Liddell Hart; Rutgers University for permission to quote from copyright material in their possession; Gordon Grey Esq for permission to quote from the letters of Major General J. F. C. Fuller to Meredith Starr; Editors of *The Journal of Strategic Studies* for permission to use material in Chapter 7, some of which appeared in a different form in an earlier article on Fuller in I (December 1978) pp. 295–312; Editor of *Military Affairs* for permission to use material in Chapter 4, some of which appeared in a different form in an earlier article on Fuller in XLIX (October 1985) pp. 192–7. If I have unwittingly infringed copyright in my honest endeavours, I apologise to those concerned.

B.H.R.

Maps

The Western Front

Source: from endpaper of B. H. Liddell Hart, *A History of the World War, 1914–1918* (London: Faber & Faber, 1934).

Cambrai, 1917

Source: B. H. Liddell Hart, *A History of the World War, 1914–1918* (London: Faber & Faber, 1934) p. 436.

Introduction

The path of nature and of truth is narrow but it is simple and
direct; the devious paths are numerous and spacious; but
they all lead to error and destruction.

Robert Jackson, *A Systematic View of the Formation, Discipline
and Economy of Armies* (London: 1804) p. 136.

Major General J. F. C. Fuller was a prolific writer and a
professional soldier. He was a rare thing in the pre-1939 British
Army, a military intellectual. The intellectual lassitude which is
popularly associated with the Army has led some to suggest that
in Britain a 'military intellectual' is a contradiction in terms.
Nevertheless Fuller was an intellectual; he was passionately
interested in ideas and their development. Throughout his long
life – he died in 1966 in his 88th year, having published his last
and 46th book the year before – Fuller was concerned with
seeking out and employing for practical purposes useful
knowledge. Past military experience bore 'lessons' which had to
be garnered for the soldier preparing for the next war. It is right
and proper that busy professional soldiers should give priority to
that information which is most relevant to preparing for their next
challenge. In Fuller's case, he wrote works of history that despite
their utilitarian character, stand up remarkably well as history.
Professional historians are, however, trained to view the past on
its own terms; that is to say, we must treat the past historically
without distorting our vision of it by deferring unduly to the
preoccupations of the present.

Consequently, although I believe that the ideas advanced by
Fuller, especially in connection with armoured warfare, retain a
continuing relevance, Fuller has been treated throughout this
book as a historical figure, though not, as I hope will become clear
after reading it, a figure purely of academic interest. The
contemporary 'relevance' of Fuller's writing, should become clear
by implication; and only rarely and then in the broadest of terms,
do I consider contemporary preoccupations in relation to his
work. But even the most casual glance at professional military
literature today, at say the pages of the RUSI *Journal* or at

1

Parameters, will show how many of those questions that concerned Fuller in the 1920s have returned to dominate the thoughts of professional soldiers. It is to be hoped that serving officers will be sufficiently engaged by historical parallels to explore Fuller's theoretical works for themselves. If Fuller himself would have disapproved of my excessively 'academic' approach, he would certainly have given his blessing to my desire to be as objective as possible, and not get involved in current controversies. In a recent lecture at the RUSI, John Terraine observed perceptively 'that the historian should get on with his history, as truthfully as he can, without too much finger-wagging, and leave the heads of the Services and the Staff Colleges to ponder what he says and draw their conclusions from it'.[1] My prime concern has been to get my history right, using the wealth of documentation now available to us and the abundant fruits of modern scholarship to reassess Fuller's military thought twenty years after his death.

The longer the passage of time, the more peculiar Fuller's career appears: he promised so much but ended up being offered command of the Second Class District of Bombay. His career is replete with ironies. The Roman historian, Tacitus, wrote sagely that 'The more I think about history, ancient or modern, the more ironical all human affairs seem.'[2] As John Keegan has pointed out, before 1914 Great Britain did not produce a military thinker of the first rank.[3] That after 1918 she produced two, Fuller and Liddell Hart, was perhaps a measure of the trauma that Britain had experienced during the First World War and the depth of feeling that something had gone wrong which had to be remedied before the outbreak of the next war. Both Fuller and Liddell Hart devoted their lives to the study of war and believed passionately that it was a serious subject which required careful study. In this quest Fuller brought formidable gifts. He was the most intellectually gifted soldier ever to serve with the British Army. Liddell Hart said of his friend and colleague: 'I regard you as a true example of genius, a term often misapplied.' 'And', he continued, 'while I do not feel that you are always right I hold that the ideas conceived by your genius have proved right so often as to claim universal respect for any you put forward.'[4] The main problem facing any scholar who attempts to tackle Fuller's prolific writings is to reduce the undisciplined products of his restless and ceaselessly diligent mind to some kind of order.

Throughout this book I have sought to interpret Fuller's ideas generally and relate them to broader intellectual currents – the majority of which flowed past the British Army which protected itself, for the most part, by a granite dam of complacent anti-intellectualism. The supreme irony of Fuller's career is that, despite the expenditure of immense effort, so little of concrete, practical military reform ensued. The American historian Garrett Mattingly, in a striking metaphor, once wrote that 'The boiling torrent of events throws up one foam-capped wave which seems to sweep everything before it, and the spectators cry "A genius!" . . . Here and there, for a moment, a rock resists, then the flood sweeps over it. . . . But the integrity of granite, not less than the fury of rushing water, shapes the final course of the stream.'[5] In Fuller's case the stream merely trickled through cracks in the granite. Compared with the ambitious goals he set himself, his writings failed to move his superiors. Fuller himself was partly to blame. Not only did he occasionally reveal lamentable judgement but he rarely gave those who disagreed with him even the benefit of the doubt. His writing on the British conduct of the First World War was scathingly critical. His sardonic wit could be merciless. Long after the Battle of Waterloo a British general noticed the Duke of Wellington writing in the margins of an account of the battle 'L' and 'DL'. On enquiring what this meant, the general received the blunt answer: 'Lie and Damned Lie, to be sure'. The moral of this anecdote is more than worthy of Fuller's scepticism. To pursue the analogy. Fuller was nicknamed 'Boney' because of his admiration for Wellington's adversary, Napoleon. Like Napoleon he lacked prudence.

A further irony is that of *déjà vu*. Despite the neglect of his writing during his own professional lifetime so much of what Fuller sought to achieve has now become commonly accepted. Consequently it is sometimes difficult to recall how novel his ideas were at the time and the strong reactions they sometimes provoked. One of his favourite themes was that 'The tools of peace are the weapons of war', and it was ridiculed; 'by these words', he explained, 'I did not mean, as certain people suggested, that soldiers should fight with the hammers and axes of workmen, but that military power derives its strength from civil industry.'[6] Today no soldier would need an explanation of the metaphor, certainly the presumptious 'educator' (as Education Officers are known in the Army) would not be thanked for offering one. Thus it needs to be asserted confidently at the outset that Fuller *was* an original thinker. His predecessors, like J. F. Maurice and G. F. R. Henderson, wrote cogently and sometimes perceptively about tactics but they rarely strayed from this narrow path. Fuller tried to discuss the problem of war in the broadest possible way and tried to link tactics with the fundamental forces that determined the conduct of war. In attempting this task he had virtually no guidance from previous military writers and little in the way of scholarly military history to support his assertions (except for the writings of Sir John Fortescue and Sir Charles Oman); consequently Fuller himself supplied the necessary historical surveys. If his basic approach to the subject of war is compared with the general intellectual outlook of the age which prevailed in many other spheres, then Fuller's originality seems less conspicuous and can be compared with the views of other thinkers. This is not to detract necessarily from Fuller's originality, only to point out that 'originality' itself is only relative, as men's views are shaped by intangible forces which are not easy to pin down with any degree of precision.

Fuller has thus been considered as a thinker with the widest possible terms of reference. I have not sought to quote every item in Fuller's work that proves his prescience because I have assumed that it could withstand detailed probing. Indeed his writings do have an integrity and an inner unity comparable with sophisticated writings in other spheres of thought, and this was achieved despite the fact that Fuller had, until 1933, pursued a busy military career, wrote only in his spare time, and had never enjoyed the advantage of, say, a university lectureship, to provide congenial surroundings for writing. Nevertheless it is important to detach any discussion of Fuller's ideas from the influence of his brilliant autobiographical writings which have influenced other historians to accept Fuller's picture of himself at his own valuation. The criticisms of the inconsistencies and vagaries of Fuller's writings that follow are not due, in so far as comparison is possible, to the possibility that military thinkers are any less able or penetrating than their peers in, for instance, economics or psychology. Comparable flaws inevitably appear in any courageous and ambitious treatment of the great forces that determine the fate of mankind, and certainly no more so than in war where ideas must be translated into action. 'I do not ask for faith in my ideas, but what I hope for', Fuller once wrote, 'is creative criticism.' This study has sought to provide creative criticism in a positive spirit.

As Fuller was a man of many parts it has not been possible, within the limits of the available space, to cover all the areas in which he involved himself. There is ample room for more specialized studies of subjects which have only been touched upon here in relation to their general impact on Fuller's ideas. A more detailed discussion of the controversy over the importance of mobility *vis-à-vis* firepower would be welcome; as would a lengthier examination of his ideas about training (a neglected area of British military history), and his ideas on the need to reform the Army as an institution, an aspect which would involve a more detailed discussion of his active military career. Neither have I assessed Fuller's historical writings, except when his books, like those on the American Civil War, have an important relationship with his theoretical works; for the same reason considerable attention has been devoted to his writings on the Second World War. On the other hand, the problem of 'influence' has not been considered in detail. It is better to establish what Fuller's thinking on any subject actually was before considering his influence.

As this is basically a study of intellectual history with a military character, considerable space has been allocated to an exposition of Fuller's personal philosophy which did so much to shape his approach to war. This has required study of subjects which do not usually come within the compass of military history (or indeed any other branch of scholarly history), such as the occult and related subjects like mysticism. I have managed to resist the temptation to become an expert in the occult. The problem of Fuller's authoritarianism has also had to be assessed. Though there can be no doubt that his association with the British Union of Fascists was the greatest blunder of his career, it must still be recalled that throughout this period many influential writers advocated similar ideas with comparable overtones.[7] However detailed his study of attitudes and prejudices, the historian of ideas nonetheless should not claim too much for his perceptions. Bernard Crick's wise cautionary words deserve careful thought. 'None of us can enter another person's mind; to believe so is fiction.' Whatever connections may be made, it is not possible to get 'inside' Fuller's mind, as 'however much we know there is no inevitable inference from these antecedent facts to what someone

actually writes.' Fuller was far too complicated (and private) a
person for any claim that we know what made him 'tick' to be
averred. An explanation can be attempted to draw links between
various ideas and their interaction; but it is only an explanation
and not clinching proof.[8]

The range of Fuller's work has presented difficulties. I do not
pretend to have a fraction of my subject's mental agility or range
of interests. For example, I have no specialized knowledge of the
Indian sub-continent. The only possible approach has been to
deploy the fruits of modern scholarship in all kinds of diverse
fields to examine and test Fuller's assumptions and the validity of
his theories. Of course, to some of the questions he poses there
are no exact (or easy) answers, only a series of hypothetical
possibilities. Given such a field – virtually the entire history of
war from antiquity to the present day – the range of issues posed
by Fuller's writing is virtually limitless. 'Historical research',
Alistair Horne once warned, 'is like a moving stair case; one thing
is certain, that when you come to the end you will have journeyed
far from your starting-point.'[9] This has certainly been my
experience and will be shared by others setting out to unravel the
military writings of J. F. C. Fuller.

Any attempt to organize Fuller's ideas must nevertheless convey
their prodigality. He was extravagant with ideas, and these
sometimes flowed from his pen too hurriedly and with varying
degrees of utility. Like all men of great ability his views were a
mixture of good and bad. Some themes recur in his writing. So
that a balance can be maintained these have not been analysed as
soon as they appear in Fuller's books; they have sometimes been
deferred for a fuller discussion when they have matured. This
method allows an analytical approach to convey more accurately
the flavour of Fuller's writing. As Liddell Hart wrote to Fuller in
1928, 'I have come to the conclusion that your conceptions owe
less to logical processes than to inspiration, and that you are apt
to use the former in a subsequent stage to explain the latter.'[10] He
was surely right even though the remark was equally applicable
to himself, or, for that matter, to most thinkers who dwell deeply
on a subject and feel strongly about the issues that lie before
them.

1

The Evolution of a Mind, 1878–1914

Oh Mahatma, what is truth?

Fuller to Mahatma Gruno Swamji, 1906

Turgenev once said that it was possible to be original without being eccentric; it is perhaps more likely that an original mind is an unconventional mind, wayward perhaps and certainly reluctant to follow existing patterns of thought or modes of conduct. After his military career was over Fuller was inclined to put his failure down to his reputation as an 'unconventional soldier', the intellectual who had aroused the ire of the orthodox and the time server. This initial chapter, which is not a detailed biographical survey of Fuller's career before 1914, is an attempt to survey the development of his mind, to analyse his reading and to assess the most important influences on his thinking before the outbreak of the First World War. Some general conclusions can be drawn about Fuller's 'unconventionality' and the attitude of the British Army to the military intellectual.

John Frederick Charles Fuller was born on 1 September 1878 in Chichester. His father was an Anglican cleric, then Rector of Itchenor. Fuller shared with Liddell Hart a religious background. His parents were intelligent and cultured; Fuller was close to his indulgent mother, Thelma, née de la Chevallerie, a strong personality who encouraged him to think things out for himself. As a small child Fuller gave no hint of any exceptional intelligence. In modern parlance he was a 'late developer'. Boredom would appear to be the keynote of his childhood. Fuller was a dreamy, sensitive and introverted child. The rote system of learning at his dame school in Chichester bored him and he preferred to take long country walks in thoughtful solitude. Throughout his life Fuller never responded to the stimulus and competition of organized learning; on the contrary, he always seemed to react against it. Following a brief sojourn in Switzerland, he attended Malvern College, which he detested. When grandfather de la Chevallerie (who lived in Leipzig) suggested that he be placed in the Army Class, Fuller was so immersed in reading *The Three Musketeers* and *The Count of Monte Cristo* that he seems to have offered no opinion on this decision taken about his future. So it was on the strength of a family whim that Fuller found himself in 1897, after attendance at the customary London crammer, ensconced at Sandhurst.[1]

The Royal Military College was at least a relief from Malvern and endless Latin conjugations, and Fuller began to show an aptitude for working on his own, seeking out those books that *he* wanted to read. Although the syllabus demanded that cadets study Philip's *Manual of Field Fortification* and Clery's *Minor Tactics*, he discovered that the latter 'was nothing like so instructive as Hume's *Tactics*, published years before, and which I read in its place'. The senility of the lecturers was at least a source of diversion. One was so deaf that if an audacious cadet asked him: 'Please, sir, may I come and kick your bottom?' back would come the stentorian reply, 'Come to me afterwards boy; come to me afterwards'. It can be safely said that the Sandhurst system of instruction left no permanent mark on Fuller except to show, to paraphrase the Duke of Wellington, how war should not be taught.[2]

In 1898 Fuller passed out without distinction, was gazetted to the 1st Battalion Oxfordshire Light Infantry (43rd) and joined his regiment at Mullingar in Ireland. He was bored by the daily routine here also, and while the majority of subalterns took advantage of the splendid opportunities for hunting and fishing, he spent most of his time reading. Fuller was entirely self-educated. Although his early attempts at widening his intellectual horizons were haphazard his restless curiosity was instinctively drawn towards the great controversies of the day. The most important was the last round of the great theologico-Darwinian debate. It has been well said that 'no one born after about 1880 could realize how terrible this conflict for faith had been'. The certainties of Victorian religious faith had been destroyed and had been replaced by a fascination with unconscious and psychic phenomena. This fascination with the non-logical and the inexplicable was to play an important part in Fuller's life.[3]

It was a gradually increasing interest in evolutionism that

shaped Fuller's intellectual outlook more than anything else. He recalled in his *Memoirs* that 'I soon became immersed in Huxley, Lecky, Samuel Laing and other rationalist writers. This, in turn, led to my first attempts in writing being heterodox.' Writing to his mother while still at Sandhurst Fuller judged that 'the world is mad, absolutely mad'; he explained some months later that he disliked materialism: 'the generality of people are cold, unfeeling, unloveable. And why? simply because Mammon bosses the show'. Fuller was already affected by post-Darwinian religious doubts and had become an agnostic. He confided to his mother that though it might 'seem funny . . . not to say ridiculous' that he should think about these matters, 'but if we are ever to think about them the sooner we begin the better, for then our ideas have a longer time to develope [*sic*] themselves'. Confidence in his own judgement is already striking. Fuller also thought instinctively in deductive terms, building upwards: 'In ten years time my ideas may have completely changed but what I think, and read now will surely in some way form a foundation.'[4]

The young Fuller preferred reading to socializing. He was a serious and grave young man, brooding and aloof. His active mind from the first was impatient with the clichés of conventional wisdom and instinctively questioned their validity. He was the opposite of the gregarious extrovert: 'going out' was a rare (and not always welcome) indulgence – a major departure from routine. This was unfortunate. Greater social intercourse might have lent Fuller's severe views a flexibility and humanity that they too often lacked. When his mother urged him to go to dances he retorted that he could not believe that he would become narrow; he made good use of his time by reading books as every 'dear friend' that he read reassured him that 'you have not wasted your time'; 'which is the best [*sic*] this or mixing with that clicking, gobbling set of apes and turkeys . . . [?]' In this, as in so many matters, Fuller went his own way and did not profit by it.[5]

Some clues can be found as to the direction of this early reading. In 1898 Fuller read *The First Philosophers of Greece*, a book which contains all the surviving fragments of Heraclitus of Ephesus, to whose terse pronouncements Fuller later attached considerable significance. Indeed so astonished was a brother officer when he discovered Fuller reading this book that he ran off to report this unhealthy development to the regimental surgeon. Heraclitus fascinated several nineteenth century philosophers, notably Hegel and Lassalle. Lassalle, author of a book on Heraclitus's ideas, was later an influence on the young Oswald Mosley. Oswald Spengler, a thinker whose massive *The Decline of the West* (1926), was later an important catalyst on the outlook of both Fuller and Mosley, completed his Ph.D. thesis on Heraclitus's thought. His chief sayings were: 'Men should know that war is general and that justice is strife. Good and bad are the same. War is the father of all things and king of all.' What seems to have impressed Fuller was Heraclitus's juxtaposition of opposites (like good and bad) and the notion that life was subject to constant change and, of course, his belief that war was the fountainhead of change – 'king of all things'. Thus at the beginning of his career, Fuller identified himself with a major intellectual current, and one that owed little to the democratic, empirical English tradition.[6]

The Boer War temporarily freed Fuller from the 'flunkeydom' – the rituals – of British regimental life and he was able to acquire some satisfaction as an independent intelligence officer scouring the *veldt*. He later wrote a book about his experiences based on his diaries, *The Last of the Gentlemen's Wars* (1937). The fundamental paradox of Fuller's military career was that he eventually excelled in a profession which ill-suited his temperament. He had the character and outlook of an artist. As a boy Fuller seems to have harboured an ambition to become an artist, but he did not press this desire on his family and acquiesced apathetically in their choice of a career for him. This artistic side to his character certainly accounts for his egotism: he could be 'difficult' and displayed what senior officers branded 'prima donna' antics. His interest in art remained strong throughout his formative years. He had a remarkable sense of colour and his imagination was of the graphic, visual kind. Art, he wrote in 1902, 'seems one of the few things worth living for[,] for to me it breathes love'. Once Fuller had decided to make the most of his military career he absorbed a great deal of the military ethos, but this always lodged uneasily with his artistic sensibility. His pictorial imagination heavily influenced the development of his written style, which was characterized by ornate and vivid imagery. Of the journey out to Cape Town in 1899 he was later to recall, 'That night I first noticed the phosphorescence of the sea, the wash of the waters glowing like myriads of opals from the bow to the stern of the ship, and then dying away in a faint ghostly sheen of silver.'[7]

The Boer War marked the first important phase in the

process of Fuller's self-education. During these years something approaching 200 volumes found their way into his hands. Analysis of some of these titles is instructive. An interest in Carlyle was already evident before Fuller left for South Africa, as he read *Sartor Resartus* in 1898, followed a year later by *Heroes and Hero Worship* and the *History of Frederick the Great* in 1902. He also devoured Laing's *Problems of the Future* and *Human Origins*, Darwin's *Descent of Man* and Freeman's *History of the Norman Conquest*. These were garnished by some serious fiction like Thackeray's *History of Henry Esmond, The Virginians* and *Book of Snobs*, Jane Austen's *Northanger Abbey* and Tolstoy's *Resurrection*. From 1899 onwards religious books hold his attention. These included Laing's *A Modern Zoroastrianism*, Allen's *Evolution of the Idea of God*, Arnold's *Death and Afterwards* and *Science and the Christian Tradition*, Wiedemann's *The Ancient Egyptian Doctrine of the Soul*, and 'Saladin', *Why am I an Agnostic?* 'The true religion of Christ', he concluded, 'has but yet a very small footing in the world.'[8]

Fuller continued to read widely in philosophy. He read Paul Carus's *A Primer of Philosophy* and Kant's *Dreams of a Spirit Seer*. An interest in science is noteworthy and titles like Laing's *Modern Science and Modern Thought* are found in his notebooks. An interest in art is confirmed by the listing of *The English Pre-Raphaelite Painters* and Cartright's *The Early Florentine Painters*. As for history, *The Secret Memoirs of Napoleon*, *The Life of George Napier*, Carlyle's *Letters and Speeches of Oliver Cromwell* (a special favourite at this time), and Sir Edward Creasy's immensely influential, *The Fifteen Decisive Battles of the World* were all consumed by Fuller's voracious literary appetite. It might be added that not all of Fuller's reading was intellectually demanding. He liked potboilers such as *More Gal's Gossip*, Conan Doyle's Sherlock Holmes stories and sentimental yarns like *Lorna Doone*, which he judged 'one of the prettiest stories I have ever read'.[9]

Fuller reflected seriously on what he had read. After reading Carlyle's *History of the French Revolution*, which he considered 'very splendid and awful', he speculated that man is but a 'veneered brute' and once the veneer wore off, man's latent savagery 'springs forth' in all its ghastly ferocity. This view of man's inherent animalism was fortified some months later when Fuller thought he had discovered the full implications of Darwin's Theory of Evolution. 'I am a believer in Darwin and Evolution[,] the whole theory is so grand, so beautiful and true.' He then

turned to Wall's *Darwinism and Race Progress* and made some
jottings on the universal application of the theory. Further grist to
his Darwinist mill was provided by a study of two books by the
Social Darwinian, Benjamin Kidd, *The Control of the Topics* and
Social Evolution.[10]

Hitherto thinking about the nature of war had not been one of
Fuller's priorities. The Boer War gave his intellect a jolt in this
direction. Reflecting on 'Black Week', the week before Christmas
1899, when British forces in South Africa were disastrously
defeated, he claimed that 'Slap dash and bang may be all very
well sometimes but that it constitutes war is obviously ridiculous';
he doubted whether 'there is one officer out of a dozen'
whose military education extended beyond the names of their
commanding generals. 'War as everything else nowadays is
reduced to a science.' However, beyond stating this claim –
obviously the fruit of his recent reading – Fuller did not yet
venture. He was also of the opinion that 'mobility is of crucial
importance' – a theme which was to dominate his thinking about
modern war.[11]

His view of the Army, notwithstanding his comments about
'Black Week', remained strictly conventional. Indeed he believed
that the Boer War had vindicated the British officer. 'I have
noticed it myself that the best sportsmen make the best officers
. . . a certain amount of intellect is of course necessary to keep
step with the scientific principles of modern warfare but animal
cunning and courage hold the first rank still.' Such platitudinous
observations, which Fuller quickly forgot that he had ever made,
did not make regimental life any more palatable. Life in South
Africa had been bearable because he had been free of its
restrictions. 'I can do almost what I like and am quite my own
master, can go anywhere, everywhere and anyhow', he told his
father. He did not look forward to returning to regimental duty
and he contemplated joining the South African Constabulary. As
leaving the Army was an uncertain prospect for an impecunious
young subaltern, Fuller decided against resigning his commission
though he admitted candidly that the Army was 'no profession'.[12]

The second phase of Fuller's self-education began in India,
where the 43rd were stationed at Simla in 1903. Here he was first
exposed to those mystical currents that were of such decisive
importance in determining his later outlook and which are closely
associated with the ideas of G. I. Gurdjieff. Fuller now subscribed

to Socrates' motto: *know thyself*. He began to develop a personal philosophy around the 'Law of Three', which enabled the mind to control phenomena by securing itself by self-knowledge: 'what we perceive as matter is in reality . . . our own sensations, our own mind; . . . I form the axis, the pole . . . and it is my inherent duty to see that this axis is based on a firm support irrespective of other minds.' His creed was now 'self-knowledge, self-reverence, self-control', and in it we find the origins of Fuller's fascination with the number three and his interest in yoga which 'enables one to maintain a sense of proportion and so release oneself from the thraldom of trivialities'.[13]

As the station officer during Fuller's time at Simla, Colonel (later General Sir) Beauvoir de Lisle recalled, 'To anyone who loves sport, India is a paradise.' Fuller was now less inclined to agree that 'the man who excels in sport excels in War', and had other ideas on how to spend his time. His isolation from the regimental world was now complete. He lacked any commitment to that feeling of camaraderie which dominated the regimental outlook. But a high degree of eccentricity is tolerated in the Army and nobody appears to have obstructed Fuller in his desire to go his own way. It is certainly difficult to visualize Fuller taking part in the mess larks, especially 'sacks to the mill', in which subalterns were thrown on top of one another so that it was impossible 'to get away from the deluge'.[14]

Indeed Fuller was attracted to intellectual currents which flowed against the establishment. He began to write poetry in the style of Swinburne. Although he did read such sober volumes as Milman's *History of Latin Christianity*, Gibbon's *Decline and Fall of the Roman Empire*, and Lecky's *History of European Morals*, his reading also included such unusual titles, for a soldier, as Havelock Ellis, *Studies in the Psychology of Sex*, Huston, *A Plea for Polygamy*, Rosenbaum, *The Plague of Lust*, *The Blight of Respectability* and Westermarck, *The History of Human Marriage*. His views on sexual morality became radical at a time when there was a marked increase in prudery. He admitted frankly that 'it is this question of sexual freedom which at the present moment interests me more than any other'. In this and in his denunciation of Victorian prudery and the need to tear off the 'mystic fig leaf . . . and stand naked and sublime in all the glory and consummation of perfect Nature', Fuller revealed himself as a most unconventional officer.[15]

It was while in India that Fuller first contacted Aleister Crowley,

writer, magician and notorious self-publicist. He saw an
advertisement offering £100 for the best essay on Crowley's works
published in the 'Travellers Edition', and 'on its arrival, I decided
to try my luck' – an indication of the extent of his leisure. Such
were the origins of Fuller's first book, *The Star in the West*. The
completion of this substantial piece of writing brought Fuller into
contact with an entirely new world when he returned to England
in 1906 – as far removed from the military as can be imagined.
Fuller won Crowley's prize and the two men became fast friends.
Crowley convinced Fuller 'that materialism . . . was thoroughly
unsatisfactory as an explanation of the universe'. Fuller had
attached himself to an intellectual fringe that was intrigued by
Oriental mysticism and disillusioned with Christianity and modern
industrial democracy. Before 1939 these groups were largely right
wing in political complexion. Other British officers – for example
Lieutenant Colonel Francis Yeats-Brown – had associated
themselves with such gatherings. None have gone so far as Fuller
in identifying himself with a civilian group of unconventional
intellectuals and misfits. His behaviour does not seem quite so
idiosyncratic if Fuller is viewed as a misplaced intellectual who
happened to be in the Army. Many other intellectuals experienced
similar yearnings as Fuller and were attracted by the likes of
Aleister Crowley. What is significant is not so much the fact of
Fuller's friendship as its date – the very point when his interest in
military affairs was at its nadir.[16]

There can be little doubt that Fuller was, for a time at least,
intoxicated by Crowley. He was to later claim that 'the most
extraordinary genius he ever knew was Crowley'. The pages of
The Star in the West teem with acclamations of Crowley's genius as
he is seen throughout as a super-man. The most important feature
of the book lay not in its contents but in Fuller's *synthetic* design.
He intended to synthesize the highest qualities of all other
religions and evolve a new philosophy of life. He claimed to find
the genesis of this eclectic system in the symbols of Crowley's
mystical poetry, and it was thus termed Crowleyanity. Another
notable feature was the importance he attached to equilibrium, or
balance. Fuller followed Hegel (and some of the ancient Greeks)
in believing that change was endemic in the universe: 'Change,
change, no stability', he declared. Dynamic forces were always
counter-balanced by those of resistance and their juxtaposition
secured a form of dynamic equilibrium. A crucial stage was

reached in Fuller's development when he grasped the importance of reconciling contradictions, what Crowley called the reconciliation 'in one harmonious symbol [of] all the antimonies'. This process of thesis, antithesis, synthesis – Gurgjieff's Law of Three in philosophical form – lay at the bottom of Fuller's theoretical approach to war and it was begotten of these early spiritual explorations. 'It is through the balancing of opposites that work is accomplished', he wrote later, 'and not through similarities.'[17]

Though still highly regarded by admirers of Crowley, *The Star in the West* is little more than a curiosity today. Its subject, a man of monumental vanity, thought highly of Fuller's effusive praise; 'for a better representation of the whole of my writings in symbolic form I cannot imagine'. To those who are more sceptical of the depth and veracity of Crowley's talents, Fuller's stylistic extravagances and the intractability of the subject render *The Star in the West* virtually incomprehensible. He was rather embarrassed by it in later life, judging the book 'A jumble of undigested reading with a boyish striving after effect. Written in the execrable English of a public school educated subaltern.'[18]

In 1906 Fuller married Margarethe Auguste Karnatz, known throughout her life as Sonia. Resident in Hamburg, the Karnatz family originally came from Poland. The consummation of the second important relationship of his formative years marks an appropriate moment to pause and consider the development of his character. His marriage revealed little of his earlier sexual radicalism. Fuller sought out and found a lifelong mate, but if the marriage had proved unhappy he would have had no compunction in divorcing Sonia whatever the social consequences. Sonia was beautiful and graceful. She was not an intellectual but an able housekeeper who enjoyed gardening. Fuller married her for precisely these qualities. A wife, in his view, was for 'quiet times' and he never discussed with her politics or military affairs, except in the vaguest terms. She played no positive part in the evolution of his thought. Neither was she interested in the occult or the macabre. Shortly after his marriage Fuller became absorbed in mystical experiences. In 1907 he recorded one of these:

For ten minutes result nil. Come down. Try again, projecting well forward. At once millions of moving stars dull green appear overhead. Behind them could be seen bright gold specks like stars on a dark night.

> The Dull Green stars form a kind of vortex ring, out of which emerge[s] a brilliant mass which gave me the idea of own obscure form . . . and then turns green. The ring grows clouds and fumes off smoke. Purple.
> Come down.

Sonia was only anxious as to why Fuller 'used to shut himself up in a room saying he must not be disturbed', and as he did not enlighten her she turned to Fuller's friend, Meredith Starr, for advice. Her influence was totally negative. She confirmed Fuller in his prejudices and suspicions and pandered to his intellectual vanity. Her cantankerous defensiveness alienated friends and relatives and increased his isolation and estrangement from the world around him.[19]

This sense of alienation is an important ingredient in the make-up of the prophet. Fuller denied in later life that he had ever been a prophet: that his latter day admirers were trying to present him as Old Mother Skipton and Nostradamus all wrapped up in one – something of an exaggeration. In truth there was always something of the missionary in him: did he not announce the dawning of Crowleyanity? Alison Starr, Meredith's wife, felt that there was something ethereal about Fuller – that somehow 'he was not fixed on the earth'; he had an urge to find open space and gained pleasure from standing on the tops of hills or mountains; while standing over the earth he would experience sudden inspirations. In 1911

> on one exceptionally hot day I was standing not far from the Martello tower overlooking Sandgate Hill, when along came the 52nd in full war paint. Somehow the sight of those decked out, sweating men horrified me . . . in an instant I decided to work for the Staff College.

Fuller also felt a compulsion to tell the truth as he saw it and this feeling was related to a marked idealism. In 1903 he tried to 'love the good in mankind and try to remedy the evil, and when one's time has come to mingle with the infinite – be able to say "I have left the world the better for my short span of life's existance [sic]"'; though his view of mankind would alter Fuller was not to be deflected from his ideal of living a productive life.[20]

Occasionally Fuller evinced scepticism about the occult but he shelved his doubts and joined with Crowley in attempting to 'convert' a hysterical Cambridge undergraduate, Norman Mudd, to their way of thinking. These efforts were unwelcome to the Cambridge authorities and the two men were banned from University premises. Fuller's faith in Crowley was still great enough for him to risk public exposure and ridicule. This Cambridge connection had however a more beneficial influence on Fuller. In 1909 he first met the poet Victor Neuburg, another Cambridge man, at the home of the agnostic writer William Ross Stewart, 'Saladin'. It was probably this circle that introduced to him the full implications of the writings of Herbert Spencer, whose works he had first begun to study in 1905. Spencer had drawn the crucial analogy from his study of Darwin's writings that institutions could be likened to the organs of the human body. It was he who had coined the resounding phrase, 'survival of the fittest'. Spencer had also added intellectual weight to an idea that appealed to Crowley and his followers, namely, that 'science' included an unknown dimension, the 'unknowable'. In his seminal work, *First Principles* (1862), Spencer argued that there was a fundamental harmony between the 'most abstract truth contained in Religion and the most abstract truth contained in Science. . . . Uniting these positive and negative poles of human thought'; but no matter how much progress was made in discovering new knowledge, the 'Unknowable' always remained beyond reach. Thus the idea of God as wonderful and mysterious confronted rationalists with a barrier of unreason and upheld an 'outer' with an 'inner' world representing the two related sides of mankind's existence. In later life Fuller could not resist the temptation of trying to penetrate this barrier and explain the influence of the unknown factor on the known and his notion of 'science' included the resources of 'hidden wisdom'.[21]

Fuller's work can therefore be related to a powerful intellectual current flowing in the years 1880–1930 and directly be compared in method and outlook to the writings of P. D. Ouspensky, Gurdjieff's pupil. Both these men adapted Gurdjieff's methodology for their own needs. The middle of the nineteenth century had witnessed the development of all-embracing philosophical systems based on assumed laws of development operating through all the various forms of phenomena. This philosophical model continued to exert influence well into the first third of the twentieth century. Spencer, according to John White, undertook the staggering task of coordinating and synthesizing all existing scientific knowledge into a single coherent system, a cosmic or synthetic philosophy, tracing the operation of the law of evolution throughout the whole of nature and society.

It was a similar heroic undertaking that fired Fuller's imagination after 1918 – to synthesize all knowledge about war into a grand theory founded on evolutionism. Spencer had cast aside the empirical, English inductive tradition preferring a deductive system. His readers were thus committed to a system, a particular point of view, before they opened one of his books. Of this Fuller could only approve and he would endeavour to follow Spencer's example.[22]

But what did Fuller mean by science? One of his earliest coherent definitions can be found in *The Equinox*, a review started by Crowley, which catered for the wide interest in the occult evident at the turn of the century. Fuller reluctantly contributed a serialized magical biography of Crowley and two short stories. (He was convinced that *The Equinox* was one of Crowley's adventures in publicity, a forum for publishing his 'own works rather than a review'.) In this biography he claimed that science 'advances by means of accumulated facts and consolidating them, the grand generalization of which merges into a theory when it has been accepted by universal inference'. Science was thus viewed as 'organized order' in which methodology was rather more important than the nature of the subject matter under consideration. Fuller certainly felt that method was the most important avenue towards discovering 'truth'. 'Truth is truth', Fuller wrote, 'and the Truth of yesterday is the Truth of today and the Truth of today is the Truth of tomorrow.' In this quest for truth Fuller never learned that one man's truth is another man's half-truth and yet another man's untruth, for truth beyonds in the realm of the unknowable: as Tacitus says, 'truth is surrounded by mystery'.[23]

The Equinox also revealed Fuller's disdain for the conventional academic mind (and one which he would never lose) which he accused of pedantry; and he was dismissive of the 'stuffy cloisters of medieval learning' he found at Cambridge. Knowledge was only of value when it could be useful, and he was attracted to the writings of William James who popularized this idea. He also thought highly of Kant's *Critique of Pure Reason*, and claimed that though it was difficult reading, the student who persevered would feel 'as if you were in a brilliantly lighted room'. This autodidacticism, though evidence of a sturdy independence of mind, had one important result: Fuller's intellect grew in haphazard and undisciplined bursts. If Fuller had attended a university and met more men of comparable ability, his extravagances might have been hammered by discussion and undergraduate intercourse into a more prudent shape. Perhaps he would have learned to tone down his tendency to take arguments to extremes. It is also possible that he might have become more conventional and intellectually less adventurous.[24]

Fuller's fascination with scientific fact-finding as the basis of a body of useful knowledge shows the influence of positivism. It is unlikely that Fuller read August Comte's *Positive Philosophy* but his mental attitudes were conditioned by a climate of opinion shaped by it. Thus he concurred with Comte's view that the physical and social sciences were governed by identical forces and could be treated in the same way. In addition, he absorbed the ideas of Benjamin Kidd and Karl Pearson as to the need for order, efficiency and discipline in the administration of all departments of state. This Edwardian vision of a technocratic elite of functional men was widely popularized in the years immediately before the First World War and, in Fuller's view, was thoroughly justified by the inept leadership shown in that chaotic conflagration.[25]

Fuller's friendship with Crowley was ruptured in 1911, ostensibly over a salacious libel case which involved Crowley and threatened Fuller with public exposure; but he had already tired of Crowley's childish egotism and the break was final; he had outgrown 'the Beast'. The abruptness with which Fuller terminated his friendship with Crowley serves as a useful juncture to estimate the influence of his occult activities on his military thought. It is important to distinguish between the mystical, philosophical currents that influenced Fuller profoundly and the magical antics he undertook with Crowley, the casting of spells and other paraphernalia with which he flirted for five years. For though he abandoned magic for ever after 1911 he never shook off its vivid vocabulary. His writings are littered with occult analogies. For example, as he was attracted to the occult because 'it exalts the human will above its usual limits', he readily saw warfare as a clash between the wills of the contending generals and later made a direct comparison between the commander who sought to impose his will on his enemy thus 'entering the world of magic; and when the magician sets out to impose his will on his victim he steps into the kingdom of war'. As Fuller placed so much faith in self-mastery, the overcoming of fear, the opposite of this, the stimulation of fear, was an obvious military objective. 'I see the horns of the Morning Star glow over this fire shot kingdom of Mars. Here I see a return to the medieval Devil – the terror of the world unseen but well furnished by the imagination of terror-stricken man.' Fuller's study of the occult added lustre to his pictorial imagination, and when he turned to the serious study of war he was wont to see it in dramatic, almost apocalyptic terms as he searched for symbols 'of the strange oneness of peace and war, of the conflict of man with nature and man with man' amid the destruction and factory methods of modern war.[26]

Fuller's association with Crowley had improved his literary skills. Crowley's claim in his memoirs that he had taught Fuller how to write was an exaggeration, but it is true that by the time he began to circulate articles to military journals he had served a useful, if unusual, literary apprenticeship. Neither was Crowley's influence in the military sphere altogether unfortunate because he introduced Fuller to Lieutenant Colonel F. N. Maude. Maude directed Fuller to the writings of Clausewitz and Napoleon, and acted as a kind of intellectual mentor – the fourth important influence on his formative years. Fuller repaid Maude's kindness with life-long gratitude. He had already studied *The Military Maxims of Napoleon* (1901) in South Africa. In 1909 he undertook to read the entire *Correspondance de Napoleon Ier* and his theoretical deductions from the *Correspondance* form the bricks and mortar of his military thought which filled out the foundations and framework laid down by his reading in philosophy. Napoleon was a dynamic genius who had a compelling fascination for Fuller. Napoleon's willpower was tremendous, for he 'supposed that events could be made' and that he could 'master the world by will alone' – he was in truth a super-man, another example of that elusive breed who entranced Fuller. Napoleon's genius was above all practical; he was largely self-educated; when in 1808 he instructed his librarian to form a portable library of 1000 volumes, he issued instructions a year later that these books be scrutinized to 'suppress anything useless in them'.[27]

From Napoleon's proscriptions Fuller drew together the diverse elements of his emerging military philosophy. It was Napoleon who brought to his attention the paramount importance of new weapons: 'The nature of the arms decide the composition of the armies, of the plans of the campaigns, of marches, of positions, of camping, of fortified places.' He also took from Napoleon the idea that it was the mind of the opposing commander that was the truly decisive point, for on his 'genius, character and talents' could plans be based. The Emperor also hinted at the psychological importance of the rear attack. And Fuller took to heart Napoleon's warning that 'one bad general is better than two good ones'. Command had to be unified. A close reading of the *Correspondance* contributed to Fuller's suspicion that there existed in war, as in life in general, some kind of basic formula of first principles. The Emperor was tantalizingly vague: 'Every enterprise should be conducted according to a system; chance alone can never bring success.' But what was this system? Napoleon did not say, except to add, 'Military science consists in calculating all the chances accurately in the first place, and then in giving accident exactly, almost mathematically, its place in one's calculations.'[28]

Another point made by Napoleon, which fitted in neatly with Fuller's general philosophical stance, that the troubles and doubts of life thrown up by a harsh fate beyond our control – the 'outer' life – could be conquered by securing the powers of the mind – the 'inner' life – was the relationship the Emperor divined in war between the defensive and the offensive. In other words, those elements that could be controlled in war and those that could not. This connection was expounded by Napoleon in terms that Fuller never tired of quoting: 'Tout l'art de la guerre consiste dans une défensive bien raisonnée, extrêmement circonspecte, et dans une offensive audacieuse et rapide.' This intimate relationship, the blending of opposite forms of war, indicated the immense importance of reserves 'to intervene at the critical moment . . . when the battle is ripe, at the point which the preliminary fighting had disclosed as the vulnerable spot'.[29]

Colonel Maude had written three books on Napoleon's campaigns, and what he had to say paved the way for Fuller's own estimate of Napoleonic warfare. Maude had also read Spencer and he provided the young Fuller with a preliminary basis for the study of the use of evolutionary concepts in the treatment of warfare. Perhaps Maude's most important legacy was the notion of economy of force, as he argued that Napoleon's primary aim *'was to economize the drain on the State by curtailing the duration of the*

campaign'. Maude underlined the importance of the time factor in
Napoleonic warfare. He asserted that the intellect was valueless in
war unless coupled with willpower. Then he pointed to the
importance of Clausewitz: 'War becomes a duel between the will
powers of the opposing leaders, and the victor would be the man
who not only concentrated the greater force at the decisive point
but the one who exercised the greater force of will.'[30]

Fuller had been involved with the Territorial Army since 1906
and volunteers rather than hidebound regulars stimulated him to
think and eventually write about military problems. His early
efforts at military writing were part of a much wider military
'renaissance'. Attempts after the Boer War to reform the Army,
and the publicity given to the Elgin Commission of Inquiry into
the conduct of the war in South Africa, and the Report of the
Esher Committee, all contributed to a desire to make the Army
more professional and to increase the intellectual attainments of
officers. The Army experienced 'a great outburst of professional
keenness', and at the Staff College 'a new spirit' was discerned as
the 'lessons' of the Boer War were digested. Fuller's interest in
war must be related to these developments. At first he experienced
some difficulty in getting his work accepted, and in the 1950s
discovered '100 old articles . . . returned . . . as unacceptable'.
Eventually he found a forum in *The Army Review*. His early essays
reveal an admirable thoroughness and attention to detail, and
already he was stressing the need for 'careful and scientific
preparation'. In 1913 Fuller published his first military book, *Hints
on Training Territorial Infantry*. It was favourably reviewed. The
sensible thesis of this book was that it was on the quality of
training in peacetime that soldiers succeeded or failed during
wartime.[31]

Fuller's early ideas embraced the importance of firepower and
emphasized that all training schemes should seek to relate every
tactical movement to the effect of fire on the attacking troops with
reference to the use of ground. They also show an interest
in arranging ideas in threes. The influence of Napoleon's
Correspondance was patent when he claimed that weapons were of
two types, projectiles and those for close quarters fighting: 'As
these two kinds are improved so do tactics change.' These
comments augur well for the future, but Fuller's discussion of
tactics in this book rarely rose above the commonplace as he
remained firmly wedded to the conventional wisdom then

prevailing concerning the moral power of the attack. This body of ideas is closely associated with Ferdinand Foch, then superintendent of the *école de guerre*, and held that if troops were sufficiently determined their assault would be victorious whatever the defensive firepower they faced. Though Fuller understood the importance of firepower, because of his adherence to the Foch school, he drew erroneous conclusions about its effect on mobility. Indeed, in view of Fuller's later contemptuous treatment of Foch's theories, the reader cannot suppress a smile when he encounters such statements as: 'At effective ranges troops advance steadily and rapidly suffer less than when they remain lying down under cover.' And that in retreat losses were heavier than in the advance. The tactical object was 'demoralizing the enemy by fire and assaulting him with the bayonet'. All this was nonsense. It was therefore misleading of Fuller to suggest in his *Memoirs* that because 'I had taken no interest whatever in things military . . . my brain was not lumbered up with conventional military doctrines . . . so far as the subject of war was concerned, I could start with a clean slate, and was in no way impeded by having to unlearn, which is far more difficult than learning.'

When shorn of the rhetoric of the *offensive à outrance*, some of the points made in *Hints on Training Territorial Infantry* can be recognized as foreshadowing Fuller's mature ideas. He underlined that 'To make war is to attack, therefore no defensive operations, if possible, should be purely passive' – a clear portent of his interest in the defensive–offensive. He also argued that 'a determined and steady advance has the greatest effect on the nerves of the defenders.' The main problem, though Fuller was yet to appreciate it, was to find a means whereby such a movement could be protected. He also recommended that advances should be carried out 'by small bodies suddenly moving forward by rushes of 20/30 paces to avoid fire' – and not in long lines. So Fuller did, to some degree, realize what some of the tactical consequences of firepower would be even though he failed to think through its outcome adequately.[32]

This book is also interesting because it offers us a glimpse at the development of Fuller's deductive methodology. He attached great importance to the 'rapid assimilation and co-ordination of facts'; he knew what he wanted to do, or thought he did, and sought out evidence to support his theory. He did not look at all the evidence to discover a theory. Fuller believed that tactical problems should be solved by dividing the work into three stages: the seeking out of knowledge, its application, and finally criticism to discover 'whether the work accomplished is of the best; if not then what imperfections are due to faulty application or faulty knowledge itself'. The first stage included mastering the principles of war. He did not as yet say what these were. The second stage involved an assessment of the ends and means available. The means were the men and weapons at hand, and the end the conditions of time and place; these had to fit the circumstances which surrounded them. Then followed criticism in the third stage: 'we make a change here and a small improvement there, earmark our shortcomings, so that they may not occur again, and throw our successes distinctly on a clear background'. In this method can be discerned the germ of what later came to be called 'operational research'. Fuller did not invent this procedure but he was certainly one of its earliest and most assiduous pioneers.[33]

Fuller's second military book, *Training Soldiers for War*, also combined fallacious Fochian tactical commentary with an impressive modern mindedness on training methods. He started from the premise that training soldiers was as much a science as an art. If the principles that determined man's character could be discovered then an efficient training system could be evolved. Without insight into psychology, training was bound to fail. He found a precedent on this score in the achievements of Sir John Moore who had successfully developed the natural abilities of soldiers through compassion and self-respect; Moore spurned fear and brutality as counter-productive and destructive of morale. This book also includes an interesting example revealing how Fuller remembered and made practical use of his reading. He took his definitions of soul and mind – those forces which shape man's instincts and thought patterns – from Paul Carus's *Primer of Philosophy* which he had read during the Boer War. He used this to develop a thoughtful thesis that a soldier's character was founded on his thoughts and instincts as 'manipulated by his spirit, which though in action is dependant upon bodily senses cannot exist apart from them'; hence in training these thought processes and reflexes could be bombarded and shaped to produce a martial spirit – morale.[34]

Stress on the value of psychology in preparing soldiers for war was quite novel in the British Army before 1914 (and indeed after). In general the Army exhibited a chronic and misplaced prejudice against any kind of scientific man management, and in this bias it reflected the values of British society. *The British Journal of Psychology* was only founded in 1904, and in the entire British Isles there were only six lectureships in psychology and little in the way of experimental facilities. Fuller was thus forced to rely on French military writers who used psychological methods, such as Grandmaison and Maud'huy. These writers, though confirming Fuller in his *offensive à outrance* reasoning, introduced him to the ideas of Gustave Le Bon. Fuller read Le Bon's *The Psychology of the Crowd* in translation. Le Bon reflected the drift of turn of the century with an emphasis on the irrational forces that controlled mass behaviour. Fuller employed Le Bon's arguments and applied them to military conditions. He contended that crowds were swayed by hereditary instincts: 'its acts are always extreme . . . and depend upon the suggestions it receives'. As a combination of minds did not lead to a pooling of intelligence but rather to a diminished collective intelligence, a crowd was impulsive, mobile and irritable, 'blindly following example, it falls an eager victim to such as use exaggeration, affirmation and repetition'.[35]

Then Fuller drew a distinction between the military crowd and the civilian crowd. The former he considered homogeneous because of the influence of military training and the subordination of the individual's desires to the will of his commander; the amorphous mass of the civilian electorate was a heterogeneous crowd because it was not harnessed by any unifying bonds. Fuller defined a military crowd as 'a mass of men dominated by a spirit which is produced by the thoughts of each individual being concentrated on one image or idea' – namely the will to win. As armies were governed by the same impulse as heterogeneous crowds, 'under the stress of war . . . [they are] ever tending to revert to . . . crowd form'; the object of training was to reduce the time this process took. The object of battle, Fuller now concluded in an original and provocative passage, was not so much the destruction of individual soldiers but the disintegration of the organization of masses of soldiers. Order and discipline could be maintained so long as military crowds maintained their organization. Once this was broken armies would revert to crowd form and become subject to the caprice of their instincts and be swamped by fear and confusion.[36]

If an officer was humane and conscientious then he could forge a relationship with his men that allowed him to understand their

behaviour and win their confidence. During the Boer War Fuller
had wished that the Army 'were a little more Democratic[,] and a
little more pliable and less narrow'; and he had played cards with
his men because British officers were 'a great deal to[o]
uninteresting for me'. In *Training Soldiers for War* he reminded
officers that their men were only human; new recruits would
encounter difficulties in adjusting to military life. They should not
be left idle, but amused as well as instructed, for idleness sowed
'the seeds of desertion, drunkenness and petty crime'. It should
also be recognized that bullying and vindictive methods were
counter-productive. Fuller recommended methods of instruction
that were both simple and amusing; 'make the men laugh;
complexity prevents concentration; make the men comfortable'.[37]

Efficient training methods demanded the evolution of a coherent
training doctrine, which should permeate every soldier's act 'until
it becomes an integral part of his spirit, his moral'. Obedience was
thus the product not of fear but of understanding, and Fuller
argued forcefully that the initiative of individual soldiers should
be developed. 'Discipline is no longer literal obedience but
intelligent obedience, for discipline aims at obedience coupled
with activity of will.' Thus an instructor must reason with his men
and *explain* the reasons for training procedures 'and show them
how to apply their training, how to use the ground, how to turn it
into a shield, and how to advance rapidly under its cover.' It
followed that training of officers should be improved, and Fuller
devoted a whole section to this problem in *Training Soldiers for
War*. He advocated a cordial relationship between officers and
men; officers should investigate their living conditions as soldiers
rarely complain openly; 'we should speak to them as if they were
our equals, but never as if we were theirs.' This was a radical
doctrine but its tactical context should not be forgotten, as Fuller
drew upon the ideas of the *offensive à outrance*. Grandmaison, in
particular, urged that 'we must never leave a stone unturned to
cultivate an offensive spirit'.[38]

The last phase of Fuller's intellectual development began with
his arrival at the Staff College in 1913. He viewed this as an
escape from 'drilling turnip headed recruits' and the tedium of
regimental duty. Only three of Fuller's Staff College essays
survive. The first was entitled 'The Tactics of Penetration' and he
trailed his coat suggesting, as had Napoleon, that tactics were
based on weapon-power and not on the generalized lessons of

military history. In the next war British tactics should be based on the machine gun and the quick firing field gun. Thus, 'The commander who first grasps the true trend of any new, or improved, weapon will be in a position to surprise an adversary who has not.' This seemed to be the authentic voice of Fuller and he went on to make some acute observations. He predicted that the 'rapidity of fire of the modern field gun' would be so great that ammunition could be massed 'opposite a decisive point, so that the guns commanding this point . . . may pour a continuous and terrific deluge of shells . . . and so enable the decisive attack to proceed against it.'[39]

This trend towards favouring the artillery was hastened by Fuller's first visit to the artillery shooting range at Larkhill, Salisbury Plain, which, followed by a close reading of *The British Officers' Reports on the Russo-Japanese War*, opened his eyes to the true value of artillery. He foresaw that artillery would become the 'superior arm' and battles static; entrenching would become widespread and infantry would merely follow the overwhelming power of the artillery bombardment. 'This logically leads to penetration in place of envelopment as the grand tactical principle of the attack, because freedom of movement will be limited by wire and field works.' These two papers were frostily received. Fuller was ordered to report before the Commandant, Brigadier General Lancelot Kiggell, later Haig's Chief of Staff, to explain himself. In the presence of a chief instructor, Lieutenant Colonel (later Major General Sir) F. B. Maurice, 'putty nose Maurice', as Fuller was later to denounce him, he was told sternly that he should study the *Field Service Regulations* more closely, that envelopment and not penetration would dominate in the next war and that infantry and not artillery would be the main arm. Despite this show of authority Fuller remained unconvinced.[40]

In his *Memoirs* Fuller quoted from these essays to show that he was untainted by Staff College orthodoxy. This was not entirely true. Fuller was thinking for himself but within strictly defined parameters. For example, the *Field Service Regulations* made reference to principles of war but failed to define them. Fuller worked out six of his own and used them in a third essay, a comparison of the Battles of Salamanca (1812) and Chancellorsville (1863), in an area where the *FSR* provided no guidance. These were discussed more fully in *Training Soldiers for War* which was completed at about this time. The first principle, that of objective,

was 'the point where the army may be most decisively defeated;
generally this point is to be found along the line of least
resistance'. The second was the principle of mass, or concentration.
Supporting these two leading principles were four others:
offensive, surprise, security and movement (rapidity). Expanding
and clarifying this list was to exercise Fuller's imagination for
more than a decade. He defined the art of war as 'imposing one's
will on the enemy – of reducing him to such a state of
disorganization and demoralization that he is unable to strike out
or guard himself'. This analysis was sensible and clear headed
but it was the means by which Fuller sought to dislocate the
enemy that was erroneous. He held that 'men may be slaughtered,
they may be annihilated, but they *will* not be conquered, and *to
will success* is but equivalent to victory'. His perceptive points
about artillery and the machine gun ('a nerveless weapon') were
vitiated by his false premises, since he failed to appreciate their
defensive strength and considered them exclusively as adjuncts to
the attack. He still lavished praise on the offensive spirit and
viewed the bayonet as 'the symbol of victory'. Yet it is symptomatic
of the stultifying intellectual atmosphere of the Staff College
before 1914 that these tentative steps away from official orthodoxy
were stamped upon. Fuller was warned that 'it was not the
business of the student to amend the book, but to study it'. His
work was 'lacking in military judgement'. Another telling phrase
used to attack him was that his ideas were 'dangerously unsound'.
Years later Fuller recalled the Commandant, Kiggell, saying, '"In
the next war we may expect very, very heavy casualties". In this
he was certainly right, but I do not think he helped to reduce
them.'[41]

Fuller was a demanding student, strident in criticism, doubtless
truculent in discussion, he never adapted easily to the discipline
of formal education. It is unlikely that any pre-1914 teacher, not
even Henderson himself, would have satisfied him. Yet Fuller
was right to condemn a system of instruction which lacked
intellectual freedom and where students were apparently eager to
accept 'the correct' procedures without demur. But Fuller always
exaggerated his objectivity and the years before 1914 were no
exception. He had perceived some valuable insights into the
character of the forthcoming war but still not shaken off the
influence of the *offensive à outrance*. It is thus an exaggeration to
claim, as did General Haking when he met Fuller in 1916, that

'This is the fellow who predicted how this war would be fought, and was sat on at the Staff College for doing so.' What is undeniable was that Fuller had developed a system whereby he could easily adapt his military thinking in accordance with 'first principles'. As he later put it, 'I was forging a piece of mental machinery wherewith I could thresh the grist from the chaff of the conventional theories of war.'[42]

But could Fuller switch this 'threshing machine' off? A contemporary recalled that he 'possessed a brilliant brain, but [his] . . . critical faculty was so highly developed that it was apt to get out of control'. His experience before 1914 had given him an incomparable breadth of mind and whetted his appetite for 'truth'. Though Fuller might have been an unconventional officer in his single minded pursuit of experience and enlightenment in all kinds of diverse fields, his thought was still in the crysallis stage; what turned him into an unconventional *soldier* was the persistence with which he demonstrated 'truth' to the Army. His attachment to 'truth', as he saw it, was a potential weakness because it reinforced a tendency to take arguments to logical extremes. Eventually this attachment would alienate those soldiers who, though inclined to agree with him, placed their faith in a higher loyalty, the Army. To such men Fuller's loyalties seemed too capricious and egocentric for comfort. But in 1914 Fuller was not yet an entirely individual military thinker. The First World War was to complete this transformation.[43]

2

The Genesis of Armoured Warfare, 1914–18

. . . he felt a heightened discontent with the wearing futility and enfeebling strain of a demand for excessive retention and dexterity without any insight into the principles which form the vital connections of knowledge.

George Eliot, *Daniel Deronda* (Harmondsworth, 1967 edn),
p. 220

Fuller says that as he has progressed from a Brigade through Division and Corps up to Army he finds intelligence progress [*sic*] in inverse ratio. The higher you get up, the more stupidity and incompetence you find.

Extracts from Letters Written in France during the Great War by Major C. L. A. Ward-Jackson to his wife, 1915–1918 (unpublished typescript), 20 August 1916, p. 320

The First World War provided Fuller with opportunities rarely offered to a staff officer to put his ideas into practice. This chapter will attempt to assess the development of Fuller's tactical ideas. The most important event of Fuller's life took place during the First World War: his assocation with the infant Tank Corps. In developing tank tactics in their infancy he had to overcome a problem that had frequently bedevilled theorists, how to make their ideas actually work; to ascertain the degree to which new ideas could be translated within the limits of technological reality. The tank was a new weapon with no antecedents in modern warfare and certainly no precedents on which to base a doctrine for its tactical employment. Fuller's ingenuity and formidable energy were tested by the challenge posed by this novelty. The years of the First World War, after a frustrating start, were the most successful of Fuller's career. He entered it an opinionated but obscure captain bordering on middle age. When the war ended he was already an international figure with a formidable reputation.

The state of Fuller's thinking before the outbreak of war was neatly summarized in an essay entitled, 'The Procedure of the Infantry Attack' published in the RUSI *Journal* in 1914. He reduced war to its essentials and postulated that battle focused on a duel between missile and shock weapons on the one hand and the protective shield on the other – ground which he had previously covered in *Hints on Training Territorial Infantry*. The shield, he wrote, 'reappears in modern warfare under the much more complex forms of cover from sight and cover from fire'. In a prophetic footnote he observed, 'The reappearance of the shield proper in modern warfare, now used by artillery, is interesting, and may lead to a further reintroduction of this essentially defensive weapon.' The duty of missile weapons was to ward off shock, but Fuller still persisted in arguing that projectiles served merely as a prelude 'to the master blow, the fight at close quarters'; and he again repeated the unhappy forecast that soldiers 'may be annihilated, but they cannot be subdued'. The foundations of Fuller's tactical outlook had nonetheless been laid. He understood the relationship between the offensive and the defensive, the mobile and the stable elements. He had also reached the conclusion that the enemy should be demoralized because 'it is not the effect produced by the arms themselves on the bodies of men, but the impressions which these arms make on their minds, which determine the conditions of modern warfare.' In 1914 he looked to artillery as the chief means of creating this dislocation of the mind. As for the advance itself, 'Advancing in long lines is unfavourable to cohesion, and is conducive to the premature opening of fire', he wrote once more. The attack could be divided into four stages, the approach, demoralization, decision, and annihilation. He attached the greatest importance to the last stage.[1]

Fuller began the war as a Deputy Assistant Director of Railway Transport at Southampton, a position acquired on the strength of his article on the entrainment of troops in the 1912 manoeuvres, and one that was most unwelcome to him. Moving to Dartmouth, he was put in charge of the disembarkation of the Canadian Corps. The vicissitudes of these early endeavours gave him a chance to show his mettle as an organizer of no small insight. He was then posted as a General Staff Officer grade 3 (GSO 3) to the

The Western Front

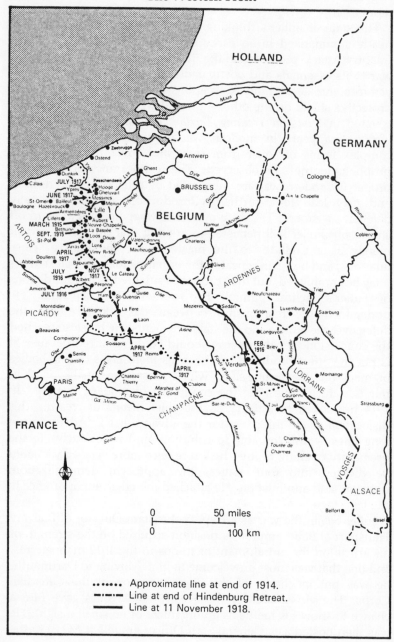

.... Approximate line at end of 1914.
–·–·– Line at end of Hindenburg Retreat.
———— Line at 11 November 1918.

Second Army at Tunbridge Wells. This frustrating posting spared Fuller from the decimation of the professional officer corps about to begin at the First Battle of Ypres. While at Tunbridge Wells Fuller addressed himself without enthusiasm to organizing various evacuation schemes, including all alcohol in Kent and Sussex and the sheep population of the South Downs, the hysterical by-products of the German invasion scares of 1914–15. When Fuller pointed out to his eccentric GOC, Brigadier General Du Cane, that the removal of millions of sheep would block the roads, the General suggested putting up signs: 'Sheep Must Not Use this Road'. Fuller's retort, that most sheep could not read, was not welcomed. 'Drink and sheep settled', he recalled, 'I was left with virtually nothing to do.' So he returned to his studies of training. He immersed himself in Sir J. F. Maurice's edition of *The Diary of Sir John Moore* and Sir John Fortescue's *History of the British Army* and produced a book called *Notes on the Training of the New Armies, 1799–1805*. This work and an article distilled from it, forms the first substantial evidence of Fuller's developing technique whereby lessons were deduced from the past to teach soldiers of the present about the needs of the future. Revised in 1923–4 this book was later published in two volumes. Frustration agitated Fuller's temper and already by 1915 that truculence which took little account of rank had come to the fore. He took the opportunity to tell Du Cane 'exactly what I thought of all this wicked waste of time', but doubted whether 'it will make much difference as he is too incompetent to realize his own ignorance and stupidity.' Relief, and a posting to France, did not arrive until July 1915.[2]

Perhaps the most important signpost for the future direction of his thinking appeared in an essay published before Fuller had seen service on the Western Front. This was a revision of one of his Staff College essays, 'The Tactics of Penetration'. Fuller's premise was that the foundation stone of any engagement was grand tactics – the art of planning and fighting battles. Grand tactics, Fuller asserted, was 'that part of the art of war which links strategy to fighting tactics, the movement of men's legs with the movement of their arms'. He then went on to suggest that tactics should be based on an appreciation of weapon-power. An efficient utilization of weapons could compensate for a numerical deficiency, an argument to which he would return with renewed confidence after 1918. He pointed out that all the great soldiers of the past had based their tactics on the weapons they employed.

Wellington, for example, had consistently employed a successful defensive-offensive, 'the soundest method ever employed by a General whose weapons were the muzzle-loading flint-lock and the smooth-bore cannon'. This argument does not reckon with the difficulty of gauging the potential accurately of every weapon immediately and employing it during peacetime. It was easy for Napoleon or Wellington to gauge the weapon-power at their disposal because it had not changed drastically since Marlborough's day. It has been justly observed that 'Fuller's ideas were too late, too difficult to integrate and too much of a minority opinion to have any effect.'[3]

Fuller also argued that if the British defences could be strengthened by machine guns, troops could be withdrawn from the front and training for the decisive attack could be intensified. When the offensive opened it would be possible to punch a hole on a narrow but decisive sector of the German front. Artillery and machine gun fire could support the movements of the infantry. Penetration could be facilitated by German tactics: their reliance on tactical envelopment and an obsession with holding ground for its own sake. These arguments went unheeded not only because of the practical difficulties (where were all the machine guns to come from?), but also because opinion was turning against the idea that firepower was decisive, and was inclined to put more faith than ever in the moral power of the attack. Also, as Tim Travers has pointed out, 'the lack of officially-encouraged methods and institutions for promoting change meant that it was effectively discouraged.' British officers continued to display a lamentable ignorance of firepower. During the Battle of Neuve Chapelle (10 March–22 April 1915), for example, one battalion of the 8th Division was ordered to close a gap of 500 yards which could easily have been covered by a single machine gun.[4]

These comments were part of a general thesis that the British Army should seek a decision on the Western Front. Fuller was a convinced 'Westerner': 'if only we had the Gallipoli army here instead of wasting it on a crazy enterprise', he wrote soon after arriving in France in 1915. Later he was critical of the Salonika expedition. The war demanded the concentration of all available resources at the decisive point – France. That said, Fuller found much to complain about in the *way* these resources were being used. He was not impressed with the muddled British trenches. 'There are heaps of gentlemen in our army', he confided to his diary, 'but very few officers (?.5%)[;] there are plenty of men but deuced few are really soldiers.' He wrote home that conscription was inevitable in order to produce enough men to withstand the German 1916 offensive which he predicted correctly would fall on Verdun. Victory, he claimed, could be snatched by that side which made the most effective use of its quick firing artillery and machine guns, for whichever side 'can throw the greatest number of projectiles against the other is the side which has the greatest chance of winning.'[5]

These early impressions confirmed Fuller's view that the method of conducting the war could be improved by clear thinking and dispassionate analysis. This required a return to first principles to prepare the ground for detailed staff appreciations. Principles, as Fuller understood them, were grounded in evolutionism. 'One can predict certain events in war as surely as Darwin could in life directly he grasped the fundamental principles of evolution.' Some of the muddle along the Western Front could be overcome if the war effort was rationalized by a more 'scientific' approach. Putting his thoughts together Fuller produced an ambitious essay on the principles of war. He began by complaining that there was a complete lack of any clear guidance to the formulation of strategy in British writing, which was true enough. As he wrote privately, 'whilst every science is run on a few definite principles, war today should [not] be run on the dice-box theory of luck'. If a number of principles related to those that governed other sciences could be defined, then strategic planning could be clarified. Fuller's solution to the problem is an exceedingly interesting one because it is his first attempt to introduce Spencer's ideas into the study of war. In *First Principles* Spencer had argued that phenomena 'are interpretable only as the results of universally co-existent forces of attraction and repulsion'. Fuller projected this idea into the realm of war by suggesting that battles represent action on the part of one combatant followed by the reaction of the other. Accordingly, as Spencer had insisted that 'the law that motion follows the line of least resistance or the line of greatest traction or the resultant of the two' governed all phenomena, Fuller interpreted this in tactical terms to mean that an attacker must seek out the line of least resistance to his own movement and that of the greatest difficulty to the counter-movements of the enemy.[6]

Although considered impressive at the time, Fuller's exposition of the principles of war in this essay is, understandably, rather clumsy, as he was tackling a subject virtually ignored by other authorities. He defined eight strategical principles: the objective, offensive, mass, economy of force, movement, surprise, security and co-operation. He added to these three *tactical* principles, demoralization, endurance and shock. He was vulnerable to the criticism that his division was meaningless if, as he conceded, both groups were not mutually exclusive, and that, for example, endurance had a strategical as well as a tactical importance. Fuller's comparison of warfare with other sciences was as yet tentative. Unlike physics, chemistry or engineering, in warfare, he pointed out, the surroundings were unstable. All the more reason then 'to hold fast to the sheet anchor or principle rather than to be tossed about in a tornado of doubt hit here and there by the lightnings of supposition'.[7]

The operation of Fuller's principles in the field depended on the relationship between pressure and resistance and the vital need to gain surprise. He commented on the command of the sea being 'a great seducer' from the principles of war though nonetheless vital. But as the principles of economy of force, movement and endurance did 'not favour one stupendous assault, which like a magnet will draw towards it every available reserve that the enemy is able to muster', he advocated a dual attack along the Arras/Namur–Rheims/Namur axis. 'The danger of such a detachment', he warned, 'is that it introduces a complexity, and consequently requires high leadership and expert staff work.' This was not forthcoming. The primary object of the attack was to secure the German artillery line. The destruction of the enemy's weapon-power rather than numbers of his men should be the primary object. Once the artillery had retired, the infantry would be forced to retreat with it. Nevertheless force would have to be concentrated for the decisive blow as 'only mass . . . will produce a force sufficiently self-sustaining' to break the German defences. Concentration should not be achieved at the expense of surprise however, as 'it is useless pushing in vast numbers of men on a narrow frontage, for the simple reason that by doing so the principles of security and endurance are so rudely violated as to nullify the result'. Objectives must be limited; unlimited objectives only led to the premature exhaustion of the men, lack of cohesion and the exposure of vulnerable flanks to counter-attack. The infantry should be methodically engaged in echelons and not thrown into the attack in unwieldy torrents. Once committed the infantry could demoralize the enemy with the aid of machine guns and supporting infantry fire, 'which should cover attackers as guns and light infantry did a century ago'; trench mortars, grenadiers and sharpshooters would gain a new importance. So would initiative in the attack, and Fuller urged again that the instilling of alertness, 'intelligent obedience' and not blind obedience, should become a crucial part of all training schemes.[8]

In this preliminary foray Fuller employed the conventional tactical framework as he found it to make some shrewd observations on the procedure of the infantry attack. Especially praiseworthy was the importance he placed on weapon-power. During the period between the Battle of Neuve Chapelle (March–April 1915) and the Battle of the Somme (July–November 1916) no attempt was made in the British Army to reappraise systematically infantry tactics in the light of the challenges posed by trench warfare. At Neuve Chapelle the objectives allotted to the infantry were unlimited and the attack ground to a halt due to its unwieldness, the soldiers 'packed like salmon in the bridge-pool at Galway, waiting patiently to go forward'. As Fuller had predicted, individual machine guns were able to dominate a locality, but no special measures were taken to defeat them. At Aubers Ridge (July 1915) 'infantry artillery' were added to individual brigades, mainly three pounder Hotchkiss guns and trench mortars, but this was an ephemeral reform. Haig believed that conventional infanty tactics would suffice once artillery tactics were so improved that the German defences would be smashed and the infantry made 'every effort . . . to press forward and gain as much ground as possible in the first rush'. No central guidance on the development of infantry tactics was thought necessary, and no General Staff pamphlets issued. Some individual commanders working on their own greatly improved the training of their individual formations.[9]

It is not surprising that Fuller, working entirely on his own and without command experience, lapsed occasionally into repeating tactical clichés uncritically. He had not thought through his arguments sufficiently to see that the day of the bayonet was over. 'The intimate co-operation of machine guns, trench mortars, grenadiers and sharpshooters will render the attack with the bayonet overwhelming', he wrote. The bullet was 'but the escort of the other arms until the act of decision begins'. Indeed given his perverse disposition it is possible that Fuller might have shed this conventional wisdom quicker if he had received central instruction in it, than if he had been left alone to repeat it in his early writings.

As he believed that the pursuit was the crucial tactical act, his reasoning as to how this should be brought about was feeble. His proposal that the BEF should form an Old Guard on Napoleonic lines was quite impractical. His ideas about the maintenance of the advance show that, though he understood the value of the machine gun in the British defences, he failed to grasp the defensive potential it offered to the Germans. It was not enough to urge that the attack 'be driven home without intermission day and night . . . so that . . . [it] may gradually work forward until the endurance of the enemy is broken down,' for as Haig was to discover, these were clarion calls which made no mention of the endurance of the attackers.[10]

Much of Fuller's writing at this date was Janus-faced. While stressing the importance of new weapons he still could not throw off entirely the influence of Foch and Grandmaison. Nevertheless his ideas about the minor tactics of the attack – how the battle is actually fought – were an advance on GHQ's thinking, especially in his stress on the use of echelons in the advance rather than the long lines reminiscent of the eighteenth century. The period ending on 1 July 1916 with the opening of the Somme bombardment affirmed that the British Army placed too much faith in the efficacy of artillery and the moral fervour of the attack. The advance was made 'in silence . . . with bayonets fixed', without small arms fire support, in long lines 'dressing from the left at a brisk walk'; seeking cover was still a court martial offence. The approach of the majority of staff officers was crude and unimaginative. At Hill 70 in 1915 one claimed that 'if only the "charge" had been sounded – and heard –all would have gone well'. Fuller was not entirely free of this kind of influence but he had moved away from 'the constant belief of the General Staff in sheer superiority of numbers [which] revealed a basic assumption that it was the weight of human beings that was the key to offensive success'. Men and weapons would have been Fuller's equation and an improvement in infantry, and not just artillery, technique. Thus although Fuller was 'glad' that his article had been appreciated, it is perhaps not surprising that he added, 'I do not suppose that it will do much good.'[11]

Fuller's last attempt to improve conventional infantry tactics before he joined the Tank Corps sprang from the work entailed in setting up a senior officers' school for the Third Army in the spring of 1916. He gave lectures on the principles of war and on 'Holding a Defensive Line' and presented 'Notes on Battle Drill'. The first students resented being sent back to 'school' and Fuller's *Memoirs* make clear that his first lectures were accompanied by a good deal of muttering and adjusting of monocles: what had junior officers to teach their seniors? They eventually discovered a good deal. They were not the only ones to learn. It was to be the pattern of Fuller's career that he would make practical use of his lectures; by teaching others he taught himself. The resultant essay, 'The Principles of Defence as Applied to Trench Warfare', was never published. It was first lost by the War Office which, when Fuller submitted a second copy, then objected that it might be of assistance to the enemy. Neither was it deemed appropriate to circulate the essay as a pamphlet which was unfortunate. Fuller firmly believed that the flooding of the trenches in the winter of 1914–15 was the fault of the occupants. 'The old saying that the British soldiers prefer [sic] to die than to dig is true', he observed. He also argued that the cherished principle of holding ground for its own sake, regardless of any tactical value, was wasteful and should be disregarded. Fuller castigated the lack of 'continuity of work or system, a labyrinth of trenches and a colossal wastage in personnel and material'. Some of his criticisms were unduly theoretical and overstated but they were on the right lines. There was room for a great deal of improvement in the British defensive scheme and it was scant consolation to point to its superiority over the French. It is debatable whether any coherent defensive doctrine was ever formulated on the Western Front. Fuller advocated economizing manpower by a more efficient use of existing resources: reverse slopes could be employed and thick belts of barbed wire and sunken obstacles laid – the very devices the Germans used in 1916–17 to economise manpower. An underground barracks should be created and not a camping ground 'where each man selects his own pitch'. Some of the muddle Fuller complained of could be put down to the Allied preoccupation with offensive strategy, but there was little attempt to rationalize the trench system even as a stable base from which to launch offensives. As General Essame observes, 'Judged as a defensive system it was a poor advertisement for years of effort.'[12]

The failure of the Somme Offensive led Fuller and many other officers to rethink their assumptions. It would be a mistake to suggest that Fuller was the only intelligent officer who thought about the war. Stephen Foot recalled how he 'used to have tremendous arguments on how the war was to be won'. The effect of this turbulent discussion among junior officers, displaying the self-confident, untrammelled wisdom of youth, was to refine

Fuller's thinking about the problems that faced the Allies. He was now of the opinion that it would take 'another three-and-a-half years to break down Germany's powers of resistance' – a rather pessimistic view as it turned out. He then read closely a lucid discussion of Allied strategy by Captain F. H. E. Townshend, called the 'MS in Red Ink' in his *Memoirs*. Townshend had shown that the German front was 500 miles long but only five miles deep. Any victorious advance would only require a limited penetration. Townshend provided no guidance as to how this breakthrough was to be achieved but thought it important to state the problem in the abstract. Fuller was by now dwelling on the need to take the enemy by surprise before he had time to man his defences. As he wrote home, 'surprise . . . is of more importance than preparation, this has always been so, but has not always been grasped, in spite of the fact that history shows its extreme importance again and again'.[13]

These thoughts dominated his mind during his transfer to the Tank Corps in December 1916. Fuller's arduous attempt to formulate tank tactics henceforth was made without any guidance from GHQ and in complete ignorance of a prophetic paper by Major General Sir Ernest Swinton called 'Notes on the Employment of Tanks'. 'It all too often happens in the military sphere', counselled Liddell Hart, 'that the drafting of theory starts afresh on a blank page – through an unawareness of previous studies that is due to a defective information system.' Throughout the war the development of tactical innovations was hampered by the lack of central guidance from GHQ. An admirer of Haig, General Sixsmith, is forced to admit that, 'What he should have done, and in 1918 did do, was to ensure a continuous and objective study of the tactical problem.' As there was no working section of GHQ giving this question the highest priority, new devices and methods were worked out in a haphazard manner by junior officers like Fuller. 'The Germans had no better brains, yet, because of their objective staff studies, they were always tactically one step ahead.' On the whole, Fuller's later criticisms of GHQ's feebleness on this count seem wholly justified.[14]

It is appropriate at this point to view Fuller and his methods within the framework of Tank Corps HQ. In 1949 Fuller exuberantly told Liddell Hart that his commander, Brigadier General (later Sir) Hugh Elles was ideal from his point of view 'because he was weak', allowing Fuller free rein as the tactical expert. This is a characteristic Fuller exaggeration. As GSO 1 Fuller did enjoy a lot of freedom to develop his own ideas. One of his former GSO 3s, Brigadier I. M.

Stewart, considered Fuller and Elles complementary. 'Elles was able, realistic, receptive, a calm and good debater, and completely in control as Commander.' He adds: 'There was no question of Fuller, the intellectual spectacular, being dominant at HQ nor did he try to be.' Fuller was a brilliant, imaginative staff officer and he needed a sympathetic commander who could transform his ideas into reality, a role ably filled by Elles. Stewart found Fuller

Approachable by his GSO 2s and ready to discuss their views. In such a small HQ even a GSO 3 was in close personal contact with him. To such juniors he was considerate and appreciative and encouraging. . . . Easy to work for though one had to be on one's toes. . . . A sense of humour and not a trace of the pedant.[15]

Fuller's first essay in tank tactics, 'Training Note No 16' showed how in February 1917 he began by grafting on to tank operations his infantry style thinking of the previous two years. He started by underlying that the tank was a 'mobile fortress' – it *protected* offensives. Here was the factor that would add that extra degree of pressure that would reduce the resistance of the enemy. If the main strategical problem was to find a way of winning a decisive battle on a wide front by advancing a few miles, then the deployment of the tank *en masse*, 'whether we have thousands . . . or only scores', would take the enemy by surprise and 'break down this resistance . . . the main tank objectives are those lines of trenches and wire which will offer the greatest resistance to the infantry advance: namely, the enemy's second and subsequent lines of defence'. In order that surprise would not be sacrified, Fuller now reversed his line of argument and pressed that the artillery bombardment be short, for if it was 'prolonged, the condition of great extension and little depth, in which the enemy is placed, cannot be taken advantage of; . . . the enemy will be able to draw reserves from his flanks to meet the attack'. Fuller showed that he could learn from experience. In an acute appreciation he now suggested breaching the enemy's defences in a period of 12–16 hours with a brief preparatory bombardment. 'Experience has definitely shown', he wrote recalling the Somme Offensive, 'that such a bombardment should not exceed 48 hours'; greater co-operation between arms was also required; all remaining preparatory work should 'be accomplished by tanks, all missile throwing weapons having but one object – the reduction of resistance offered to the advance of the infantry bayonets'.[16]

These conclusions bore a marked resemblance to those reached by Swinton. Fuller shared Swinton's belief that a breakthrough 'in one day may be contemplated as a feasible proposition'. In other words, the trench deadlock could be broken by a decisive battle of Napoleonic proportions. Fuller now began to develop his ideas on the line of least resistance. He saw that it was the tank and not the infantry which was the true demoralizing agent. If the enemy could be thoroughly disorganized then the advance through his second and third lines would 'savour more of a pursuit than an assault'. The object of penetration was the creation of flanks. He came to the conclusion that every grand tactical act was based on the movement of armies *against flanks*, or the line of least resistance. If none existed then they had to be created. Once prised open and a flank exposed from a continuous front an advance would revert from a penetration to an envelopment. The process of penetration was nonetheless intricate. When attacked the defensive line must be split and the gap widened; an envelopment of the two artificial flanks must follow rapidly. The tank was the ideal creator of flanks because it combined offensive power with the necessary defensive strength to withstand small arms fire.[17]

Fuller thus moved towards a concept of the Napoleonic battle applicable under modern conditions. Each detailed tactical appreciation he made stimulated a more general development of his thinking. For example, after suggesting that tanks move in section columns towards definite points, creating flanks 'and so driving the enemy underground or cause him to bunch and offer tangible targets to the infantry's rifle and bayonet', and that a series of temporary rallying points could be established behind the enemy's lines in order to sustain the advance if it ran into difficulties, he came to a fresh conclusion: 'For infantry the use of the Tank is very similar to the use Napoleon made of his heavy cavalry.' Fuller now vaguely realized that weapons fulfilled certain tactical functions. After 'the infantry attack in column covered by skirmishers or massed artillery fire', he wrote, '. . . [came] the charge of the heavy cavalry, which profiting of the disorder caused in the enemy ranks by the first, accentuated it by lance and sabre. Last came the Old Guard who completed the victory.' The British Army could thus be organized according to function:

artillery, machine guns and rifles, then tanks, and finally infantry bayonets. Or, as he neatly labelled them, 'Disorganizers, Demoralizers and Despatchers'.[18]

He also began to seek further historical support for his ideas. He read Colonel Theodore A. Dodge's volumes on Alexander the Great. Years later he recorded, 'It struck me how modern were Alexander's campaigns, and how much could be learnt from his battles which might be applied to tank warfare'. He found other analogies in medieval warfare, claiming that the armoured knight had reappeared in the guise of 'modern science'; the tactics he thought most similar to the tank's were those of Ziska during the Hussite Wars (1419–36). These were based on a mobile 'block-house line' of carts, which afforded 'a secure and mobile base behind which the cavalry could retire and through which it can advance at will'.[19]

In 'Training Note No 16' Fuller made little effort to expose the limitations of tanks. Comments on these appeared some months later. He pointed out the difficulties of communicating between tanks and their limited field of vision; he also commented on their tendency to 'belly' (jamming the superstructure on the ground so that the tracks could not propel them forward), and their low speed. Tank crews moreover became exhausted quickly as they worked under the most primitive conditions. Fuller was wise to underplay these. After all he was not writing academic treatises. It would have been impolitic to circulate information that could have been thrown back at him in conference. 'There is perhaps a tendency', he wrote, 'to judge by failures rather than by successes; if this tendency were always followed, heavy artillery would have been abolished many months ago.'[20]

Fuller's thinking took another step forward in June 1917 with another ambitious paper on tank tactics. Repeating his assumption that a victorious advance need only be made a short distance on a wide front, he refined it by claiming that the prime difficulty was not breaking the German line but *moving through it*. The real German strength lay in their adept support of the second and third lines with artillery fire. By withdrawing to these the enemy 'was able to draw the attacking infantry away from his artillery support and eventually place him . . . in a worse position than the one he was in at the start'. And by holding back a reserve, once the British had moved beyond the range of their artillery, a counter-attack could throw them back. Fuller then asked: how could movement be sustained in face of communication difficulties, demolished houses, 'swarms of guerrilla machine guns' and the capacity of the enemy to withdraw his guns because of the *time* it took to advance the British artillery?

Even before the opening of the Third Battle of Ypres (Passchendaele, June–November 1917) Fuller had realized that a link existed between the time factor and mobility in trench warfare, and that the pace of the advance was being slowed down by imaginative German defensive methods. By now his thinking was far in advance of GHQ who persisted in organizing an offensive around the movement of infantry to a series of coloured lines marked on the map, regardless of tactical conditions on the ground. The Germans had long since abandoned rigid, linear defence. They employed small groups of machine gunners who moved into the craters caused by shell fire and were thus able to bring enfilading fire down upon the advancing British infantry. Fuller proposed to deal with these by a combination of tank action and rolling barrages.[21]

For the most part he still emphasized the necessary subordination of the tank to infantry, as 'it is the infantryman with his machine gun and bayonet who is going to decide the battle'. Still, the tank had an important role in the pursuit; as soon as the breakthrough had been achieved every medium tank should be moved 'independent of guns and infantry, into the destroyed area in rear of the enemy's gun positions', and thus prepare the way for the movement of other arms. Another point emerges in Fuller's papers at this time, namely, that the tank could economize infantry power. By its action infantry casualties could be reduced for greater gains. As regards infantry tactics, Fuller repeated his earlier arguments. At all costs infantry should avoid moving in rigid lines. Instead he recommended files covered by machine gun fire 'which should smother the objective with bullets'. Fuller was later to claim that there was nothing new in these tactics, as he had simply modified them from Xenophon's *Cyropaedia* – a striking example of his practical use of historical reading.[22]

These developments did not go hand in hand with any changes in his view of the nature of war. His opinions still remained conventional and there was no hint yet of a desire to limit war. Its object was 'the destruction, pure and simple of the German Empire . . . and a 10 years military occupation of the country'. The German devastation of the French countryside during the

Cambrai, 1917

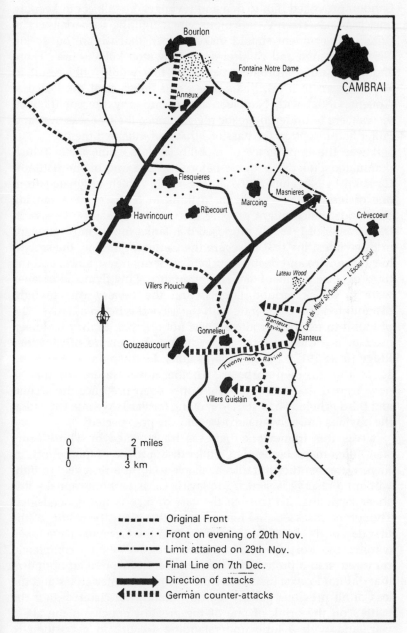

Bourlon

Fontaine Notre Dame

CAMBRAI

Anneux

Flesquieres

Masnieres

Marcoing

Crèvecoeur

Ribecourt

Havrincourt

Lateau Wood

Canal du Nord St.-Quentin – L'Escaut Canal

Villers Plouich

Banteux Ravine

Gonnelieu

Banteux

Gouzeaucourt

Twenty-two Ravine

Villers Guislain

0   2 miles

0   3 km

- - - - - - - Original Front
· · · · · · Front on evening of 20th Nov.
—·—··—· Limit attained on 29th Nov.
———— Final Line on 7th Dec.
➤➤➤ Direction of attacks
◀▪▪▪▪▪ German counter-attacks

retreat to the Hindenburg Line and the early bombing raids on London provoked him to demand revenge. 'To talk about keeping one['] hands clean is ridiculous when fighting barbarians.' The British Government should make it clear 'that we are out to kill German women and children until they stop killing ours'. There should be no compromise peace, as this would only result in another war 'in a few years time', and Fuller cited the Peace of Amiens (1802) with Napoleon as an unhappy precedent. Such views were to undergo drastic revision once the war was over and Fuller had forgotten the passions that had inflamed them.[23]

It was the importance of mobility and the time factor which dominated Fuller's thoughts before the opening of the Battle of Cambrai in November 1917, the germ of which originated from one of his papers. He began to think in terms of demoralizing tank raids which might prepare the way for a major offensive in the summer of 1918. He proposed that tanks should move forward in three lines: the first to secure the German gun line; the second to cut the wire and destroy pockets of German resistance; and the third to seize points of tactical importance. Low flying aeroplanes were to attack ground targets, and the cavalry was to fight dismounted and co-operate with the second echelon of tanks. The proposal to use fighter aircraft was not original; as they had been used in a ground support role during the seizure of Messines Ridge (June 1917), but Fuller was quick to grasp its potential and adapt it for his own purposes. Another novel feature was that he now argued that artillery should only open fire once the second and third echelons had started moving forward: 'we must abandon the obvious and rely on surprise and the unexpected.'[24]

It was this framework that was transformed by Third Army staff into a major battle plan. Fuller disapproved of their efforts as there were insufficient tanks available to form a reserve. 'To fight without a reserve is similar to playing cards without capital – it is sheer gambling. To trust to the cast of dice is not generalship.' Though he disassociated himself from this plan, the results of the first day of the Battle of Cambrai, when the Germans were taken wholly by surprise and their defensive lines completely ruptured, had a profound effect of Fuller: it inspired an optimism that did not lose its lustre after the German counter-attack and the loss of all previous gains. 'We now stand', he claimed after the battle, 'on the brink of one of the greatest epochs in the art of war, and with a little understanding we are in a position to proclaim it.' Hugh Elles's decision to lead the attack in person – which Fuller had initially opposed – lingered in his memory, a glimpse of glamour in a war lacking in heroes but full of drab pedants and dull bureaucrats. 'There is some periodical bringing out the *famous* generals of this war,' Fuller wrote tartly, 'Elles deserves better company.' Above all, the dramatic success of the advance had an invigorating effect on him. 'I believe the attack was one of the most magnificent sights of the war, great numbers of T[anks] forging ahead in lines of battle followed by infantry.'[25]

One important point failed to dent Fuller's enthusiasm – the strategic effect of the material factor. He rightly believed that he was advocating the use of weapons which would reduce the time required to bring about a decisive victory and increase the drama and moral effect of the attack. Only a limited number of tanks had been available for the Cambrai offensive, and it is arguable that if tanks had been held back in reserve, the strength of the initial attack might have been weakened. Fuller was theoretically correct to make his stand, but other considerations determined the course of planning of which he had, as yet, little experience. He did not square up to the fact that a shortage of tanks and their tactical imperfections rendered them less than invulnerable; some degree of scepticism on the part of GHQ was therefore understandable.

This is not to suggest that Fuller's thinking was overly visionary. He was capable of coming to grips with technical problems. His use of fascines, a large bundle of sticks tied together, permitting tanks to cross trench lines, showed a grasp of detail and practical ability of no common order. His next paper on tank tactics continued to display shrewdness. He pointed to the weakness of heavy artillery as an offensive weapon; the landscape of craters created by shells only served to throw up yet another barrier against the attacker. There could be no pursuit in trench warfare until the use of artillery was modified and the German reserves exhausted, not only those behind the battlefront, '*but also those on the flanks of the decisive attack*'. If these were not held they would move inwards on the salient created. An effective pursuit demanded that 'the gap must not be less than one third to a quarter of the battlefront'. Such had been Napoleon's method, reasoned Fuller: 'attack everywhere, then watch, select the front for the decisive blow and hit hard at the point selected'. This was a novel interpretation of Napoleonic warfare and illustrates clearly Fuller's concept of the tactics of penetration.[26]

The point here was that it was easier to see the problem in the abstract than it was to realize the solution. 'If we employ mechanical means', wrote Fuller, 'it [the attack] becomes feasible with a comparatively small force'. But where was this mechanical force to come from, at least in the short term? Tanks had not been produced in large numbers in 1916–17, partly through short-sightedness, but mainly because of the justifiable reason that they used up large quantities of scarce resources that were needed elsewhere, at a time when their value was far from proven. Only large numbers of tanks could have an overwhelming effect – the Germans had recovered quickly at Cambrai – but these were not available.[27]

Though this paper moved some way towards the kind of thinking formulated in 'Plan 1919', the actual spark that inspired the arguments behind this celebrated plan was ignited by the conduct of the retreat during the German Spring Offensive in March 1918. In the months prior to the offensive Fuller had returned to a study of the campaigns of Napoleon, and read Colonel J. B. M. Vachée's Napoleon at Work (1914), 'as it might give me ideas'. He observed keenly, once the storm broke on the British armies, that it was the moral effect of the withdrawal of Corps and Army HQs which induced chaos. Then suddenly – and the location is no coincidence – 'It occurred to me on the top of Mt St Quentin . . . whilst I was watching the déroute of our troops in March 1918. Why were they retiring? because our command was paralysed'. Fuller was so contemptuous of the way that the retreat had been handled, that after Clemenceau's famous speech, later dressed up to good effect by Churchill in 1940, (when he declared that 'we will fight them on the beaches') Fuller commented sarcastically that British generals could be relied upon to get their troops to the beaches.[28]

'Plan 1919' must be the most famous unused plan in military history – certainly the most highly praised, and most of this praise is deserved. The plan is an accurate insight into the future character of war. Yet the same difficulties present themselves when appraising 'Plan 1919' as had marked his earlier papers: was it a practical proposition for conducting this war? Glimpses of the future are not necessarily the best guides for the present, given the conditions of 1918 and the resources available. It involved the use of a new and untried weapon, the Medium D tank. This had a radius of action of some 200 miles and a speed of

18 mph. It was a great improvement on earlier tank design, with a lower hull and wire rope suspension. The Medium D's speed was its greatest asset. Here was the answer to the problem of military time. 'The introduction of the tank on the battlefield entirely revolutionizes the art of war . . . petrol enables an army to obtain a greater effect from its weapons in a given time with less loss to itself than one which relies on muscular energy'; it was possible to project that 'it superimposes Naval Tactics on Land Tactics . . . it enables men to discharge their weapons from a moving platform protected by a fixed shield'. The argument that tanks merely escorted the bayonet into the German defensive system was now banished. Fuller stressed instead that the side which fielded the best weapons technology would win, because technology 'saves Time – the controlling factor in war'.[29]

The analogy drawn between naval and land warfare was not his own. Fuller borrowed it from a paper written by his GSO 3, Captain (later Lieutenant General Sir Giffard) Martel, a young officer whose views at this date were more radical than his own, called 'A Tank Army', originally written in the spring of 1917. What distinguished Fuller's concept from that of Martel was the comparison he made between an army and the organs of the human body. This had existed in Fuller's mind in a crude form for years. Now he declared baldly that 'the potential strength of a body of men lies in its organization; consequently, if we can destroy this organization, we shall have gained our object.' Thus he reduced fighting battles to attacking the enemy's body – the bodies of his soldiers – or attacking the enemy's brain – his command organization. 'The brains of an army are its staff – Army, Corps and Divisional Headquarters'. If these could be knocked out, 'the collapse of the personnel they control would [follow] . . . in a matter of hours.' If the enemy's supply system could also be located 'his men will starve to death or scatter'.[30]

This new set of assumptions allowed him to state confidently that the object of the next offensive should be 'to destroy "command", not after the enemy's personnel had been disorganized, but before it had been attacked' – a theory which represented the optimum use of surprise. This had important implications for his developing concept of the decisive battle. He now argued that Napoleon had refused 'to break the enemy's front and then when his own men were disorganized risk being hit by the enemy's reserves; but instead to draw the enemy's reserves into a fire fight and then once these had been worn down, to break through or envelop them.' A devastating pursuit then followed. The real secret of winning a victory, Fuller now divulged, lay in avoiding a premature wastage of reserves; that is, 'pursuing with troops disorganized by victory'; new weapons economized manpower and it would therefore be possible to organize a reserve around the tank. Once achieved the results could be spectacular. 'Plan 1919' 'represented the winning of a war in a single battle'.[31]

The tactical details were worked out in accordance with this Napoleonic rationale. The German Army HQs and not their artillery line should now be the main objective. Objectives should be marked by aeroplanes dropping coloured smoke by day or lights at night – another striking portent of the future. The RAF was to concentrate on attacking road and rail centres, but not signal communications, for Fuller hoped that by allowing German units to communicate with one another 'they would be reduced to a rabble which could be mopped up at leisure.' 'Bad news confuses, confusion stimulates panic', he wrote. In order to achieve his aim of disorganizing the enemy's reserves before they were attacked, the attacking force was organized according to its tactical function: the Breaking Force that would disrupt the German defences; the Disorganizing Force that would disrupt the German command system; and the Pursuing Force. The pursuit was to begin once the penetration had been made.[32]

The idea of demoralizing the enemy had been relevant to Fuller's thinking before 1917. Its logical development – paralysis of command – probably had its origins in Napoleonic practice. Napoleon had declared at St Helena that the true objective in war was upsetting the balance of the enemy. But earlier examples of attempts at dislocating the enemy's command can be found. Perhaps the most striking was the attempt to kill the King of Sweden, Charles XII, by the Russians at the Battle of Rajowka (1708). Twenty squadrons of cavalry had been allotted to this task, and Charles only escaped by masquerading as a Russian officer. Fuller was unaware of this example in 1918. The historical incident which did most to shape his idea was to be found in antiquity: the conduct of Darius III, King of Persia, at the Battle of Gaugamela (331 BC). When Alexander the Great attacked the centre of his army, Darius 'nervous as he had been all along, saw nothing but terrors all around, he was himself the first to turn and ride way', recorded Arrian. Thereupon the Persian army disintegrated. 'It was through reading Arrian's *Anabasis* of him [Alexander] which did more than any other thing to detonate in my mind my "Plan 1919", as well as open up to me a new vista on war', Fuller recalled many years later.[33]

The ultimate feasibility of 'Plan 1919' depended upon the validity of the analogy Fuller drew between an army and the functions of the human body. It is true, and especially true of the period 1914–18, that an army does resemble a biological organism. The armies along the Western Front during the First World War were largely immobile, and therefore their vital organs remained stationary and could be located more easily than if they were on the move. And, because of their size, they were dependent on lines of communication; their organization did resemble a brain (the HQs) and a nervous system (signal communication and telephone lines). This analogy was accentuated by linear trench lines and a complete absence of operational radio communications. An army devoured vast quantities of ammunition, food, petrol, spare parts, equipment, clothing and still, in 1918, forage. These were sucked into the fighting organs and operational limbs through vulnerable supply lines. There is, in short, much truth in the analogy, but, like many others, it can only be used as an illustration – not concrete proof. An army is more complicated than an organism because its component parts can exist independently of one another. Brains, courage and fighting power are not compartmentalized, and a crisis can throw up a relatively junior officer who can provide the guidance formerly given by higher authority.[34]

As generals commanding higher formations of troops are chosen because of their powers of leadership, it is rash to assume that every attempt to gain surprise will result in panic. Brigadier Bidwell rightly comments, 'This is to elevate the principle of surprise to a law of nature, and this is going much too far'. It can nonetheless be said in Fuller's defence that the conditions favoured such an effort in 1918. German morale had been steadily declining during the summer, exacerbated by Ludendorff's policy of filling the storm troop divisions with the best officers and men; the remaining *eingreff* divisions were very shaky.[35]

The possibility existed that Fuller's strategical aims could have been fulfilled. His main thesis that the German Army could be defeated if only a short advance on a wide front could be sustained was sound, and eventually proven by the military history of 1918. 'If the enemy continued to attack with even ordinary vigour', wrote Ludendorff after his defeat at the Battle of Amiens (8–11 August 1918), an offensive with strictly limited objectives, 'we should no longer be able to maintain ourselves west of the Somme.' He added: 'a great enemy victory was possible'. The factors of time and space underlying Fuller's thesis had been complicated by the German Spring Offensive, as the Allies had to regain some forty miles of ground before penetrating the main German defences. Once these had been passed the war was brought to an end by a pursuit which advanced only another forty miles beyond the Hindenburg Line. The campaign of 1918 also showed that psychological paralysis was efficacious. Ludendorff complained afterwards that one of the main reasons why the German defences at Amiens were ruptured so completely was that tanks continually surprised divisional staffs in their headquarters. Mercurial in temperament, Ludendorff's own personality was a factor favouring 'Plan 1919'. He lost his temper and panicked when matters went askew. He would hardly have provided a steady guiding hand if the shattering blows envisaged in 'Plan 1919' had rained down upon the German Army.[36]

But could the tactical means fulfil the strategic end? The thorny problem of the technical limitations of new weapons again complicates the practicality of theoretical schemes. The aircraft of the period were capable of fulfilling the role allotted to them in the plan. The reliability of the Medium D tank was much less certain. The battles of 1918 (when the more primitive Mark IV were used) revealed that the tank had severe weaknesses as an offensive weapon. Its vision was very restricted. So thick were the mist and smoke on the morning of 8 August before Amiens that tanks 'could not see each other, nor the targets except for flashes of discharge'. Tanks were extremely uncomfortable and made tremendous demands on the stamina of their crews. One tank crew was gassed during the initial breakthrough at Amiens by engine fumes. Tank casualties were very heavy during the battle and the percentage loss increased with each day. On 9 August there were only 145 tanks fit for action out of a total of 415. All these drawbacks reduced the mobility of the tank and its ability to economize military time.[37]

The Medium D tank was, of course, a considerable advance in design on these earlier models, but could it overcome their limitations? As Martel pointed out twelve years later, 'Plan 1919' marked a step towards the division, as in earlier times, between the mobile and close quarter fighting arms; that is, the tank would eventually emerge as the main instrument of victory and not remain as an adjunct to the infantry. Much of the evidence would seem to suggest that such a division was not yet practical. Both the official historian and General Essame remark on the success of the tank in co-operating with other arms: 'working independently they had overcome many machine guns posts and small centres of resistance, and by their moral effect carried the surrender of many prisoners'. The real lesson of Amiens was the success of 'all arms skilfully acting in combination with one single aim' – and this was concealed by the writing of Fuller and Liddell Hart on the role of the tank in the First World War.[38]

This line of argument does not in itself vitiate the kind of thinking that lies behind 'Plan 1919'. The military history of 1918 confirms that the kernel of the plan was sound. The tactics of a particularly effective formation during the Battle of Amiens, the Australian Corps commanded by General Monash, were designed to concentrate all the available mechanical aids on the battlefront to protect the infantry. His method, though it saved infantry lives, contributed to an *increase* in the proportion of tank casualties, mainly because 'the effect of the initial surprise had not been utilized to push the enemy over the devastated trench area near the old trench-warfare front.' If this caution had been replaced by greater adventurousness, tank casualties could have been reduced. The Germans had shown that woods, villages and machine gun posts could be neutralized by artillery and trench mortars; they did not always require the intervention of tanks in penny packets. These could have been kept in reserve. As the Official History observed, 'it is to be greatly regretted that no massed tank attack was made, nor even planned, and that no attempt to raid behind the enemy lines was made, except by the 17th Armoured Car Company.' This raid was a successful venture, which shot up a Corps HQ at Fameville and captured a plan of the Hindenburg Line, 'a striking fulfilment in miniature of Fuller's "Plan 1919" vision', as Liddell Hart noted. It was possible, then, to use armoured vehicles in the audacious manner conceived by Fuller.[39]

If grounds for optimism exist it must nevertheless be recalled that the Medium D tank was a new weapon untried in action. Its reliability was uncertain, and this was, as Fuller conceded, crucial to the success of the plan. Its specifications, as Martel pointed out, were far in advance of anything yet manufactured and would no doubt have led to grave difficulties. Experimental trials revealed that the engine was troublesome. Fuller thereupon suggested that a prototype, the Medium C, be put into production. He already displayed that disregard of technical difficulties in producing new weapons so characteristic of the inter-war reformers. Fuller was a hard-headed thinker but his vision was invariably couched in highly coloured and sweeping, romantic terms which, it must be admitted, sometimes avoided practical realities. The designer of the Medium D, Major (later Lieutenant Colonel) Philip Johnson, recalled that 'being entirely unmechanical himself, he [Fuller] used to question me as to whether some particular project could be converted into actuality.' Johnson had to temper Fuller's enthusiasm constantly. When difficulties confronted the Medium D, Fuller urged that its engine should be immediately changed. Johnson found this exasperating and replied that if this was done 'we might find ourselves after a fortnight's work, in the position of having to change engines in every one of the available Tanks, the position being naturally complicated by the fact that they would probably all go down at the same time.'[40]

In sum, 'Plan 1919' faced formidable difficulties. Martel eventually concluded that it was unlikely that a reliable Medium D could have been produced in time for the summer of 1919. The desperate attempts to use tanks straight from the factories during Operation 'Battleaxe' in June 1941 does not provide an encouraging portent for what might have happened had 'Plan 1919' been launched. Another factor to be considered was the German decision to build large numbers of anti-tank guns at the end of 1918. The final verdict on 'Plan 1919' must be that it was a hazardous undertaking involving prodigious difficulties, not least the co-ordination and control of an expensive and untried weapon. There was a real danger that numbers of tanks might be trapped and destroyed piecemeal behind the German lines beyond the aid of supporting infantry. When all this is said, it might still be replied that the plan had a chance of working so long as German morale continued to decline, and that the moral impact of the initial attack could be sustained by overwhelming Allied material resources. With the American build-up this factor at least was assured. No military plan ever succeeds in its entirety. Fuller's experience at Cambrai had shown how an original statement can be transformed by later planners; perhaps later refinements would have borne no resemblance to Fuller's original scheme.[41]

Any attempt at assessing whether an untried weapon would work under battle conditions inevitably enters the realm of speculation. The unhappy fact must be faced that no really firm conclusion can be reached. The First World War ended before 1919. The plan was left to languish as a lucid theoretical statement. It represented Fuller's coming of age as a military thinker. It provided not only the foundation stone for his own later refinements but a basis for the efforts of all the pioneering advocates of mechanization: the essential starting-point. 'Plan 1919' reflected a romantic yearning to bring back glamour to the field of battle. Mechanization, Fuller contended, 'would enable a comparatively small tank army to fight battles like Issus and Arbela [Gaugamela] over again'. The utility of battle would be restored. He later wrote that 'Plan 1919' 'would have ended the war with a stupendous drama, the only satisfactory way to win a war'. He predicted optimistically that 'As the mobility of the Tank increases so must it be realized that the opportunities of using Tanks as mechanical cavalry can become greater and greater'; therefore it followed that the armour 'should not be hampered by being tied to the close Infantry co-operation based upon slower types of tanks'.[42]

Fuller's development of these arguments, and his attempt to synthesize them into a general theory about war is the subject of the next chapter.

3

The Reformation of War, 1919–23

In spite of this [the Battle of Hamel] it will take a long time yet before the flintlock way of thinking dies out.

Fuller to Mrs Fuller, 8 July 1918, FP IV/3/232

He [Lucullus] was now so sure of his aim that he concealed it no longer from his men; [he] called them together, and told them with great triumph, in a few days he would gain them a great victory which should not cost one drop of blood.

'Lucullus', *Plutarch's Lives*, J. and W. Langhorne (transl., London, 1898 edn) p. 345

Fuller's prophetic document, 'Plan 1919', had predicted the dawning of a new era in warfare in which tanks and aircraft would co-operate closely to restore the utility of the decisive battle. 'As the mobility of the tank increases, so will it have more and more to rely on the aeroplane for its security and preservation.' Thus 'Aeroplanes will bear to tanks a similar relationship as cavalry to infantry in the old days.' In the years immediately after the First World War Fuller developed his initial ideas about mechanized warfare. Much of the writing of this period simply amplified the precepts of 'Plan 1919' in an attempt to gain for them some degree of official recognition. These essays sketch out the problem in the most visionary and colourful terms. Fuller's 'picture was painted with sweeping strokes', wrote Liddell Hart, 'and in an extremely futuristic style avoiding detailed treatment of problems. But anything less extreme might have had a less startling effect.' Fuller deliberately adopted the methods of the seer, the sermoniser and the prophet. He tended to exaggerate the offensive potential of the tank, and sometimes deliberately so. His arguments, though often crude and overstated, were an attempt to come to terms with the 'lessons' of the First World War.[1]

A fundamental paradox lies at the heart of this process. Fuller's interest in restoring the utility of the decisive battle was the product of his perception of the influence of technology on conflict. He believed that the pace of the Industrial Revolution would determine the nature of future warfare. Thus the next war would be unlike the last; the machines produced by modern industrial society, like the tank and aeróplane, would have a profound influence on tactics. Indeed he predicted that the dynamic potential of these weapons was so great that they would usher in a new type of warfare in which physical destruction would eventually be overtaken by psychological dislocation as the main aim in war. He therefore suggested that a link existed between technological development and the character of war. If such weapons as the tank and aeroplane were employed in a way so as to maximize mobility, the velocity of warfare could be accelerated and its time scale reduced. A belligerent could be demoralized and annihilated (especially if it was unprepared for the onslaught) before a stalemate set in and thus the *overall* degree of force required to gain a decisive victory could be reduced. As be put it in 'Plan 1919', 'Every principle of war becomes easy to apply if movement can be accelerated and accelerated at the expense of the opposing side.'[2]

Fuller expanded on this potential in a highly romantic and visionary way, frequently overlooking practical difficulties. Yet at the same time, he demanded that the increasing technological character of war required sober objective analysis conducted in an atmosphere of scholarly detachment – the essence of what he called 'scientific thinking'. Fuller was the first to flout the standards he demanded of others. His posturing did much to undercut his call for a scientific approach to the study of war. This idea was crystallized in the opening paragraph of an essay that was awarded the RUSI Gold Medal in 1919.

To understand the past and to judge the present is to foresee the future. To understand is to see through, to judge is to value and decide, that is to think logically before a decision is arrived at; consequently, in order to appreciate the worth of a proposition, it is necessary to discover the facts which underlie it and to reduce these to the general terms of a theory; in other words, to think and work scientifically.

Fuller's desire to synthesize what he regarded as the lessons of the First World War into a new theory about war forced him to advertise the value of the new arms, and he did this so effectively that he undermined any faith that other more sceptical soldiers might have had in the merit of the scientific concept.[3]

Fuller's own experience in 1914–18 obviously helped determine which were the most important 'lessons' that he drew from its conduct. He wrote in his autobiography of 'the main event in my life – the war of 1914–1918'. His indictment of the conduct of that war in his two books, *Tanks in the Great War* (1920) and *The Reformation of War* (1923), was scathing. 'It is incredible', he wrote in the latter, 'that anyone, who has the welfare of humanity at heart, can wish to repeat this devastation.' Generals commanding the armies had not only miscalculated the character of the war they were called to fight but failed to overcome the stalemate that had checkmated them: 'traditionally educated and trained armies have but one chance of success, that is the initial operation they undertake'. Thereafter the influence of industrialization and technological change was so great that new weapons created new conditions of war which in their turn required new tactical solutions. GHQ was quite incapable of providing these. It became obsessed with quantities of shells – 'artillery mania' – which prolonged the war rather than curtailed its duration. Faith in ever increasing numbers of men, guns and shells required a corresponding growth in the size of the supporting and administrative services; armies expanded, grew more difficult to administer and therefore more cumbersome to command. In a striking metaphor, Fuller characterized the armies of the First World War as 'pot bellied and pea brained'. Hence the deployment of increasing accumulations of destructive power which devastated for no corresponding advantage and thus required further ill-co-ordinated and costly offensives to sustain the position of the belligerents. These were incapable of bringing the war to an end quickly and only added to the economic and social dislocation of Europe. This experience (especially the Bolshevik Revolution of 1917) pointed to the supreme importance of the 'inner front' in future wars, and its vulnerability to a new kind of attack.[4]

It is difficult not to have sympathy with Fuller's criticisms of the judgement displayed by many of the generals of the First World War. The majority of their miscalculations, he pointed out, were based 'on chance and the misinterpretations of events rather than

skill and foresight'; though it is much less easy to sympathize
with his preremptory dismissal of the appalling difficulties they
encountered. Fuller was heavily influenced by Social Imperialism,
the late Victorian doctrine that welded together Social Darwinism
and Imperialism, which envisaged widespread social reform and
a rationalization of the structure of the British Empire to strengthen
Britain's place in the world; already fear of 'decline' was a
pervasive issue, even at the height of *Pax Britannica*. Fuller, like
other Social Imperialists, believed that if only 'order' and
'efficiency' could be introduced into all the departments of state,
and the detestable liberal glorification of the amateur – the 'all-
round chap' – eradicated, then incompetence could be to large
extent banished from the conduct of human affairs. This was a
widespread Edwardian delusion. No matter how absolute the
reign of intelligence, it is mistaken to assume that the activities of
life can be regulated by reason alone. Certainly Fuller himself was
not free of the vice of 'misinterpreting events'.[5]

In one very important respect Fuller's criticisms were certainly
justified. 'In retrospect it seems astonishing', writes Brian Bond,
'that virtually no official attempt was made to garner the
experience of the First World War while it was still fresh.' No War
Office department was set up to study the tactical trends of that
war. Fuller branded the General Staff 'monastic in mind', though
this was more the fault of the system under which they worked
than from any lack of ability in their ranks, as 'their ability and
brain power are swamped by routine'. Fuller suggested the
formation of a grand strategical organ which could think of war as
a political instrument and treat it 'as one subject', therefore
achieving a high level of co-ordination between the three services –
an ideal far from realized during the First World War, or for that
matter in the Second. Fuller wrote that

> the Navy forms the strategical base from which the other two
> defence forces operate and that when it comes to land warfare,
> the Army forms the base for the Air Force. To think in separate
> terms of sea, land and air is, I feel, entirely wrong, but under
> existing circumstances, I fail to see how any close co-operation is
> to be obtained unless we can institute a body of thinking men
> who will talk of war as one operation in place of three.

It was also important to attach to the Imperial General Staff representatives from the specialist arms, and bring into 'intimate relationship weapon power and tactics'. Fuller was not the only writer to grasp that these measures would inevitably result in the formation of a Ministry of Defence, though he was one of the first to point this out, and the one that devoted most attention to the co-ordination of the three services.[6]

No matter what justification may be found to support Fuller's critical views, it must be understood that he could not resist the temptation to twist the evidence to suit the requirements of a particular theory – the result of his deductive reasoning and the movement from the general to the particular. A clear example was Fuller's treatment of the tank in the First World War. Fuller recapitulated his wartime thesis that as motion resulted in a clash between force and resistance, the tank had overcome the inertia of the entrenched battlefield and restored mobility to the battlefield. The maintenance of the offensive 'demanded as a necessity that the endurance of the attack should be superior to the resistance of the defence'. The vulnerability of the infantry to small arms fire could not be overcome by increased artillery support because longer artillery barrages created 'a new resistant' – shell craters which destroyed communications – 'as severe an obstacle to movement as wire'. By combining protection from bullets with offensive power and mobility, Fuller claimed that the tank had overcome the German defences virtually unaided. This was not true. He was also prone to assume that as artillery had revealed limitations on the Western Front, it would be downgraded in the next war and have no significant part to play in the mobile battle. This was not true either. Thus Fuller not only exaggerated the importance of the tank in 1914–18 *vis-à-vis* other arms, he went on to exaggerate the offensive power of the tank in the future. It should also be recalled that he had been intimately involved in the development of tank tactics and was hardly an unprejudiced observer.[7]

This tactical trinity of protection, offensive power and mobility was central to Fuller's discussion of the tank's potential. It had, claimed Fuller, falling back on his earlier work,

> equilibrated movement and fire and by doing so has superimposed naval tactics on land warfare; . . . it now enables the soldier, like the sailor, to discharge his weapon from a moving platform protected by a fixed shield.

This was an elaboration of the assertion made in 'Plan 1919' that land warfare could be likened to naval warfare. A year later he now judged the impact of the internal combustion engine on war to be potentially '*stupendous*, for it has opened a new epoch in the history of war to which we can find no parallel in land fighting, the nearest approach being the replacement of sails by steam as the motive means in naval warfare'. In other words, the tank would be able to circumvent those restrictions which had previously hampered the movement of armies. It also meant the centralization of weapon-power on capital intensive, mobile units, the technological (and tactical) implications of which have still to be fully worked out.[8]

Technological change would introduce into warfare quite novel conditions. Tactics would thus vary with the pace and the character of these changes and be decisively influenced by the increase in velocity afforded by the tank. Future wars would no longer open with stately declarations of war and long periods of mobilization. There would be no repetition of the immense battles of attrition of 1914–18 between armies contesting linear entrenchments and supplied over long lines of communication. The next war would open abruptly and focus around pivots of manoeuvre. Fuller's clearest description of this type of warfare can be found in a lecture delivered at the RUSI in 1920.

> I see a fleet operating against a fleet not at sea but on land: cruisers and battleships and destroyers . . . there appears an aeroplane [carrying] . . . the Commander-in-Chief. . . . Suddenly I see the fleet is moving a few points north-east; the Commander-in-Chief has spoken to it by wireless telephony. I sniff the air; . . . Is it gas? The Tanks submerge; that is to say, batten down their hatches. The battle begins.
>
> Out go the minesweepers; we are in the enemy's land. A series of detonations show that the act was not executed a moment too soon.
>
> The enemy's fleet concentrates their fire on the gaps made. The Commander-in-Chief is again talking. A small squadron moves to the north, tacks east, and huge clouds of smoke pour across the sky. New gaps are made and the fleet moves through.
>
> Then I see the old scene re-enacted – the contest between armour, gun-fire and mobility.

The enemy is disorganized, demoralized; his flag aeroplane has been brought down; his brains are paralyzed; it is now the pursuit.

This is a good example of Fuller's prophetic, romantic style. Veterans of the battles in North Africa in 1941–2, especially Operation 'Crusader' and the Battle of Gazala would doubtless recognize the description. Of particular interest is the argument that technological improvement would have important implications for command methods. Lieutenant General Sir Alan Cunningham arrived in the Western Desert ignorant of radio-telephony and 'he is remembered fumbling helplessly with a radio-telephone, trying to use it like an ordinary telephone'. Generals would also take to the air – like Rommel; though no general was rash enough to take the risk of actually conducting a battle from an aeroplane in 1939–45, this is common enough today.[9]

Major General Sir Ernest Swinton and the remainder of the audience at the RUSI were unanimous in praising Fuller's lecture as 'the best exposition, the clearest vision of what warfare is likely to become'. Yet, 60 years later it is necessary to examine Fuller's predictions more critically. His general picture is sound, but the details are either distorted or quite wrong. The question of gas will be considered shortly. As for the general proposition that the tank could paralyse an enemy unaided, Fuller's major assumption that tracked vehicles could negotiate the earth like a skater glides over ice was exaggerated. He was on surer ground when he suggested a correlation between fighting-power and road-power, so that if communications were inadequate an advance would grind to a halt. Thus even though 'fronts are breakable . . . as long as supplies are tied down to roads it is practically impossible to exploit a penetration'. Yet Fuller's optimism that mechanization would solve this problem, as armoured units would be self-contained and able to move across country, was not wholly realistic. The prospect of advances over a radius of several hundred miles in a week, though possible (and there were several such operations in 1940–1), were difficult to sustain over long periods. Men must eat and sleep and cannot maintain such exertions for long periods of time without losing efficiency, as Fuller would soon recognize.[10]

This is not to suggest that Fuller was mistaken in stressing the tremendous potential of cross country movement, far from it. The Fall of France in 1940 was in part due to skilful 'avoidance of

villages . . . and all major roads; movement straight across
country, thereby ensuring a surprise appearance in the flank and
rear of the enemy', in Rommel's own words. Fuller however
underestimated several qualifying factors. It was misleading to
suggest that movement would become the norm in battles fought
in Western Europe. Here broken terrain ensured that such
potential could only be realized under exceptional rather than
normal conditions. Patterns of settlement as well as physical
features delimit possible lines of advance. Only over ideal terrain
such as the Western Desert, was unlimited cross-country
movement possible. Tracked vehicles are delicate and cannot
endure prolonged strain. As it was discovered that large numbers
of vehicles were required to sustain any sizeable advance, wheeled
vehicles were found to be both more reliable and cheaper. Under
the strain of war strategical paralysis of the enemy might result in
the paralysis of the victor also – the result not of enemy action but
the pace of his advance. Rommel's hectic and chaotic push to the
position at El Alamein in July 1942 is surely a case in point. In
short, it was too glib to assert 'that the Tank delivers the goods to
the firing line, not to a point one or more miles in rear of it' – a
remark that glosses over too many practical problems.[11]

Implicit in Fuller's arguments was an observation of profound
importance that transcends his discussion of tank tactics. Fuller
deduced that the emergence of powerful armaments due to the
technological advances arising from the Industrial Revolution of
the nineteenth century would introduce a qualitative differential
between armies. This theme was expanded in the final chapter of
Tanks in the Great War. The tone of this chapter is sober and lucid.
Here Fuller stated that the introduction of a new weapon
demanded a corresponding change in the art of war. 'That in all
wars, and especially modern wars . . . no army [equipped with
weapons] of fifty years before any date selected would stand a
"dog's chance" against the army existing at this date, not even if it
was composed entirely of Winkelrieds and Marshal Neys.' Thus
the power most highly prepared for war would be in the best
position to win a rapid and decisive victory over an ill-prepared
opponent. Courage in itself could not compensate for a deficiency
in weapon-power. As the German Chief of Staff, Halder, said of
the German victory over Poland in September 1939, the Germans
'would have had to be very poor soldiers not to win the war in
Poland with one hand tied behind their backs'. It redounds

greatly to Fuller's credit that he had fully grasped the implications of this by 1920. At the RUSI he warned: 'If we do not step forward today we shall be marking time, and if we mark time now . . . believe me, we shall be marking time in our own graves.'[12]

Fuller vaguely perceived that 'the ideal army to aim at is *one* man, . . . one man who can press a button or pull a plug and so put into operation war-machines evolved by the best brains of the nation during peacetime'. Periods of peace were likely to become just as important in war as periods of hostility. Yet, impressive as his prescience is, this qualitative differential begs several important questions about the ultimate value of strategic paralysis. Does one side have to be overwhelmingly superior in men and morale? Fuller seemed to suggest that a determination to control operations alone would suffice. 'The "Fog of War" very frequently does not exist at all', he wrote, 'or is, at most, but a thin mist. A careful study of the enemy's forces, his lines of communication and the tactical features and conditions which prevail . . . from the start reduce the fog of war very considerably.' What fog prevailed after this preliminary study 'should get less and less if a thoroughly good intelligence service is established'. If both opposing generals stood firm, however, calmly made their dispositions and notified their subordinates of their intentions, under what conditions could one be strategically paralysed by the other? Strategic paralysis demands similar conditions to those which prevailed in 1918 or 1939–40 when the belligerents were half defeated before the offensive onslaught began. Even the death of a commanding general does not necessarily lead to a complete rout, though the contending armies might be of similar size. At this early, optimistic stage Fuller did not realize that strategic paralysis would lead to a return of attrition. Strategic paralysis demands a degree of technological superiority before it becomes efficacious. It might be added that in attempting to build a theory of war around strategic paralysis, Fuller was simply trying to stretch a good idea too far.[13]

Perhaps the most enduring legacy of Fuller's interest in naval aspects of mechanization was his contention that mechanization would harmonize the tactical development of naval and land forces. Much to the disgust of the Admiralty he won the RUSI Naval Gold Medal Prize Essay for 1921. 'It is rather amusing as a soldier', wrote Fuller mischievously, 'having beaten the sailor at his own job.' The main theme of Fuller's naval writings was that in the future, command of the sea would be exercised by submarines, which presented a major threat to Britain's commercial lifelines. Privately, he believed that the capital ship would endure for another ten, or more likely twenty years. Fuller could see no reason why tanks should not follow similar lines of development as submarines and become amphibious; at the very least tank landing craft could be developed. In a brilliant description, Fuller envisaged them as travelling 'under the protection of the fleet at 25 to 30 knots the hour'; 'these machines being conveyed across the ocean and launched into the sea near the coast carrying fuel to move them 300 or 400 miles inland'. Sound though these predictions were, Fuller did allow his enthusiasm to run away with him, foreseeing the days of a 'floating mechanical base' from which the 'ships will launch our floating mechanical army. This force propels itself ashore, crawls up the beach . . . [and] it moves straight inland at a speed of ten miles an hour, and within twenty-four hours of landing is 150 miles within the enemy territories'. Fuller believed that such forces could spread chaos, 'and, when threatened by a superior force, it can make for the coastline, possibly several hundred miles away from its original point of landing, swim out to the fleet and re-embark'.[14]

It can be said confidently that such an operation, at least on any sizeable scale, is not feasible; apart from logistics Fuller had entirely overlooked the possibility that mechanization would actually make amphibious operations *more* difficult. That is to say, lorries and tanks could move to the coast more rapidly to reinforce shore garrisons than ships could reinforce landing forces thrown ashore. Moreover, any amphibious scheme had to give top priority to the capture of a major port. This contingency greatly reduced the strategic flexibility conferred by mechanized seapower. The importance attached by the 'Overlord' planners in 1944 to the early capture of Cherbourg is a clear example. The kind of results claimed by Fuller in 1920 could only be achieved against a power totally unprepared for war.[15]

These trends in Fuller's thought form the prelude to the publication of *The Reformation of War* in 1923, his most important book to date. In it he attempted to synthesize his ideas within the context of a general theory of war. The book had a chequered history. It was written within a month, mainly

between 9 and 10.30 plus an occasional Saturday afternoon and

Sunday. I limited myself to 65,000 words simply because publishers fight shy at longer books. It has many imperfections, this I know, and many omissions – I could easily have made it twice the length.

Fuller then had great difficulty in finding a publisher and sought Liddell Hart's advice. By 1922 the friendship of the two military thinkers, first begun somewhat tentatively by Liddell in 1920, had developed into something approaching equality; Fuller was still by far the senior figure but he respected Liddell Hart's ability and was not so conscious of his dignity that he would refuse to ask the advice of a younger man – one of his more pleasing traits. He also submitted the manuscript of the book for War Office approval and a 'frightful fuss' ensued. Though allowed to publish Fuller was recommended '*not* to do so!!'. The book was then hurriedly revised while the Fullers holidayed in Austria. 'I have been busy at this during the last 14 days', he informed Liddell Hart in October 1923, 'and have nearly finished the extra work.' Writing a book was no easy task for a serving officer; as he confided to Liddell Hart, 'I do want to get quit of this work as my future movements are uncertain.' *The Reformation of War* was finally accepted for publication by Hutchinson after a long struggle which entailed another revision. Fuller simply had to face up to the fact that 'military books are not in v[ery] great demand'.[16]

These vicissitudes account in part for a number of the book's unsatisfactory features. Fuller admitted candidly that *The Reformation of War* 'is simply a potboiler or rather a means of advertisement' so that he could secure the acceptance of a weightier book on the science of war. Field Marshal Lord Carver, reflecting half a century after its publication, claims that it contains some 'nuggets of gold' scattered in an argument otherwise cluttered by a 'profusion of high-flown language and exaggerated claims'. It is probably true, as Lord Carver suggests, that the great majority of officers found some of Fuller's claims 'little better than science fiction', but the book was not aimed primarily at a military audience. It was intended also to make educated civilians think about the future of British military policy. It was therefore provocative and some of Fuller's exaggerations were deliberate as he struggled to justify the tank before an audience of civilians – who were hardly noted for their interest in things military during these years. As a means of self-advertisement *The Reformation of*

War was perhaps too vulgar and rebounded on its author. That said, and also once it is conceded that it is difficult to estimate the degree to which Fuller would wildly assert an argument merely to provoke discussion, and that such posturing reduced the intellectual stature of the book, *The Reformation of War* does have an important place in Fuller's *oeuvre*. It forms an introduction to all that follows it, and *The Foundations of the Science of War* (1926), *The Dragon's Teeth* (1932), and *Lectures on FSR III* (1932), the three most important books of his maturity, all grew out of its leading arguments. The publication of *The Reformation of War* was a noted event: the first full-length attempt to work out a military theory based on the 'lessons' of the First World War which bore little relationship to conventional wisdom. Fuller believed that 'it is by exaggeration that man's mind is aroused', and Fuller's imprudent but stimulating book had an effect on young, thinking officers that was almost as important as its contents. For Captain Liddell Hart, *The Reformation of War* was 'the book of the century'.[17]

The starting point of Fuller's discussion was the tension he perceived between mobility and stability. In the military sphere this relationship was expressed in the link between the offensive and the defensive, 'for these acts form the halves of the diameter of the tactical circle, the circumference of which is the fight'. The weapons employed by men accentuate this connection – shock (close quarters) or projectiles. 'In all circumstances missile weapons must be employed to facilitate or ward off the shock.' Most of these points had appeared in earlier commentary but Fuller expanded them in this book by discounting the notion that the defensive was concerned merely with holding ground or resisting attacks, 'for it is just as much a part and parcel of every forward movement as every holding or retrograde one'. It was within this context that Fuller introduced Napoleon's dictum that the whole art of war consisted of a circumspect defensive followed by an audacious offensive. Fuller had his own use for this saying. Napoleon himself rarely employed the defensive-offensive. Of the great generals only Wellington made consistent use of it. During the Second World War the defensive-offensive technique as envisaged by Fuller was developed by Rommel (and later by Montgomery) in the Western Desert and also by Slim in Burma, who argued that a general 'seizes ground his enemy must recover at all costs and destroys him in the course of his counter-attacks'.[18]

There was another reason why the defensive-offensive appealed so much to Fuller. The concept embodied a contradiction. Fuller was greatly attracted to the philosopher Hegel's prescription of thesis, antithesis, synthesis. He attempted to synthesize material that sprang from the juxtaposition of contradictions into 'an integration'. There was no 'death to H when uniting with O it forms water . . . only a higher integration'. Such connections seemed to indicate the existence of tactical cycles, as every improvement in mobility had given rise to a new defensive form, and this had been overturned by a more efficient offensive means. 'Every increase in weapon-power not only leads to a new means of protective power being adopted but to an increase of moving power in order to avoid having to carry extra protection.' There were two types of protection, direct, which included earthworks and fortifications, and indirect, which nullified the effects of blows by employing mobility to move away from them. Fuller accordingly believed that the second was the most important protective form because 'any change in location necessitates a change in the enemy's tactical organization, and consequently a loss of time for destructive effect'. This remark was the origins of a persistent error in Fuller's later analysis of future mechanized operations, namely, the overestimation of the protective power of speed. In his view the deadlock of the First World War would not occur again because both sides would find it more advantageous to move in order to protect themselves rather than to halt and construct immobile defensive positions – an excessively optimistic view which he would have occasion to revise.[19]

These cyclical ideas were still only vaguely worked out in Fuller's mind. In *The Reformation of War* he contented himself by arguing that the First World War formed the culmination of an epoch in war when tactics were based wholly on increasing numbers of men and quantities of destructive power. The machine age was being ushered in and this would mechanize armies and reduce their dependence on muscular power and thus on numbers of men; consequently, their size and destructive power would be reduced. The First World War, he contended, had been

> based on a gigantic misconception of the true purpose of war, which is to enforce the policy of a nation *at the least cost to itself and enemy*, and, consequently, to the world, for so intricately are the resources of civilized states interwoven that to destroy any one country is simultaneously to wound all other nations.

Fuller had drawn this justification for limiting the destructive scope of war from a reading of John Maynard Keynes's immensely influential denunciation of the Paris Peace Settlement of 1919, *The Economic Consequences of the Peace*. Keynes attacked the punitive clauses of the Treaty of Versailles because they would hinder the economic recovery of Europe after the war. This prompted Fuller to call for an adaption of the military instrument to protect the growth of civilization and more readily suit the needs of the international environment. For the first time he introduced his readers to an appreciation of the work of the Polish banker, I. S. Bloch, who had predicted the deadlock of the First World War but been treated with derision by military audiences before 1914. Bloch received high praise in *The Reformation of War* for understanding that a nation's weapons developed from out of its industrial potential and that, given the conditions of 1914, any war between the great powers would have resulted in stalemate. Bloch was therefore 'able to visualize the nature of the next war more clearly than the most eminent of General Staff officers'. The next step was to assert that Bloch's reasoning could be overturned and the utility of war restored if its destructive effects could be reduced over a shorter time period. Thus the degree of force employed by a belligerent should be commensurate with its war aims. If a war could be ended swiftly and decisively, then the degree of force used could be reduced over the long run. The potential to reduce the length of wars depended on the use of new, more powerful weapons which the enemy might lack. This whole line of argument was derived from an interpretation of military history inspired by the Theory of Evolution as propounded by Herbert Spencer. The essential components of social evolution were, *progress* – that is, ceaseless change – necessity, adaption, continual modification until perfection is reached. It is important to identify these elements in Fuller's thinking before 1923.[20]

In his RUSI Gold Medal Essay and in *Tanks in the Great War*, Fuller argued that warfare had progressed under the influence of the Industrial Revolution, weapon-power became more powerful and the human target became smaller and more difficult to hit with projectiles. Whereas during the Thirty Years War (1618–48) ranks in the armies of Gustavus Adolphus were eight men deep, by the time of the Peninsular War (1808–14), Wellington had reduced them to two men deep. The Franco-Prussian War (1870–1) had witnessed wider and wider extensions, so that by the Boer

War (1899–1902) these had increased to fifteen paces per man. The Russo-Japanese War (1904–5) had seen large-scale entrenching and by 1914 'the spade was supreme', though most generals had not realized it. The trench deadlock was broken by the tank – a 'mechanical skirmishing fortress' – and by gas, which was a projectile like a high explosive shell, except that it allowed the 'attacker to "hit" an invisible target and increased the destructive effect of artillery fire many times'. Machine power and not manpower had become the most significant factor in the First World War. These changes would have an important influence on the future of war, Fuller predicted. 'That war will be eliminated by weapons, not by words or by treaties or leagues of nations: by weapons – leagues of tanks, aeroplanes and submarines – which will render opposition hopeless or retribution so terrible that nations will think not once or twice but many times before going to war.' This was a controversial view to air in 1920. Its prophetic insight hardly requires comment. 'That we have attained the final step on the evolutionary ladder of war', he concluded, 'is most unlikely, for mechanical and chemical weapons may disappear and be replaced by others still more terrible.'[21]

The Reformation of War was an important step in Fuller's work because he began to argue that *in battle* new weapons 'humanized' warfare. The heart of the problem was relating tactical novelty to an economical strategy; if battle could fulfil the strategical end more decisively then warfare would become more efficient and less destructive. Destructiveness was the measure of an inefficient system of warfare not an efficient one. This contention was at the heart of his belief that strategic paralysis combined with the tactical use of the tank would usher in a new epoch in war. As evidence for his proposition that weapons humanized war – the antithesis of popular wisdom that sophisticated weapons barbarize war – Fuller advanced the idea that projectiles reduced the savagery of hand-to-hand fighting. This was an idea taken from Clausewitz's great work, *On War*; this book remained an important influence throughout Fuller's career. Clausewitz believed that the experience of war had taught men 'more effective ways of using force than the crude expression of force'. He also predicted that in the future wars 'will again be severely restricted' and not 'so monumental in character'. Projectiles, he considered, 'instruments for the understanding; they allow the feelings the "instinct for fighting" properly called, to remain almost at rest, and this so much the more according to the range of their effects is greater'. If 'a certain degree of anger' accompanies the firing of a sling shot, 'there is less of this feeling in discharging a musket, and still less in firing a cannot shot'. The obscurity of the language and the clumsiness of the translation of Clausewitz read by Fuller should not conceal its valuable insight. It was because hostile emotions remained latent that Fuller declared projectile weapons a humanizing influence. Also, soldiers do not see the damage caused by their projectiles, while the action of men hewing with swords and axes under conditions 'nearest to the pugilist encounter' is all too evident as they tussle to overcome one another. Therefore as the size of the battlefield increased soldiers became insulated from the carnage of war.[22]

These arguments about the humanizing of war through technological changes reveal a striking ambivalence. Fuller was now inclined to the view that the potential of modern technology was so great that the ultimate goal of the progress of war was in reach, 'a bloodless war': 'it could dispense with the old custom of killing and could do something far more effective – it could petrify the human mind with fear . . . and will vastly reduce bloodshed'. Of course, to ensure this restriction, the opening phase of the next war would have to be terminated abruptly. At the same time, although shying away from bloodletting, Fuller continued to hold to a view popular before 1914 that war had a firm moral purpose – to enhance national character and sweep away moral decadence. Yet he shrank from the logical conclusion that this would entail, violence on a sizeable scale for a prolonged duration. Instead he claimed that if war was a continuation of peace policy, then it was linked with the post-war policy that followed. 'During peace man's policy is to live and not to die: consequently, if war be a continuation of this policy, then soldiers should not be sacrificed like rabbits in an Australian hutch.' Fuller could only have this argument both ways if future wars could be reduced in destructive scope. The relevance to Fuller's thinking of William James's celebrated essay, 'The Moral Equivalent of War' is clear. Fuller had read a lot of William James's work in his youth and found it stimulating. At the heart of his ambivalence lay an inversion of the argument underlying James's essay. James called for the introduction of the moral equivalent of war in peacetime, as the martial virtues 'are absolute and permanent goods'. Fuller conceived the need for a moral equivalent of peace in wartime.

Peacetime ethics, business efficiency, technical skill and fraternal care should take their place with the martial spirit – courage, duty and self-sacrifice – in warfare and enable it to reach a 'higher ethical position'. His conception depended on the technology fulfilling its promise; if the ethics of war and peace were to become indivisible then warfare would have to become more decisive, more *useful* a human activity and the traditional boundaries between war and peace lessened. After the French invasion of the Ruhr in 1923, in an attempt to force Germany to meet its reparations commitments under the Versailles Treaty, Fuller wrote:

> It all depends where one draws the line . . . If there is no line then the Ruhr operations are operations of war. If the line is the recognized one, then they are preparations for the next war. Every next war, so far, has been a developed form of the last.[23]

His vision was only partly realized because the technological development of weapons and the employment of devices such as psychological paralysis opened a veritable Pandora's box. The battles of 1939–41 could be likened to Fuller's ideal, the fruit of preparation for war, followed by abrupt periods of hostility of short duration, rather like the various Napoleonic Wars. The years afterwards became even more brutal and destructive than the First World War. For example, psychological paralysis, if taken to its logical conclusion, would require the systematic assassination of opposing generals. When a young officer asked the Duke of Wellington on the field of Waterloo for permission to shoot Napoleon, the Duke was appalled. 'No, no. Generals commanding armies have something else to do than to shoot at one another.' Fuller would have agreed with the chivalrous spirit behind this remark. A degree of chivalry did mark the North African Campaign, nonetheless the British did not flinch from attempting to kill Rommel in the Keyes Raid of 1941 before the opening of Operation 'Battleaxe'. Fuller had no patience with such efforts. 'To enter houses at night[,] shoot up sleeping enemy soldiers and run away is not war.' Surely this was the logical culmination of strategic paralysis?[24]

The value of Fuller's prognosis was dependent less on the validity of the conclusions he drew from the conduct of the First World War than on his calculation that new weapons had actually opened a new epoch in the history of war. This was far less certain. He greatly overestimated the moral effect of new weapons, especially the impact of tanks, gas and aeroplanes on the rear of the enemy's army, and strategically against his rear – the civil will. To take aircraft first. The role of strategic bombing played a far larger part in his thinking than in that of Liddell Hart. Fuller believed that the appearance of 500 bombers carrying 500 ten pound bombs or quantities of mustard gas could 'cause 200,000 minor casualties' and throw a city the size of London into confusion 'within half an hour of their arrival'. He continued:

Picture . . . what the result will be: London for several days will be one raving Bedlam, the hospitals will be stormed, traffic will cease, . . . the city will be in a pandemonium. What of the government at Westminster? It will be swept away by an avalanche of terror. Then will the enemy dictate his terms, which will be grasped at like a straw by a drowning man. Thus may a war be won in forty-eight hours and the losses of the winning side may be actually nil![25]

This is a much quoted passage: it is splendid journalism. It would appear, however, that Fuller had been reading too many H. G. Wells novels. Even allowing for deliberate exaggeration, this lurid description is a grotesque distortion of reality. It assumed the maximum preparation on one side and the minimum on the other. Fuller's earnest desire to acquire 'scientific detachment' seems to have deserted him when he considered the future of air power. His writings actually supported, rather than detracted from, the conventional wisdom of the time. Fuller was typical in that 'when the officers of the older services were not directly involved in the battle between the services, they were often voicing similar conclusions about air war as the most dedicated air power enthusiast'. Fuller's low opinion of the fighting qualities of the great mass of his fellow citizens (which was not exceptional) led him to conclude that 'panic' would lead directly to the 'collapse' of the war effort. This included the dislocation of industrial production as well as the resignation of the government of the day. No such organic link actually existed. Outbursts of panic had occurred during the First World War after air raids. In 1915, for instance, Hull had to be policed by 'Voluntary Patrollers' after the first Zeppelin Raids. Fuller and other pundits drew quite misleading 'lessons' from these examples.[26]

Strategic bombing raids worked as a catalyst which reinforced a resolve to fight on – a development which quite undercut strategic paralysis. There is no correlation between fear and cowardice, and this is perhaps the greatest flaw in the theory. Fuller made no allowance for movements in the population of cities, particularly by evacuation, and failed to take into account that the cumulative effect of bombing would have greatly reduced effects after the first raids – a kind of strategic law of diminishing returns. His predictions of likely casualty rates were greatly exaggerated. As far as industrial production was concerned, he took the available figures from 1914–18, when indeed the dramatic and unexpected appearance of Zeppelins and Gotha bombers had temporarily halted production in isolated areas for varying periods, and then applied them across the board. He overlooked precautions that might ensure the continuation of production, like the dispersal or concealment of factories. Nor did he allow for the ameliorating effect of constant public discussion of the air problem. Of course Fuller was by no means alone in these miscalculations: 'the interwar years in Britain', writes Barry Powers, 'were not ones of very logical and dispassionate thinking about the future air threat'. Fuller's mistakes arose largely from his attempt to fit all military developments into the framework of a new theory of war. He twisted the evidence and from this faulty interpretation predicted developments that, in his view, seemed to fit a new trend.[27]

The same criticism can be made of his treatment of gas warfare in *The Reformation of War*. Fuller had shown no interest in gas warfare during the First World War. His plans for Cambrai and 'Plan 1919' had made no reference to its potential. Fuller now subscribed to the provocative thesis that gas was a demoralizing weapon *par excellence*, 'as it can terrorize without necessarily killing, it, more than any other known weapon, can enforce economically the policy of one nation on another'. Then, basing his argument on United States statistics, he claimed that only 1.87 per cent of gas casualties proved fatal. It was accordingly more humane than other projectile weapons. There is some truth in Fuller's claims. Gas was one of the most feared weapons employed on the Western Front. It caused, in the words of one soldier 'frightful pandemonium' as men struggled to get their gas masks on; two or three gas alarms a night were frequent. 'Gas shock was as frequent as shell shock.' Nevertheless once again there were several important qualifying factors that reduce confidence in Fuller's predictions. The ethical question is a complex one. Fuller certainly had a point when he claimed it was otiose to draw moral distinctions between ghastly shrapnel wounds and the effect of chemical agents. There are however degrees of human suffering; the side effects of these gases were horrific and their moral impact was not mitigated by the development of non-lethal gases. The risks of precipitating war are so great that commanders prefer to clinch their gains by using lethal means. Developments in chemical warfare became more rather than less inhumane, and during the Second World War no power dared use gas because of the retribution it might provoke. Fuller's prediction that 'gas will not only effect an equally great revolution of means [as gunpowder], but also a revolution in idea', was wrongheaded. It might be consistent with his addiction to method but not necessarily with the evidence.[28]

Fuller's initial post-war concern with the tank was guided by a similar theme. He tried to show that it could attack the morally weakest part of the enemy's battle body – his rear. In his discussion Fuller pursued the analogy he made in 'Plan 1919' that an army resembled the organs of the human body. He conceived a battle as a series of fights 'compounded of the elements of war operating concentrically round the problem of how to give blows without receiving them'. These elements could be reduced, as Fuller had already shown, to four acts: the assembly, the approach, the attack and the pursuit – the 'dividend' of victory which was the tank's forté. 'I maintain', wrote Fuller, 'that a pursuit nearly always requires fresh troops and if possible, troops of a more mobile nature than those which have been defeated.' Infantry pursuing infantry or cavalry pursuing cavalry 'has seldom proved effective because the pursued are racing for their lives, whilst the pursuers are only attempting to take the lives of others'. Fuller deduced that 'it is here that the Tank becomes such an important weapon since cavalry are practically useless in a modern pursuit'. The battles outlined resembled those of 1918 and not battles between mechanized forces.[29]

Fuller's interest in the pursuit was inspired by a combination of experience and Clausewitz's writings on the subject. In *On War* Clausewitz claimed that no victory was truly effective without a pursuit. He wrote: 'pursuit makes up the second act of the victory

and in many cases is more important than the first'. He also
analysed the value of cavalry, pointing out that though it was a
subsidiary arm in the main engagement, its powers were most
fully realized during the pursuit. Without an efficient mobile arm
warfare is slowed down and an advance 'has to be organized
more carefully'. Fuller dwelt nostalgically on the romantic character
of past cavalry charges. 'Of all operations in war it was the most
rapid and the most effective, for though its killing power was
seldom as great as that of infantry, its disorganizing and
demoralizing power was terrific.' In the pursuit Fuller claimed
that the tank would be devastating: 'rousing hostile bivouacs . . .
they will reduce the enemy to a demented mob'. Only the means
behind the cavalry charge had altered.[30]

The actual mechanics of battle operated through an interaction
of movement and protection. 'An attack should aim', wrote Fuller,
'at pushing forward a series of bases of operation, a new force
operating from each base successively.' These bases must be
given stability, and as the time factor was of supreme importance,
and resistance along the whole front was unlikely to be equal, it
'becomes necessary to fix a period at which each base halts, for by
doing so, it will enable the new base to be pushed forward'. By
the early 1920s Fuller had already understood that future battles
would revolve around the offensive power of the tank and the
defensive power of the land mine – a modern equivalent of the
medieval moat. Hence a careful delineation of the priority allocated
to the approach and the attack in battle. 'I do not agree with you
as regards the bad influence of limited objectives', he informed
Liddell Hart in 1920, 'objectives are limited by human endurance
and by the possibility of pushing in fresh reserves directly the
battlefront as a whole is becoming exhausted'; this argument was
also drawn from Clausewitz, and was to underpin Fuller's later
writings on future armoured operations. Clausewitz stressed: 'the
envelopment must be tactical; a strategic envelopment concurrent
with a major blow is a complete waste of strength'. This line of
argument was also to lead to a major difference of view with
Liddell Hart within a decade.[31]

Had the cavalry been as decisive in battle as Fuller contended?
In 1922 he wrote to Liddell Hart comparing the results of the
Battles of Ligny (1815) and Jena (1806). 'The Prussians were
dislodged at the first but were not destroyed, at the second they
were dislodged and destroyed, destruction being effected by

cavalry.' Fuller interpreted military history in his own favour. The opposite case could easily be made: The decisive act of battle was the infantry versus infantry encounter with the cavalry consummating the success won by the infantry supported by the artillery. The most decisive battles of the Napoleonic Wars, Leipzig (1813) and Waterloo (1815), were both decided by infantry action. A devastating cavalry pursuit was mounted after Waterloo, but this merely clinched the rout of the French Army thrown into confusion by the repulse of the Old Guard – an infantry versus infantry engagement – which Wellington followed up by a counter-attack. The French were driven from the field when he linked up with the advancing Prussians.[32]

Fuller's view of future mechanized operations was also supported by two other historical examples. The first was Alexander's Macedonian Army which first began to engage his attention during the First World War. Fuller likened Alexander's tactical problem to that facing the generals in 1917. If he increased the weapon-power of his phalanx of infantry by adding to the length of the sarissa (the Macedonian pike) he would reduce his mobility – exactly as increased artillery fire had in 1916–17. Alexander thus made 'extensive use of cavalry directly the enemy's ranks were broken' and his greatest victories were completed with a cavalry charge. The future evolution of armies would follow that of Alexander: hoplites would disorganize the enemy and cavalry would annihilate him. The second example was drawn from the Middle Ages, a time according to Fuller, when 'the armoured knights ruled the battlefield, infantry were employed merely to garrison castles, or to hold tactical points such as swamps, forests or hill-tops . . . localities in which knights could not move'. He did not suggest that modern wars would resemble those of earlier periods, but with a cyclical view in mind, argued that no matter how weapons might change, they fulfilled certain tactical functions, and these were unchanging.[33]

Like a column of heavily armoured knights, Fuller envisaged mechanized forces of the future moving across country, accompanied by 'tank mine layers' and the infantry 'in cross country transporters'; cross country diggers would have replaced the spade so, when halted, the infantry would seek protection in entrenched (but mobile) camps. Speed would be their greatest asset: 'from the military point of view, one hour is not 60 minutes, but what is accomplished in 60 minutes'; and as the armoured

forces drove deep into the enemy's rear they would be co-
ordinated by wireless. This foresight is acute but Fuller tended to
exaggerate the moral influence of tanks. He argued, for example,
that armoured forces moving under cover of smoke would
confuse defenders; but smoke was a double-edged weapon if
employed against a skilful enemy. It broke up control of the
attacking forces and it was they rather than the defender who was
likely to be confused. If smoke clouds fell short of the enemy's
positions then tanks usually presented clear and vulnerable
targets.[34]

Fuller nevertheless continued to believe that the moral power of
the tank was overwhelming. In *The Reformation of War* he
dogmatically predicted that infantry would be reduced to the
status of field 'police and the defenders of positions – rail-heads,
bridge-heads, workshops and supply magazines'. It is unlikely
that these tactless comments advanced the cause of mechanization.
Instead of claiming that infantry would be rendered impotent by
the tank, Fuller should have rounded upon and demonstrated the
falsity of certain misconceptions about its future role. The CIGS,
for instance, Lord Cavan, failed to understand that tanks were
most effective in turning flanks. He persisted in arguing that
'Under even the worst fire men will often cling to their positions;
it is usually safer than to run away.' If the enemy was forced to cling
to his position and then out-flanked, that very act of obstinacy
would contribute to his annihilation. Cavan also believed that it
was 'the actual physical threat of steel' that forced the enemy to
retreat, 'and this threat the mechanized battalion is comparatively
powerless to give' – an extraordinary argument. In private, or in
his essays, Fuller was more prudent. He conceded the need for
'closer and closer co-operation with the infantry, [because] . . . of
the ever increasing number of machine-guns rendered possible by
cross-country tractors'; and companies of tanks would have to be
attached to infantry battalions. The evolutionary process of
weapon-power would eventually change these proportions and
'we may expect to see the future battalion represented by three or
four tank companies equipped with one or more types of machine,
and one company of mechanically transported infantry'. Fuller was
also anxious privately not to give the impression that he thought
infantry valueless. Unfortunately in *The Reformation of War* he
branded infantry as the 'queen of fortresses' – a blatant and

flippant gibe at their description in the *Field Service Regulations* as the 'queen of battles', more likely to annoy than to make an officer think about his assumptions.[35]

The legacy of *The Reformation of War* was a mixed one. This book was important and influential in suggesting that the impact of technological development on war would become the cardinal factor: speed of invention was crucial because the next war would largely be waged by the machine. Fuller was also correct in foreseeing the need to introduce self-propelled artillery and improve training procedures. Ceaseless rifle drill 'deadens the brains and does not produce a reserve adaptable to reinforce the other short range arms.' The introduction of mechanization required training methods to ensure that '*No individual, once he had finished his individual training, should be considered fully trained unless he can take the place of his immediate superior.*' Especially praiseworthy was his understanding of the need for a body of engineers to take their place 'in the van of the battle'; though this need was not fully met until the Royal Corps of Electrical and Mechanical Engineers was founded in October 1942.[36]

The Reformation of War was however responsible for spreading two fallacious arguments: that tanks would economize on the numbers of infantry required, and that these would stand aside during the tank battle. Official thinking about mechanization was rightly sceptical about its influence on infantry fighting. Cavan thought it possible that one day each battalion might 'be transported in its own land-ship' but, if general efficiency was considered, he rejected any idea that mechanization would reduce the numbers of infantry battalions; thus mechanization *in toto* did 'not hold out to the politician nearly such attractive prospects of effecting savings'; Cavan added: 'Some day, we may pull our infantry into tanks and assault with them', but that day would be far off and they were still needed. The danger posed by armoured forces could actually be cancelled out by *increasing* the size of infantry forces. This nullified the strategic flexibility attained with mechanization. A country could reduce the likelihood of amphibious invasion, for example, by mobilizing sufficient manpower resources to guard its shores. The continuing need for infantry however was simply due to the fact that Fuller's calculations were only partly accurate. The defenders of infantry argued that they could shelter behind obstacles and only the opposing infantry could drive them back. Fuller replied that 'They may be dislodged by gas or some other means'. Yet this did not occur and infantry remained to dominate future battlefields, a much tougher species than he had reckoned on.[37]

4

'The Dawn of a New Era in Military Thought'? 1924–8

If you will permit me to say so, it [the science of war concept] is the forerunner of the dawn of a new era in military thought – the product of an 'organized' brain, which has hitherto been entirely lacking in all British military writing and rare even abroad.

Liddell Hart to Fuller, 14 June 1920, LHP 1/302/3

As for the philosophers, they make imaginary laws for imaginary commonwealths; and their discourses are as the stars, which give little light, because they are so high.

Francis Bacon, *On the Advancement of Learning* (London: Dent edn, 1954) p. 206

The greatest danger to the Staff College is a swollen head.

Brigadier General F. P. Crozier, *Impressions and Recollections* (London: T. Werner Laurie, 1930) p. 132

'I cannot even to pretend to understand the mentality which . . . shelters itself behind regulations and dares not face criticism', wrote Colonel (Later General Sir) Bernard Paget to Fuller in December 1923. Twelve months earlier, in January 1923, Fuller had taken up a Staff College appointment as a chief instructor. Camberley was, he quipped to Liddell Hart, '35 miles from London but 3500 miles from civilization'. During his period there he wrote about a hundred lectures and from these distilled a weighty volume entitled *The Foundations of the Science of War*. Many progressive officers had urged Fuller to undertake this work. Paget had claimed that such a book 'would fill a gap, which no one except yourself had yet had the courage to fill'. This chapter is devoted to an analysis of this book and two others that form historical appendices to it, *Sir John Moore's System of Training* and *British Light Infantry in the Eighteenth Century*, both published in 1925. The publication of *The Foundations of the Science of War* was marked by a heated controversy which damaged Fuller's career. Although he looked upon the book as his *magnum opus* and believed it carried forward progressive hopes, the book's appearance was ridiculed or ignored. In retrospect this hostility was but a pretext for airing a dislike of Fuller that had built up in established quarters, and had as its focal point an anonymous review in *The Army Quarterly*. The danger of Fuller's book, commented the reviewer, 'is that the young might take it too seriously'. The reviewer would no doubt have been annoyed by Paget's belief that 'I, with so many others, look to you to lead the way to progress and a better way of things.' The main theme of this chapter is that, though many of the criticisms of Fuller's faulty presentation of the argument were justified, the neglect of this book was not. A belated recognition of Fuller's important role in evaluating the principles of war, and the increasing attention which these are now receiving from military commentators, more than justifies a lengthy study of this book and the controversy it aroused in the British Army.[1]

The Foundations of the Science of War also fulfilled an important educational function. The British Army has always insisted that 'character' was the most important component of successful generalship. This was not at all odd. The whole thrust of British education before 1945 had aimed to develop 'character' at the expense of intellect, and the public school system was geared to learning by rote and the painstaking translation of classical texts. The humanities and the sciences were neglected. The military schools were modelled on similar lines and required the learning of received truth. Fuller was of the opinion that the Army could not be adequately reformed until this method of instruction was changed. He also insisted that in modern warfare there was a connection between character and intellect. As Napoleon said, 'The military leader must possess as much character as intellect – the base must equal the height.' To broaden the base Fuller introduced into his Staff College lectures a study of psychology, philosophy and the influence of technology on weapons and tactics – subjects which had been conspicuous by their absence previously.[2]

Fuller's intention has been aptly summed up by Mrs Alison

Starr: *The Foundations of the Science of War* could be read as 'the foundations of the science of life'. In Fuller's view there was an intimate connection between war and society, 'to understand war . . . you must understand peace: the psychology of the people . . . the nature of their institutions, their industry, commerce, politics and finance'. As part of this experiment Fuller introduced radical teaching methods. 'The Staff College was run like a school (absurd)', he wrote in 1926, 'I, in my division, changed it into a university. I did not care whether the students worked or not – and they worked all the harder for it.' He also announced, 'Nothing clarifies true knowledge like a free exchange of ideas; consequently, because I happen to be a Colonel and you a Captain or Major, do not imagine for a moment that rank is a bar to free speech.' No matter what its other deficiencies may be, *The Foundations of the Science of War* formed an important point of departure for radical new ways of thinking about war.[3]

The main thesis of this book was that war could be reduced to a science with definite principles and laws which governed the operation of the whole – the art of war – 'the conditions of the moment . . . by the laws of existence – action and inertia'. Fuller sought amid the chaos of war clear and distinct principles as a guide to strategical action. 'These laws', writes Michael Howard, 'created a pattern of behaviour uniform throughout the world, and by observing a part one could deduce the principles which operated the whole.' This revival of interest in classical military thinking reflected a renewed interest in laws and principles sparked off by evolutionism; such laws resembled but were by no means identical to those perceived by eighteenth century *philosophes*. Fuller's own starting point were the references made by Napoleon and Clausewitz to the influence of scientific phenomena on war. For example, Clausewitz said that 'Action in war is like movement in a resistant element.' Also he added, *'immobility* and *inactivity* are the normal *state* of armies in war, and *action is the exception'*. In his logical way Fuller turned to the scientific literature of his day and asked: upon what evidence are such assertions founded, and if valid what implications do they have for the conduct of war?[4]

The disciples of Darwin had not been slow in advancing opinions about the character of the forces that influenced the development of the universe, and it is to these writers that Fuller turned for enlightenment. Herbert Spencer and his disciples held that all phenomena, including man himself, depended on the 'incessant and indestructible motion which pervades all bodies and all space, and which acts according to invariable laws'; namely, that stronger forces overcame weaker ones. The human body was also subject to this contradiction between action and reaction. Thus the central unity of phenomena was as central to Fuller's concept of warfare as to that of Clausewitz. More controversial was Fuller's personal view of this unity which he saw reflected in the threefold order – that the world was three dimensional and that man's thought and action reflected these dimensions. 'This three fold order I believe to be the key to the understanding of all things; it is my postulate.'[5]

Fuller, again like Clausewitz, projected a thesis, antithesis and synthesis in the manner of Hegel. He had employed this device in his earlier writings but had declined to give it such prominence. In *The Foundations of the Science of War* he considered 'The 3-fold order . . . the key . . . 3 main and all embracing quantities. . . . The whole question is the Expenditure and Maintenance of Force.' This philosophical leaning shows the heavy influence of German idealistic philosophy. There is little evidence that Fuller was acquainted with either Hegel or Lasalle in the original; he seems to have absorbed their ideas through the medium of Spencer's synthetic philosophy or the writings of Henry Maudsley, an English Hegelian whom Fuller greatly admired. Yet whatever its antecedents, the three fold order was, as both Jay Luvaas and General Trythall have pointed out, a personal fancy elevated to the heights of philosophic truth. It was a hostage to fortune. Reflecting on Fuller's belief that we conceive nature as 'earth, water and air, and mankind as men, women and children', *The Army Quarterly* reviewer, Brigadier General J. E. Edmonds, the official historian, observed, 'besides we might add, wearing "coat, trousers and boots" and using "knife, fork and spoon"'.[6]

A second aspect of the three fold order which Fuller emphasized was that 'the most economical military organization is the one which expresses the closest relationship to the organization of the human body'. The structure, control and maintenance of man's existence reflected on the activities of his body, brain and soul; these were founded on a negative element (stability), a positive element (activity), harmonized by a relative element (co-operation). From these elements were derived 'three modes of force which must be expended, controlled and maintained in war': the desire to protect life (stable); the power to fight (active); and the ability to move (co-operation). This kind of biological argument was not new in his thinking either but its reiteration in *The Foundations of the Science of War* was more highly developed. From this physiographic basis Fuller drew a connection between the elements of existence and the defensive, offensive and mobility. In armies these were expressed in tactical functions and implemented by principles of war. Like Jomini he believed that though weapons and methods of war may change, the principles of war remained constant.[7]

Fuller then gauged that the main tactical problem was overcoming inertia and maintaining velocity, Clausewitz's 'resistant element'. The finest example that Fuller could find that was able to employ mobility to the best effect was the army of Alexander the Great. Following on from his brief discussion in *The Reformation of War*, Fuller argued that Alexander's troops fulfilled three tactical functions as they were based on three arms, the light infantry (*psiloi*), heavy infantry (*hoplites*) and cavalry (*cataphracti*). The heavy infantry provided stability and from this base the light infantry moved out to harass the enemy. The light infantry were the co-operative element because the heavy infantry lacked mobility and were vulnerable to cavalry action if they tried to pursue.

> Thus [the light infantry] compel the hostile soldiers to protect themselves; that is, to stabilize their activity. The phalanx then catches up with the fixed enemy and breaks his organization into pieces. Eventually the cavalry follow and destroy the scattered fragments.

The relationship between stability, activity and mobility remained the perennial basis of tactics.[8]

Once these tactical functions had been evaluated then a science of war could be established, 'a workable piece of mental machinery' that could expose military values. Fuller was advocating systematic research and preparation along similar lines to that carried out by the German General Staff. This would render the planning and conduct of military operations the permanent sphere of officers equipped mentally to develop the study of war into a solid body of knowledge that could be handed down to their successors and adapted to changes in military conditions. However, in trying to justify the abstract reasoning on which his ideas were based, Fuller plunged into a quagmire of his own making; a trap laid by his intellect and sprung by his conceit. He aimed to 'obtain so firm a mental grip on war' that the unintellectual and unprofessional British officer 'with his hands will accomplish what our brains have devised'. Fuller's mental 'grip' was not as tight as it should have been. His search for a common body of doctrine for the Army was laudable, but he failed lamentably to present it simply and clearly.[9]

Liddell Hart's appreciation of his basic ideas was enthusiastic. After perusing an early draft of the original lectures he found them 'difficult reading' and perhaps confusing; but 'After a second reading the impression is that they are the most brilliant contribution to scientific military thought that has ever been made', and claimed that 'The man who cannot understand these lectures is totally unfit to hold high command or staff appointment in modern scientific wars.' Regrettably there were too many officers who could not understand them. Fuller conceded that Liddell Hart's initial criticism was just. 'I *know* there *is* something missing in it, the whole argument do[es] not as yet go home with a click. I shall get it right some day, meanwhile I think it is sufficiently right to form a working basis.' Nonetheless Fuller neglected the problem of fluency and concentrated on the integration of the book's ideas. The overall structure of the book is cogent. It is the style which mars its clarity, being repetitious, erratic and self-conscious. Fuller should have paid more attention to achieving literary grace (after all the book would be finally judged on this score), and less to exposing philosophical vagaries. 'The Science of War. Idea (? 5 seconds), gestation (15 years), writing (3 months). Remember that logic is but a means to an end. Sometimes the end requires it to be rigid, sometimes flexible, sometimes fluid, sometimes illogical.' In the abstract this is true, but with a military audience in mind, and one not fully acquainted with such philosophical subtleties, it was urgent that Fuller acquired readability and simplicity of exposition. Even as late as February 1925 Fuller still had not settled the book's general format, but he was pleased to report that 'I have got the principles more logical.' As Spenser Wilkinson warned Liddell Hart, no matter how good Fuller's ideas were, soldiers would not study books that were difficult to read.[10]

Fuller committed a grave blunder in attempting to explore and elaborate in detail his ideas about science. It was the introduction of scientific vocabulary into the study of war which provoked such scorn. 'What did you think of Fuller's latest book?' asked a vocal conservative general, Montgomery-Massingberd, of Liddell Hart. 'I hope someone will stop him making such an ass of himself.' When Liddell Hart inquired whether Montgomery-Massingberd had actually read the book, it emerged that, though he had been greatly amused by hostile reviews, not least Edmonds's in *The Army Quarterly*, he had not even lifted the dust cover. 'It would only annoy me!' This remark has now acquired some notoriety as a typical 'blimpish' outburst. Montgomery-Massingberd found it 'impossible to take him [Fuller] seriously or derive any pleasure from reading what he has written'. Fuller's intolerance and ostentatious display of his own knowledge invariably provoked such 'blimpish' denunciations from conservative officers. 'There are two classes of people I have no time for –', declared Montgomery-Massingberd. 'Those who run down and crab everyone above them and those who think that because they have read a little Military History everyone else is an ignoramus . . . Fuller comes into both Categories!' In this instance, Fuller advanced ideas that instinctively repelled conservatives; and he did so in an unduly complicated style calculated to befuddle the mind of the average British officer. He left himself exposed to the criticism that his ideas were so pretentious and high flown that they were irrelevant. Edmonds took some delight in suggesting 'that those who "can't", teach' and then teach nothing of interest for the practical soldier. This was far from being the case, but the clouds of Fuller's phrases obscured the shafts of insight and the book's fundamental value. Paget had thought Fuller's earlier lecture on the 'Science of War' a 'model of clear and thorough thought expressed in logical sequence'; and other friendly critics thought that Fuller's short essays were much more lucid than *The Foundations of the Science of War*.[11]

Two points need to be advanced concerning the book's hostile reception. First, Fuller's arrogance had stimulated a resentment which rebounded on the ideas he advanced, irrespective of their merit. His thesis indicted by implication a whole generation of British officers as amateurs, or worse. ('I am trying to work out a science of war and not a *vade mecum* for fools.') It was hardly likely that it would make many friends if expressed in tactless language. Fuller should have cushioned the blow with a little diplomacy, but he seemed to go out of his to annoy his seniors. His truculence when the CIGS, Lord Cavan, ('a little rabbit of a man') refused him permission to publish *The Foundations of the Science of War* when it was first mooted in 1923, upset the War Office. Cavan's attitude he branded 'only 800 years out of date'. Fuller was, of course, expressing so much post-war idealism in these attacks, that the foolishness of past military thought and doctrine must be swept aside and replaced by more radical ideas, and he received considerable support from middle-ranking officers. Paget complained of Cavan's prohibition that it 'depresses me beyond measure because it means that so much of the sacrifice of the war has been in vain and that we are not to progress'. He was not cheered up by the thought that 'we are expected to rely on mental sustenance entirely upon the training manuals' as these were 'neither so super-human in their wisdom nor so satisfying in their sufficiency that we can hope to keep the military body and soul together.' Nevertheless idealism and diplomacy must work together in the cause of reform. Much as one may sympathize with Fuller's frustration, his manner of expressing it must be deplored, and threats to 'indulge in a little frightfulness – the *Daily Mail* etc' must be viewed as counter-productive. His tussles with the War Office were conducted in a curiously fatalistic mood. 'I shall end by having my throat cut – it is inevitable.'[12]

Fuller treated the controversy over his book, secondly, as further evidence that he was surrounded by fools. 'What is wrong with us is that we hate thinking', he observed. 'No one had to think over the *Reformation of War* but over the *Science of War* they must think a little, therefore the book is a bad one in the eyes of our "men of action".' There is some justice in this complaint; but hostility was by no means a uniform reaction; Fuller did receive support from other journals, though the editor of *The Army Quarterly* sided with his reviewer in warning Fuller that he should learn to be more concise, as men of action lacked the time to read long and complicated books. Also, the controversy over the book did not prevent the announcement of Fuller's appointment as commander of the new Experimental Brigade in December 1926, which was to conduct detailed manoeuvres with mechanized forces. The degree of intellectual intolerance to be found at the highest reaches of the Army can be exaggerated. What was not inevitable was that Fuller would cut his *own* throat by resigning this command petulantly. The upshot of these developments was that the debate over the science of war was conducted in a facile but superficial way. It concentrated on the forms rather than the substance of the question. Areas of mutual agreement were ignored. It is certainly paradoxical that a book devoted to objectivity, reason and scientific thinking should generate a discussion so charged with emotion. Given the author perhaps this is not surprising.[13]

From the outset Fuller's critics cast doubt on the originality of his concept. Both Edmonds in his review and Montgomery-Massingberd in correspondence with Liddell Hart, denied that Fuller was writing about anything new in *The Foundations of the Science of War*. 'Surely that has been done before but in clearer language?' asked Montgomery-Massingberd. He was probably thinking of Henderson's *Science of War*; though in this and other books the fundamental question *why* was war a science was not asked. Fuller did try to ask this question though with limited success. Yet the concept was not entirely his own. His greatest debt was to Colonel F. N. Maude. In July 1912 Maude had given a lecture entitled 'The Science of Organization and the Art of War', in which the themes of Fuller's later writings were first rehearsed. Maude defined the science of organization as 'a synthetic science the principles of which are involved in the applied sciences'. He went on to link this with the conduct of war, suggesting that war was both a science and an art, 'connected by a common link or blood relationship to one another'; such a relationship, Maude argued, was governed by an axiom and three principles. The three principles included the line of least resistance and the axiom that society was an extension of the individual. Maude's presentation of the argument was highly mystical in tone, showing an interest in the arrangement of threes and in the qabalistic drawings that Edmonds found so amusing in Fuller's book. Indeed it has been recently suggested that 'A cautious parallel may be drawn between the rhetorical styles of Maude and J. F. C. Fuller, though the two writers are not of comparable intellectual stature.' They both possessed 'an almost mystical sense of the study of war' and an attachment to first principles, of the 'existence of which neither had the slightest doubt'. The parallel may be more than cautiously stated. By asserting that economy of effort 'is indeed the predominant principle underlying all natural

Development and the Law of Evolution', Maude was pioneering the kind of thinking that Fuller developed to its logical conclusion after 1918.[14]

If Fuller's ideas were not as esoteric as his critics claimed, what value did these 'scientific' ideas have for the conduct of war? Within three years of the publication of *The Foundations of the Science of War*, two other books had appeared refuting his thesis that war could be reduced to a science: V. W. Germains, *The 'Mechanization' of War* (1927) and Major General Sir Frederick Maurice, *British Strategy* (1929). The debate was therefore fruitful. Fuller had noted the ambivalence of writers when discussing principles of war. Some writers refused to believe that they existed (and Germains does not list them); others agreed that they influenced warfare but did not trouble to define them; another group referred to principles only by inference 'without much scientific proof'. Fuller agreed wholeheartedly with the main conservative authority, Maurice, when he warned that 'War being a very serious and practical matter, knowledge of its principles in the abstract is of very little value.' Writing with the approbation of the CIGS, General (later Field Marshal Lord) Milne, Maurice claimed that principles did not provide foolproof formulae but only laid down guidelines for thinking about war. Thus, when Liddell Hart began to draw elaborate diagrams showing the interaction of the various principles, Fuller cast them aside in exasperation. 'I really cannot follow your qabalistic tables. . . . This is all playing at war.' Liddell Hart was at a loss to explain an ambivalence that Fuller so bitterly denounced in others. If this was his view, he wrote, 'why did he, Fuller, subsequently write a whole book on these lines?! – i.e. his 1926 book *The Foundations of the Science of War*.' Of course Fuller's attitude can be justified, and was consistent with Clausewitz's wise caution that laws and principles provide a soldier only 'with a frame of reference for the movements he has been trained to carry out, rather than to serve as a guide which at the moment of action lays down precisely the path he must take'. Nevertheless he was less free of the ambivalences of the majority of his profession than he liked to think.[15]

Fuller's conception of principles of war and their value is derived from a study of Napoleonic practice in which reasonably small armies (of about 150 000 men) moved quickly and secured decisive results. He stressed how Napoleon 'refused to accept circumstances as they appeared . . . he went into alliance with them, and turned them to his own advantage'. Principles could reduce the caprice of fate to a significant degree. They enabled a commander to think in terms of the essential, wasting no time on details and led him to take quick and clear-cut decisions. The flow of this stream of thought was implicitly anti-intellectual and depended on the importance of the 'inner' meaning of things as much as on reason. Here Fuller owed a clear debt to the writings of William James, especially in his advocacy of common sense. Fuller was convinced (and rightly) that generals should not be dominated by the intellect and argue over ideas for their own sake. Ideas had to have utility: thought and action had to be nicely balanced. The means of achieving this was through common sense. 'Common sense', he explained, 'is thought, sentiment or action adapted to circumstances and circumstances are those innumerable conditions which surround us, some of which are stable and others in a permanent state of flux.' A paradox lies at the heart of this approach. The anti-intellectualism implicit in its development tended to undercut the very intellectual approach that Fuller advocated. On the very last page of *The Foundations of the Science of War* Fuller declared boldly that the art of war could be reduced to one simple maxim, 'When in doubt, hit out'. If this was indeed the case then many officers could be forgiven for doubting whether Fuller required 335 pages of intricate scientific analysis to explain his position.[16]

Maurice agreed with Fuller that war was both a science and an art; but the scientific aspect only encompassed preparation for war. There was no room for scientific methods in the formulation of strategy. 'A leader in war can never treat his task as a scientist treats his', Maurice wrote. '[H]e can never know what is exactly in the mind of the enemy.' Germains's argument was more extreme. There could never be a science of war but there was a *technique*. 'To have a *science* of war, it would be necessary to deal with fixed and definite quantities.' Fuller's scientific terminology was brushed aside as 'solemn sounding nonsense . . . old truths restated in a pretentious and pedantic form'. Fuller never at any stage contended that war could be reduced to an exact science; rather, he suggested, following Napoleon, that the number of 'unseen' factors could be reduced; that knowledge of the enemy would increase by increments – perhaps with the aid of technology. Neither did Germains have any patience with Fuller's mystical language. 'It is emotionalism, not "science" to talk about "Witches Sabbaths", "Black Masses" and the rest of it.' The modern reader has some sympathy with this criticism. However, Germains's criticism was too severe. The importance Fuller attached to the value of meditation, for instance, was overlooked. Montgomery considered it 'absolutely vital' for commanders to free themselves from the tyranny of paperwork and minor details. 'No commander whose daily life is spent in the consideration of details, and who has not time for quiet thought and reflection, can make a sound plan of battle on a high level or conduct large-scale operations efficiently.' The difference between Fuller and Maurice, on the other hand, was really of degree rather than of kind. Fuller's point was not that artistry was of no account, quite the contrary. He urged that an understanding of scientific methods enhanced artistry, as every improvement in artistic standards was based on scientific advances.[17]

The criticisms of both Maurice and Germains were founded on the assumption that society could not support science on any sizeable scale during wartime, and also that intelligence would be rudimentary. The Second World War revealed that they were completely wrong and Fuller right. Since 1919 Fuller had attempted to introduce the British Army to the idea of operational research, and in his RUSI Gold Medal Essay of that year wrote: 'It is remarkable, indeed, to consider how completely the civilian with his knowledge of civil science, and not the soldier with his drill book, has revolutionized the entire art of warfare.' The operational research developed during the Second World War showed how perceptively Fuller had anticipated this trend. It has been defined as 'a scientific method of providing executive departments with a quantitative basis for decisions regarding the operations under their control'. It is a highly organized activity employing definite scientific methodology (though not the three fold order) in solving complex problems, the character and scope of which were foreseen in *The Foundations of the Science of War*. Highly trained civilians were used in large numbers to decipher and interpret the data secured by such sophisticated intelligence methods as 'Ultra'. It was material such as this, acquired through technology, which could permit the scientific treatment of military operations called for by Fuller.[18]

If it is accepted that science is a cumulative branch of knowledge 'with a solid and universally accepted core of accumulated knowledge and a growing outer edge of new knowledge', then warfare, too, can be regarded as cumulative and thus treated as scientific. For example, the 'Overlord' landings took place on the same beaches as those on which Naval Intelligence had begun their first crude studies in June 1940. 'The skimpy collection of photographs pasted on to brown paper of folio size, linked with the text, was to become the elaborate and beautifully produced work, in thousands of copies of a University Press.' Nevertheless the limitation of scientific procedures must be noted. Fuller seemed to suggest that scientific method was uniform based on hypothesis and observation of facts. No such uniformity actually exists among the sciences; these vary according to the type of evidence handled and the prevailing conditions; the results recorded often vary. In warfare the factors cannot be abstracted and isolated like chemical elements in a laboratory. Armies on the ground move too quickly, and when such results could be applied in the Second World War, it was discovered that situations in the field were much more variable than in the air or at sea. So operational research was of least value in land warfare and rarely influenced tactical encounters.[19]

Fuller's scheme was much more ambitious than simply working out a method of intelligence evaluation in battle. He sought nothing less than the introduction of evolutionism, that is, the synthetic philosophy, into the study of war. He aimed 'to establish a foundation so universal that it may be considered axiomatic to knowledge in all its forms . . . [then] not only shall I be able to work from a solid base, but I shall be able to bring the study of war into the closest relationship with the study of all other subjects'. Herbert Spencer had argued that it was the 'persistence of force' which determined the character of the universe. Indeed the persistence of force 'must be at the basis of any scientific organization of experience'. For Fuller this discovery had a significance of the first importance. If motion governed physical force it must also determine the expenditure of military force. As 'all motions were the resultant of the pressure and resistance exerted by one or more forces on another . . . I called the law which governs these changes the law of economy of force'. There was another factor. One of the leading British Social Darwinists, Karl Pearson, from whose writing Fuller had learned much, had indicated the crucial importance of inertia in estimating forces in motion. The 'fixed stars providing the frame of reference against which the motion of bodies is measured'. This tied up neatly with Clausewitz's view that immobility was the normal state in war. Given the friction between mobility and immobility, Fuller seemed to find confirmation of his thesis that these forces overcame one another in cycles. An understanding of history was therefore vital in establishing the 'progress' of war; 'natural history, the evolution of organic nature, is at the basis of human history', wrote Karl Pearson and Fuller did not forget these words.[20]

Fuller spent more than three years trying to define precisely how these forces affected warfare. This was an intricate and frustrating process. He agreed that concentration of force had to be allied with economy of force and co-operation. 'Personally', he wrote, 'I do not consider liberty of action a principal [*sic*] of war.' And neither was liberty of movement. The capacity to manoeuvre was the product of 'compounds of an intricate nature' and these could only be achieved by the 'condition resulting from the application of the principles'. It was therefore 'the offspring of two wills rather than the force engendered by one. . . . It is manifested through a general will, a general endurance, a general co-operation.' From this discussion Fuller drew four principles: objective, offensive, mobility and security. Four others reinforced their application: surprise, co-operation, concentration and economy of force. These are the eight principles that Fuller wrote into the 1924 edition of the *Field Service Regulations* and included in *The Reformation of War*. Maurice also used them in *British Strategy*. They were a notable achievement in themselves – as Colonel Paget, a member of the War Office committee working on the formulation of the principles, recognized: a trenchant and clear exposition of those fundamental elements underlying the conduct of war. Yet Fuller still remained dissatisfied.

> I look upon conservation of military energy in [the] same line as conservation of physical energy. At present economy of force, in my system, deals only with fighting force like economy of petrol consumption in a car . . . I think my idea is right – perhaps the words are wrong.

When Liddell Hart queried whether mobility was a principle of war, Fuller was quick to defend his premise. 'As long as you exclude movement as a principle my system is unworkable and so

I think is yours.' Yet these remarks show that he was looking beyond the definition of principles to discover another governing element – the key to the system.[21]

The principles as they appear in *The Foundations of the Science of War* date from 1924. Fuller increased their number from eight to nine, thus completing the symmetrical process of arranging an interlocking series of trinities. He also changed their names. The principle of the objective was renamed direction; those of economy of force and co-operation became distribution and endurance respectively, and a ninth, determination was added to the list. The solution to Fuller's problem was now revealed in one governing law – that of economy of force: 'one law grasped by one brain which controls [all the principles and] . . . which, when in harmony, produces co-operation. This may be called the philosophical basis of my science.' In practical terms 'the object (pivot [or] purpose in the brain of the commander) takes control and co-operation is towards the objective – perhaps a single sniper.' As for this new law, 'Economy of force works . . . outside the mind' but economic *expenditure* of force is the result of the workings of the principles, if correctly applied. 'If perfect it will coincide with the law. To make it coincide is our work.'[22]

Maurice had included economy of force as a principle in *British Strategy*. Germains considered the whole idea ridiculous; 'looking at the thing in the cold light of common sense', he asked, 'how can you have any *law* of economy of *force*?' The degree of force employed at any one point was dependent surely on the actions of the enemy. Commanders should either 'give battle wholeheartedly or . . . avoid battle wholeheartedly . . . To attempt economy of force means in practice to adopt half-measures, which usually means disaster'. There was no room for laws in warfare. Germains's comments illustrate the terminological character of the debate sparked off by the publication of Fuller's book. Although Germains refused to contemplate scientific terminology he did concede that there was a technique of war which was largely 'an exaggeration of the technique of peace'; this included a theory and mechanics of war. The former consisted of a body of speculations drawn from military history upon which it was possible to base 'certain broad principles of Strategy and Tactics' – the groundwork of the mechanics of war. Shorn of Germains's polemics, these remarks seem little more than a watered down

version of Fuller's ideas without his terms: an example of the
worst kind of pre-1914 writing which refers vaguely to principles
without defining them.[23]

Germains, furthermore, quite misunderstood what Fuller meant
by economy of force. Fuller interpreted this term in a nineteenth
century sense to mean careful husbanding of resources, not
merely their restricted use. Such an interpretation was wholly in
line with Clausewitz's comments on the subject. Germains's odd
references to Clausewitz do not inspire any great confidence in
his grasp of the subtleties of On War. It is true that Clausewitz
was sceptical of the value of laws in war, though this does not
prevent him from using them on occasion to express a general
idea. The Foundations of the Science of War was not a sweeping
criticism of Clausewitz as the prophet of mass along the lines that
Liddell Hart undertook in 1932. Indeed Fuller was indebted to
Clausewitz for his understanding of economy of force, particularly
on the relationship between concentration and the use of reserves.
'The commander and the army', the latter wrote in On War, 'who
have come closest to conducting an engagement with the utmost
economy of force and the maximum psychological effect of strong
reserves are on the surest road to victory.' This is the essence of
Fuller's thesis, not what Clausewitz also called 'mere stinginess'.
As he told Liddell Hart, 'what is wanted is just the right amount
of strength – any fool can throw in all he has'.[24]

The law of economy of force was an all-embracing concept and
such an idea clearly involves some problems of application.
General Trythall is certainly correct when he argues that the law is
tautological. Nevertheless it represents an effort to postulate a
military factor that determined policy at both grand strategical
and grand tactical levels of military action. Fuller seems to have
been one of the few military commentators in the mid-1920s who
understood that British generals could never again be as profligate
with the lives of their men as they had been in 1916–17. 'The good
general', Montgomery realized in the next war, 'must not only
win his battles; he must win them with a minimum of casualties.'
The lack of enthusiasm with which British infantry contemplated
close order fighting in the Second World War, coupled with a
chronic shortage of manpower, meant that economy of force
acted as a restraining influence lurking at the back of every British
general's mind during the Second World War.[25]

Fuller's analysis forged the closest link between grand strategy and grand tactics – war at the top and war in the general's tent. He suggested that 'military strength does not reside in individuals, but in the cooperation of individuals and masses'. If therefore this co-operation could be shattered with the utmost speed then decisive results would follow in the victor's train.

> As grand strategy secures the political object by directing all war-like resources – moral, physical and material – towards the winning of war, grand tactics secures military action by converging all means of waging war towards gaining a decision.

Thus if the velocity of war could be increased then the overall amount of force expended in war could be economized – even if it is brutally deployed in the opening stages of a war. 'Politically the decisive point is the will of the hostile nation, and grand tactically it is the will of the enemy's commander.' *The Foundations of the Science of War* therefore brought *policy* back into focus at the centre of Fuller's philosophy: 'it is all but a certainty', Fuller warned, 'that the energies of the next great war will mainly be directed against this objective [the national will], and relentlessly waged by every means at the disposal of the belligerents'; it was vital that Britain ensured that demoralization did not set in 'before war be declared, for on our national endurance will depend the future success or failure of our arms'. The collapse of France in 1940 and the survival of Great Britain points up the wisdom of this chilling warning.[26]

In order to bring this dislocation about, Fuller considered that the principles governing military activity were best applied in three interdependent groups, reflecting military functions and types of force: pressure, resistance and control; the latter reflected the will of the commanding general to impose a decision on his opponent. The side which endured the longest would win, if it could mount a degree of pressure commensurate with the resistance offered. Thus a victorious commander should aim at acquiring a superior means of movement and striking power over his opponent. Fuller pointed out that the aim of tactics was to secure military activity – protected offensive power. Strategy sought to secure movement – protected mobility. Conversely, the 'object of strategy is to disintegrate the enemy's power of co-operation, and that of tactics is to destroy his activity'. These arguments were an extension of the thesis that speed was the most important protective element. Though the word 'mechanization' was conspicuous by its absence in *The Foundations of the Science of War*, it was around this factor that Fuller built *Lectures on FSR III* and his points deserve the closest attention.[27]

Fuller suggested that 'our battle problem [is] the maintenance of a moving *organized* body of men'. Movement required organization and the enemy attempted to prevent this not only by inflicting casualties on military formations but by trying to disrupt their organization. 'We must, therefore, protect our men and their organization, and we do so to a great extent through offensive action. By hitting we reduce the chances of being hit.' The object of movement was to deprive the enemy of the power of movement, and therefore of the capacity to attack. One way of doing this was to reduce him to a state of psychological incapacity by striking at his rear. The enemy should first of all be pinned to his position. 'This is the true act of attrition which should precede the decisive attack. Its supreme value lies in the fact that the enemy is being demoralized by manoeuvre in place of by attack, consequently the whole of the forces engaged may be held in reserve.' This line of argument reveals that economy of force was largely a product of *mobility*. As the most profitable mode of attack was the rear attack which reduced the enemy to a state of psychological incapacity, it followed that the 'application of force does not necessarily mean physical force but moral force, and that the greater the moral pressure we use in war the less need be the physical force we concentrate for the decisive battle'. The degree of force required would depend on the prevailing conditions of war. At any rate it should be recognized that the 'maintenance of the initiative does not . . . lie so much in physically destroying the enemy as in reducing him to a moral wreck'.[28]

This development of *blitzkrieg* was an attempt to up-date Napoleon by fusing manoeuvring and fighting into one indivisible activity. Hence with greater mobility and commensurate striking power, greater strategic flexibility could be conferred on an audacious commander. These arguments represent, in varying degrees, a divergence from the teaching of Clausewitz, and were certainly a long jump away from the tactical wisdom of the 1920s. In the short term Fuller was right to advance the kind of grand tactics thus envisaged; subsequent experience has modified rather than overturned his thinking. Mechanization did enable commanders to secure a more effective form of protected offensive power which through rapid movement could catch an enemy strategically off-guard to an extent hitherto unparalleled in the history of warfare. Maurice, too, conceded the protective power of mobility. Both Maurice and Fuller agreed that the most important objectives in the next war would not be the bulk of the enemy's army but his communications – his rear areas, administrative centres and supply depots. Air power added a new dimension to the argument. It was possible to foresee, Fuller predicted, 'an army holding at bay another, whilst its aircraft are destroying the hostile communications and bases and so paralyzing enemy action'. Improvements in mobility thus allowed an attacker to feint in one direction, draw the enemy away from his chosen position, gain liberty of movement and simultaneously deprive the enemy of it, and once the feint had succeeded attack another section of the front: 'draw an enemy away from his communications and then force him to fight for their security'. As the Emperor claimed: 'The secret of war lies in the secret of the lines of communication. . . . Strategy does not consist of making half-hearted dashes at the enemy's rear areas; it consists in really mastering his communications, and proceeding to give battle.' The total demoralization of the enemy held up the possibility of a 'bloodless victory' – another Ulm. As Fuller warned:

> If our luck be out, or if our adversary be mentally superior to ourselves, we shall be annihilated, because whilst in 1914 we misjudged weapons – weapons which could be countered by the use of trenches – in the next war we shall have misjudged movement, which has rightly been called the 'soul of war'.[29]

In Fuller's conception of the principles of war, those of resistance, endurance, security and distribution, were regarded as stepping stones upon which an offensive plan could be mounted, 'which through force of circumstances, cannot at once be put into operation'. Thus 'we must think in one term – the *protected attack* – whether we are advancing, retreating or standing still.' He thus took issue with Clausewitz for suggesting that the defensive was the stronger form of war. 'What is the stronger form of war is a well secured offensive operation.' This was a hasty comment, as Clausewitz does allow that the defensive 'enables one to take the offensive after superiority has been gained', though Fuller was quite justified in roundly condemning the French Army for thinking mainly in defensive terms, as 'security without reference to offensive action is no security at all, but merely delayed suicide'. The relationship which lay at the heart of his conception was the defensive-offensive and this was further developed:

> Security is, therefore, a shield . . . merely a prelude to the accomplishment of the military object of war – the destruction of the enemy's strength by means of offensive action augmented by defensive measures . . . a well-secured offensive operation.[30]

The real problem in evaluating Fuller's conception lay not in the defensive-offensive, which was imaginative and valuable, but in coming to terms with the persistent tension that can be perceived between the law of economy of force and the principle of war which governed it – mobility. It is not surprising that a theory as all-embracing and ambitious as Fuller's should produce a tension between the parts and the framework into which those parts slotted. Fuller had inherited the difficulties that Spencer had encountered when developing the synthetic philosophy. There is another fundamental paradox lying at the heart of this effort to introduce evolutionism into the theory of war. Fuller tried to show that a unity existed in military action when successful, a tendency to economize force. Yet this unity was achieved in spite of an infinite variety of perplexing circumstances and unstable conditions. He tried to resolve this paradox by claiming that the range of possibilities could be reduced by a single system sanctioned by nature – the principles of war. When it came to practice, however, the field of action, the changing conditions of war had shown by 1943–4 that force could not be economized by rapid manoeuvre. Those generals who actually succeeded in economizing force, notably Montgomery, actually *reduced* the velocity of war. Montgomery's technique enshrined caution as the soul of war with every conceivable variant and contingency having been catered for in the so-called 'master plan'. Economy of force and velocity in warfare, in the long run, are not compatible. It was a dilemma that Fuller never satisfactorily resolved.[31]

The Napoleonic bent of Fuller's arguments render the comments of his critics all the more perplexing. The importance that he attached to manoeuvre in *The Foundations of the Science of War* was held up as evidence that Fuller underrated the importance of battle. Maurice wrote, 'I am not amongst those who believe that in these days of tanks and aircraft we have nothing to learn from Napoleon and other great commanders who had not these weapons of war.' He seemed oblivious of these areas of broad agreement (as was Fuller). Yet as he contributed a foreword to Germains's book, he must have sincerely believed that Fuller neglected the problem of battle. This was a complete misunderstanding. From the first Fuller made it quite clear that the science of war was based on the assumption that battle was the 'crucial act of war'; the purpose of strategy was to 'bring about a tactical encounter under the most favourable circumstances possible'. In *The Foundations of the Science of War* there is actually less emphasis on the line of least resistance, and Fuller held that any decisive point in the enemy's distribution was likely to be that most closely guarded. If overwhelming strength could be concentrated against this point, then it will 'normally follow the line of greatest traction'; if an attacker is vulnerable to counter-attack then the line of least resistance should be chosen; but whichever line is chosen, resistance mounted against the advancing forces must be reduced by manoeuvre or surprise.[32]

If changes in civil life demanded changes in the means of waging war, Fuller also contended that so also did they demand changes in the means of preparing for it. He defined the principle of the object as the means of destroying the enemy's strength, 'which is centred in his will to command, and which finds expression in the organization of his forces and endurance in the *moral* of his men'; this was achieved 'by the application of brute force and . . . by fear and terror leading to panic'. Modern war demanded that morale be carefully studied. If the fear of soldiers was not balanced by morale then soldiers would become victims of rumour and panic. Training should attempt to cultivate leadership, as 'each man as an individual must be able to lead himself and the team to which he belonged'. Fuller believed, probably rightly, that British soldiers during the First World War had lacked initiative; this problem would get worse in the next war which would be dominated by machines and these needed new tactics and these, in turn, would require new training methods. Fuller had been advocating such reforms since 1914 and the appearance of *Training Soldiers for War*. In 1925 he published his manuscript on the training methods of Sir John Moore in two volumes, *Sir John Moore's System of Training* and *British Light Infantry in the Eighteenth Century*, and they provided *The Foundations of the Science of War* with valuable supporting evidence.[33]

Fuller was a light infantryman and it was natural that he should take pride in the achievements of his own regiment, the 43rd/52nd Oxfordshire and Buckinghamshire Light Infantry. Indeed the evidence indicates that he became interested in Moore – perhaps the greatest light infantryman produced by the British Army – while still a subaltern. There was one other reason for his interest. Moore, who had studied the writings of Robert Jackson and Henry Lloyd, was a good example of the soldier-intellectual who could put his ideas into practice. Moore's famous training camp at Shorncliffe was *'an active service camp*, and his men were actually trained *under war conditions* by a master *trained in war'*; and Fuller was keen to point out that 'no true system of discipline can be set forth between the covers of a book'. Moore had quickly understood that tactics were dependent on fire, and that these portended looser formations requiring intelligence and not merely drill. Fuller tended to identify strongly with Moore. He was sure that if Moore had been alive in 1925 he would have called for another training camp like Shorncliffe, 'another Experimental Brigade to try out new tactics, weapons and systems of discipline'. And Fuller made this call in a lecture given at the RUSI. From it sprang the Experimental Brigade of 1927 which would concentrated on working out the new tactics of armoured warfare.[34]

In considering the new system of discipline required, Fuller advanced two arguments. The first was that discipline would have to take into account increasing educational attainments among soldiers. 'We may vaunt our old discipline of 1914'; he wrote, 'it was magnificent, but it was the discipline of the magazine rifle.' This kind of mechanical discipline degraded the soldier and brutalized war; attitudes were transfixed by a 'guts *versus* guns' equation; and in the past if weaknesses were discovered in military organizations remedies were always sought 'in making demands on the *moral* of the soldier'. The second argument was that self-preservation determined a soldier's behaviour on the battlefield, and this instinct had to be controlled by morale. Fuller continued to subscribe to the view that armies resembled crowds. No matter how well an army was trained, its homogeneity was liable to break down under the strain of war.

The object of improving training was to slow this process down, 'so that, when intellect and reason fail, man is not ruled by his instincts and sentiments alone, but by his *moral*, which has become part of his very nature'.[35]

The main burden of his historical proof was drawn from a close reading of the writings of Jackson and Lloyd, two eighteenth-century theorists whom Fuller admired and thought of as kindred spirits; they shared his predilection for principles and laws and improvements in training methods. They had both criticized the draconian discipline of Frederick the Great's army. Fuller had likened the heavy infantry of the First World War to Frederick's well dressed lines, believing that both he and Haig had overlooked the offensive value of light infantry. Another interesting example of the repetition of this historical cycle was General Braddock's defeat on the Monongahela (1757); this revealed the futility of advancing (as in 1916–17) 'in dense and heavy formations, against agile and skilful sharpshooters, who depended on themselves as on each other, and who were as skilful with their rifles as they were dexterous in using cover'.[36]

Robert Jackson believed that there were two kinds of training, the artificial and the natural. The artificial relied on rigid discipline. 'In itself it is not wrong', commented Fuller, 'for the crowd has at times to be mechanically manoeuvred, but when alone taught and untempered by individual, or what Jackson calls "natural" training, it becomes faulty to a degree.' Natural training – the inculcation of initiative and self-reliance – required that 'knowledge of each individual must be possessed by the officer so that he can make the most of each individual soldier'. Only knowledge and trust could provide a solid foundation for improving a soldier's military aptitude. 'Don't dishearten a man, appeal to his heart, don't crush it.' Of course the British Army worked on the opposite principle: that the private soldier could not be trusted under any circumstances, and only officers, and then NCOs, could take decisions. Although Fuller never mentions them directly, the Australians, those 'enemies of pomposity and humbug' as Denis Winter calls them, would appear to be his model soldiers – a combination of healthy scepticism and virile, martial virtue, with the added benefit of promotion from the ranks. Fuller's ideas implied a modification of the class structure of the British Army. Moore had insisted that young officers drilled with their men on joining the regiment and got to know them as human beings. 'I hold in detestation and abhorrence all *Button* and *Buckle* officers', wrote Sir John Moore, and Fuller detested them no less.[37]

Fuller here made some interesting and perceptive points, and his arguments are distinguished by experience and authority, as he had proved himself a brilliant trainer of troops. Nevertheless it is important to distinguish between his criticisms of blind obedience for its own sake and his attachment to the formalities of military discipline. He clung tenaciously to the traditional military values such as saluting and smartness. When in uniform a soldier, he wrote, must always act as if on parade, 'he must be smart, obedient and alert'. Initiative did not imply slackness or disobedience but 'obedience without orders . . . obedience with reference to the general plan . . . as governed by the conditions of the moment'. Another important recurring theme was the importance Fuller gave to the need for a commander to provide a personal example. Moore spent much of his time among the troops and understood them; it was easy for him to appeal to what Fuller called 'the primary object of discipline' – their sense of honour. He also paid tribute to Moore's kindness as an important factor in gaining the affection and loyalty of the troops. Moore's method of instruction was, depending on the intelligence of his men, either lively to stimulate interest, or repetitive, and this provided a good model for improving British training methods in the 1920s, which were, in Fuller's opinion, banal and tedious in the extreme. An instructor should 'guard against turning himself into a human gramophone, for even repetition requires skill and individuality'; but, judging from most of the training methods used by the British Army in the Second World War, Fuller argued in vain.[38]

On the specific historical comparison, Fuller exaggerated the similarity between the Frederician Army and the British Army before 1914. Some officers, like Evelyn Wood had attempted to develop the initiative of individual soldiers, realizing, as Lord Roberts put it, that they could no longer be trained like machines. Though the individuality of Fuller's suggestions can be exaggerated, they were nevertheless laudable and modern-minded. The men of 1939–45 were more questioning than their predecessors of 1914–18. Montgomery described the soldiers of the Second World War as men who could think for themselves and 'definitely prepared to criticize'; military movements had to be explained to them, and this Montgomery did with great skill. Consequently, young soldiers were 'more readily disillusioned by unnecessarily repetitive training' and uninspiring leadership, which, it must be admitted, was too frequently found in the Second World War. Fuller's attempt to stimulate interest in psychological methods was not successful but the Moore tradition did have an influence on training methods in the Second World War through the medium of Fuller's friend, Paget, who subscribed, while GOC 21st Army Group in 1943, to the idea of the 'thinking and fighting soldier', and introduced it into the training programmes that preceded 'Overlord' in June 1944.[39]

What is the final verdict on *The Foundations of the Science of War* and those books related to it? Fuller commented to Liddell Hart just before its publication that it was 'going to start a new epoch in military thought or join the limbo of lost causes'. He also predicted that few people would really understand it. He was right and the fault was entirely his. 'I shall give it about five years before I re-write it; as it stands it is only a draft.' The presentation of the book led many people to conclude that Fuller's feet were not entirely on the ground – a quite unfair accusation; 'while your vision is admitted', Liddell Hart reported, 'it is suggested that you would never make a practical commander'. He continued:

> Your thought . . . is on a higher plane than your exposition – by comparison; that as a writer you are apt to vary between a dazzling brilliance and a certain mistiness . . . Thus I have not yet met anyone who shares my opinion of *The Foundations of the Science of War*. My opinion of its intrinsic merits is unshaken but I am afraid that it may not have the practical effects which I hoped.

Fuller's failure to provide a lucid and accessible basis for a doctrine for the Army seriously undermined his efforts at reform; he was discredited and after his departure from the Staff College in December 1925 it no longer remained at the centre of an intellectual ferment; this was perhaps the most disappointing of the 'practical effects' that Liddell Hart had cherished. Yet, though *The Foundations of the Science of War* was not adopted officially, some of its ideas had a more informal influence; scientific modes of thought were gradually adopted by 1939. In 1946 Lieutenant General Sir Frederick Morgan, responsible for the initial 'Overlord' planning as Chief of Staff to the Supreme Commander, wrote to Fuller acknowledging his influence. Morgan admitted that he had been 'vastly intrigued by your writings from which, I for one, derived immense benefit. If only your sage advice had been taken in days gone by with regard to the necessity for thought, I am certain we should be in rather a less of a mess today than we actually are.'[40]

By comparison, however, with the goals Fuller had set himself the publication of the book was a dismal flop. Thirty years later he conceded that *The Foundations of the Science of War* 'like the curate's egg, was only in parts good. I set out to do something which at the time I was not sufficiently equipped for mentally. It is too mechanical.' But the most lasting fruit of this book was that a preoccupation with evolutionism led Fuller to take an interest in the relationship between war and social forces. Fuller regarded war as a social science like economics which, though responsive to certain laws or principles, nevertheless experienced a high degree of uncertainty. He pointed out how 'My Science of War is only a bit of a Whole', which entailed a study of the nature, causes, restriction, ethics, economics and 'Scientific Management of War', which included grand strategy. When he had written books on this formidable list of subjects, 'I will then write my *one and only* book on war. I write these things to educate myself not others'. Fuller's intellectual tools may have dated quickly but the areas they introduced to him resulted in the breaking of new ground in the study of war. *The Foundations of the Science of War* was but a glimmer in this process; the 'new dawn' would not be finally realized until the publication of *The Decisive Battles of the Western World*. Thus the true significance of *The Foundations of the Science of War* is to be found within the corpus of his own thought. For this reason it is difficult to dissent from Fuller's observation in 1935: 'You are right. *The Foundations of the Science of War*, in spite of its many faults, is the best book I have written.'[41]

5

Student of Generalship, 1929–33

Military history in all its aspects is itself a *source of instruction* for the critic, and it is only natural that he should look at all particular events in the light of the whole.

Clausewitz, *On War*, II, 5, p. 165

Do not look around thee to discover other men's ruling principles, but look straight to this, to what nature leads thee, both the universal nature through the things which happen to thee, and thy own nature through acts which must be done by thee.

The Meditations of Marcus Aurelius, VIII, 55, p. 205

Fuller once described the mind of a historically trained soldier as resembling not a dusty old lumber room but a highly tuned laboratory. *The Foundations of the Science of War* ended with a brief section on the application of scientific method to the study of military history. Even before this book was finished Fuller was contemplating the problems raised by a critical study of history. He agreed with Clausewitz that the development of military theory was intimately related to the study of history: it lay at the heart of any sophisticated treatment of warfare. This chapter discusses Fuller's use of military history in relation to his development as a theorist. It will assess the 'lessons' that Fuller deemed most instructive after a study of the American Civil War (1861–5) analyse the historical foundations upon which his interpretation rests, and discusses whether Fuller's limitations as a historian vitiate them. Finally it will evaluate the conclusions he reached about the character of future generalship.[1]

Fuller believed that the decisive watershed in any study of generalship was the First World War. Much of the generalship displayed during this war had been lamentable. He felt that it was

107

the role of the critic to look back at past wars and discover what elements had been successful so that the disastrous errors of the past could be avoided. His three books on generalship, *The Generalship of Ulysses S. Grant* (1929), *Grant and Lee* (1933) and *Generalship: Its Diseases and their Cure* (1933) form an attempt to fill out the theoretical framework of *The Foundations of the Science of War* with historical evidence, and Fuller hinged on to this interpretation his mature ideas on strategy and command. He tried to drive home the lesson that the study of war should be wide ranging. A student should ask 'the "why" and "how" of success or failure [in war] in a series of campaigns, and not [gather] . . . microscopic knowledge of any one campaign'. If an individual war had to be studied, then it should be the last great conflict which had preceded the war just concluded. The war which bore the closest resemblance to the First World War was the Civil War.[2]

Fuller's approach represented nothing less than a damning indictment of the pre-1914 Army's teaching on higher command. British soldiers had followed the campaigns of the Civil War closely since the bombardment of Fort Sumter in 1861 and General Sir Garnet Wolesley, Queen Victoria's most distinguished field commander, had accompanied General Robert E. Lee's Army of Northern Virginia at the height of its success. This interest reached a peak in 1898 with the appearance of Colonel G. F. R. Henderson's *Stonewall Jackson*, a romantic and highly effective account of Jackson's campaigns, reflecting the pro-Confederate bias of British military studies of the Civil War. Fuller, chose as his hero, not a Confederate but a Union general, Grant. He thought ill of the British Army's traditional heroes, Lee and Jackson. They were 'certainly not more than third degree. Jackson I think has been somewhat overestimated', he observed in 1923. Fuller was a natural pioneer who was attracted to neglected historical figures. As he recalled to an American in 1950, 'I became interested in your Civil War because I felt that U. S. Grant had not received sufficient credit.' Fuller had also been stung by the criticisms of *The Foundations of the Science of War* and was anxious to produce a distinguished contribution to Civil War literature, one that would stand comparison with, if not supersede Henderson's *Stonewall Jackson*, and he succeeded. His mentor, Ironside, a future CIGS and Commandant of the Staff College while Fuller was a chief instructor, thought *The Generalship of Ulysses S. Grant* 'distinctly good and very well written and he has put in no pseudo-scientific terms to mystify people'.[3]

Fuller, with Grant as his didactic vehicle, judged the issue of command to be the central issue of the Civil War. It was the last great war in which direct, personal command had been exercised. In his view soldiers had ignored its lessons and foolishly followed the example set by Moltke's victories during the Franco-Prussian War (1870–1). Fuller disliked Moltke's system of command because it allowed too much freedom to subordinate generals and prevented the commander from stamping his will decisively on operations. Moltke's system had been taken to extremes during the First World War, so that the commander-in-chief had been totally out of touch with reality. 'When things went awry', Fuller wrote, 'Grant went to the front and so did Lee . . . and had a few of the generals of the First World War gone forward when their men went back, many a reverse would have been avoided.' This kind of initiative was impossible under Moltke's system. Worse, Fuller held that Moltke had refused to study the Civil War, claiming that it was a contest 'between two armed mobs chasing each other around the country, from which nothing could be learned'.[4]

The substance of Fuller's analysis required the restoration of the Napoleonic system of command as utilized by Grant and Lee. The commanding general should be in the forefront of decision-making. In his judgement a commander should 'understand himself, and see himself as the enemy sees him'. This was the chief reason for Fuller's interest in Grant's mysterious personality, and why this enigmatic man made such a valuable subject. Grant was a man of immense intelligence but little formal education. Diffident but self-reliant, his shyness and modesty concealed immense reserves of self-confidence. Grant, wrote Fuller, 'was never petrified by numbers or situations, and never through fear or caution did he exaggerate the strength of his enemy'. He was always calm, confident, reasoning, energetic and forceful. His success was based on a 'quick and rational grasp of conditions, his determination to see things through and the rapidity with which, once he made up his mind, he moved and acted'. Moreover, Grant's generalship seemed to justify that strand of anti-intellectualism that runs through Fuller's thought like a red thread. He was at pains to point out that Grant was a man of action not an intellectual, 'typically non-academic; thinking in facts and not in theories; . . . always willing to listen to others . . . when he believed in them, but seldom if ever led by them'. It was precisely because Grant's education had been so rudimentary and the war so unprofessional and civilian in style that Fuller found it 'so vastly interesting, and its generalship so brilliant and instructive' – a sharp contrast to the rigid, clockwork professionalism of 1870–1.[5]

The governing thesis of *The Generalship of Ulysses S. Grant* was that the higher art of generalship could not be taught. Fuller believed that the greatest generals antedated the rise of military professionalism. 'Since the advent of the war schools native genius has been crippled by pedantry, not because sound military education in itself is detrimental (such a contention would be absurd), but because the easiest thing to do in a school is to copy the past'; professionalism, in Fuller's opinion, was 'the dry rot' of generalship: 'it does not probe into the viscera of living war, it merely rattles the skeletons of our military ancestors'. As a reviewer in *The Army Quarterly* observed, 'There is something to be said for this contention, and something to be said against it.' Fuller was again suggesting that soldiers should study rather than learn the doctrines advanced in military schools. Grant was now held up as a model. The bogey of Fuller's books of the Civil War was Major General Henry W. Halleck, later President Lincoln's Chief of Staff but an indifferent field commander. Fuller disliked Halleck because he epitomized the worst kind of fussy, narrow-minded, studious staff officer: 'a cautious, witless pedant who had studied war, and imagined that adherence to certain strategical and tactical maxims constituted the height of generalship . . . Halleck was worth much more than the proverbial army corps to the Confederate forces.'[6]

Fuller here developed the thesis expounded in *The Foundations of the Science of War* that a connection existed between common sense and the application of the principles of war. A general did not require a great deal of learning to operate them; he only needed to show a talent for adapting his actions to prevailing circumstances, not a clear memory for recalling something read in a book. Hence Grant's success where other more highly educated generals like McClellan and Halleck failed. 'Grant's common sense is so remarkable', commented Fuller, 'that it constitutes a military lesson of no small importance, namely, that the art of war – strategy and tactics – is nothing more than action adapted to circumstances.' There is no mention here of the three fold order. Fuller exaggerated Grant's 'civilian' approach to war, as it was quite unexceptional. The United States Military Academy at West Point provided a satisfactory free education biased in favour of the sciences, but little formal military instruction. Only seven days were allotted to the course on strategy before 1861. The keen cadet was forced to supplement his meagre knowledge of war by recourse to informal societies like the Napoleonic Club. The majority of cadets left the Academy without imbibing much theoretical knowledge. Indeed most left the US Army shortly after graduating. 'At the beginning of the war, Grant knew as much about the theory and history of war as the average West Point graduate and regular army officer, which was not very much.'[7]

Fuller then compared this mental climate with that prevailing in the British Army before 1914, much to the disadvantage of the British. Military professionalism in the British Army had produced soldiers 'to whom all things are to be measured on the bed of Procrustean regulations'. There was an obsession with trivia and routine. The very success of Henderson's *Stonewall Jackson* had contributed to the closing of minds. Fuller considered this book 'an admirable exposition of the generalship of small semi-professional armies'. For all its qualities however *Stonewall Jackson* lacked any understanding of the impact of industrialization on war. Modern warfare demanded the mobilization of whole nations. It was not so much Henderson that was at fault, as the system – one dominated by what Fuller branded the 'Bradshaw mind', that is, 'the meticulous memorization of facts and of useless detail'. Fuller claimed that he had collected so many useless facts about Jackson's campaigns in the spring of 1862 that he could have told his examiner the weight of kippers eaten by Jackson for breakfast at selected camps along the Shenandoah Valley. Henderson's signal influence is made clear by Montgomery-Massingberd, Fuller's enemy, in a letter to Liddell Hart in 1926, and many other officers would have agreed with him:

> *Stonewall Jackson* was my first introduction to Military History . . . and the impression it left on me, on account of the very human tone of it, has never faded. Many decisions I helped to arrive at during the war date back from those early readings and the impression it left on me.

Fuller took the opposite view. A study of Grant's campaigns set within their social and political context would have provided a much more valuable introduction to the problems facing commanders on the Western Front 1914–18.[8]

The Generalship of Ulysses S. Grant began with a discussion of what Fuller called the 'Natural History of War'. This chapter evinced his increasing concern with war as a social and political phenomenon. The phrase 'natural history' was borrowed from Karl Pearson. Few historians would now agree with Fuller's discussion of the causes of the Civil War, though his other comments are of enduring value. His main thesis was that the American Civil War was an outgrowth of American society, and that its conduct reflected not only developments inherent within American society before 1861, but also the divergent forms that had developed within that society. The Civil War was just as much a war between two differing societies as between two opposing groups of commanders. He then suggested that the varying ways the Confederacy and the United States chose to conduct the war reflected the mores of the parent societies. In *Grant and Lee* he took this reasoning a stage further and argued that these two generals were model representatives of the conflicting sections. This was a new point of departure for the study of military history in Britain. The best work in this genre was restricted to the multi-volume campaign narratives of Sir Charles Oman and Sir John Fortescue. Fuller had followed Clausewitz's lead in suggesting that there were three sources of strategy – the purely operational, the political and the social. Modern nation states were able to mobilize these resources to a greater extent than hitherto because of the profound influence of the Industrial Revolution on war. The Civil War was 'the first great conflict begotten of the Industrial Revolution, the second was the World War of 1914–18; consequently, in the natural history of war these two stand in close relationship'.[9]

Both wars demonstrated the influence of technology on modern war. Although the earlier conflict was based on steam-power and the later on oil and electrical power, technical developments link the two together not only in structure 'but their influence on the means of waging war is similar; for both in 1865 and 1918, war is brought to an end by the collapse of the industrially and financially weaker side'. This was a perception of the first importance. As Michael Howard observes, Northern generals like Grant were able to 'deploy in such strength that the operational skills of their adversaries were rendered almost irrelevant'. Fuller's interpretation added another dimension to the study of strategy in the British Army. The battles in Virginia in 1862–4 resulted in 'an attrition of man-power, but it was the moral attack of Sherman in Georgia and the Carolinas, and the economic attack of Sheridan in Virginia, which brought the Confederacy to its knees'. Purely *military* operations were but one part of the warmaking process.[10]

Fuller was also concerned to draw out the link between these developments at the strategical level and their influence on the battlefield. Improvements in weaponry had resulted in the domination of the rifle bullet and the supremacy of the defensive; the Civil War ended as a large-scale siege. The speed with which inventions such as the observation balloons, wooden trench mortars and hand grenades were introduced led Fuller to conclude that 'we can easily transport ourselves from 1864–5 to 1914–15'. Any attempt to assess Civil War generalship raised several problems because of the speed of invention. Each battle was shrouded by a tactical doubt produced by the tactics the general had been taught and those he was forced to adopt. Hence tactics became 'the more uncertain branch of the art of war'. The most confusing developments were the obsolescence of the shoulder-to-shoulder charge and the need to deploy men in short rushes covered by skirmishers. The defender was well entrenched and held his fire until the attacker broke cover, whereupon a deluge of bullets broke his cohesion and threw him back in confusion.[11]

Some of Fuller's strictures on Civil War generalship were overstated. In the main his discussion is to the point. He was correct in his estimate of the comparative value of arms. The bayonet was useless. In 1862 the German observer, Heros von Borcke, studied the results of a bayonet fight during the Peninsular Campaign in Virginia in 1862. The three or four corpses that he found with bayonet wounds had received them after being hit by bullets. He concluded that 'as far as my experience goes . . . bayonet-fights . . . exist only in the imagination'. Even during the Battle of Spotsylvania (8–21 May 1864), in which hand-to-hand fighting took place, only 14 bayonet wounds were recorded, compared with 7046 bullet wounds. During the entire war Union hospitals treated 246 712 wounds; of these only 400 were bayonet wounds – mostly self-inflicted cases or the result of brawling between soldiers. This is far from suggesting – as Fuller was prone to do – that hand-to-hand fighting did not occur, it did, but American soldiers were more likely to club one another with their rifle butts than use bayonets. These features of the Civil War contributed to the broadening scale of the battlefield, the duration of battles, and the rare sighting of enemy soldiers on the field. It cast a glimmer of damning light on the stubborn adherence to the tactical importance of the bayonet during the First World War and after.[12]

Fuller used Grant's conduct of the 1864 campaign to condemn prevailing attitudes towards firepower. Grant like many after him fell too easily into the delusion 'that battles can be won by masses of men; . . . that human tonnage is the coefficient of victory'. Fuller thus returned to elaborate on one of the most important arguments to emerge from *The Foundations of the Science of War*: superiority of numbers and resources were important but they should not be squandered, and they would be if generals forgot that 'on a modern battlefield it is not men who count, but weapon-power – bullets and shells'. Fuller had come to the conclusion that the frontal assault would no longer prove to be the main grand tactical act in battle; out-flanking would take its place. He tended to overlook some of the difficulties confronting Civil War commanders. They favoured retaining compact formations not only to keep control over their men but because under certain conditions coming to grips with the enemy was more important than deploying firepower. The Civil War showed, moreover, that out-flanking was not a decisive manoeuvre for muscle-bound armies. As Russell F. Weigley observes, 'strong entrenched positions are not carried by men moving in driblets from one shelter to another; the end of the assault had to be some semblance of the traditional massed charge'. Weapons were not yet sophisticated enough to replace men on the battlefield. Indeed 132 years after the end of the Civil War projectiles still have not driven men from the battlefield.[13]

Despite these qualifications, it was Fuller's keen appreciation of the difficulties posed by trench warfare and the implications of social and technological change that marks out his writings on the American Civil War as original. It must be underlined though that Fuller's book on Grant was only the logical culmination of much pre-1914 writing on the American Civil War. Fuller's predecessors, Henderson, for example, had written of the Wilderness Campaign in Virginia in 1864 as providing 'a better clue to the fighting of the future than any other which history records'. Perhaps more typical though was C. F. Atkinson, who in a study of Grant's campaigns published in 1908, wrote that 'attacking entrenchments was not a matter of principles but of particular cases'. By showing that this was far from being the case, Fuller made an important contribution to Civil War literature, as well as to military thought, for no British soldier has shown more discernment than he in evaluating the general character of the American Civil War.[14]

His analysis of Grant's greatness as a field commander has been no less influential. Crucial to this was his acute perception of the intimate relationship between grand strategy and grand tactics. Grant was a model *generalissimo*, in Fuller's estimation. If the aim of war was 'to defeat the enemy decisively', then in the industrial age this could only be done by a rational mobilization of the nation's resources and their careful utilization on the battlefield. Grant was a consummate grand strategist, capable of taking the larger view. He interested himself in the political complexity of the war and trimmed his strategy to match political priorities. He grasped more firmly than any other Civil War general the three prongs of grand strategy: the military, economic and moral (political) attack – the social movements (Clausewitz's 'popular passions') which the conflict expressed. As a study of command, *The Generalship of Ulysses S. Grant* was more than a mere campaign narrative, as it reached out to assess those forces which lurked beyond the battlefield, but were of no less importance in the study of war than the movements of armed forces in the field.[15]

It is timely to consider the historical 'foundations', to use one of Fuller's favourite terms, upon which this important and ambitious book rests. As a self-educated soldier, Fuller had no formal training as a historian, and, like so many who have never formally studied history, he was fond of pontificating on the value of its study. After completing the manuscript of *The Generalship of Ulysses S. Grant* in 1929 he gave Liddell Hart his forthright views on the writing of history.

The one lesson I have learned . . . is that seventy-five per cent of history is fallacious. . . . History is most unreliable, so unreliable that I cannot help feeling that a little speculation, even if it is not immediately related to facts is sometimes more illuminating than an outline based on the facts themselves.

This book, his first work of history, was not an exercise in impartial scholarship; on the contrary, it formed a historical platform which allowed him to invigorate the facts with a 'little life' – his own strongly held views. In this respect, *Grant and Lee* was even more radical. He rejected the conventional view that Lee was a very great general, finding him instead 'one of the most incapable Generals-in-Chief in history – so much for school education'.[16]

Though he might have scant regard for the pretensions of other historians, Fuller was prone to claim for himself the objectivity they lacked. The quality of his scholarship must therefore be assessed. Fuller read widely. *Grant and Lee*, he claimed, 'has four years reading behind it'; but the width of his reading was rarely matched in depth. For example, apart from the memoirs of Grant, Sherman and Sheridan, Fuller had read few of the recollections of other serving officers of the period. He was not acquainted with publications in scholarly journals. To his credit he had mastered the *Official Records* – the most important Civil War primary source – not an inconsiderable achievement for a serving officer constantly on the move. A glimpse of the difficulties he faced can be found in a letter to Liddell Hart complaining, 'How I am going to correct proofs in Germany [where he was posted to command a brigade at Wiesbaden] I don't know, especially as I hear that I shall be in camp from Aug 20 to end of Sept.' It is a tribute to Fuller's remarkable energy that he also wrote several months later, 'Grant is finished and I feel lost.'[17]

Fuller used the sources at his disposal to argue the case for Grant most effectively, if a little too aggressively. Liddell Hart commented (although these remarks were equally applicable to himself): 'Although you occasionally criticize Grant, I feel that you have held your critical faculties more tightly in check than is your wont.' He added two months later: 'one so often has the feeling that you don't sift evidence but simply search it for something to support an opinion already formed'. Fuller was often 'most obstinate in refusing to modify your original deduction when an inconvenient fact or argument turns up later'. It was coincidental that Fuller and Liddell Hart, two 'seekers after truth', became interested in the American Civil War at the same time. Fuller felt that the American public 'ought to be extremely flattered'. An American reader might be bemused by the ensuing fuss, for not only did Fuller and Liddell Hart expend more effort over researching and writing about the American Civil War than any British war (except possibly the First World War) but it was the cause of their first serious quarrel.[18]

Both men battled against the complacency of the 'official view' – the numerous publications of writers, including the official historian of the First World War, Brigadier General J. E. (later Sir James) Edmonds, who deliberately concealed the truth to protect the reputations of their masters. It is difficult not to have considerable sympathy with Fuller and Liddell Hart's noble aspirations to seek out the 'truth'. Yet Fuller and Liddell Hart, especially Liddell Hart, took them to extremes which occasionally bordered on the ridiculous. Fuller was at least by now rather sceptical about 'the truth'. 'I know what friendship is, but what is Truth?' he asked at the end of 1929. He was eighteen years older than Liddell Hart and after a number of disappointments was losing his youthful idealization of 'truth'. It was therefore ironical that in their search for historical truth both men, when contemplating the interpretation of the other, accused him of the same omissions and failings. Hence the mutual irritation that their arguments sparked off. Fuller, for instance, rebuked Liddell Hart for sending him ' "corrections" as if you were a schoolmaster and I a little boy' – criticisms that Fuller did not think sound.

To you they must be so, and because I have not swallowed them in one gulp your self-pride is wounded, so deeply wounded that you talk of 'getting at the truth', do not delude yourself, for what you are getting at is your own glorification.

These differences were eventually patched up but what this exchange reveals is that all the talk about 'truth' was fundamentally a synonym for emotional commitment. Fuller and Liddell Hart were as emotionally committed to their subjects as any sympathetic biographer could be. Any talk of detachment was, as Fuller observed, delusion.[19]

Fuller's exceedingly high opinion of Grant's generalship and his concern for an unprejudiced treatment of it raises the question also of whether his contention that Grant had been unjustly neglected was valid. This is doubtful. Fuller was right to complain of his neglect in British military colleges, but he shared the 'Grant complex' of so many of his admirers who constantly reiterate the complaint that Grant's share of the laurels had been lavished on his defeated opponent, Robert E. Lee, by both British students of the war and American historians. It is true that in the pantheon of American heroes 'Grant's memory has never inspired the sentiment of tenderness of Lincoln's or the majesty of Lee's'. Yet Grant has remained 'lodged in the cloudy Valhalla of myth' as the saviour of the Union. It is quite wrong to suggest that Grant's talents were dismissed as trivial by military writers. The internal evidence of Fuller's own book would suggest this, as he found many writers to quote who praised Grant. Fuller was fond of argument by quotation, advancing themes by reference to other writers. Liddell Hart advised him to check this tendency. 'Least of all do I like quotations from military historians of a later generation e.g. Atkinson. The reader wants Fuller's own criticisms not those of some second rate pedant.' American and British writers had praised Grant before Fuller, though they were less convinced of his ability as a strategist. Even Lee's biographer, Major General Sir Frederick Maurice, wrote of him kindly as a great general. Finally Fuller's portrait owed a great deal to the earlier semi-official biography written by Grant's military secretary, Adam Badeau. Fuller's Grant was cast solidly in Badeau's mould. For all his contempt for 'official history', Fuller did repeat uncritically assertions made by an official historian when it suited his purpose.[20]

By concentrating heavily on the individual, Fuller's writings on the Civil War are characterized by a singular overestimation of the role of the great man in military history. Fuller magnified Grant's talents as a grand strategist. Following Badeau, he argued that Grant aimed to bring the Confederacy to its knees, after he had been appointed General-in-Chief in 1864, by striking at its rear. This was the 'grand manoeuvre' which had been foreshowed in the Vicksburg Campaign in the summer of 1863. Then Grant 'by cutting loose from his base . . . protected himself against an attack in rear by leaving himself without a rear to be attacked'. If Sherman struck deep into Georgia while Grant pinned Lee down in the forests of Virginia, then the triumph of Vicksburg could be repeated on a greater scale. It mattered not that Grant seemed to fare badly in the field against Lee, so long as Lee remained fixed. 'Though means vary, his idea remains constant; he holds fast to Lee, so that Sherman's manoeuvres may continue.' Liddell Hart doubted whether Grant was the omniscient *generalissimo* depicted by Fuller: 'you ascribe to Grant a subtlety and range of vision which is Fulleresque but which is in contrast to the very picture you paint of Grant's normal character'.[21]

Much of Fuller's analysis is distorted by special pleading. The degree to which Lee was fixed is debatable. He was defending Richmond because he chose to, and was thus reacting just as much to his own desires as conforming to Grant's movements. It is much harder in practice than in theory to fix an army, as Lee was to show by pushing Early's corps up the Shenandoah Valley in July 1864 to threaten Washington after Grant had supposedly pinned him down. Grant's failure in Northern Virginia and the consequent Siege of Petersburg (June 1864–March 1865) were excused by Fuller on the grounds that it prevented Lee from assisting General Joseph E. Johnston against Sherman. This supposed that Grant and Sherman had worked out a coherent strategy before taking the field; this was far from being the case. The initial correspondence about Sherman's role does not mention Atlanta; no clearly defined economic or moral purpose was assigned to Sherman, and after he reached Savannah, Grant considered transferring Sherman's army to Petersburg, which suggests that the siege was an end in itself rather than the expedient praised by Fuller.[22]

When questioning whether Grant had the strategic vision claimed for him by Fuller, Liddell Hart made the valid point (though its obvious implications for Sherman may be disregarded) that 'It is easy of course to show that Grant had a vague general idea of pushing across ultimately to the Atlantic coast. But there is no originality in this "idea", which had long since been mooted by Halleck, even McClellan, and hundreds of others.' That the strategic debates of Grant and Sherman were matters of wide discussion – and not fruits of unique strategic genius – is made clear by the suggestion of Major General Benjamin F. Butler (himself a discredited field commander) to the Joint Committee on the Conduct of the War in the spring of 1863 that a force should take 'supplies ruthlessly from the country' and sweep through Alabama, Georgia and the Carolinas. 'For to take the producers, to stop the production of the country and everything else contributing to the power of the Confederacy' should be the aim of the Union armies. As a prediction of Sherman's eventual course this cannot be bettered, but it lays bare the historical deficiencies of an approach that competed the talents of one individual against another – one to which Fuller and Liddell Hart made such an influential contribution.[23]

When assessing Grant's generalship in the field, Fuller sought out evidence of his application of the principles of war. Grant's campaigns have a certain symmetry that made them an admirable basis for such a study. He gradually matured as a commander and his forces became successively larger. Fuller's use of the principles of war is not intrusive, and though they underpin his entire discussion he rarely mentions them by name. To take one example. In planning for the advance into Virginia in 1864, Grant's 'central idea was concentration of force from which he intended to develop a ceaseless offensive against the enemy's armies, and the resources and the *moral* of the Confederacy'. Then 'Having decided on his main line of direction, the next problem was one of combining security and concentration of force.' Had Grant thought along these lines? We return to the fundamental paradox of *The Foundations of the Science of War*. If the principles of war were immutable then they existed by their very nature. If that was so, then his treatment of them in *The Generalship of Ulysses S. Grant* would have to show convincingly that Grant had employed them. The trouble with Fuller's argument was that he provided only empirical evidence of a kind – namely his own interpretation of Grant's actions rather than clinching proof. In his analysis Fuller does not cite any of Grant's comments made at the time which show beyond doubt that he thought in terms of principles of war. There was a further difficulty. The anti-intellectualism implicit in Fuller's thinking only served to obscure the issue. Grant made no reference to principles in his published writings. The *Personal Memoirs* only remark, 'My general plan was to concentrate all forces possible against the Confederate armies in the field.' This was of little help to Fuller. Also, Grant made several comments that deprecated any idea that military theory was of value. 'The art of war is quite simple enough. Find out where your enemy is. Get at him as soon as you can, and strike him as hard as you can and keep moving on', said Grant in his laconic way. Ultimately, Fuller's advocacy of common sense rebounded upon him. If principles of war were all a matter of the unconscious, then Fuller could not demonstrate beyond a shadow of doubt that they had been practised in the way he claimed.[24]

That Fuller had imposed a system and order on Grant's

generalship which did not in fact exist becomes clearer on a further examination of the Virginia campaign of 1864. On marching through the Wilderness area in Northern Virginia, Grant aimed, according to Fuller, 'to get through it with the minimum of fighting'. 'It was a manoeuvre and not an advance to an attack. It is true that he [Grant] did not overlook the possibility of a flank march, but it is untrue that he intended to march on Lee and engage him.' On the contrary, it is doubtful whether Grant had any clear cut ideas as to the nature of the coming engagement. On the first day of the advance, his instructions read: 'If any opportunity presents itself for pitching into part of Lee's army do so without giving time for disposition.' Grant did not distinguish between the need to fix Lee with a well prepared and supported attack and piecemeal assaults. Grant's control over operations, moreover, was frequently minimal and this feature of the Civil War was not conveyed by Fuller's account. He spent long hours surrounded by the fog of war – usually whittling – a factor often underrated, or at least underplayed, by Fuller's account of military operations.[25]

Grant's vindication, according to Fuller, arose from his keen conviction that he would win eventually because of his overwhelming material superiority. Fuller was nonetheless keen to refute the notion that Grant had won by numbers only, that he was 'a bludgeon general, . . . an extraordinary conclusion, for no general in this war, not excepting Lee, . . . made greater use of manoeuvre in the winning of . . . his battles'. Fuller had to show, in other words, that Grant was imaginative; in a word, no Haig. This was at the bottom of his differences with Liddell Hart over the American Civil War. A convinced Sherman partisan, Liddell Hart saw Grant as a prototype Haig whose 'obsession' with fighting battles was 'faithfully imitated with even greater lavishness and ineffectiveness' on the Western Front. It was wholly appropriate, given their varying approaches to the study of war, that Fuller chose as his hero a hard fighter like Grant, and Liddell Hart a soldier who, if he never lost a campaign, never won a battle.[26]

Fuller's assumptions about Grant's greatness however require careful probing as they illuminate flaws in his reasoning. His initial exposition of the principles of war was based on the Napoleonic system of warfare – the product of a largely pre-industrial society. *The Generalship of Ulysses S. Grant* assumed that industrial change would promote conditions that would facilitate the use of the classical principles of war. A part of Fuller's case for Grant was that he was Lee's peer on the battlefield; they could be judged by the same criteria; but Grant, as the commander of armies which enjoyed the benefit of vast industrial resources had an immense advantage over Lee. Grant enjoyed the initiative and need not fear that operational considerations would be undercut by logistics. Fuller never made this point explicitly. This is hardly surprising. Grant's campaigns show that profitable application of force required, not economy of force, but a *preponderance* of force. In an industrial age the principles of war do not have a universal application. Grant's crossing of the James River in June 1864 and his pursuit of Lee after the fall of Richmond in the spring of 1865, which were held up by Fuller as textbook examples, were discussed by him in operational terms as if Grant and Lee enjoyed comparable resources, when they did not. Fuller's books on the Civil War integrate the technological and social factors with the personal more successfully than any other of his writings by showing that Grant and Lee were representative commanders of two conflicting cultures. Patently the defeat of the Confederacy showed that the use of principles of war required a massive technological and numerical superiority over the enemy. In order to advance the case for Grant, however, Fuller had to underplay those very technological and social factors that he had brought so successfully to the fore in the study of war, and instead argue in terms of personalities. Hence, when dealing with Lee, he could not resist the temptation of clinching his case by placing all the blame for the Confederacy's failings, not on general structural weaknesses of the South, but on Lee's shoulders, judging him one of the worst quartermasters in history.[27]

For all of Fuller's futuristic vision he was still tied to the conventional criteria of generalship in which the talents of individual commanders were pitted against one another in 'league tables'. This gap in his thinking was symptomatic of a fundamental flaw: an inability to understand that increased technological and industrial sophistication would delimit the activities of great men, forcing them to become more dependent on the brains and energy of their staffs. Nevertheless, *The Generalship of Ulysses S. Grant* and *Grant and Lee* both made an important contribution to the study of war in the modern world. Although Liddell Hart warned Fuller that his excessively pro-Grant stance would expose him 'to the ripostes of the modern American historians', modern scholars tend to support Fuller's case rather than that of Liddell Hart. Although some inconsistencies and flaws in his reasoning do indeed qualify some of the assertions made in these books, in purely historical terms they were an undoubted success. When a second edition of *Grant and Lee* was published in 1957 Fuller could congratulate himself on divining correctly the future direction of Civil War historiography.[28]

From his studies of the Civil War Fuller distilled later in 1933 some general reflections on the higher art of generalship in the next war. This little book, *Generalship: Its Diseases and their Cure*, acquired a degree of notoriety out of all proportion to its contents. It began life as an article for the Royal Artillery *Journal*, which was rejected on the grounds that it might offend the CIGS, Milne. The book was certainly brazen in tone. In the Preface Fuller recounted a story in which a brave and meritorious officer, Colonel Clement was wounded in the head and carried off the field of Waterloo. Napoleon was so impressed with his courage that he decreed that he should be promoted immediately to the rank of Brigadier General. On arrival in the hospital he was so badly wounded that the surgeon general, Larrey, removed the top of his head and took out the brain. Then suddenly an *aide-de-camp* from the Emperor arrived and announced his promotion. Revived by the news Clement rubbed his eyes, jumped up, picked up the top of his head and ran out of the hospital. '*Mon général*, your brains!' shouted Larrey. To which the gallant Clement, running faster, replied, 'Now that I am general I shall no longer require them!'[29]

With this opening it is hardly surprising that the general drift of conservative opinion was that *Generalship* was a 'hasty and unconvincing piece of writing' really 'designed to throw discredit on British generals and the British General Staff'. This unfortunate impression was reinforced by Fuller's bitter attacks on the proliferation of military bureaucracy that had occurred since 1865. The growth of the General Staff resembled a 'paper octopus squirting ink and wriggling its tentacles into every corner . . . It creates work, it creates offices, and above all, it creates the rear spirit'.[30]

This remark was unfair and the resentment that similar comments aroused did much to obscure the valuable parts of the book. Like the other books on Grant, *Generalship* had grown out of the arguments of *The Foundations of the Science of War*. Here

Fuller had recommended that command be split into two so that operational aspects of generalship could be separated from management. The commander would be free to concentrate on the battlefield 'free from all routine duties'. This would restore a Napoleonic style of command and allow the general greater freedom of action. The underlying theme of *Generalship* was that '*The more mechanical become the weapons with which we fight, the less mechanical must be the spirit which controls them.*' No doubt Fuller was unfair in referring to the 'shell-proofing' of generals along the Western Front, but there was more than a grain of truth behind his accusations that a great difference existed between the living standards of the fighting troops and the staff. He was also right to complain that until 1918 GHQ exercised an insufficiently tight control over operations.[31]

When Fuller turned to the narrower question of command in the next war he was at his best and divined perceptively the pattern of command employed by the most successful generals of the Second World War. As Patton emphasized, a general should 'lead in person': 'see with your own eyes and be seen by your own troops while engaged in personal reconnaissance'. Montgomery organized his headquarters along similar lines to those suggested by Fuller, with a Tactical HQ where Montgomery commanded in person; the Main HQ where detailed planning was completed; and finally the Rear HQ where administrative matters were handled. Montgomery also adopted Fuller's suggestion that a commanding general should lighten his burdens by appointing a highly trained executive officer, a deputy – a role filled to perfection by de Guingand. Montgomery also agreed with Fuller's desire that a commander should exert his personality. He 'should never bring them [his subordinates] back to him for . . . a conference; he must go forward to them. Then nobody looks over his shoulder. A conference of subordinates *to collect ideas* is the resort of a weak commander.'[32]

Fuller suggested, again following Napoleon, that a commander could keep tight control over military operations by employing a number of *aides-de-camp* who could act as his eyes and ears. They should deliver his orders and ensure that they are carried out – a suggestion put to practical use by both Montgomery and Patton. They sent out liaison officers from their advanced HQs in jeeps, reporting directly by radio. If there is a flaw in Fuller's reasoning it is to be found in the undue isolation of the commander which this kind of personal command promotes. Montgomery, for example, became unwilling to consider matters which did not interest him or distracted him from the narrow task of fighting battles. Such a system does not promote harmony among allies, when a variety of interests were at stake or conflicting ideas emerged about how a war should be conducted.[33]

Fuller added that war was a young man's business. The majority of the greatest generals – and he appended an impressive list enumerating their ages – were young men. He contended that the British Army should be streamlined so that the most able officers in the age bracket 35–45 could be selected for the highest commands. He inveighed against the cramping effect of peacetime routine – which bore no relation to war conditions: 'in our existing system, though self-knowledge cannot be denied, self-expression very largely is, because it so frequently clashes with the regulations'. Then, giving vent to his pent up frustrations, Fuller wrote, 'The soldier who thinks ahead is considered, to put it bluntly, a damned nuisance.' Support for Fuller's view came from a surprising source, the official historian, Edmonds, who complained of 'dubious methods of selection for promotion and the absence of searching medical tests before promotion to general's rank and before Active Service'. It was less what Fuller said that caused offence than the way it was said.[34]

If the broad line of argument was correct, Fuller's fascination with youth was exaggerated. He had a point that the world's greatest soldiers had been young men: Alexander the Great was only 32 when he died; Napoleon and Wellington were both only 46 in 1815. The experience of the First World War had not been edifying in this respect. General Sir James Grierson had died of a heart attack en route to France in 1914; Fuller, who had watched him depart from Southampton, said that he looked like an advertisement for OXO beef extract, rotund and with rosy (almost purple) cheeks. The candidates for the Sulva Bay expedition during the Gallipoli campaign in 1915 were hardly in the first flush of youth. One, General Ewart, was too fat for trench warfare. Youth was on the side of the victors in the Second World War. The average age of corps and divisional commanders in 21st Army Group was 48; that of regimental officers 35. In the BEF of 1939–40 it had been 54 and 45 respectively. Still, youth was not a guarantee of success. Wavell in his book on *Generals and Generalship*, pointed out that Caesar and Cromwell had started

campaigning at 40; and Turenne, Marlborough, Moltke and
Roberts had won their most admired victories after they had
passed the age of 60. There is no direct correlation between age
and incompetence. Patton, the most dynamic Allied commander
of the Second World War, was 60 in 1945. As General Essame
observes, there should be no arbitrary age barriers raised in
wartime: 'the ratio of clever to stupid being about the same in
both young and older age groups. It may be true to say that there
"is no fool like an old fool" but historically the young ones have
always run them close.'[35]

In *Generalship* Fuller claimed that generals should lead their men
into battle. This was firmly in the Moore tradition. Moore, like
General Sir Ralph Abercromby, enjoyed the din of battle, and
both were killed, Moore at Corunna (1809) and Abercrombie at
Alexandria (1801). Surely Fuller was going too far. The question
posed by his argument has been well summed up by Douglas
Southall Freeman: 'whether the gain to troops' morale at the front
was compensation for the fatal exposure of leaders whose death
hastened the doom of the Confederacy'. In the Army of Northern
Virginia alone, Stonewall Jackson, A. P. Hill and 'Jeb' Stuart were
only the most famous of the high-ranking casualties of highly
personalized command. Wavell opposed the use of generals as
front line troops; their lives were too valuable to fritter away in
fruitless adventures – surely the most sensible stance to take. In
any case, generals could not control *both* the strategy and tactics of
a great war, even when armies remained small. Fuller's attempts
to show that Grant was a general capable of exerting influence
over these dual functions was not convincing.[36]

Notwithstanding these qualifications, Fuller at least provided a
starting point for an assessment of the influence of political, social
and economic factors on strategy and generalship. It is a damning
indictment of the blinkered approach to military education
between the wars that these elements were almost totally neglected
in the British Army. This was a penicious consequence in part of
the terminological debate over the science of war. Fuller had
moved from the science of war to the 'natural history' of war and
Grant. Those soldiers who insisted that war was an art tended to
conceive of its study in exclusively operational terms, as
exemplified by Stonewall Jackson's campaign in the Shenandoah
Valley. The individual generals of the American Civil War thus

attained a symbolic status in the British Army which had only a tenuous connection with their historical significance.[37]

It must be conceded that Fuller's strictures on the quality of British generalship shown in 1914–18, which he compared so adversely with that of 1861–5, hardly helped his cause, but opposition was not confined to his harsh verdict on the First World War. Conservatives were genuinely fearful of the effect on young and impressionable minds of Fuller's writings on the Civil War. In 1933 it was decided to include *Grant and Lee* along with Liddell Hart's *Sherman* on the reading list for the officer's promotion examination; the subject set for the military history paper in 1933 was the American Civil War. Edmonds, wishing to curry favour with the new CIGS, Montgomery-Massingberd, whose rabid dislike of Fuller was well known, wrote to warn him of the likely consequences of a wide circulation of *Grant and Lee*. He did not enclose with his letter a copy of the article he had written on the 'diseases' of generalship agreeing with Fuller. Major-General Vesey, the Director of Staff Duties, replied that the CIGS 'fully concurs that it is a most undesirable book to include for study', and orders were issued restricting the syllabus to a detailed study of the Virginian theatre, 26 June 1862–14 July 1863, campaigns covered in a few pages in *Grant and Lee*. Montgomery-Massingberd wrote to thank Edmonds personally. 'I confess I was horrified when I saw it [Edmonds's letter] and cannot make out how and why these books were chosen.' Thus Fuller's efforts had boomeranged. His attempts to broaden the study of military history had resulted in a tightening of bureaucratic control over its study. Grant remained a neglected historical figure in the British Army. As Fuller told Liddell Hart bitterly,

though books of this kind may not sell well in America, the few who read them do seem to appreciate them, which is more than happens in our own country. I have never had a single letter of appreciation from an English soldier, not even when I presented a book free. We are a race dead from the neck up.[38]

6

'The Natural History of War', 1930–2

As a writer my works fall vaguely into two series, those
written up to about 1930, and those written since. The first
impinges on the technical and tactical aspects of war, and the
second increasingly become more historical and political.

Fuller to Jay Luvaas, 8 July 1963, Luvaas Papers

Fuller's books on the Civil War demonstrated his increasing
interest in the political and social aspects of warfare. The final part
of *The Generalship of Ulysses S. Grant* was entitled 'The Generalship
of Peace'. 'Stress the last part (Part IV)', he asked Liddell Hart, 'it
is the only part worth reading, and it has nothing to do with
Grant.' The latter duly obliged in his review in *The Daily Telegraph*.
The main points of this section were to be expanded in a series of
books written during the years 1930–2, *India in Revolt* (1931), *The
Dragon's Teeth* (1932), and *War and Western Civilization, 1832–1932*
(1932). Fuller wrote them while on half-pay between postings
when he had a good deal of leisure time on his hands. 'I have 20
more books in my head, and 20 more articles at present, and want
to make hay whilst the ½ pay sun shines so amicably upon me.'
Ironside felt that, despite this chance to write more, Fuller would
soon get bored. 'I always have an idea that he will get out of the
Army', he predicted in 1929. 'That little wife of his is always
pushing him to get away and little drops in the end wear away
the hardest of stones.'[1]

The main drift of Fuller's thought during these years was an
increasing preoccupation with what he termed the 'Natural
History of War'. Fuller had emphasized throughout *The Generalship
of Ulysses S. Grant* that the study of war could not be divorced
from the study of peace, and that the conduct of war had to be
related to its social, political and economic context. He regarded
his studies in the science of war as 'but stepping stones towards

the development of my main idea which is, that war is a world force and must equate with the progress of civilization generally'. War was thus an agent of change and was itself influenced by that change:

> if you look back over the last three thousand years you will find that the main occupation of mankind has been war. In fact war has been the main pivot of religion, politics and economics and, unless this undoubted fact is recognized, religion, politics and economics cannot be correctly understood.

From this major premise Fuller developed in more detail the historical and philosophical ideas that he used to justify mechanization. Despite their historical scope these three books were really thinly disguised polemics on the need to limit war. They thus complement Fuller's more technical treatises, *On Future Warfare* (1928), *Lectures on FSR II* (1932) and *Lectures on FSR III* (1932), which will be discussed in the next chapter.[2]

Fuller started off in both *The Dragon's Teeth* and *War and Western Civilization* by explaining that during the last century the destructive scope of war had expanded at the most alarming rate. If this was not checked it would continue to grow. He had no truck with the rhetoric of the 1920s that the Great War was the war 'to end all wars'. He took up a prediction that he had made in a little book called *Imperial Defence, 1588–1914* (1926). He believed that another war was inevitable; and that it would be fought with Germany over the integrity of the new East European republics. He also warned that each attempt to restrict armaments had resulted in their increase. Hence conflict would continue, given the existing degree of dissatisfaction with the Versailles Treaty; while the abolition of weapons could not prevent war breaking out as 'armaments are the outward and visible sign of inward discontent'.[3]

Then Fuller tried to show why this was so. He agreed with Rousseau that war was the product of organized societies; the two were inseparable. So long as nation states existed and upheld their interests against others, then war would exist. War 'is an instrument of policy and armaments are instruments of war; consequently disarmament, as well as war, is the outcome of *policy'* – and policy rested ultimately on *force*, as each nation pursued a policy commensurate with its interests. Relations between states were thus political and not amicable. Like Hobbes, Fuller believed that the international system resembled a jungle. In *The Foundations of the Science of War* he had argued that 'man had no right to live but did have the power to protect that life and this became the right to safeguard it'. Primitive and social man could be compared. Fundamentally, Fuller asserted that there were three causes of war: security of life based on the instinct of self-preservation; the maintenance of life based on the instinct of hunger; and the continuity of race based on the instinct of sex. In the complex world of international relations these basic causes naturally had to be modified.

> The animal man fights for a mate, the social man for peacefulness. The biological cause thus passes into the ethical cause – the maintenance of peace – and the same energy which is expended in the establishment of peace is utilized to preserve and secure it.

Thus Fuller perceived a profound truth among this archaic biology of war: that the most potent military cause of war was the *search after security*. As security was the 'pivot' around which the nation state system revolved, peace was secured by force. During peacetime force could only be exerted indirectly, and nations could only threaten to use it; 'the desire for security leads to a search after strong or unattackable frontiers'. In other words, a search for peacefulness often led to war. This kind of reasoning led Fuller to conclude in 1926 that there was no essential difference between peace and war. The difference in the struggles between nations was purely relative. Ultimately, he predicted, if war grew out of peace, then logically peace would have to be modified to stamp out war.[4]

Turning to the problems of Europe, Fuller rightly saw that the First World War had destroyed the balance of power in Europe, and substituted a number of small states some of which lacked the resources to sustain themselves. The Treaty of Versailles and the accompanying League of Nations Covenant, had elevated nationality as the bedrock of the post-war international system; 'self-determination' would eradicate war by setting up national states which could match the national aspirations of minorities and remove a source of discontent. Fuller, with no little relish, brutally exposed the contradictions inherent in this liberal outlook.

(He had once confided to Liddell Hart that 'For a poor man the joy in life is really to be without fear.') All it did was introduce disruption pregnant with war. How was it possible for the League of Nations to eradicate friction between states, as its enthusiasts eagerly hoped, when it upheld the principle of nationality – the very cause of the tensions that led to war? How could any agreement between nations be enforced without the (threatened) use of force? Furthermore, the League of Nations upheld the *status quo* and French hegemony in Europe, which only served to exacerbate German suspicions rather than allay them. A truly national outlook was reinforced by the League of Nations and not that international spirit claimed for it.[5]

In *The Dragon's Teeth* the proposition that there was no essential difference between peace and war was forcefully restated. 'Peace is war without blows and bloodshed, and war is peace with them; therefore . . . instruments of war must be such as can control strife in both these spheres of human activity.' Fuller now added another dimension to the argument: economic rivalries precipitated fears about security. 'War is a continuation of economic policy in another form; consequently the causes of war are to be sought in economics. The present world turmoil is not due to arms, but to economic systems which demand arms to protect them.' Here Fuller reflected a more general interest in the influence of economics on the world order. 'Were every nation to adopt free trade', he wrote, 'war would be eliminated. . . . Every tariff is a cannon shot, and if nations are unprepared for war, wars are long, and the longer they are the more barbarous do they become.' The new system of nation states introduced by the Versailles settlement had brought the introduction of free trade no nearer. On the contrary, since 1921 virtually all the major powers had engaged in a tariff war. 'Debts', Fuller justly observed, 'like tariffs and cannon are instruments of policy.' No degree of international stability could be achieved without free trade, he argued. 'With twenty-six tariff walls in an area less than that of the United States, Europe (less Russia) cannot develop full prosperity.' Implicit in his comments was the assumption that only another war could create those conditions under which free trade could flourish.[6]

His thesis acquired an additional interest when he suggested that the First World War had accelerated a discernible trend towards the grouping of nations into cartels. Fuller viewed the First World War as a 'European civil war'. He predicted that 'the whole civilized world is rapidly circling towards the whirlpool of war. Not a war like the last one, but like the Thirty Years War, a war which will eliminate economics as the bone of contention.' Out of this conflict would emerge 'a federated Europe, in which each nation will be politically autonomous but economically internationalised.' 'Federal unions', he claimed, are nearly always beneficial, because nationalism demands security, and security demands federation.' Thus 'it may one day become . . . impossible for Germany to declare war on Europe'. Fuller also foresaw the rise of China as a great power, and eventually expected the emerging American and Russian super-states to dominate the world; '[once] the economic necessities are placed on a rational footing, the present age of wars will pass and we shall enter another age of war; not wars between nations but wars between continents'.[7]

These predictions bear out the clarity of Fuller's vision. He was certainly justified in underlining the importance of the economic factor in increasing international tensions and creating an atmosphere in which nations were prepared to go to war. Paul Kennedy has commented on the 'insidious appeals to chauvinism which so frequently lay beneath the surface of protectionist arguments'. He concludes that 'economic developments were related to national strategy and internal politics; ideas about power were intertwined with those about profit'. In his opinion the most important cause that contributed to the growing Anglo-German enmity before 1914 was economic. However, though it is widely agreed that the economic factor before 1939 – and particularly the economic strains unleashed by German rearmament, which might have led to an earlier outbreak of hostilities than the Germans had planned for – played an important part in triggering off the Second World War, there was no *direct* link between the operation of economic factors and the decisions made by statesmen in both 1914 and 1939 to commence hostilities. Fuller was nevertheless right in showing that military, economic, financial and diplomatic policies hung together and should not be studied in compartments.[8]

What also redounds greatly to Fuller's credit was that he saw just as clearly as Sir Halford Mackinder, the eminent geopolitician, that the world would in the future be dominated by states which occupied continental land masses. Both Fuller and Mackinder noted the influence of geography on the character of empires.

Every great power was dependent upon the territory it occupied, for as Mackinder argued, 'defence is essentially the protection of the means of economic subsistence; and the distribution of products, being conducted in chief measure along lines of least resistance, follows and prepares the paths of strategic opportunity'. Both Fuller and Mackinder were of one mind in advocating that there was a link between strategic factors and the economic intercourse enjoyed by nations. Strategic points were usually trading centres of the first importance.[9]

Fuller's analysis of the interaction of balance of power, economic policy and war has now taken its place as part of the stock currency of the study of war. 'War is born of peace', asserts Professor Sir Harry Hinsley, in a standard work on international relations, 'or at least of the precautions which men have taken for the purpose of achieving durable peace.' In the inter-war years, however, such views were not greeted with any great enthusiasm. The traditional liberal view of the world order, which *The Dragon's Teeth* sought to refute, saw trade as automatically 'good' and peacefully beneficent, whilst war was not only detrimental to trade but far worse – it was an appalling 'evil' and therefore not worth studying. Such views have not altogether disappeared. According to Fuller this Manichean outlook was not only misguided but had a distorting effect on the political outlook of democratic nations. Moral judgements lavished on 'war' and 'peace' were irrelevant to the main issue. His principal point was that it was precisely a desire for trade and new markets that led states into competition and ultimately down the road to war. As Kennedy remarks, a 'country could be both commercial and warlike without the basic pattern of expansion being affected'. Throughout the analysis, Fuller's moral relativism, his belief that good and bad were intimately connected, is striking.[10]

Thus if statesmen would understand that there was no essential difference between war and peace they would be better equipped to tackle the problem of war. Fuller argued that the modern world had seen the opening up of the 'inner front', in which guerrilla tactics and propaganda were of far greater importance than brute force. With increasing dissatisfaction growing within the European colonial empires, Fuller went so far as to suggest that war was now '*within* the civilized world itself'. Consequently the iniquities of peace were just as relevant to the war problem as the evils of war. Each attempt to disarm had overlooked the relationship between social discontent, revolution and war. Fuller took as a germane example, China, a signatory of the Pact of Paris (1928) 'outlawing' war; 'yet during the last ten years this country has been harrowed by unceasing civil war. It is the perfecting of peace far more than the elimination of war which is the true war problem.' No state of peacefulness could be established which ignored civil disruption. Thirty-one wars since 1800 – half the conflicts of modern times – have been heralded by civil unrest, and this factor in international relations has hardly diminished since Fuller wrote in the 1930s.[11]

Fuller was thus concerned to point out the immense complexity involved in the study of conflict and its causes. Most writers who thought about war in the 1920s claimed that war was a simple problem that could be easily solved. Fuller wrote that the best way to understand peace was to understand war. If the problem of peace was complex, then so was the problem of war. In the second book of *The Dragon's Teeth* Fuller contented himself with making some suggestions as to how the war–peace relationship could be better understood. In support of his thesis that conflict was engendered by national rivalries (or by those seeking to secure their national identity), Fuller pointed to Kant's treatise, *Perpetual Peace*. Here Kant had argued that mankind had been forced into ever larger social groupings despite himself – what Kant termed 'social unsociableness'. That is, there was a connection between cycles of war and its elimination: 'that in the long run wars tend to unite the human race', Fuller wrote, 'because grouping lessens the incidence of war. Nature's goal is unity and her driving force towards it is war.'[12]

Apart from Kant, the other influence on his thinking was Oswald Spengler's *Decline of the West* (1926) which popularized the cyclical theory. Fuller read it on its first appearance in England and joked with Liddell Hart that *The Foundations of the Science of War* was a 'child's book' compared with it. Fuller's perusal of Spengler confirmed him in his existing outlook. It did not, on the whole, change his mind on any subject. He agreed with Spengler that the crisis facing the West was comparable to that which overtook the Roman Empire in the West in the fifth century AD. To think in terms of a 'crisis' of the West was a commonplace of the age: a reaction against the unprecedented trauma of the First World War which affected even those who had not been directly involved in the fighting. Fuller, in particular, had long been addicted to the notion that Western civilization was heading for the abyss. In the opinion of both Fuller and Spengler, 'Western' civilization was a distinct cultural entity, quite separate from that of Eastern Europe.[13]

When examining the warmaking potential of a society, Fuller pointed to the signal influence of geography. This determined the structure of a civilization and therefore the character of its armed forces. Thus in Ancient Greece it was the mountainous terrain and the influence of the sea which 'were the two halves of the mould in which Greek tactics and grand strategy were cast'. The food stocks were in the valleys, and battles were fought for their possession; heavy infantry were best suited to fight under these conditions. The Greeks also took to the sea to break the land blockade of their cities. Fuller's treatment of war was thus wholly related to aspects of the totality of the parent society. He argued forcefully that if Pericles based his strategy on the prevailing geographic and economic factors, then his measures could not be understood 'in their true perspective unless related to the civilization of this period'. Fuller did not study warfare as the product of a 'cause' which was self-contained and no business of the student of war, while he concentrated on the campaign, ignoring the 'result'. He studied the whole process in the round. Thus he wrote of the interminable wars between the Greek city states that their

> struggles [were] . . . one and all are based on food supply. The command of the sea, as in modern times, is all important. The quarrel of Corinth and Athens over the island of Corcyra was not a mere pretext for the outbreak of the Peloponnesian War, . . . for Corcyra was the strategic focal point of Sicilian and Italian trade.[14]

Fuller is perhaps guilty again of exaggerating the importance of the economic factor. Nevertheless his studies did introduce a new dimension into the study of warfare. In the Middle Ages he observed how the relationship between economic development and social change influenced the art of war and that warfare played a major part in forming the modern nation state. Fuller can perhaps be forgiven for overestimating the influence of gunpowder in his zeal to link together the political, social and economic factors with the military in a characteristically sweeping passage:

> Gunpowder . . . first restricted and then eliminated the feudal
> order, it abolished private wars, consolidated kingdoms, policed
> them, and with the merchant led to the emergence of another
> order and form of civilization – the Modern Age.

As T. H. Wintringham pointed out, Fuller's analysis veered rather
closely to the Marxist view of the dominant influence of the
productive elements of society. It is curious that given his earlier
emphasis on the importance of the great man in history, that
there seemed to be little room for the personal factor in this
strictly determinist view of social development. Fuller had once
tried to reconcile this anomaly by observing: 'History is like a vast
organ, the keys are fixed but according to the genius of man can
the tune be varied . . . Historical relationships are in form spirals.'
Fuller himself had shown how social changes had wrought
significant alterations in the art of war in which great men had
played no part. His generalization was therefore not entirely
convincing.[15]

Other such distortions as emerge in Fuller's historical treatment
were largely the result of his prescriptive intent. If Fuller was
right to adopt Kant's notion of 'social unsociableness', then he
had to show that patterns did exist in the ultimately unifying
process of history. This approach was symptomatic of a general
love of paradox. Societies were bound together by a brittle cement
which threatened to fracture and splinter under the impact of the
corrosive yet unifying force of war. If these trends could be
discovered, then it might be possible to find ways of mitigating,
perhaps eliminating, the destructive propensities of war. What
Fuller was really attempting was to extend the structure so
painstakingly worked out in *The Foundations of the Science of War*
into the study of the relationship between man, war and society.[16]

This system was Fuller's own. Spengler's *Decline of the West*
played its part in refining the theory, and in fortifying Fuller's
belief that cycles existed. As early as 1920 Fuller claimed to
discover 'certain tactical cycles . . . which like comets, travel along
fixed paths and reappear at stated intervals, the periods being
measured . . . according to the evolution of weapons, means of
movement and protection'. Fuller thought that Spengler's
theory of civilization's decline was overly complicated and too
metaphysical. This was ironic because Fuller had been accused of
the same fault. *India in Revolt*, for instance, had mystified some

reviewers. Fuller explained: 'I tried to write it in an Oriental atmosphere, this is why some reviewers can't understand it.' Fuller termed the interaction of war and society 'social geomorphology' – the change of form in societies. 'These are largely due to diseases which with almost mathematical regularity afflict mankind until they are prevented or cured.' If historical inquiry, he continued, was likened to a post mortem examination, 'then it follows that there is nothing extraordinary in the coincidences which the histories of peoples and civilizations offer us'; but he agreed that such similarities were not necessarily inevitable. It must also be said that throughout his life Fuller was rather profligate with definitions and as he wrote so much, he tended to forget that he had concocted them, and this sometimes leads to confusion when the main lines of his thought are delineated.[17]

One theme which is not difficult to establish is the thread of Darwinism which runs through his writing. It would not be desirable or very easy to attempt to show that Darwinism dominated *every* level of Fuller's thought. But he thought deductively, establishing a firm basis and then moving up – his favourite 'foundations' – and the concrete of those foundations was provided by the Darwinism which he had absorbed as a young man reading Herbert Spencer's *First Principles*. Spencer had held that those elements which best adapted themselves to changes in conditions were the best suited to survive, and Spencer perceived in this mechanism a law of development which operated in his biographer's words, 'in all those endless abstract products of human activity which constitute the environment of daily life'. Fuller found this law useful in expressing a basic military concept from which strategy and tactics could be extrapolated; the military aspects themselves bore little connection with Spencer's thought but the concept itself was a Darwinian progeny. In 1932 Fuller declared that there was a *law of military development*. If civilization was the environment in which armies existed, then they must 'adapt themselves to its changing phases in order to remain fitted for war'.[18]

The law of military development impinged on society through the interaction of mobility and stability, fluidity and fixity; a reaction would automatically follow any progression. As weapons became more sophisticated man tried to protect himself by eliminating danger from combat. Hence the *constant tactical factor*.

Every improvement in weapon-power (unconsciously though it may be) has aimed at lessening terror and danger on one side by increasing them on the other; consequently every improvement in weapons has eventually been met by a counter-improvement which has rendered the improvement obsolete; the evolutionary pendulum of weapon-power, slowly or rapidly, swinging from the offensive to the protective and back again in harmony with the speed of civil progress; each swing in a measurable degree eliminating danger.

The influence of industrial change so perceptively divined by Fuller, operating through the social mechanisms of evolution introduced a new variable into warfare, a *differential tactical factor*. In the twentieth century 'civil progress being so intense . . . that no army can in the full sense be kept up to date', its equipment would need constant improvement and its commanders would have to keep abreast of the most recent technological developments. An 'arms race' would develop between those able to field the most advanced weapons and those countries less able or inclined to field them would fall behind. Such a qualitative differential, resulting in the rapid introduction of new weapons, meant 'that the army which is mentally the better prepared to meet tactical changes, will possess an enormous advantage over all others'. It also meant that decisive superiority in striking power would be proportionate to the degree of technological superiority attained. In an arresting metaphor, Fuller alleged that even the Earl of Raglan could have defeated Napoleon at Waterloo if he had been equipped with machine guns.[19]

These components had had an important bearing on the development of Fuller's thought since the First World War. Both *Tanks in the Great War* and *The Reformation of War* show the influence of Darwinism and reflect the same kind of thinking. *The Dragon's Teeth* revealed a more precise formulation stated against the background of a philosophy of history and with the full panoply of Spencer's terminology. Fuller had also drawn heavily upon Pearson and Gore in working out the supporting evidence for the interaction of mobility and stability. It is upon this pivot that the pendulum swings back and forth. Fuller filled out the psychological basis of the theory by relying on the work of William James, whom he had also read in his youth. Fuller argued that it was the tension between the will and instinct that formed

the mainspring of the constant tactical factor: 'the one urges man
to close with his enemy and destroy him, the other urges man to
keep away so that he himself may not be destroyed'. He had
adapted this contention from James's thesis that all human actions
were the result of a tension between our impulses and our
inhibitions, and James refers to the soldiers' 'dread of cowardice
impelling him to advance, his fears impelling him to run'; this is
evidently the origin of Fuller's idea.[20]

The other dimension of his methodology was the cyclical device.
In *The Dragon's Teeth* Fuller held that the civilized world had
experienced two great military cycles which had corresponded
with the Classical and Christian epochs. Each of these had
witnessed three tactical cycles; likened to organisms, each
tactical cycle germinated into youth, sprung into maturity and
degenerated into old age. In primitive – that is, rural – societies,
weapons were made for hand-to-hand fighting (or shock). As
civilization advanced, and became increasingly urbanized, so did
the numbers of projectiles increase. Fuller arbitrarily began with
the Classical projectile cycle which he dated from c.332 BC. Of the
Christian cycle, he dated the shock cycle c.650–1450; the shock
and projectile cycle c.1450–1850; and the projectile cycle from
c.1850 onwards. His main aim was to draw Spenglerian parallels
between the Classical and Christian projectile cycles, and show
how industrialization, in different but comparable degrees, would
influence the conduct of war.[21]

This cyclical idea had been developed throughout the 1920s.
After its initial appearance in the *Cavalry Journal*, Fuller concluded
that the end result would be a dawning of a new cavalry cycle,
with mechanically propelled weapons reinstating cavalry action.
Critics were sceptical; some were hysterical. One of the more
measured, Lieutenant Colonel Howard-Vyse observed that it was
possible to vitiate Fuller's argument by pointing to intermediate
periods which 'would lead to the opposite conclusions'. Howard-
Vyse's understanding of Fuller's argument was less than sure, as
he went on to claim that on Fuller's reasoning 'we must now be
moving for the third time towards an era of cavalry supremacy' –
which was Fuller's point, though in mechanized form in
accordance with industrial change. Fuller's critics usually failed to
grasp the significance of the social and technological dimension of
the argument, though on occasion they did score debating
points.[22]

When Fuller adapted this essay for a contribution to the journal, *The Nineteenth Century and After*, Lieutenant Colonel A. G. Baird Smith, a knowledgeable conservative, wrote a rejoinder which possibly influenced Fuller to discard the practice he had hitherto followed, of naming the cycles after the dominant arms in each, namely, cavalry, infantry and artillery, to those adopted in *The Dragon's Teeth*. Yet Baird Smith missed the point about the interaction of war, society and the technological factors that was at the bottom of Fuller's imperfect formulation. Instead he concentrated on refuting the idea that fear was the basis of any constant tactical factor. Courage, he argued, was just as much a constant in battle as fear, and men 'stood or marched forward . . . with no better protection than trust in their luck' – hardly a sophisticated argument, if not a red herring, as fear and courage were closely interlocked in the chain of Fuller's reasoning. The broader implications of the argument passed Baird Smith by.[23]

Both Howard-Vyse and Baird Smith were right to point out, however, that Fuller's conception was incorrigibly didactic. Historians are now rightly suspicious of the kind of historicism so readily indulged in by theorists like Fuller. Its real value lay not in the sphere of historical scholarship but as a justification for mechanization. Hence the close parallel that Fuller drew with the Classical projectile cycle, which saw important developments in artillery, so that 'we see a steady increase in the use of projectiles until battles became markedly modern in nature'. There were two features of warfare in this period that he underlined. The first was the possibility that generalship might fall behind inventiveness. The second was the likelihood that sources of economic and technological strength which sustained armies might become equally important targets for attack as the armies in the field. Weapon improvements, he contended, shifted the aim of war away from killing soldiers 'to killing, or terrorizing, civilians and so depriving an army of its economic as well as its moral foundations. It is a curious and unexpected development, and yet not only logical but inevitable.'[24]

The other important 'lessons' that Fuller emphasized in his treatment of the shock and shock and projectile cycles was the importance of armour when encountering unarmoured troops. Fuller took examples from the battles of the Crusaders at Hazarth (1125), where they lost 25 men but the Saracens lost more than 2000; Arsouf (1191) when their losses numbered 700 to the Saracen

7000; and Jaffa (1191) when only two knights were killed against the Saracen 700. The shock and projectile cycle that grew out of the social and technological changes of the fourteenth century saw an increase in the numbers of infantry and the increased deployment of projectiles which broke the dominance of the mounted arm. Its importance returned in the seventeenth century when it was supported by artillery. Lines of infantry held one another while the cavalry manoeuvred to launch the decisive blow. This system, Fuller wrote in a rather breathless survey, reached its zenith under Frederick the Great of Prussia; the use of artillery was increased and, as the infantry advanced, the cavalry broke into the enemy's rear areas and routed him. This system took Napoleon to the apogee of his power.[25]

The Industrial Revolution, which was already under way by the end of the eighteenth century, broke down the components of the Napoleonic tactical system. This depended upon shock weapons, supported by projectiles, striking the decisive blow and driving the enemy from the battlefield. The projectile cycle rendered this a near impossibility by introducing technological changes which made hand-to-hand fighting difficult. As Fuller observed, 'The percussion cap signed the death warrant of the cavalry charge, and the conoidal bullet revolutionized tactics' – it forced the gun back, increasing the size of battlefields, and because of the range of the rifle, cavalry could no longer charge home. The impact of industrialization, the growth of the power and resources of the nation state and the strategic flexibility conferred by railways all contributed to a great increase in the size of armies. 'As democracy, in the form of one man one vote, was the final expression of the French Revolution, so was that of the nation in arms, one man one musket, the military expression of this same upheaval.' The result, more men firing more projectiles, more efficiently, virtually dislocated the decisive battle and led to a complete tactical stalemate.[26]

It would be surely fair to say that Fuller had introduced some brilliant insights into the study of warfare, but they are only insights, and his all-embracing Darwinist terminology raises some problems of evaluation. It has been rightly observed that a peculiarity of Darwinism is that it explains *too* much. It can be employed retrospectively to explain virtually every range of phenomena or human condition. 'Natural selection explains why things are as they are: it does not enable us, in general, to say how they will change or vary.' Thus it is important to note that weapons did not, and do not, develop as sequentially as Fuller suggested in his law of military development. In medieval England, for instance, the battleaxe was used long after it had been rendered obsolete by archers and armoured knights. In the twentieth century when developments have become far more rapid, mechanization has gone hand in hand with a widespread dependence on horsed transport. Antiquated methods of transport usually survive long after they have been superseded by more advanced forms. In September 1939 Germany attacked Poland with tanks and aircraft. Yet 37 German infantry divisions were equipped for this campaign with a total of 198 875 horses requiring 4 375 250 tons of fodder, transported by 135 railroad cars per day. One of the most perplexing problems facing planners in May 1940 during the attack on France was finding enough harnesses to equip this host.[27]

Though it might be difficult to establish cast-iron laws of military development, such a formulation is a step in the right direction; it attempts to lay down the pattern of vague trends – but no more than that – trends 'which show progress along certain lines and establish a possibility of further progress'. This is valuable even if the overlying paradigm can be rejected. As J. D. Bernal sums up, the weapons of 1939–45, 'the walkie-talkie, the DUKW [a landing craft fitted with wheels which, like a duck, could move out of water], and the jeep are just as characteristic of the Second World War as the self-propelled gun, the super-fortress and the atom bomb itself'. No organic link exists though between civil and military progress, the one following automatically from the other. Sir William Tarn clarified this with regard to the Ancient Greeks who, 'apart from military needs, . . . invented next to nothing in the way of machinery'. Modern man has harnessed atomic energy because of its military potential; this was not recognized after it had been utilized by civil industry but before.[28]

The comparison with the Ancient World is an apt one because Fuller's cyclical theory drew the closest possible parallels between these phases of Western Civilization, especially with the need for a new 'model' army akin to the Macedonian Army of Alexander the Great. Mobility was the key to this comparison, despite vast changes in the conditions of war. Fuller's diagnosis of the stalemate on the Western Front showed once again that what had been required was a revival of movement. Thus, 'As long as wars continue, and they must continue until their causes are eliminated, the only military solution to this problem is to shorten their length.' Fuller's interest in Alexander's tactics reflected a much wider revival of interest in Alexander the Great during the inter-war years as a unifier of the world. In Fuller's opinion Alexander's army was 'probably the most wonderful ever devised by a single man, and more scientifically perfect than any existing today'. Alexander had understood the moral effect of a continuous advance combined with a mobile thrust into the enemy's rear. Fuller studied Alexander's victories closely and came to the conclusion that numbers could not stand before superior weapons. At Issus Alexander had overthrown King Darius III of Persia with 35 000 against 600 000; at Gaugamela he had defeated Darius's 1 000 000 with 47 000; and at the Hydaspes King Porus had been crushed by a mere 14 000 men. 'The scientifically organized, well armoured, superbly disciplined, highly offensive and wonderfully mobile *little army* invariably destroyed the *horde*.'[29]

Fuller's analysis provided the most sophisticated justification among the pioneers of mechanization for what Lindsay called 'the true implications of mechanization . . . [a] reduction of numbers', and Hobart felt the same. New technology would economize on the manpower required to field a certain degree of weapon-power. Guderian also looked for the emergence of a 'modern Alexander' who 'must bend modern technology to his will and instil it into his soldiers' – a widespread romantic reaction with deep roots in German thought. But was it true? Fuller was not scrupulous in his use of classical sources, though he had read widely. There is good reason to doubt some of his claims. At the Battle of the Granicus, Alexander's first victory over the Persians, he had outnumbered them. One eminent authority asserts that it was possible that Darius III's army was outnumbered by Alexander at Issus also. Indeed the only battle in which Fuller's generalization has any degree of validity is Gaugamela, and it is most unlikely that the disparity in numbers was anywhere as great as Alexander's apologists among the classical writers claim.[30]

Though on the whole Fuller's wide ranging analysis shows that perhaps Clausewitz was rash in claiming that 'The further back one goes, the less useful military history becomes', generally speaking he was right and Fuller wrong on a number of detailed points. Recent history has not seen another Marathon. There was *some* truth in Fuller's claims, but the overall validity of his discussion is more suspect. He was wise in underlining the primacy of weapon-power. Clausewitz had agreed that tactics were based on weapon-power and that when one side deploys a new weapon the 'other side promptly copies them'. An imbalance was however unlikely because 'European armies are comparable in equipment, organization and training'. Thus replacing 'articles of arms and equipment . . . takes place only periodically, and therefore seldom affects strategic factors'. Fuller had convincingly shown that this line of argument was now redundant, that changes in weapons since Clausewitz's day had been 'bewildering' and were likely to get more so. One country could achieve a significant qualitative advantage over another, even with a short lead in the arms race; but this line of reasoning did not justify two of his leading assertions: that weapon-power was an adequate substitute for manpower and would thus reduce the size of armies; and that mobility could outweigh the firepower of the infantry mass.[31]

Technology actually favours numbers. The Second World War revealed that the Soviet Union could survive colossal losses in the opening phase of Operation 'Barbarossa' in June–July 1941 and still equip vast armoured forces. The United States was able to fight two wars in different parts of the globe, and provide massive quantities of equipment not only for the Soviet and British Armies but for the Free French as well. As Professor Braudel so wisely sums up, 'Technology weighs heavily in war as in peace. But even if technology does not favour *all* dense populations equally, it is more or less always a product of numbers.'[32]

If this is accepted, then Fuller's claim that mobility could destroy larger immobile forces looks suspect as an all-embracing generalization. He was perceptive in 1932 when claiming that the French Army was 'no better than the hordes of Darius dressed up in twentieth-century uniforms'. It should nevertheless be recalled that the German Army that defeated it so decisively in 1940 was supported by a large infantry mass. The appearance of the tank did, to some extent, revive the technique of the armoured knight. Fuller was also right to show how a combination of movement and protection could allow armoured forces to penetrate and outflank on a scale unattainable in 1914–18. Thus infantry would evolve into motorized troopers. 'We shall then have two types of petrol-driven cavalry . . . armoured cavalry and mounted infantry'; and as in the sixth century mobile soldiers would be both armoured and unarmoured. 'Casualties amongst the armoured troops will become ridiculously small when compared to the casualties of unarmoured troops during the World War.' Again, there is *some* truth in this also, but it is not the whole truth. Fuller's stress on mobility and mechanized forces as the dominant arm too narrowly restricted his perception. Consequently, any return to the defensive was viewed purely in terms of the mechanized arms, as 'anti-tank defences will strive to destroy the protection armour affords by gun fire'. Infantry did evolve in the manner described by Fuller but they have not become a subordinate arm. No attention is given in these historical works to the impact of infantry fighting on armoured warfare, though Fuller's predictions are correct as far as they go. 'Thus the pendulum of war swings back, and we return to the footsoldier, not infantry trained to attack, but trained to defend. Not infantry armed with rifles and bayonets, but engineers equipped with anti-tank weapons.' A return to mass – and infantry fighting – was implicit in this statement, but Fuller did not acknowledge that mobility was only profitable in modern warfare when generals could muster sufficient resources to *move a mass army*. Mobility and mass armies were complementary rather than contradictory instruments of war and so they still remain.[33]

This flaw undoubtedly reduced the value of Fuller's analysis of future prospects for disarmament – a major preoccupation of the inter-war years. In *War and Western Civilization* he developed two subsidiary themes. The first was the existence of a constant tension between social mores and the adoption of new inventions, which were usually taken up most reluctantly. Hence 'excessive bloodshed was caused not because the new weapons were more barbarous than the old, but because generals persisted in using them as they used the old'. Soldiers were usually one or even two generations behind the pace of civil change in their technical understanding. The second was that the expanding destructive scope of war could largely be put down to the democratization of war and the influence of public opinion. Fuller, like Clausewitz before him, pointed to the importance of the French Revolution as a milestone on the road to 'total' war; '*sans culottism* replaced courtiership, and as the armies grew more and more the instruments of the people, not only did they grow in size but in ferocity'. As the influence of the electorate over the actions of its government increased so did its policy become more bellicose. There had been 13 wars in the first 40 years of the period 1814–1914; there had been 33 in the last 60 years of that period. 'During the Napoleonic Wars, science, literature and art still maintained their international spirit. In this war [1914–18], so potent was popular opinion that they were degraded into instruments of international strife.' Thus the ethical spirit of the First World War 'was but the unleashed spirit of the peace which had preceded the war, social sadism released from its conventional bounds'. These two factors thus contributed to the indecisiveness of modern war and the dominance of attrition. It would be idle to deny that popular passions have played an unfortunate part in the history of the past century and a half, but Fuller surely exaggerated their influence, and certainly strained his evidence to show that the power of the press had been decisive and had driven the great powers to war in 1914. As Paul Kennedy observes, 'Perhaps the real significance of the press lay not so much in its official policy but in its ability to worsen the political atmosphere.'[34]

More convincing was his criticism of qualitative disarmament, disarming by negotiating the 'abolition' of certain categories of weapons judged 'offensive', like tanks, aircraft and submarines. The war potential of any country, Fuller claimed, was the equivalent of its peace potential: 'war being a continuation of peace policy in another form . . . draws its strength from peace industry'. Given that nations steadfastly pursued their own interests to the detriment of others, and that qualitative disarmament assumed a contentment with things as they were, no concrete basis for any such agreement could be achieved so long as nations dissatisfied with the *status quo* were determined to circumvent disarmament agreements. Fuller pointed out that not all nations were satisfied with the *status quo*: 'Fear remains as deep-rooted as ever, and it is the elimination of the causes of fear and not the search after the definition of aggression which is the true problem of disarmament.' Furthermore, if war was inevitable, and nations went some way to deprive themselves of those weapons which made wars shorter, then they would be forced to rely on attrition – the economic attack – 'the most brutal of all forms . . . because it does not only kill but cripple'; and the next war, if allowed to become a repeat performance of the Great War, was likely to cripple the economic prosperity of the world.[35]

Also perceptive was Fuller's warning that disarmament negotiations usually have an unexpected consequence: increased rearmament, because 'when nations talk of peace they think in terms of war'. Liddell Hart, who favoured qualitative disarmament, shrewdly pointed out that if certain categories of arms were restricted, 'this may hinder an aggressor getting his way' and reduce the initial advantages of the attack. Fuller replied with a simple question: how could such agreements be enforced? Industrial development required that factories which produced goods in peacetime would produce the sinews of war.

Bombing aeroplanes are built in the same workshops as commercial aeroplanes; machinery which turns out typewriters and calculating machines can be adapted to turn out rifles and machine-guns; railway and tractor works can build tanks and lorry works armoured cars; . . . cellulose is used for artificial silk and smokeless powders; glycerine for soap or dynamite, etc., etc.

Fuller overestimated the ease with which this transformation could be made but his general point is sound: nations that had the capacity to manufacture the weapons they required would do so irrespective of treaties; indeed they would gain an advantage over those who adhered to agreements limiting offensive weapons. Qualitative disarmament might then have another wholly unexpected consequence: it might actually promote war. The only real concrete arms limitation agreement of this period, the treaties signed after the Washington Conference (1922), supported Fuller's sceptical view. It was agreed that cruisers should not exceed 10 000 tons in size or armament of eight inch calibre guns, stipulations which encouraged naval powers actually to build up to this size, and new vessels were more powerful than those they replaced. As Captain Roskill observes, 'a conference on naval *limitation* can reasonably be said to have ensured a substantial increase in the size and armament of one important class of ship'.[36]

An untrammelled arms race or a repeat of the First World War might be avoided by *use* of the new weapons like tanks and aircraft, and a swing of the constant tactical factor which might 'humanize' war. If not, then 'the next great war will be no less brutal than the last'. It therefore followed that if the military instrument changed, so would the military craftsman. Warfare might become more sophisticated, more refined, as scientific improvements caught up with generalship, or, as Fuller observed sarcastically, *vice versa*. 'If surgery and medicine were still treated as war is now treated, we should today be using grated unicorn's horn and butcher's knives in our hospitals.' Mechanized operations did not effect such a transformation; but even if war could be 'humanized' in the short term, Fuller still expected a reaction to follow, and that the accentuation of danger would once more become the aim of weapon development. The offensive might become so powerful that statesmen might acknowledge that 'the game of war was not worth the candle'. Weapon improvement would eliminate the human element in war. 'The method of fighting would become perfect, and absolutely diabolical.' The elimination of danger was inherent in the elimination of war, as war without danger was absurd.

> Conversely, the accentuation of danger, until it embraces civilian and soldier alike carries with it a similar conclusion . . . for universal danger becomes as absurd a means of lethal argument as no danger at all.

Technological improvement in weaponry has as its logical conclusion the linking of one weapons system to one brain, rather than many individual weapons to many brains. Warfare would become a ridiculous solution to human quarrels and lose all utility. Thus, 'wars will at some time in the future be relegated to the dustheap of things which have failed', though Fuller thought this change was unlikely until man evolved a social order in which resort to war held no promise of gain.[37]

Fuller's three books on the 'Natural History of War' were all well received, and civilian reviewers compared him with Spengler in range of knowledge, penetration and the stimulating nature of his conclusions. He was certainly far in advance of his time in believing that 'Strategy [is] not only concerned with mobility on the battlefield but with all the sources of mobility in civil life.' Likewise, tactics is not only concerned with protected weapon-power, 'but with many other powers besides, such as finance, ethics, economics etc'. It must nonetheless be emphasized that Fuller's treatment of the 'Natural History of War' exposed most sharply the contradiction between his stress on the importance of material factors and the significance of the great man. Fuller's emotional commitment to the great man blinded him to the logical deduction from his own reasoning: that the next war, like the last, would be a mass conflict in which the winning side would command the greatest resources. Quality *and* quantity marched behind the victor's train. His writing was however an honest attempt to treat war rationally during a period when such study was conspicuous by its absence. 'The truth would appear to be', Fuller wrote in 1932, 'that we are living in one of the most warlike periods the world has ever seen because our interest in war has fallen to zero. When no interest is taken in cleanliness vermin will abound.' He was not mistaken.[38]

7

The Mechanization of War, 1928–32

> Of course you must on no account even think of leaving the Army. After all, the real workers in this business, ie those who have really thought deeply on the subject and really understand what we call the IDEA, are very few, and in spite of every disappointment and set back we must stick to the work – and try and see it though.
>
> Lindsay to Fuller, 11 September 1930, Lindsay Papers.

Fuller's fame as a military thinker arose principally from his tireless advocacy of mechanization. It was the lynchpin of his military thought, and in a stream of articles and lectures he had propagated his ideas throughout the 1920s, but it was not until five years after the publication of *The Reformation of War* that he began to organize them in more precise and satisfying terms. This chapter will attempt to discuss three themes. The first is Fuller's development in both strategical and tactical terms of the idea of strategic paralysis. This was made possible by the mobility of the tank: 'for the more mobile is its [war's] form and the quicker a decision is arrived at, the less time will there be to methodize destruction'. Secondly, it will focus on the way in which Fuller's thinking on mechanization differed from that of Liddell Hart. This question has been clouded by Liddell Hart's own contribution to the history of mechanization which has done so much to influence the judgement of other writers, usually to Fuller's detriment. And finally, how do Fuller's predictions withstand evaluation when compared with the practice of war – and especially the campaigns of the Second World War?[1]

It hardly needs pointing out at this stage that Fuller's position in the Army was becoming difficult. Neither were his relations with the other pioneers of mechanization intimate. He had sacrificed the priceless opportunity of putting his ideas into practice by his high-handed resignation from command of the Experimental Brigade in 1927. This isolation is reflected in the kind of appointments Fuller held thereafter. There is an overwhelming sense of anti-climax. He was posted as GSO 1 to the 2nd Division at Aldershot commanded by Ironside (a true foul-weather friend at this juncture) in 1927. In 1929 he took command of an infantry brigade in the Allied Army of Occupation on the Rhine and was promoted to Major General in 1930. None of these appointments were beneath his rank or experience but they are not on the fast track to the highest positions in the Army. Unlike Hobart and Lindsay he had little contact with armoured vehicles and did not grapple daily with the problems of maintaining or supplying them. Hence his growing isolation, which had first become noticeable as early as 1925. 'I had a talk with Fuller', Hobart reported.

> Rather disappointed. He is inclined to 'lecture' – or rather one gets the feeling that he is under the impression that no one else has thought about tank tactics at all, so he continues to communicate his views in general rather than to attempt to meet any considerations one may put forward oneself.

Fuller had by now completely alienated Swinton, an early ally, who thought him 'damned silly' with a 'sort of buffoon reputation'. Hotblack informed Lindsay of an example of this silliness at the Tank Corps Christmas dinner in 1929.

> Boney was needlessly offensive in his speech . . . and spoke in a tone that was out of date. . . . It is a pity, for having done so much to get the Idea going, he has dropped completely out of the work of turning that Idea into reality.

His isolation was the product of an increasing disenchantment with the Army. 'I am now, I feel, the complete soldier', he mused to Lindsay in July 1930.

> I have been a Brigadier a year, and have done absolutely nothing during 342 days out of 365, on the other 23 days . . . I was on leave. Command in this country is the nearest approach to zero that any scientist has ever got down to.

His irritation and boredom – he claimed that his most taxing task
in 1929 had been the supervision of the polishing of taps in the
men's lavatories at Aldershot – is even more marked in his letters
to Liddell Hart, in which he admitted frankly that he was 'very
tired of soldiering' and compared himself to Ovid singing his
songs in Colchis. 'I know what should be done with the Army
and [know] what will be done with it, but I am not destined to
live a 1000 years, and consequently am looking forward to
freedom and usefulness in life.' He was now of the opinion that
'Ridicule is . . . the only weapon, for reason is impotent
against the bastioned ignorance and stupidity of our army –
"muddleization" in place of "modernization" is the order of the
day.'

Fuller looked for support among the junior officers with a
confidence that was largely justified.

> As regards my *senior* critics and traducers I care nothing, for
> none of my books are for them – they are past praying for; but I
> should like to hear what the junior people think, though it will
> take 30 years before we get a *true* junior outlook, at present it is
> so contaminated with spittle-licking.

His books on tactical matters were largely written with this
audience in mind. In 1928 he collected a series of essays and
published them as *On Future Warfare*. Two years later he gave his
officers at Catterick a series of lectures on the *Field Service
Regulations* explaining how changes in weapon technology would
influence tactics. These were written in fourteen days and
published in 1931 as *Lectures on FSR II*. Fuller also started work on
a new study 'deal[ing] with the speculative tactics of all new arms
in all the circumstances in which we are likely to use them. . . .
Hitherto, weapons have always been ahead of tactics, and the
result has been a gross lack of economy of force.' This study
developed into Fuller's most important book on mechanization,
Lectures on FSR III. Like the earlier volume it began life as a series
of lectures; undelivered, they were published in 1932.[2]

The underlying themes of these books reflected the arguments
of *The Dragon's Teeth* and were based on the simple proposition
that weapons change because the character of civilization changes.
'As the present age is largely a mechanical one, so will the wars of
this age take on a similar complexion, because military organization

follows civil organization.' Then following the constant tactical factor through to its logical conclusion, if the basis of all weapon development was the sword (offensive) and the shield (protective), then the basis of all generalship was audacity tempered by caution. Defence was as 'closely related to the offence as is the left arm to the right arm of the boxer'. Fuller expected that the defensive-offensive would play an important part in future warfare, 'the enemy being first misled and persuaded to commit himself, and then strongly attacked when in a false position'.[3]

It is also important to define closely Fuller's approach to war. Here his position has been distorted by the tendency of writers to link him closely with Liddell Hart – often rightly. However, because of the greater familiarity of most historians with Liddell Hart's work, it is believed – often wrongly – that they shared the same interests and assumptions. Fuller rightly judged their efforts to be those of 'Partners, not actually working in collaboration, but towards the same goals by road which suit our fancies best . . . in detail there is very little in common in our respective work.' What is so little appreciated, and the chapter on Fuller's writing on generalship should have clarified this difference, was that it was the fighting and winning of battles and the means of securing decisive victory economically that dominated Fuller's approach to war. Liddell Hart sought in his writings to find all possible means of avoiding battles. Hence it was grand tactics, battlefield planning, and not field strategy, the manoeuvres that preface battle, that formed, in Fuller's opinion, the truly vital sector of military activity, and that which most tightly linked military organization with civil developments. The return of decisive battles was 'the surest protection of the civil population' because 'as this object grows in importance, so will it become important to concentrate every available weapon in the battle area'.[4]

Reinstating *quality* and not quantity as the norm in future warfare, technological improvement would banish the mass armies of the First World War from the battlefield, and 'cavalry, infantry and artillery, as we know them today, have entered the stage of obsolescence'. The velocity of war was increased by the speed and power of the tank and aircraft to strike at the military and civil will, so that Fuller predicted that 'physical destruction . . . will gradually and increasingly be replaced by attempts to demoralize the will of the enemy in its several forms, and so not only disorganize his armies but unnerve his people'.[5]

A review of these arguments reveals, with some reservations, that Fuller drew a remarkably clear picture of the nature of future warfare as it developed until about 1941. The trenchancy of his analysis remains 'relevant'; that is to say, he confronted the major problems of 'conventional' strategy so directly and provocatively that his fundamental approach can be used to dissect warfare beyond 1945 – for as Fuller himself would have claimed, no matter how much weapons change, the principles of war remain constant. Nevertheless, the direct comparison with the actual operations of the Second World War would have pleased Fuller most, as he wrote with the practical problems of the next war very much in mind. Several qualifications have to be made to this favourable assessment. Firstly, Fuller believed that mechanized operations would occur 'in highly populated and developed areas'. Yet it was in regions that were not industrialized – the Western Desert and the rolling steppes of Soviet Russia – that the naval analogy developed in 'Plan 1919' and adumbrated in *The Reformation of War* found some expression. Secondly, in the campaigns in Western Europe where armoured forces achieved spectacular successes, these were gained by armies that were indifferently mechanized. As Liddell Hart put it, the Wehrmacht in May 1940 was only 'a few vital degrees more advanced than its opponents'. Fuller assumed in *Lectures on FSR III* that decisive success could be attained over opponents matched equally in mechanized sophistication. This question, thirdly, raises the problem of scale. Fuller persisted in arguing that the great cost of mechanized forces would reduce the size of armies. This was a mistake, and there can be little doubt that on this score the conservative sceptics were a much surer guide.[6]

The thinking behind *Lectures on FSR III* was almost entirely Fuller's own. There are no major important influences on his thinking – apart from the fruit of his own consideration of this problem for almost fifteen years. One document that he did read by another soldier was Lindsay's 'Suggestions Regarding the Best Means of Rendering the Royal Tank Corps in Particular and the Army in General More Suited to the Probable Requirements of Future Warfare' (1926), but there was little new in this. 'The real change in my outlook', Fuller recalled in 1948, 'of the early 20s and in the early 30s came with the advent of an effective A[nti]-T[ank] weapon, and in my *Lectures on FSR III*, I built my idea around tank and anti-tank'. In *The Reformation of War* Fuller visualized tanks as mechanized cavalry acting against a non-mechanized foe. In *Lectures on FSR III* future operations were seen as completely mechanized. Men fighting on their feet played little part in the battle. Tanks combined, Fuller averred, the most important tactical elements, offensive power, defensive power and mobility 'in a higher degree than any other arm'. Given this assumption, a certain number of conditions and the probable characteristics of the supporting weapons, Fuller held that 'it is possible to develop a sound tactics from all but theoretical data', and the book is Fuller's best effort at sustained prediction.[7]

The next war would thus be one in which, during the opening phase at least, speed and demoralization would be the key to victory. The rear attack would become a common method of overthrowing the enemy. Fuller correctly suggested that armoured formations would advance 'immediately before the declaration of war, or simultaneously with it'. Rushing forward to seize the most favourable ground, they would then establish 'a protective fulcrum upon which to move an offensive level'; this lever would strike a paralyzing blow deep into the rear of the enemy's army so that he would be boxed up and forced to surrender. In order to strike at the enemy's rear, Fuller held that it was vital to fix the enemy's front and pin him to his position; in the opening advance this was *the* paramount objective; 'the next step is to circumvent this fixed point and by a rapid movement strike at the enemy's vitals in rear of it. Should this be accomplished, then this front itself will crumble to pieces'. This is a prescient sketch of the manner in which the Germans won their initial victories in the period 1939–41. 'Only when an enemy is held is liberty of movement gained, and liberty of manoeuvre carries with it freedom of action which is the aim of all generalship', Fuller stressed.[8]

Thus it was clear that mechanized operations would make arduous demands on commanders. He had pointed out in *Lectures on FSR III* that plans must be flexible, including alternative objects, as 'to economize time in action will become the soul of every plan'. Hence the need for a commander who would 'be with his fighting troops, he will be *in* the battle and not outside of it'. This portends the day of what might be termed 'tank buccaneers' like Guderian and Rommel. 'I work out my plans early each morning', wrote the latter, 'and how often, during the past year and in France, have they been put into effect within a matter of hours?'

The qualities that would be most needed by a commander, Fuller predicted, would be balance, quick intelligence and decisiveness. The last was particularly valuable because the 'bulk of the fog [of war] will remain just as dense, for increased mobility will cause situations to change rapidly, and constant and often conflicting information from air and ground will bewilder [the commander] as much as complete ignorance will render him cautious'. This would also lead to a prevalence of oral rather than written orders. Such is the accuracy of Fuller's predictions that they could be taken as a description of the conditions characterizing Operation 'Crusader' in Cyrenaica, in November 1941.[9]

It was implicit in Fuller's thinking that strategic paralysis operated at both grand strategic and grand tactical levels. He therefore extended the speed and dynamism of conflict between armies into struggle between states. 'War in its philosophical form', he wrote in *On Future Warfare*, is a struggle of two wills in opposition. Each of these wills is protected by economic resources, ethical codes, social rights and military forces.' Industrial nations had become so sophisticated, 'so sensitive and centralized that an extensive and vulnerable moral target was offered – the paralyzation of the national will'. The Second World War did reveal that the complete paralyzation of a nation state was possible. As General Spears observed of the French leaders in 1940, 'That they should have been surprised was understandable, that they should have failed to react with clarity and courage was not. There seemed to be no plans.' France literally collapsed like a house of cards; the confusion following the breakthrough at Sedan 'led to stupefied bewilderment over wide areas. From prefects to village mayors no one knew whether to believe or disbelieve, obey or disregard an order.' Yet the continuing resistance of Britain in 1940 against the German onslaught must call into question the validity of strategic paralysis when employed against a steadfast opponent. 'As I hurried into my clothes', recalled Lord Ismay after the invasion of Norway in April 1940, 'I realized for the first time in my life, the devastating and demoralizing effect of surprise.' Britain nevertheless fought on. The Germans did wage a successful 'war of nerves' in the period 1939–41, but this proved decisively successful only against ill-organized countries whose morale was vulnerable before the crushing *coup de grâce* was delivered; and Fuller was to realize this in 1943 when he admitted that his belief that demoralization rather than destruction would become the aim of future warfare was an 'overstatement'.[10]

Fuller's views on the importance of strategic bombing had undergone a revision since 1923; they were to be modified again; but at this stage they were correct. He cautioned his readers not to expect decisive operations at the beginning of the next war, at least between the great powers, because of the importance they would attach in any 'war of nerves' to gaining the support of neutral opinion. He doubted whether any belligerent 'will risk bombing its enemy's industrial centres and cities for fear of being branded an international criminal'. Strategic bombing attacks would not begin 'until excuses can be found to justify them'. This was indeed the case in 1940 with both the British and the Germans claimed that the other had started the bombing. Fuller concluded that the civil will was intimately linked with the progress of the armies in the field; thus it could be more effectively attacked by defeating them decisively than by the more indirect methods of aerial attack; such action would also restrict the quantity of destructive power inflicted upon a belligerent.[11]

On the battlefield Fuller had an acute grasp of the potential of strategic paralysis, but he exaggerated the moral effect an attack on the opposing commander's mind would have on the outcome of an engagement. General Sir Alan Brooke commented in June 1940 on

the lack of sleep, irregular meals, great physical exertions of continuous travelling in all directions, rumours, counter-rumours, doubts, ambiguous orders and messages, lack of information . . . and the thousand and one factors that are hammering away at one's powers of resistance.

As generals are appointed because of their resilience, it is not wise to depend on the dislocation of command. Brooke recalled of his own experience during the retreat to Dunkirk, 'I had reached a stage when the receptive capacity of my brain to register disaster and calamities had become numbed by successive blows.' Of course, not every general had Brooke's stamina but it was unwise of Fuller to project at every turn the cumulative effects of strategic paralysis. Some generals instantly gave way under psychological strain; but some did not, and their obstinacy often formed the dividing line between victory and defeat.[12]

A clear example is Auchinleck's conduct of the closing phase of Operation 'Crusader' in November 1941, a campaign which accords closely with the conditions laid down in *Lectures on FSR III*. It shows that even in battles between small armies, speed and dramatic strokes were not enough in themselves to dislocate an enemy's forces. Rommel's counter-attack during the Battle of Totensonntag (23 November 1941), was followed by the famous 'dash to the wire' deep into the rear of 8th Army. Rommel succeeded in creating chaos and General Cunningham, GOC 8th Army, was on the verge of losing his nerve but, after the initial shock had worn off, as General Jackson comments, 'it was found that remarkably little damage had been done. The fighting units had not panicked and were hanging on to the flanks of the Afrika Korps as it plunged eastwards.' While Rommel's thrust degenerated into a series of unco-ordinated actions, the British took the opportunity to restore morale and recover at the very point that Fuller had predicted maximum panic. Auchinleck remained unflinching in his resolve to defeat Rommel and it was the Afrika Korps that was forced to retreat. Methods that the British themselves had used against the Italians the year before were of no avail against courageous soldiers led by a resolute commander.[13]

The least realistic part of Fuller's ideas about strategic paralysis was that dealing with motorized guerrillas. These had not featured in his earlier thinking, and were an attempt to find a mechanized equivalent of Alexander's slingers or Napoleon's *tirailleurs* – light troops who would harry the enemy before the heavy troops came into action. During the First World War Fuller had shown a marked interest in the activities of German guerrilla machine gunners. About 1925 he took note of General von Seekt's attempts 'to reinforce the small, long service and highly trained German Reichswehr by a militia', one which was motorized and trained on guerrilla lines. His idea of motorized guerrillas was not conceived as partisans, 'but as uniformed soldiers who could search the area of advance etc', and thereby clear the avenue of advance.[14]

There was nothing wrong with the tactical function that Fuller sought to express, it was the means that was impractical, and no force resembling these motorized guerrillas appeared during the Second World War – though guerrilla forces were occasionally motorized. It is true, as Fuller was quick to point out, that the German advance through France and the Low Countries had been preceded by swarms of motor cyclists. This is straining the analogy. These troops certainly spread panic and uncertainty. As Spears wrote, 'The general sense of insecurity and nervousness that these methods added to the moral blow of a terrible defeat need not be stressed.' Yet Fuller was inconsistent in his view of these guerrillas. He thought of them as 'irregular pure and simple', and also claimed that there was a possibility of 'pillaging and other irregularities' occurring. Though he was quite justified in predicting a general increase in guerrilla warfare, and on the Eastern Front this kind of harrying did take place, there was no overall blending of the regular with the irregular. German troops, for instance, did not use civilian motor cars, nor were they employed in an irregular way – crucial differences that vitiate Fuller's claims. As he also admitted, motorized guerrillas were restricted to road movement, thus 'swarming' was impossible, and the guerrillas would be vulnerable not only to air attack but to small arms fire, as unarmoured vehicles are just as easily incapacitated by rifle fire as horses. There were motorized forces like the Long Range Desert Group and the 'Jock Columns' formed by the British Army, which undertook raiding and reconnaissance duties, but these always remained part of the regular military establishment.[15]

How does Fuller's doctrine of strategic paralysis compare with Liddell Hart's strategy of the indirect approach? On strategical matters the two thinkers are usually linked together. It is important to point out that Fuller was sceptical of the value of Liddell Hart's cherished theorem of the indirect approach. He warned Liddell Hart in 1929 that:

> It is wrong to look upon an indirect approach as a cure-all. The object is to defeat the enemy and if this can be done by direct approach so much the better. The indirect approach is usually a necessary evil. Which should be employed depends entirely on weapon power.

Liddell Hart judged this adherence to what he called 'conventional strategy' limiting. Fuller and Liddell Hart had disagreed over the relative merits of the indirect approach as exemplified in the campaigns of the American Civil War. In his *Memoirs* Liddell Hart later maintained that while Fuller expounded '*deep tactical penetration*, he did not advocate the *deep strategic penetration*, as I did'. That is, Fuller preferred mobile forces to be employed against 'the opposing army's immediate rear, rather than its communications far in the rear'. After reading *Lectures on FSR III* Liddell Hart felt that 'there is rather too much emphasis on the mechanism of tactics and not enough on the art, or on strategy'. Also he believed that Fuller 'concentrates too much on the old idea of "battle" and does not point out how the strategical use of armoured forces may produce the opponent's downfall without a serious battle'. Liddell Hart's assessment depends on the assumption that 'deep strategical penetration' could be effected without battle. Fuller thought that it could not. Hence the importance he attached to fixing the enemy. "Liddell Hart looks upon fixing', he once explained, 'as a purely tactical operation – it is really a strategical one.' Thus it is quite legitimate to evolve plans in strategical terms whose execution depends on tactical means – the direct approach. The variation in emphasis renders the approach no less strategical. Thus even though they shared broadly similar aspirations, not least the desire to reduce the destructive scope of war and substitute paralysis for destruction, Fuller and Liddell Hart differed fundamentally over the *means*: the former thought that armies should seek battle to achieve it, Liddell Hart that they should manoeuvre and avoid battle.[16]

Fuller's concept of the nature of the mechanized advance raises another comparison with Liddell Hart, namely, the place of the infantry in future battles. Liddell Hart is usually credited with calling for a 'balanced' force of all arms. There can be no doubt that in this regard Liddell Hart has been highly successful in persuading historians to accept his version of history. His viewpoint is summarized in his *Memoirs*:

> Fuller had come by now [c.1927] to think that the tank alone would dominate future battlefields, and that the infantry would not be needed except to garrison the country that the tanks had conquered . . . I argued that there was both need and scope for a more mobile kind of infantry to co-operate with the tanks . . . I visualized them as what I called 'tank marines'.

This interpretation has been accepted hitherto, and has become a commonplace of military criticism. In this period Liddell Hart was apparently fertile in suggestions for the efficient co-operation of tanks and infantry which made 'little impression in British quarters, but caught the attention of fresh-minded soldiers in the

German Army'. These were supposedly poured into a little book called *The Future of Infantry* (1933), which he claimed had been used in the training of the German Panzer Divisions. Liddell Hart's wisdom – and the folly of those who spurned his advice – was proved with deadly effect when the 'balanced' Panzer Divisions (combining both tanks and infantry) swept all before them in the years 1940–2. There is distortion in these comments, though they are not wholly wrong, but Liddell Hart did misrepresent Fuller's position and thus, by implication, his own, for, in this period, Liddell Hart's views were very similar to those of Fuller.[17]

All commentators agree that Fuller's general framework was grounded on an overstatement, namely, that in mechanized warfare mobile armour would replace static earth as the main determining tactical factor. This he termed the primary tactical function, which aimed at maximizing protected offensive power. The tank could thus replace the man, as his physical energy was replaced by the internal combustion engine, his 'legs and feet the tracks, his shield the armour, his sword the machine gun'. Thus the bullet would be eliminated as offensive power became increasingly based on shells and armour-piercing projectiles and protective power was based on bullet-proof armour. Fuller's view of mechanized battles was therefore to some degree a distorted one. He suggested wrongly that there was no room for the infantry assault. The decisive act of battle would be the tank versus tank encounter or, depending on conditions, the tank versus anti-tank gun. Tanks should be armed, then, with small calibre armour piercing guns which could destroy their own kind.[18]

These arguments suffer from one significant defect: if tanks are to move out and fight decisive battles, they must be supported by their own infantry. Fuller did allow for supporting anti-tank troops but not for conventional infantry which he regarded as 'useless'. Thus 'on all ground where tanks can move, infantry will disappear as the decisive arm and will be replaced by these machines'. In his estimate, and it is a wholly justified one, to link poorly equipped, marching infantry with mobile forces was 'tantamount to yoking a tractor to a carthorse'. As before, he recommended that infantry should be mounted in cross-country buses and move in support of the tanks. Nevertheless they should remain a subordinate arm in tank country, and 'must be organized

and trained for mountain, swamp and wood fighting, and not as
hitherto, mainly for warfare on the plains'. This statement only
has validity when the terrain favours armour; as Rommel said,
'Everything [then] turns on it [the tank], and other formations are
purely auxiliaries.' In the European theatre of war the tank was
not such an omnipotent weapon, and Fuller's view was
overstated.[19]

The conservative critic, Germains, was quite right to question
whether it was wise to assert dogmatically that infantry would
never stand against tanks whatever the circumstances. Indeed, in
On Future Warfare Fuller agreed that infantry would get used to
tanks, but despite his stubborn refusal to concede the case for
infantry in principle, when it came to specific points he was much
less dogmatic. He did acknowledge that the future role of infantry
was to hold the enemy's infantry. There would be no scope for
the assault, 'but, by threatening to assault, to fix the enemy's
infantry, and hold them so that the [armoured] cavalry may
manoeuvre, charge them in flank, or attack them in rear'. This
could be achieved by smothering the enemy position with gunfire,
so that the tanks could get round the flanks. 'Should no flanks
exist, then again the infantry should hold and bullet-proof heavy
cavalry, protected by artillery, should assault and penetrate.'
Machine gunners should move forward to occupy a position
'from which the enemy can be pinned down by fire'; the assault
would be made by the bullet and not by the bayonet. 'I do not say
that small parties of infantry cannot at times experience the
extreme satisfaction of prodding one another [with the bayonet]',
Fuller wrote sarcastically. 'But for large numbers to attempt to
wield any of these weapons is surely an unprofitable task.'[20]

These comments reveal a much greater flexibility than Liddell
Hart's 'all-tank' interpretation would suggest. Indeed such a view
would require Fuller to deny some of his best teaching – that
which advocated the use of light infantry. The contrary was
actually true. He did suggest to Liddell Hart that 'Mixing up steel
and muscle is no good and frontal attacks are genuinely absurd
unless purely fixing operations.' This standpoint was not mistaken.
The German advance through France in 1940 was hastened by the
ability of the armour to break away from the supporting infantry
mass. What Fuller was really getting at was that the old heavy
infantry of the First World War, the 'footsloggers', would be
replaced by a much lighter, more mobile kind of soldier as there

were 'marked resemblances between the tactics of light infantry and tank tactics'. Hence all infantry would have to be mechanized – a trend that reflected changes in civil life. 'Again we are ceasing to be a walking race – a Birmingham man doesn't walk more than he can help, therefore he does not join the TA.'[21]

Fuller was also prepared to admit that there was room for co-operation between tanks and infantry, as tanks could not move everywhere unaided. In wooded areas, for example, 'riflemen should precede the machines under cover of the wood on each flank of the track, ready to open fire on any anti-tank weapon which may block the way'. Three types of infantry were therefore needed: field pioneers with anti-tank guns; field police to hold and occupy; and light infantry to co-operate with the tanks. He even realized at one point that tanks would require infantry support in the tank battle:

Frequently the ground will be of half and half description in which close co-operation between tanks and infantry becomes necessary . . . the infantry line of advance [should be] sufficiently close to that of the tanks to enable the infantry to rush forward under cover of the confusion caused by these weapons.

Despite these occasional passages in his articles (usually found in professional journals), Fuller still showed himself incapable of realizing that infantry would have to be integrated within the structure of the armoured division, and he is still open to criticism on these grounds. This was the result of a tension between the practical need for infantry in the immediate future, which Fuller conceded (however reluctantly), and his desire to look ahead to an ideal future of completely mechanized operations. He was also stung by the lack of progress that mechanization had made by 1932. The conservatives seemed to carry the day. Montgomery-Massingberd held that tanks could never achieve any degree of surprise in battle because of the noise made by their engines. He passionately believed that calvary were 'more sensitive to ground', a point which could 'hardly be exaggerated'. The increasing prevalence of this view provoked Fuller to cut out all the qualifying statements that feature in his earlier essays and concentrate instead on perfecting the symmetry of his arguments in *Lectures on FSR III*.[22]

The important point to emerge from this discussion is that

during the same period Fuller's undeniably restricted view of the future of infantry differed little from Liddell Hart's. In *Great Captains Unveiled*, Liddell Hart analysed the military methods of the Mongols with an eye on future needs, pointing out that mobile troops need not necessarily 'rest on a stable infantry base'. Such a comment bodes ill coming from the self-appointed champion of the infantry. Turning to a later book, *The Remaking of Modern Armies*, his opinion of the 'effective role of infantry is now limited to "mopping up" the ground that the tanks have conquered and to holding it' before the enemy brings up machine guns. 'And with the development of the six-wheeled carrier even this transitory role disappears, for the machine gun can be rushed forward more quickly than the infantry.' Though indicating, as did Fuller, the need for infantry to hold the enemy's infantry, Liddell Hart judged, moreover, that 'the proper role of infantry is that of land marines', by which he meant troops to engage in hill and wood fighting. In other words, Liddell Hart's view of land marines was a good deal narrower than he later claimed; it made no mention of large-scale co-operation between tanks and infantry. A tank force sometimes required infantry to protect it from snipers: 'But to attach a whole embussed infantry brigade to it seems a mistake; it cramps its freedom of manoeuvre, and doubles the target.'[23]

In *The Future of Infantry* Liddell Hart followed Fuller's lead in stressing the need for light infantry, particularly in areas unsuited to tanks. Under other conditions 'Infantry . . . cannot replace the need for modernized cavalry because they cannot strike quick enough or follow through soon enough for decisiveness in battle.' He noted also that in the next war motorized guerrillas would make their appearance. To sum up, despite Liddell Hart's disclaimers to the contrary, his outlook was very similar to Fuller's over the composition of future armoured forces. Indeed it is possible to suggest that the usual comparison between these two military thinkers should be reversed: that their views on strategical questions were dissimilar while their writings do show a broad measure of agreement over the formation of future mechanized forces.[24]

Fuller's vision of completely mechanized operations in which hand-to-hand fighting was eliminated and thus 'humanized' was not fulfilled. This was due to the fact that the tank did not drive the foot soldier from the battlefield. The bullet was not eliminated from the tank battle. Neither did the tank have the moral effect claimed for it by Fuller – certainly not among armies enjoying a comparable degree of mechanization. During the Battle of France, French officers had panicked: they spoke of an *'attaque foudroyante* by legions of tanks' against which their men refused to stand. This was perhaps a special case. In Finland in 1940 panic was ignited by the appearance of the Finnish Army's only armoured car among their own troops. 'A cry of "tanks are coming" caused a retreating column to flee in panic abandoning all its equipment, until the men got behind the main position.' The Finns eventually got used to tanks; they not only imported 37mm anti-tank guns, but were confident enough to tackle them at close quarters with petrol bombs. By 1945 even armed civilians would tackle tanks, sometimes with great success. It was therefore unconvincing to claim that the tank would render hand-to-hand fighting obsolete. Even in the Western Desert scope was found to use the bayonet and in the jungles of East Asia it remained an important weapon. In general terms such evidence indicates the limitations of *Lectures on FSR III* with its implicit European bias. In retrospect General Auchinleck considered that British generals had been 'led astray by the idea that the tank was omnipotent on the battlefield, and that the others – the unarmoured horde – must perforce look on until the armoured battle was won, when it would be safe to move'. Auchinleck now realized that *'good* infantry with *good* artillery can look after themselves' and would not be demoralized by the unexpected appearance of tanks.[25]

The extent to which this misconception was due to a study of Fuller's writings is difficult to determine. It is accepted widely that *Lectures on FSR III* was not studied extensively in the British Army before 1939, so it does seem perverse to blame Fuller for all the things that went wrong with British armour in the Second World War, though this particular line of argument was mistaken. One theme that deserved the closest study and was wholly misunderstood was Fuller's exposition of the defensive–offensive The naval analogy which he employed in his writings on mechanized warfare was taken up rather glibly. It was visionary and involved practical problems of which Fuller was aware. 'I do not suggest that identical changes are going to take place', he explained,

because nations live on the land and not in the sea, but I do suggest that, as navies are the creations of industrialism, and that mechanized armies must also draw their strength from industrial power, there is a common link in the evolution of both.

Fuller never suggested at any time, when advocating the naval analogy, that armoured forces should move out from their bases without reference to anti-tank forces, as General Cunningham did at the beginning of Operation 'Crusader'. Fuller envisaged that the future mechanized battle would follow the pattern of the Battle of Hastings (1066): 'an advance to engage the enemy, a withdrawal to persuade him to advance against anti-tank defences, and then once more a forward movement to strike him before he can re-organize'.[26]

The four phases of the tank battle that were drawn up in *Lectures on FSR III*, the initial movement from the anti-tank laager (or base), manoeuvring and feinting, forcing the enemy to fight under a disadvantage (or blockade him), followed by the movement of the anti-tank base forward, were firmly stated within the context of the defensive–offensive. Fuller argued persuasively that anti-tank guns should

> take up a position which the enemy will have to attack in order to carry out his plan, then it will generally be to the advantage of his opponent to let him attack, and directly his attack begins to succeed, or fail, to launch a counter-offensive in full force against him.

Anti-tank forces facilitated mobile defence, a method used by Rommel with devastating success, and one which Cunningham had not contemplated. He pushed up anti-tank guns under cover around 8th Army's flanks – a deadly supplement to tank fire. 'Their fire', Fuller predicted, 'can drive tanks into areas where counter-attacks can defeat them.' In the attack, especially in desert warfare, Fuller recommended the use of what he called 'dustpan and broom' tactics, using tanks as bait to draw enemy tanks on to concealed anti-tank fire. Likewise in the defence or retreat he suggested the deployment of a 'funnel' formation, in which anti-tank guns were thrown out on the flanks of the tanks and they withdrew behind the screen – a technique effectively employed by Rommel to frustrate the British pursuit during the closing stages of Operation 'Crusader'.[27]

On one point Fuller can be criticized justly. In *Lectures on FSR III* he claimed that 'encounter engagements are likely to become more frequent, especially during the opening phases of a campaign'. This was only in part true. In France and the Low Countries in 1940, the Allies were determined to avoid an encounter battle with the advancing German armoured forces. Thus Fuller's prediction that armour was 'likely to be distributed over a wide area rather than to remain concentrated' was sometimes unhelpful; but he did not advocate that tanks should move into battle dispersed; indeed one advantage conferred by the naval analogy was that moving like a 'fleet' the armour was automatically concentrated at the decisive point. Armoured forces should then be distributed in the order that the troops were required, and advance 'as rapidly as possible with the idea of engaging the enemy . . . by manoeuvring him into difficult ground . . . fire will seldom pin down a mechanized force, it will have to be boxed up by manoeuvre'.[28]

If it is accepted that Fuller's predictions stand up remarkably well to scrutiny, and that he sketched correctly an accurate guide to the trends of future warfare until 1941, then it is important to assess the limitations of his vision. Fuller's prescience until Operation 'Barbarossa' in June 1941 is impressive. 'As they [the Germans] drove or marched in dusty columns through the villages and towns of Flanders they felt that they had revived the "classical" warfare of manoeuvre and thrust in the tradition of Frederick, Clausewitz and Moltke.' Some evidence suggests that under certain circumstances the introduction of armoured forces did refine the brutality of warfare. The armoured component of the Wehrmacht was small and highly professional. The German victories had been remarkably swift: Poland conquered in three weeks, Norway in two months, France and the Low Countries in six weeks. Moreover, as Fuller had predicted, casualties were low. In Scandinavia the Germans lost 5926 men and the British 1869. In the Balkans the Germans lost 5000 casualties and captured 90 000 Yugoslavs, 270 000 Greeks and 13 000 British prisoners. This dynamism introduced into warfare, as Fuller had discerned, a new uncertainty. Before Operation 'Crusader' Auchinleck warned his political overlords 'what a peculiar battle it is to be, and how everything hangs on the tactical issue of that one day's fighting, and on one man's tactical ability on that day.' He concluded, 'All these months of labour and thought can be set at nought in one afternoon; rather a terrifying thought?' Also, in battles between small armies there was a return of chivalry. It could be argued that *blitzkreig* had humanized war. 'The *blitzkreig* operations', writes John Lukacs, 'hurt the conquered less than had many of the wars of the past. What hurt them were the deprivations and the tyranny of the occupation that followed.'[29]

Though the tank lent a new decisiveness to warfare, and many of Fuller's predictions were fulfilled, the lightning victories of 1939–41 gave way to a less dynamic form of warfare. *Blitzkreig* had insulated the German civilian population from the war and thus limited it, but the nihilistic Nazi ideology always threatened to come to the fore in any discussion of German war aims. The onset of total war and the limitations of Fuller's faith in decisive battles reveal a number of flaws in his thinking. His faith in reason as a limiting factor in war was only valid when the belligerent states shared a measure of cultural similarity. Fuller had calculated that wars could be limited by statesmen once their armies had been reduced in size by the imperatives of mechanization and a new instrument that could terminate wars decisively had been placed in their hands; and also, to limit wars was the reasonable, sensible thing to do. Reason does not invariably prevail in international politics, and neither is it a quality readily associated with the Nazi leaders; in the last resort they only understood one thing – brute force. When nations are forced to fight for their very existence, they are not chary about the methods they use. Also the peace factor – industrial development which in turn influenced weapon development – gave determined states the ability to wage war on a scale barely conceived of in *Lectures on FSR III*. The cost of mechanization did not reduce the size of armies. From 1942 onwards it was numbers and productive capacity, 180 million Russians and 150 million Americans and 'their willingness to fight even more than the quality of their equipment, [that] decided the war'.[30]

A return to mass was implicit in a great deal of Fuller's thinking, but to explore this possibility went against the grain of his most cherished assumptions. For instance, he agreed that war would be limited ultimately by the character and the resources of those who waged it rather than through any idealistic desire to limit war. 'It is the overwhelming blow which above all others paralyses an enemy's will, and in the future the object will undoubtedly be simultaneously to strike such a blow on the ground and in the air.' Fuller was also aware that if this blow was unsuccessful then operations in both the air and on the ground would gain in intensity. In his opinion, attrition was always latent in military operations and would develop if 'both sides are determined to fight it out, which will seldom be the case'; nothing could be further from the truth. Moscow and Leningrad in 1942 faced not only obliteration but extermination and the fighting became accordingly bitter and bloody. These elements of passion were neglected in Fuller's business-like exposition of future wars between small, highly professional armies.[31]

The defensive, moreover, returned to dominate battlefields. The concluding campaigns on both the Western and Eastern fronts in 1944–5 led to a reduction in the velocity of operations, and not to an increase as predicted by Fuller. Yet is is mistaken to assume that he did not take this into account. His conception of the constant tactical factor led him to expect a return of the defensive. As he wrote:

> Unless command of the air is absolute . . . it should be accepted as a rule that an enemy *is always within striking distance*. . . . Protection will force itself more and more to the fore, not only in the form of armour, but in that of fortifications and defensive distributions.

Lectures on FSR III develops this line of argument. 'Field warfare always begets siege warfare, it did so in the last war, and will do so in a war between armoured forces, but with this difference: Whilst in the World War fronts were fortified, in a war between armoured forces areas will be so instead'. He went so far as to suggest that it was possible for conditions 'as static as those experienced in 1914–17' to return.[32]

Fuller also further developed the ideas of *The Reformation of War* concerning defensive techniques: that future measures would include mines, which would replace barbed wire, and networks of strong points would replace linear entrenchments. Defences would centre upon a series of fortresses and shielded anti-tank guns. The most successful defensive systems, Fuller claimed, were those which combined protective power and mobility. British defensive positions in the Western Desert, like the ill-fated Gazala Line, failed because they were static and held without reference to the disposition of mobile forces. Rommel's defences at El Alamein wrought a close relationship between the static and mobile troops, and consisted of three belts of minefields which, as Montgomery observed, 'were sited to canalize any penetration we might make'. Rommel's development of them in Normandy goes far to sustain Fuller's argument. He took advantage of the *bocage* to mount a powerful screen of anti-tank guns supported by tanks sited in hamlets and hedgerows in the area. He also held that a number of anti-tank guns should be ready to be rushed to any threatened points. On the Eastern Front mines were used in vast quantities. At the Battle of Kursk in July 1943 the Russians laid 30 000 mines per day. On the Central Front alone there were half a million mines with a density of 2400 anti-tank and 2700 anti-personnel mines per mile. The anti-tank positions bear out Fuller's predictions. They were based on carefully hidden anti-tank guns, with ten commanded by one officer, so that enfilading fire could be brought to bear on threatened points. Fuller was also right to underline another important point about future defensive positions:

> I consider it likely that valleys and defiles will play an important part in future defensive warfare, for when the defender can rest his flanks on natural obstacles, all he will then have to consider are the artificial defences on his front.

This clearly envisaged defensive systems like the Gustav Line and Gothic Lines in Italy, which would be 'of earth, concrete and steel' and aimed at 'canalizing' attacks; counter-attacks would have to be *selective*, aiming to secure the maximum co-operation between minefields, tanks and anti-tank forces, with anti-tank guns held in reserve. Not only Kesselring in Italy, but Rommel in Normandy, imitated these measures almost to the letter. These passages are military commentary of the highest order. The only criticism that can be made of Fuller's analysis is his estimate of the size of the defensive forces, which is much too small.[33]

A gap emerged in Fuller's thinking at this point because, though he had clearly thought out the implications for the defender of moving into areas of high ground – as the Allies did in Italy in 1943 – he totally ignored the consequences for the attacker of fighting in towns and villages. He kept repeating that 'villages are unsuitable localities for tanks to fight in', but did not seem to realize that urban areas would have to be seized and held. Spears observed in 1940 that if only the French towns and villages had been held (as the Germans were able to do in 1944), the German penetration could have been blunted. Fuller's neglect of this factor was the pernicious consequence of a persistent error: his assumption that speed would remain a constant protective factor; therefore to protect themselves armoured forces would move round urban areas and blockade them; but defensive weapons developed on a par with offensive ones. Fuller had assumed complacently that speed alone would neutralize urban areas, leaving the infantry to mop up behind. This was a prime miscalculation. Faced by a determined opponent, towns and villages placed a deadly brake on the freedom of movement of armies. At Stalingrad the most effective weapons in street fighting were the grenade and the machine gun; and the tank was reduced to the role of an infantry support weapon. Similarly in Italy street fighting revealed the tank's limitations. The advance was blocked by craters and fallen houses. 'Each position had to be taken with the bomb or the bayonet.' Such conditions were quite alien to those outlined in *Lectures on FSR III*. They also show the continuing value of infantry in a guerrilla role, supported perhaps by a tank and several anti-tank guns, lurking in the woods or in ruined houses, waiting to harry armoured forces with grenades or 'sticky' bombs; they did not require motorization to fulfil this function. Fuller went some way towards acknowledging his error in 1943 when he conceded that 'I overestimated the protective power of speed and underestimated the likelihood of a general thickening of armour to neutralize a rise in the calibre of tank and anti-tank guns.'[34]

Whereas Fuller had calculated that small armies of comparatively equal strength would move into open country to fight battles of manoeuvre accomplishing decisive success quickly, this proved to be an unduly optimistic expectation. Decisive victory can only be achieved by bringing overwhelming strength to bear on a weak and broken enemy – at least between armies of comparative strength and technological sophistication. Given a disparity in degrees of mechanization, the force fielding inferior equipment usually refused to manoeuvre into the open and dug itself in. Consequently, it was not until the German Army Group 'B' was

annihilated at Falaise in August 1944 that Montgomery could
declare that, 'The proper tactics are for strong armoured and
mobile columns to by-pass enemy centres of resistance and to
push boldly ahead creating alarm and despondency in enemy rear
areas.' Likewise on the Eastern Front, the German offensive at
Kursk had to be smashed before the Red Army could, in two
immense leaps, advance to the frontiers of Rumania. In other
words, the tank could not fulfil under every circumstance a
specific tactical function; if there was no scope for an armoured
thrust, then tanks were relegated to the subordinate role of
supporting the infantry advance. *Lectures on FSR III* took the
defensive factor brilliantly into account; but attrition preceded the
armoured thrust; this book tended to assume that it would set in
only afterwards. Fuller perceived accurately the course of the
Second World War but the initial campaigns were fought between
armies which were unprepared for armoured warfare; *Lectures on
FSR III* assumed comparative preparedness. Whatever conditions
prevailed there was an overwhelming need for large numbers of
infantry who broke down the enemy's defences – they were (and
are) vital and not just mere tank auxiliaries.[35]

There are two other points that deserve consideration. The first
is Fuller's view of air power. The emphasis that he placed on the
movement of armoured forces to and fro from an anti-tank
'laager', though not wholly wrong, did ignore the danger of
tactical air power. Fuller did underestimate the future potential of
fighter/fighter-bomber aircraft, and here Liddell Hart's criticisms
are better founded. For example, he claimed that 'one limiting
factor in air offensives is the difficulty in hitting small targets'.
Though infantry were vulnerable to air attack, armoured columns
were not, as they moved rapidly and in dispersed formations; and
should one tank be hit 'it is unlikely that any other machine will
suffer'. The real answer to air power, he claimed, was mobile
armour, as 'armour "strikes" at air power itself by denying moral
effect to inaccurate bombing' – that is, bombs would be so small
that they would bounce off tank armour. This is a feeble piece of
special pleading. Fuller's observations in *Lectures on FSR III* only
amount to the need to gain 'local command of the air'. Elsewhere
he did remark on the necessity for bombing communications, but
this needed further amplification. Fuller could not perhaps have
foreseen the advent of the 'tankbuster' aircraft like the Hawker
'Typhoon' which could destroy tanks even when they were dug

in, but his excuse that *Lectures on FSR III* was not concerned primarily with air power was undermined by the fact that he never grasped the significance of the Ju87 'Stuka' bomber. Another factor that Fuller used to underpin his argument, namely, 'that there is a close relationship between mechanization on the ground and motorization in the air', which would result in the intimate co-operation between tanks and aircraft, as tanks drove forward to seize the enemy's air fields, was valid. Once the range of aircraft increased though, this factor became less important.[36]

The second point concerns the problem of maintaining mechanized forces in the field. Many of Fuller's suggestions are worthy of high praise, especially his earlier prediction that field, mechanical and electrical engineers would be found in the forefront of battle. During the drive to the English Channel after the breakthrough at Sedan in May 1940, the courage and efficiency of the German engineers did much to maintain the speed of the advance. A more general proposition, that mechanization would render the grip of supply on strategy 'far less tenacious' was rather less convincing. The contrary was actually true, even in terrain which favoured armoured vehicles, mainly because it was so inhospitable. The weather had an important part to play here – either freezing cold or boiling hot. In his first flush of enthusiasm, Fuller claimed that mechanized units would be able to free themselves from the apron strings of fickle Mother Nature. Never again would the weather be able to frustrate military operations as it had during Passchendaele (Third Ypres, July–September 1917). The experience of the Second World War showed that this was far from being the case; it is probable that mechanized and air forces 'are more rather than less susceptible to weather'. The result was that mechanized armies demanded vast armies of supporting vehicles to keep them in the field. The dream of small self-supporting armies, as Michael Howard observes, 'turned into the reality of huge armies with massive "tails", highly vulnerable to enemy air attack and demanding considerable logistical ingenuity to keep them moving at all'. The 'horde army' did not disappear from the battlefield; on the contrary, it continued to grow in size.[37]

General reflection on Fuller's views on mechanized warfare as advanced in *Lectures on FSR III* suggests that in his expectation of a revolution in warfare he was mistaken. The introduction of the tank produced only (to employ the title of an earlier book) the *reformation of war*. Armoured warfare led to a reassessment of the older arms and (with the exception of the cavalry) not to their abolition. As Fuller's arguments were based on an overstatement, he was able to indulge himself in some wishful thinking about the size of armies which flew in the face of reality. This notwithstanding, it is clear that Fuller's contribution to the debate over future mechanized operations was his most mature – and enduring – contribution to technical military literature.

8

Military Critic as Fascist, 1934–9

When in the Army, I was not against Authority but against Lethargy posing as such . . . until our political traditions go our defence forces cannot rise.

Fuller to Liddell Hart, 5 May 1937, LHP 1/302/280

The politicians never forgave him [Fuller] for having played with the Nazi idea.

Field Marshal Lord Ironside to Colonel R. Macleod, 13 February 1959, Macleod Papers

Lindsay's plea that Fuller 'stick to the work' was made in vain. The publication of *Grant and Lee* in 1933 testified to the continued variety and depth of Fuller's interests but he had for some time been looking for employment outside the Army. Two years earlier Ironside had reported to Liddell Hart, 'Boney Fuller is at Eastbourne and doesn't think that he will be given any appointment. I am sure he will not as long as Uncle George sits in his seat.' Once Montgomery-Massingberd had been appointed CIGS on Milne's retirement Fuller's chances of being usefully employed shrank to zero. As Ironside wrote in 1933, 'I am not saying that he has not been stupid, but he was not handled properly just because his critical spirit was considered disloyalty' [*sic*]. In November 1933 Fuller was offered command of the Second Class District of Bombay. He refused on the grounds that his previous experience would be wasted. Privately he considered the offer an insult, which was no doubt the reason why it was made. Ironside thought Fuller 'a difficult man to place and not everybody's man. But, he is straight and fearless and ingenious. How many of our leaders are that? Very, very few.'[1]

A taste of Fuller's 'critical spirit' could be savoured in *Grant and Lee*. He wrote acidly: 'Since 1917, . . . I have preached almost daily that the answer to half an ounce of lead is half an inch of steel; . . . This would seem so obvious . . . as to require no accentuation.' Then came the sting in the tail: 'my failure has been complete but not altogether wasted; for my efforts have led me to appreciate why for a hundred years the chivalry of France, in spite of dreadful losses, continued to charge the English archers.' Ironside was thus correct in predicting that 'when he does retire he will begin to be vitriolic. If the WO is thin skinned they won't like what he says.'[2]

Fuller was placed officially on the retired list in December 1933. There is a clear connection between his interest in political fringe groups and his disillusionment with the Army. He had already lectured to the New Britain Group by 1932, a fascistic grouping typical of the kind of associations, weary of democracy's failings, that were spawned by the Great Depression. Within six months of retiring he had taken the serious step of joining the British Union of Fascists. Despite the complaints against 'politicians' which pepper his writings, he was the most politically committed of all British generals. Fuller later claimed that he joined Sir Oswald Mosley's new fascist party because the latter had consistently advocated a completely mechanized army. This was only one factor in his decision. To a very large extent Fuller's political ideas were rationalized prejudice of a rather commonplace kind. They were dominated by the professional soldier's instinctive dislike of 'politicians' and all their works. Sir Oswald Mosley has emphasized that Fuller had a very conventional soldier's view of politics. Hence the appeal of fascism: it was a political movement with a military character. A premium was placed on leadership, military terminology was used and a uniform worn (until this was outlawed by the Public Order Act of 1936). The BUF was a favourite political cause of retired officers from all three services.[3]

Fuller's fascism was technocratic in character, emphasizing order and efficiency in government – a rational management of resources that was not possible with democratic muddle. This concern was most evident in *Empire Unity and Defence* (1934) – the least ideological book of Fuller's fascist phase. This began life as a lecture delivered at the Imperial Defence College in 1933. It was structured around a series of interlocking trinities, though they were not as obtrusive as in *The Foundations of the Science of War*. It once more covered the ground which Fuller had earlier traversed in the 1920s. He called for a unified command and the setting up of a Ministry of Defence, 'not so much to replace the three Service Ministries, as to found a grand strategical brain which could equate policy with strategical requirements and the resources available'. He roundly criticized the existing arrangements because 'each Service . . . looks at every problem from a departmental point of view, the result is a series of half measures'. Fuller's ideal arrangement in British defence planning has still not been fully realized fifty years after the completion of that book.[4]

Fuller's specific military criticisms were well made and convincing. He was certainly justified in attacking the sloth and lack of direction in British defence policy; when disagreements between the Services were referred to the Committee of Imperial Defence, a committee (including Cabinet ministers) co-ordinating defence questions, they were frequently referred back to the Chiefs of Staff, the very body that had 'failed to solve them'. But his assumptions about the place of the British Empire in the world were rather more suspect. He was surely right in thinking that 'Unconsolidated, it [the Empire] cannot risk another European War, for . . . it is likely to be sucked down piecemeal in the general maelstrom.' Fuller assumed that if the Empire could be given adequate institutions it had a future as a world force. He commented on 'the mutual ignorance between the various parts of the Empire'. He suggested that an Imperial Council be set up along the lines recommended by the Haldane Report (1918). This would act as 'a great Bureau of Information', and help form an intelligent Imperial public opinion, thus giving the Empire a measure of cultural identity. Fuller was prepared to concede that the Empire was 'latently disruptive' but he did not realize that the Dominions would resist any attempt to formalize by institutional reforms the unprecedented imperial co-operation achieved during the First World War, though they might pay lip service to Imperial unity as an ideal. Thus Fuller's preference for a policy of isolation from European affairs, 'and, in place of mixing ourselves up in the tangled net of international politics, we should economically develop our Empire', was impractical as there was no guarantee that any such consolidation would take place. We must recognize, however, that such a harsh judgement might smack of the false wisdom of hindsight; Fuller would never have agreed that the collapse of the British Empire was inevitable. He made cogent recommendations for its future, and as these followed in the Imperialist tradition of Joseph Chamberlain and Lord Milner, they were eminently respectable.[5]

The strong element of social imperialism in Fuller's thought which led him to criticize the muddle of British defence institutions, provided the background for a series of books ridiculing the social ethos of the British Army – mainly for its amateurishness. In *The Army in My Time* (1935), *Memoirs of an Unconventional Soldier* (1936), and *The Last of the Gentlemen's Wars* (1937), Fuller with no little comic talent, dissected the flaws of the Army with devastating effect. His reminiscences had a polemical purpose, as they were designed to reveal the defects of the Army and show by implication how they could be rectified. The *Memoirs* especially were a higher form of political pampheteering. They also indirectly contributed to the flood of anti-war literature in the 1930s that poured scorn on the character and achievements of the Army. Fuller, naturally, had no intention of undermining the Army, he only wanted to reform it. He was at pains to point out that when he criticized senior officers and their methods, 'my criticism is aimed against their craftsmanship and not against their integrity as soldiers'. His books were part of a wider concern within the Army that reform was urgently needed, as exemplified in Captain J. Russell Kennedy's book, *This, Our Army* (1935). Writing to his friend, Meredith Starr, Fuller was pleased that he enjoyed the *Memoirs*, and added that he might now realize why there was a war memorial in every town and village. 'A change in our system of command I think will be more common sense than the yearly two minutes silence. We should act instead of standing still.'[6]

The mocking tone of *The Army in My Time* and the *Memoirs*, and the many amusing anecdotes they include, depicting the average British officer as an ill-educated fool, did not make many friends in the upper echelons of the Army and therefore did not advance the cause of reform. Swinton wrote of *The Army in My Time* that there was a great deal of truth in the book, but that it was 'put in a way to exasperate and cause doubts as to the author's motives and judicious sense'. Fuller himself conceded that '*The Army in My Time* is not exactly a pot boiler, for there was little to be made out of it; but it is spiritually in that class.' Liddell Hart thought the book's criticisms too sweeping but still believed that they were valuable and not invalidated just 'because he failed to emphasize all the time that there were exceptions to his indictment'. He assured Fuller that he would do everything possible to prevent it being dismissed by 'one of the "old gang" reviewers, and so would like to do what I can to ensure it a better fate'.[7]

The main target for Fuller's ridicule was a social system that not only protected amateurishness but glorified it. On joining the Army, Fuller claimed that he had been 'appalled by the ignorance which surrounded me and the immense value attached to it'. The regimental spirit of the Army, 'the self-worship of the amateur', was 'the prime cause of military inefficiency'. Hence the complacency which dominated the upper echelons of the Army. 'This fear of the truth creates a discipline the aim of which is not to foster originality, but a universal damping down and standardization, which ends in creating an all-pervading mediocrity of spirit, in which genius and talent are the demons to be exorcised.' The Army was thus isolated from social and technological forces which surged outside the barrack walls. Before 1914 the Army had prepared for 'a dream war which would vanish with the first actual cannonade'. In a brilliant vignette Fuller encapsulated the level of reading of the average British officer before 1914. He remembered in 1913 'a Major recommending Henderson's *Stonewall Jackson* to a brother officer, and then . . . when this book was being discussed, committing the error of supposing that "Cross Keys" was a public house in Odiham and Jackson the name of the man who ran it'. Then he added sarcastically, 'Yet even to recommend it, though unread – what an advance!'[8]

Fuller returned to the charge over this issue in his *Memoirs*. He substantiated his charges by a skilful presentation of his own experiences with a graphic style and pungent turn of phrase. The book begins with a brilliant description of Fuller's time as a cadet at Sandhurst where, it would appear, the teachers were almost as old as the military doctrines they taught. The class in military law, like much else, 'was a jest'. The cadets exhausted their energies poring over 'those sections [of the Manual of Military Law] dealing with murder, rape and indecency' and then, filling in time, 'either destroyed Her Majesty's property with our pen knives or twiddled our thumbs'. Fortunately the monotony of the classroom was alleviated by the senility of the teachers. Still, Fuller's point was a serious one: he argued that the British officer was uneducated and when some attempt was made to improve his capacity to think, it was usually counter-productive.[9]

The Staff College was designed to provide the Army with the intellectual stimulus so lacking in regimental life. Fuller found this quite unsatisfactory. The examination system was mentally cramping rather than stimulating; 'do not study in order to fit yourself to become a Staff Officer', he warned, 'but solely in order to pass the examination'. He was particularly scathing about the pernicious effect of 'crammers' on the minds of young officers. As for the Staff College itself, Fuller condemned it, not only because it failed to encourage creative thought, but because it stifled curiosity by overwhelming students with doctrine which they were expected to *learn*, and forced them to memorize mountains of useless facts about military history. Fuller's own attempts to think things out for himself had been discouraged. The Staff College was 'just parts of a machine created to produce standardized thinking, and to think in a standardized way is a great relief to an instructor, for otherwise he might be caught out'.[10]

The vast scale of the First World War resulted in a blossoming of this conformist, bureaucratic mentality. At Field Marshal Sir Douglas Haig's Headquarters Fuller depicted this flowering as not only luxuriant but virtually impenetrable. Forms were signed by the ton, but no soldier sitting behind its cosy walls seemed to think deeply about the nature of the tactical problems facing the British Army. As the leading staff representative of an infant branch of the service, the Tank Corps, it was not surprising that Fuller found this inertia frustrating. Of General 'Kitten' Wigram, who was responsible for the organization of the British Expeditionary Force (BEF), he wrote, 'Often did I visit his office in Montreuil, invariably to find him standing by a desk, sallow and tired out, as in deepest thought he extracted a cook here and a batman there from whatever establishment was before him.' For all of Wigram's 'charm, sincerity and self-sacrificing hard work', Fuller claimed that he was typical of the British military mind, a type who 'through a profound sense of duty, coupled with a microscopic vision of the reality of things, spent hours every day blowing blue pencil-dust into the military machine'; and he characterized any attempt to secure even minor changes in the Tank Corps organization as 'like playing golf on course with a hundred bunkers between each green'.[11]

The result was command by consultation – always an anathema with Fuller. His best depiction of this occurred during the planning for the Battle of the Somme. He recounted in detail the final conference before the battle of VII Corps divisional commanders and their GSO 1s. Fuller attended also because his GSO 1, Berkeley Vincent, 'was somewhat deaf'. Around this fact Fuller penned a brilliant description with consummate comic skill.

It was a typical Conference. To begin with, the Corps Commander delegated his responsibilities to his Divisional Commanders, who explained how they in turn would delegate their shares in his responsibilities to their respective Brigadiers, who, had they have been present, would have delegated their shares to their Battalion Commanders until in the end, a trembling line of Platoon Leaders, Sergeants and Corporals would have the entire responsibility loaded upon their shoulders.

Command, the prerogative of the Generals, having been atomised, a trivial discussion arose on what the men should eat before they went over the top. Eventually it boiled down to a choice between pea soup and porridge. Berkeley Vincent was straining to hear what was being said. He was a highly educated officer, a great strategist and had been attached to the Russian Army during the Russo-Japanese War. Dreaming of some cunning penetration or overwhelming turning movement, and hearing nothing but a jumble of voices, suddenly, as a lull in the conversation occurred, he turned to me and whispered: 'What has been decided on?' And I, for the moment forgetting that he was deaf, replied: 'Pea soup'. 'Pea soup?' he exclaimed incredulously. 'What do you mean?' But the final conference was at an end and 'pea soup' was the decision. A gathering of Battalion cooks would, I think, have displayed certainly an equal generalship.

This is a striking description and highlights a number of features of Fuller's outlook. The aplomb with which he juxtaposed 'cunning turning movements' with 'pea soup' hardly requires comment. If the story has a moral, it is that a conference at this level should not be immersed in trivial detail. That the business of war should be reduced to manageable, but fundamental simplicities, not swamped by crowds of staff officers brandishing papers on routine matters. Otherwise the result would be the wholesale abdication of responsibility. Fuller's indictment was savage but not unjustified. The *Memoirs of an Unconventional Soldier* was Fuller's revenge on the British Army; literary retaliation for many frustrations in both war and peace.[12]

After 1918 this narrow conservatism became entrenched behind the walls of the War Office. There was not attempt to study the lessons of 1914–18, only persistent pen pushing and an obsession with returning to 'real soldiering'. Hence there was no reform, only stagnation. The 'paper wars' of the War Office were interminable. 'To write "I agree" on the flyleaf of a branch memorandum, . . . is the height of bad form unless the agreement is qualified; because to agree to a suggestion is apt to shorten its questionable life'. Work would be curtailed and appointments threatened; bureaucracy only breeds more bureaucracy. Fuller discovered that it was possible to 'write a minute on any subject in such a way that the department to which it was addressed would be compelled to forward it to some other department, which in turn would be compelled to forward it to some other department, and so on'. This process would take up to twelve months before the minute returned, thereupon some rewording would suffice to send it back on its contentious but circular journey. The tyranny of bureaucracy had another unfortunate by-product. The Army allowed no freedom of expression. Fuller cited as an example the reaction of Lord Cavan, then CIGS, to *The Foundations of the Science of War*, whose publication he refused to sanction. 'Imagine a surgeon, a lawyer, a chemist or an engineer objecting to active members of his profession writing a book for other members to read!' he asked.[13]

These charges are serious ones, and they have heavily influenced the views of later historians. Other authorities support Fuller's general picture of a War Office machine clanking along, clogged with routine paper work. Pownall, Assistant Secretary of the Committee of Imperial Defence, complained in 1936 that the 'War Office machine is working very slowly . . . [it] seems very badly bogged'. It should also be remembered that such was the dynamism of British military institutions at this time that Pownall managed to teach himself German in CID time. This instance supports Fuller's view that many officers were so bored with routine that they spent their working hours reading books. Any attempt to prepare seriously for war would be enmeshed and throttled by a bureaucratic 'jungle'.[14]

Some of these criticisms are just, but there can be little doubt that most are exaggerated. Fuller had, as Mosley observed, 'perhaps an almost exaggerated intolerance of bureaucracy of any kind'. He may have encountered a comparable degree of obstruction from the established institutions of civilian professions. He endeavoured to make out a special case against the Army: its amateur spirit and the lack of any rational decision-making system had resulted in the domination of petty minds and bureaucrats. Yet it is by no means clear whether simply rationalising the system would have eradicated inefficiency – though it might have helped. Fuller supposed that reforming complex military institutions was a simple matter and that these changes were themselves untrammelled instruments of good. It was a fallacy spread by Social Imperialism that if only the administrators of policy could be changed, then a new, more efficient policy could be introduced. Fuller believed that if a highly trained group of staff officers could take over the management of the War Office then its more objectionable features would disappear. He had adopted as his motto a saying quoted frequently by Karl Pearson, *la critique est la vie de science*. Alas, intellectual power by itself does not overrule the weaknesses of human nature. Pearson had also warned against the consequences for any branch of thought of introducing 'a scientific hierarchy which would brand as heretical all doubts as to its conclusions, all criticisms of its results'. Surely the institutionalizing of intellect required by Fuller unfortunately leads to that very aversion to criticism which so appalled him. Clever men are just as prone to vanity and stupidity as the less clever; perhaps they are more rather than less vulnerable. Goethe once said that 'Men are oftener separated by opinions about things than the things themselves'. The extraordinary blunders and uncommon arrogance displayed by the German General Staff in its preparations for war with Soviet Russia in 1941 reveal the human failings of the most professional of military staffs.[15]

The highly critical tone of Fuller's *Memoirs* was partly due to a reaction against his own shabby treatment. This book also reflects a much deeper loss of interest in military affairs. After reading a series of articles by Liddell Hart in *The Times* on the need for a change in the Army's structure, Fuller frankly admitted that he had 'lost interest in our Army, for I am of [the] opinion that there is no intention of modernizing it'. Thus he agreed with Liddell Hart that under no circumstances should the Army in its present state be committed to a European war; 'if we do, it will prove nothing short of a suicide club'. Pointing out the dire necessity for reform now that all European nations were modernizing their forces, he made an unflattering comparison between the Army and the RAF:

> Personally, I would not spend a penny more on our present army, for it is dud from top to bottom – even Austria has more tanks than we have. I would put every penny on the Air Force, for even should the machines not be what we want, pilots will gain in training, whilst in the Army we de-train our men and render them unemployable.

This interest in the air was stimulated by fascism, which attached great importance to the aeroplane, as it combined futuristic technology with individual skill and daring. But even as early as 1930 Fuller claimed that freedom of speech, or at least some freedom, was RAF policy, although the smug and uncritical acceptance of the clichés of strategic bombing and its importance in the next war hardly provides evidence of clear or scientific thinking in the youngest service.[16]

A good case can actually be made suggesting that, compared with the Army, conditions were actually *worse* in the senior service, the Royal Navy. Like the Army, the Navy had experienced a great increase in the number of its permanent senior officers, so that men of seniority rather than talent monopolised the highest posts. The Navy had no permanent general staff before 1918. There was a comparable degree of prejudice against specialists like electricians. Indeed the Navy showed an even greater degree of blindness towards the impact of technological factors than the Army. Admiral Sir Herbert Richmond had demanded that the 'future of the battleship must be approached in a far more scientific manner', and that the Admiralty must rid itself of an unreasoning commitment to these capital ships. Though the Admiralty admitted that the potential of aircraft carriers was great, it still regarded them as information carriers, and concluded that 'there is nothing in the present offensive qualities of aircraft carriers which render them a menace to the capital ships'. The career of the brilliant but peppery and outspoken Richmond is comparable to that of Fuller, and Richmond was retired early on a similar flimsy pretext by senior officers irritated by his fearless criticisms.[17]

In terms of tactical doctrine the 1920s were for the Army, like the Navy, a period of sterility. Nevertheless Fuller did exaggerate the conservatism of the Army towards the tank. It remained in the vanguard of mechanization until about 1930. Where the Army failed was in evaluating a tactical doctrine for the use of tanks in battle. As Fuller wrote in exasperation in 1928 of the mechanized experiments of that year: 'The "Armoured Force" is now the "Armoured Farce" as you suggest . . . The CIGS would not lay down what it was for, so it has drifted into what it is not for.' Fuller claimed that the results of this kind of drift were obvious. 'When tanks', he wrote in 1937, 'are used by soldiers who have no training, no tactics, no administration and no organization – what can one learn?' Yet he did underestimate the practical difficulties of mechanizing the Army. He may well have been right to claim that in the long run it was not a true economy to finance an obsolete army but a waste. On the other hand, he failed to take into account the fact that any large-scale mechanization programme demanded levels of capital expenditure for which the funds were not available. There were no trained mechanics in the Army; nor were there garages, workshops or spare parts. 'It is no use producing costly machines unless proper accommodation is available for housing them.' Finally, the Army faced a dilemma because the numbers of available places to train officer cadets at both Woolwich and Sandhurst were not being filled. The General Staff faced an upheaval if mechanization was adopted. This was an excuse rather than a convincing reason for opposing reform. Still, it is equally valid to suggest that factors which operated outside the Army's control could not be overcome by reforming its structure.[18]

Fuller was nevertheless justified in attacking a social ethos which not only held back the cause of reform but petrified the minds of even mildly progressive officers. The regimental system, whatever its important role in fortifying *esprit de corps*, also promoted laziness and a narrow parochial outlook. The peacetime British Army was little more than a series of 'clubs' of varying degrees of social exclusiveness in which officers pursued their favourite hobbies. The amount of free time available to junior officers was enormous; regimental routine rarely took up more than two or three hours each day and could be handled by the adjutant; the rest of the day was free, and the actual details of supervising the troops were carried out by the NCOs. 'In those days', recalled Brigadier Fergusson, 'the most devastating criticism that could be made of a soldier was that he was "ambitious".' Such men were 'unsound'. The most serious consequences of the lassitude and prejudices of regimental life were that these foibles were carried over into the institutions that were supposed to impart a more serious aspect to the study of war, such as the Staff College. 'It was considered', General Sir Frederick ('Tim') Pile recalled, 'rather a bad mark if one did not hunt with the Drag, though it was always claimed by the Directors that it had no influence on the final results.' The Drag was a foxhunt that accompanied the Staff College course. Parochialism and needless rivalry was also promoted by the regimental 'house' spirit between the different arms of the service. Fuller had long advocated that manuals be written in a more general way to facilitate a co-operation of arms – a co-operation which the British Army found it extremely difficult to achieve throughout the Second World War.[19]

The widespread lack of professionalism prevailing in the Army between the wars contributed significantly to the weaknesses of the British military leadership during the Second World War. The wartime CIGS, General Sir Alan Brooke, wanted to replace a good number of the Army and Corps commanders as they lacked 'character, imagination, drive and powers of leadership'. He continued: 'but heaven knows when we shall find anything . . . very much better'. Fuller's criticisms though often just were not always fair. Major John North wrote to Fuller in 1936 praising the *Memoirs*. 'The apostles of a new doctrine can only hope that those who come after will benefit from their martyrdom.' North was depressed because he realized that the General Staff 'are more disconcerted by your *ideas* than by the manner of their presentation'. This was only half true. Fuller brought much obloquy on himself. The *Memoirs* did not take account of the efforts of mildly conservative officers like Brooke and Major General (later Field Marshal Sir) John Dill, who were certainly not fools, labouring to reform the Army from within while remaining unconvinced as to the benefits conferred by mechanization. Neither was there a correlation between favouring mechanization and insisting upon the desirability of reform. Field Marshal Sir Philip Chetwode, the champion of the cavalry, was just as anxious as Fuller to widen the intellectual horizons of officers. The picture of heroic progressives striving to overturn the lethargy of the cavalry clique, as portrayed in Fuller's *Memoirs*, was simply not true.[20]

It might be added that any Army in the world might have had difficulty in accommodating an intellectually dynamic force on the scale of Fuller. Liddell Hart, never one to defer to the dictates of false modesty when assessing his own talents, believed him to be 'the greatest intellectual power I have ever come across, a Triton amongst minnows'. Fuller *knew* he was very clever, did not bother to disguise that he knew it, and did not tolerate fools – let alone gladly. It was widely held that Fuller and his mentor, Ironside, were the two 'most conceited men in the Army'. Fuller's role as an *enfant terrible* was reinforced by the structural weaknesses of the Army, as it lacked an operational research organ which could harness his talents adequately. Yet Fuller's grave weaknesses of character were, as Liddell Hart later came to realize, surely the decisive factor in his isolation and eventual failure. Fuller was often lacking in generosity ('lacking the milk of human kindness' was how Swinton once describe him) and sweepingly unfair; his predictions could be wild and his utterances dogmatic. As Liddell Hart claimed, he had suffered 'for years from an outer circle of bitter hostility and an inner circle of pure adulation – with practically no mean'. The 'inner circle' was no doubt a reference to Sonia Fuller who tolerated no criticism of her husband. Fuller was resentful of criticism, 'proclaims the essential value of truth and free criticism, yet inconsistently cannot tolerate it himself'. All these faults found their way into the *Memoirs*, which one reviewer called an 'egotistical work'. Yet this book also supports Liddell Hart's final verdict that Fuller was 'the chief military pioneer of the post-war [post-1918] era, and one of the few significant figures that the Army has thrown up in modern times'.[21]

The publication later in 1936 of *The First of the League Wars* was to highlight these fissures in Fuller's development and the increasing influence that fascist ideology was exerting over him. He applauded the spirit of free inquiry in the Army and yet sought to supply it by the introduction of an authoritarian political system. He looked to fascism not only to restore heroism and glamour to war, but simultaneously provide the means for intricate preparation which seemed to set heroism at nought. *The First of the League Wars* was the most ideologically committed of all his books, though it did not taint his reputation as a military commentator. Even Swinton believed it 'thought provoking'. Douglas Jerrold, later chairman of the publishers Eyre and Spottiswoode, believed it to be 'one of the most important books which Fuller has written'. *The First of the League Wars* was written in an unmistakable style, that 'queer compound of mysticism and realism, which makes his writing, . . . unmistakable'. It was evidently a mystical book. In 1934 he confided that all his writings 'are in a way Qabalistic. All activities are but expressions of one activity'. Thus, 'As my occupation was soldiering I selected "war", because if you want to live a full life, qabalistically or otherwise, you must live with your occupation as if it were your wife.' The interdependence of war and life could serve as a *leitmotif* in the corpus of his life's work.[22]

There was an important mystical connection between Fuller's anxiety about the approaching tyranny of materialism, the influence of the machine on war, and the character of the next war. He had become anxious about the increasing standardization of life which resulted from the growth of the machine. His prime concern was 'liberating [man's] mind from the mechanical monster it has created . . . [and] directing the power of the Machine Age to intellectual and spiritual ends'. The most potent influence on this kind of thinking was Lewis Mumford's *Technics and Civilization* (1932). Those states who could master the potential of the machine under a new moral order would be able, due to superior organization and morale, to steal a march on those nations who had not prepared for war. From these assumptions proceeded an analysis of what Fuller called 'dictatorial warfare', the ruthless pursuit of state interests in a world bridled by the false ideals of the democracies.[23]

The underlying thesis of *The First of the League Wars* held that so long as the Western democracies defended the *status quo*, and Germany and Italy remained equally determined to change it, then another World War would ensue. The 'first' League War had led to the Italian acquisition of Abyssinia in 1936. The 'second' would probably involve Germany in Europe. Fuller's view was biased in favour of the fascist dictatorships and often misguided; the deductions drawn from it were not. In *Empire Unity and Defence* Fuller calculated that whereas in 1914 'our main naval question was that of the maintenance of supremacy in the North Sea, today it is the economic control of the Atlantic and strategical control of the Pacific Oceans' – as the Second World War was to show decisively. Fuller supported this contention by relying on the conventional wisdom of the time that the blockade of Germany had proved the decisive factor in Germany's defeat in 1918. Consequently without mechanized forces the economic attack was the stronger form of war. Historians are now much more sceptical about the validity of some of these claims. Fuller himself revised this view after visiting Abyssinia, and asked: if the dictatorships attacked the vulnerable civil will of the democracies, then 'what place is there for the cumbersome machinery of the League, with its slow-moving sanctions and collective security?' The attempt to blockade Italy in 1936 with sanctions had failed because Mussolini had moved too quickly for economic pressure to have any effect; in short, collective security lacked utility, for security which had to be collected was not security at all.[24]

This line of reasoning was further developed in *Towards Armageddon*. Fuller predicted that Hitler would attempt 'to cash in on every crisis' by an overwhelming 'war of nerves'. He would 'make so warlike a grimace that he will deflate them [the democracies] and gain what he is seeking without firing a shot'. Thus future war would 'take the form of a *coup d'état*: a conspiracy instead of a mobilization, and a bolt from the blue of a cloudless sky instead of a declaration preceded by political thunder'. The full reason why Fuller had urged a rationalization of British defence institutions now became clear. As the British Chiefs of Staff had no thinking or research organs to assist them they were forced to waste time considering matters of detail. Faced with 'dictatorial warfare' the British decision-making machinery was simply too cumbersome to acquire the necessary speed of decision that would be vital in a war of movement. Britain would risk a crushing defeat in the opening phase of the next war.[25]

It was crucially important that British statesmen realized that 'the scientific method must be applied to an entire nation' with total mobilization of all warmaking resources. 'Plans have to be made years beforehand', he wrote, 'so that their demands may be prepared for, and normally speaking, execution will depend more upon preparation than individual generalship.' Fuller was not wrong, indeed he was right, but this statement seemed to undercut so much of his earlier teaching. The 1930s witness a change of direction in his thinking. There is much less emphasis on the importance of mechanized forces as the most important weapons of the moral attack. If the civil will was the most vulnerable link in the nation's armour, then the only weapon that could attack the civil population effectively was the bomber – which Fuller now called the tactical 'master-weapon' around which the other weapons may be deployed. His attitude towards bombing thus veered around to the uncritical faith expressed in *The Reformation of War*. He was now convinced that armies and navies would become bases for air action, 'from which aircraft can be projected against the enemy's cities and vital points. Logically, this is the sequel to the siege warfare epoch of 1914–18.' Ground forces were of secondary importance, 'Ultimately, as complete mechanization is approached (which obviously does not exclude unarmoured troops), the entire Army should organically and tactically be so shaped that it may fulfil its final tactical function' – supporting air action. 'As aircraft set the pace, so must landcraft exert themselves to the uttermost to keep up with it', he wrote. Consequently, as armies would remain small there was no need to introduce conscription, which would hinder rather than aid preparation for war.[26]

A degree of prescience can be discerned in these views; but on the whole Fuller exaggerated the power of the bomber, and either ignored or underestimated the technical limitations of this weapon. He was misled less by its destructive potential (indeed he criticized politicians for exaggerating the quantities of bombs aircraft could drop) than by a miscalculation of its moral effect. Fuller, like virtually all commentators, overestimated the effect of a single raid on a community. Thus the notion that civilians would respond hysterically if exposed to bombing was overstated in his books. After the first raids in 1940, for example, people '*talked* about nerves and shock, [though] they showed no sign of either'. The German attack on Coventry in November 1940 resulted in an 'unprecedented dislocation and depression', and this city did exhibit hysteria, terror and neurosis. 'Women were seen to cry, to scream, to tremble all over, to faint in the street, to attack a fireman, and so on.' This attack was not followed up and Coventry recovered. Fuller's quite ridiculous view of the corruption and inefficiency of democratic rule led him to underestimate the contentment of the British people with their lot. Tom Harrisson was of the opinion that the technology of the period was incapable of 'knocking out' any state where the populace was 'broadly satisfied with their own society', and there is no shortage of evidence to support this view.[27]

Fuller was given an opportunity to test his assumptions during the Spanish Civil War (1936–9) and he visited Spain three times. His recorded impressions compiled for the War Office indicate that his capacity to adjust his ideas and absorb the lessons of experience was in inverse proportion to his ideological commitment to fascism. So much for 'scientific detachment'. The Spanish Civil War showed that the capacity of bombers to unhinge the civil population was greatly exaggerated. On his arrival in 1937, Fuller was surprised how 'insignificant' bombing damage really was; during his second trip in October of that year he noticed what 'little damage was done by aerial bombardment'. 'People go to shelters as they like. I witnessed two alarms at Saragossa, there was absolutely no disorder though the streets were full of people.' Fuller nonetheless persisted in making the case that it was the 'moral effect of air attacks' which was truly demoralizing. 'It is the tension between the attacks, quite as much as the suddenness and violence which seems to effect people's nerves . . . I have felt this myself.' Thus 'an undisciplined people will always panic under air attack, for it is only natural that they should'. Here regardless of political affiliation, Fuller was only voicing the fears of the British governing class, what Tom Harrisson rightly judged 'the inability of the highly educated to "think down" into the hearts and minds of the less fortunate, then commonly termed "the working classes"'.[28]

Fuller's overall viewpoint was overstated, but he drew from it, as was frequently the case, some perceptive comments about air tactics. He pointed to the future importance of air power in the narrow seas. In the Mediterranean, for instance, he predicted that the battleship would be helpless when attacked from the air. A new kind of blockade would follow, 'the aim of which is not to bottle up a harbour or scour the seas for the enemy merchantmen, but to keep the enemy's ports under constant or intermittent bombardment [from the air]'. This was accurate, and attacks on dock emplacements did become as important as attacks on the enemy's main fleet. The Japanese committed a signal blunder when attacking the United States fleet at Pearl Harbor in December 1941 when they neglected to destroy the dock installations. At sea, the aircraft carrier would replace the battleship as the most important capital ship, and 'cruisers, destroyers, submarines and possibly also battleships, will become their auxiliaries, the moving sea-fortress from which their aircraft will operate. . . . Bomb-power is the key, because air-carried bombs vastly out-range gun-fired shells.'[29]

As offensive power increased in the air, so would it, Fuller was increasingly arguing in the late 1930s, decline on the ground. In 1935 he published an article in the Daily Mirror showing how quickly Abyssinia could be conquered by tanks. 'Why does he write such tripe?' asked 'Tim' Pile, a leading advocate of mechanization within the Army. Though Pile's question could have been levelled more justly at some other of Fuller's less happy contributions to the popular press, in this case Fuller was right and Pile was wrong. Thereafter a change in emphasis was evident. Fuller still believed that entire countries could be overrun in weeks, but he made fewer claims for the success of ground forces. He underlined the need for good roads (previously he had discounted these) and strong bases; he also emphasized the need for anti-tank defences which would aim 'at entangling the enemy's forces in a tactical net of fine mesh, from which, should he break through it, he will find himself caught in a strategical net of wider mesh'. While in Spain he had observed that under 'conditions of modern warfare the attack is vastly more costly than the defence', but he did not go as far as Liddell Hart in claiming that the defence was stronger than the offence, and he made fun of 'clichés (slogans) or Liddell Hartisms'. He engaged in a brisk correspondence with Liddell Hart pointing out that opportunities for the attack were still present, like at the Battle of Malaga in 1937. 'The entire operation was a stampede, there was practically no fighting.' In 1939 he considered that the Battle of Madrid 'gave the lie direct to those critics who proclaimed the defensive as being the stronger form of war'. This was an indirect but unmistakable attack on Liddell Hart.[30]

Finally, Fuller completely changed his mind over the future of gas warfare. While he had enthusiastically welcomed the Italian use of gas in 1936 as a 'simplifier of tactics', within twelve months he had reversed this view, and referred to the 'clap-trap' spoken about gas warfare: 'the likelihood of an enemy using this "missile" is remote, because high explosive and incendiary bombs are more effective', and he was perfectly correct.[31]

Fuller's friendship with Liddell Hart had already undergone some strains in the late 1920s, and by the mid-1930s the pressure on it was so great that the bonds of friendship snapped (temporarily as it turned out). The fundamental cause was Fuller's fascism. The full extent of Liddell Hart's abhorrence of this creed can be gauged by a private reflection written in 1937; but he laid aside these feelings and continued to champion Fuller's cause with an admirable pertinacity considering the circumstances. 'I wish you would give me bigger scope by writing something fresh on mechanized warfare', he wrote in 1937, 'especially now that armies are busy trying to mechanize.' In truth Fuller had lost interest in armoured warfare. *Towards Armageddon* disappointed Liddell Hart because whereas 'in the Army . . . Fuller is essentially liberal-minded. Outside it he advocates the very authoritarianism, and encourages the very attitude which forced him out . . . to the Army's loss.' He could not understand why a man who claimed to value free discussion wanted to muzzle representative institutions, and how could this be reconciled with his attitude to liberalizing training methods? In *Towards Armageddon* Fuller attacked close order drill 'because it relieves a man of the necessity of thinking at all'. Liddell Hart scribbled in his copy, 'like Fascism!' It was all very well Fuller praising the 'intellectual freedom' he found in Berlin under the Nazis, but he agreed with the regime; what if he disagreed? Liddell Hart was convinced that the only result of authoritarianism would be the growth of 'the familiar type which tried to suppress your light and eventually drove you out of the Army'. With cruel irony he claimed that under the Nazi system 'You would have been in prison long ago under such laws.' This was the last letter they were to exchange for five years.[32]

The naivety and inconsistencies of Fuller's fascism may be put down to the possibility that his political adventures were no more successful than those of other professional soldiers. For this reason, *The First of the League Wars* and *Towards Armageddon* are among the most difficult of his books to appraise. They do contain interesting insights, though they are also riddled with pro-fascist propaganda and anti-semitic gibes which, as North pointed out, 'cheapens your argument'. In a way Fuller was nonetheless proved right. The Second World War was to show that 'today war is far too complex for any one man to handle', and that its preparation would have to be 'total', but his perception of this trend was flawed by an ability to see that conscription and the 'horde army' were an inevitable concomitant of the Warfare State. To conscript the nation's civil resources without conscripting its military resources was a contradiction in terms. Fuller's flirtation

with fascism had one final unfortunate consequence. His visits to
Nazi Germany had so impressed him that he was deluded into
thinking that the Nazis had really introduced a 'scientific' state.
Nothing could be further from the truth. Throughout the Second
World War Fuller mistook the character of Britain's adversaries;
he gave them the benefit of the doubt when they did not deserve
it.[33]

9

'A Watcher of War': Critic of the Second World War, 1939–66

These are the words of a watcher of war and that is the sole significance of the title [of *Watchwords* (1944)].

Reflection scribbled in FP IV/4/63

Really I could not stick another dose of Monty [at the 1953 Cambrai dinner], but naturally I gave no hint of this [in declining his invitation]. Last night L.H. called up and asked whether I was dying? Reply – very slowly!

Fuller to Martel, 3 December 1953, Martel Papers
P242/GQM/6/3b

The Second World War was the most significant upheaval of the twentieth century. In terms of casualties, destruction and political results this war was of greater moment than the First World War. It was natural that Fuller, a journalist of great ability, would focus on its leading issues, discuss the validity of the policies pursued in his inimitable manner and their relation to the evolution of his own theories. This chapter discusses Fuller's final contribution to military thought, especially in connection with the conduct of the Second World War. Fuller was a pioneer of the 'revisionist' view of the war, one which has not yet received much scholarly attention. There are very few new ideas in Fuller's books published after 1939, but there were some interesting modifications which show him coming to terms with the reality of war. His theories were thus refined and placed into a historical perspective. Increasingly during this period Fuller devoted himself to a study of history. This important contribution to historical study has not been probed in any detail in this chapter, but it does discuss how Fuller again used history to buttress his theories and justify his prescience, which was increasingly acknowledged as the peace so dearly bought in 1945 degenerated into 'Cold War'. His writings are a signal tribute to Fuller's consistency. There may be nothing more corrupting than coming to terms with the 'establishment', but Fuller could claim that 'they' had come to terms with him. Consequently, his writings stand out in bold relief and reveal his strengths and weaknesses as a military thinker.

Fuller's reputation as a military commentator had undergone a not undeserved decline in the years 1938–40. His volumes on *Decisive Battles* appeared shortly after Britain declared war on Germany, and although his accounts of the individual battles were first rate, it was fortunate for Fuller's reputation as a historian that most of the stock of this book was destroyed during the 'Blitz'. The quality of the historical writing is obscured by a welter of polemical matter – a shrill fascist interpretation of history. Fuller maintained his close contacts with Sir Oswald Mosley and lunched with him in June 1940 shortly before the issue of Defence Regulation 18b, an Order in Council empowering the Home Secretary to detain any person who gave 'reasonable cause' that he was involved in 'acts prejudicial to the public safety or the defence of the realm'. As a result Mosley (and then later Lady Mosley) and 747 other members of the BUF (though not Fuller) were arrested. It was probably his membership of the BUF that scuttled his chances of being re-employed by the Army. Fuller was not arrested thanks to Churchill's generosity, but his activities were closely scrutinized by MI5. In 1941 General Sir Alan Brooke, C-in-C Home Forces, interviewed the 'Director of Security to discuss Boney Fuller's Nazi activities with him'. Brooke concluded, 'I cannot believe that he has any unpatriotic intentions.' Fuller had brought this surveillance on himself. His anti-semitic article, 'The Cancer of Europe', was reprinted in *Die Aktion*, and the Nazis made propaganda use of indiscreet comments in another article on the Jewish influence over British foreign policy. The blots on Fuller's copybook were more than faint smudges.[1]

The quality of the works that followed *Decisive Battles*, *Machine Warfare* (1942), *The Decisive Battles of the United States* (1942), *Watchwords* (1944) and *Thunderbolts* (1946) did much to retrieve Fuller's besmirched reputation. *The Decisive Battles of the United States* formed a half-way mark between the discordant fascist overtones of the original *Decisive Battles* and the broader, more mature treatment of the later three volumes. *Machine Warfare*, though imbued with an irritating self-justificatory tone, was a valuable preparation for his more extended study, *The Second World War, 1939–1945* (1948). Liddell Hart thought *Machine Warfare* 'one of the most significant' books that Fuller had yet produced. He did not agree. 'Personally, I was not very pleased with the book. There was nothing much new in it, and writing sense on the war is all but impossible, and I am afraid will be for several years after its conclusion.' This judgement was too severe. Fuller conveyed successfully the all-important message: 'War today is total, therefore it includes everything.' Combatants would have to understand that there was an ethic of war, a science of war, an economics of war, a mechanics of war, and an art of war, just as their equivalents governed life in peacetime. 'War is not fisticuffs only, because war is no more and no less than living violently instead of argumentatively.'[2]

Machine Warfare, *Watchwords* and *Thunderbolts* show Fuller attempting to come to terms with the deficiencies of his own thinking and adapting it accordingly. He was always inclined to underrate the value of the last two books – selections of press articles. 'I send you this little book', he joked with Liddell Hart about *Thunderbolts*, 'which has one thing remarkable about it. It is that I succeeded in finding a publisher to put his name to it'. Yet these witty and lucid essays provided an ideal forum for refining his ideas. He now affirmed that the power of naval blockade was declining relatively to land power. He also acknowledged the great difficulties facing amphibious operations when mounted against an occupied shore. His ideas on strategic bombing were completely transformed – their fourth and final change. He now understood that repeated bombing attacks tended to lose their psychological potency. Their only effect, he predicted, would be the eventual scattering of German factories. Only persistent bombing of all cities could guarantee success. 'But intermittent bombing of a few centres at a time is morally useless, for panic . . . is purely local. Neighbouring towns are unaffected, and when their turn comes those previously bombed have recovered their nerve.' When criticizing the apostles of airpower who had exaggerated the power of the bomber, he failed to mention himself.[3]

These three books also develop the thesis that the tactical elements which had contributed so decisively to the success of armoured warfare in the years 1939–41 were breaking down. A new weapon or at least a new tactical system was required to reinstate mobility. In *Machine Warfare* Fuller congratulated himself on the grounds that 'If in my writings on the character of present day warfare I have shown precision, it is not because I am clairvoyant, but because I saw in mobility, which I prefer to call "velocity", the key to both offensive and defensive operations of war and refused to consider either *per se*.' The Allies had fallen into this trap and Fuller branded the Maginot Line the 'tombstone of France'. Despite his praise for the German General Staff, he contended that the Germans had been unable to secure a decisive victory because they had failed to think through their tactics. Before Operation 'Barbarossa' they had neglected to ensure that their defensive means were as strong as their offensive power; as the Panzer Divisions lacked motorized holding troops, the Russian armies, though mauled, had escaped, and the German gamble on bringing the first mobile phase of the war to a close had failed. A diminution in the velocity of war would inevitably follow.[4]

Fuller still maintained that the main strength of the tank rested in its power 'to attack the credulity of its enemy, his nerves and his morale'; and that the Germans had shown 'that *velocity of attack is more important than methodical preparation*'. The British Army had failed to learn this lesson and 'ever since the Battle of El Alamein we have jumped straight back to those [tactics] of 1916–17 – the mass artillery battles of the last war'. He roundly criticized the bombardment of an unguarded shore before the Anzio landings in January 1944 as typical of methods which sacrificed mobility for weight of metal; it 'would enormously damage port facilities and the shore-line, and in consequence delay disembarkation'. The revival of mobility demanded more than simply a return to the 'old and familiar fire tactics of the last war'.[5]

In *The Second World War* Fuller dovetailed his earlier discussion into an analysis of the breakdown, as he saw it, of the vital relationship between grand strategy and grand tactics – the end and the means. In *The Foundations of the Science of War* Fuller had predicted that this relationship must become closer for war to retain any utility. This was a most stimulating and original approach and distinguished Fuller's critical and provocative analysis from the more bland and pedestrian accounts of his contemporaries. It had the additional advantage of ensuring that Fuller's book gave sufficient space to a discussion of tactical developments. Too often books on the Second World War detail the movements of formations about the battlefield and give space to strategical commentary without assessing the manner in which the war *was actually fought*. On the tactical level, *The Second World War* can still be read with profit even though much also has dated given the paucity of the source material at Fuller's disposal, the opening of the archives, and the completion of numerous and substantial official histories. The book is also a fine example of Fuller's ability to digest and cogently organize his material into a convincing and rounded whole. The argument fits together easily and readably.

It is nevertheless important to consider some of Fuller's assumptions about the character of the war. In June 1942 Fuller and Liddell Hart had patched up their differences. After the first meeting since their estrangement in 1936 Liddell Hart was pleased to see Fuller 'still remarkably clear-headed, shrewd and perceptive', but noticed 'a curious psychological symptom' as Fuller 'worked himself up almost into a frenzy in discussing various foolishnesses of Government policy – thumping the arm of his chair, and repeating himself in a risingly strident tone'. Fuller can hardly be classed as an unbiased student of the war. 'I have reason to believe that history will one day prove me right', he wrote after that meeting, 'when I say that our guarantee to Poland in 1939 was given in order to render war absolutely inevitable . . . history's dictum will be that it was we and not he [Hitler] . . . who detonated the present conflict.' And Fuller still refused to commit himself in 1942 as to the result of the war.[6]

He continued to believe – like Mosley, Lloyd George and Liddell Hart – that 'it would have been better for Europe and ourselves had we come to terms with Hitler in the summer of 1940'. Churchill's determination to fight on had rendered a settlement impossible and the war had become 'a police court operation' in which policy was negated and transformed into 'a hangman's job'. 'The war as it is being run', he wrote acidly in 1942, 'is just a vast Bedlam with W[inston] C[hurchill] as its glamour boy: a kind of mad hatter, who one day appears as a cow puncher and the next as an Air Commodore . . . to many the war is a Hollywood show'; 'Democracies should never go to war'.[7]

It is difficult to explain the venom behind these remarks. Throughout the 1930s Churchill, the champion of rearmament, had held a high place in Fuller's esteem. As a pioneer of the tank he was one of the few men to emerge from Fuller's *Memoirs* with credit. In 1937 he believed that Churchill was one of the 'two most energetic politicians in the country'. The other, of course, was Sir Oswald Mosley. Churchill continued to interest himself in Fuller's ideas but within a decade this relationship had changed drastically. 'That man, when he gets into the next world – basement or attic, will wreck it', he wrote of Churchill in 1946. 'His greatest claim to history is that he is the greatest mountebank since Nero.' Repeating a similar claim to Liddell Hart three years later, Fuller explained that when Churchill particularly annoyed him, 'to relieve my feelings I returned to my Suetonius. Like Nero he is an expert in somersaults . . . in short a highly popular clown, who in the Press has been transformed into a supreme artist.' Perhaps what caught Fuller's eye was Suetonius's comment that Nero (like Churchill) had a thirst for popularity and was prone to 'jealousy of men who caught the public eye by any means whatsoever'. It is striking testimony to the perversity of Fuller's judgement that he supported Churchill during his years in the wilderness, when he was mocked and despised, and yet denigrated him when he was applauded as the saviour of his country.[8]

Emphasis cannot be given too strongly to this important feature of Fuller's personality. He had a temperamental aversion to siding with the popular view on any subject, insisting instead on the minority position. 'I have just finished a history of the war', he wrote in 1947. 'In part at least a psychological study of the folly of man.' There was a strong streak of intellectual sadism in Fuller's make-up. He enjoyed attacking as idiotic and fraudulent the achievements of the Second World War – Great Britain's last and 'finest' hour as a great power. Some grounds did exist for treating with scepticism General Eisenhower's claim to preside over 'near perfection in Allied conduct of operations' in North West Europe 1944–5. Yet Fuller took this critical stance to extremes. Though his strictures make for stimulating reading, some of them need to be treated with caution. 'Really', he burst out in 1948, 'I think, God intends that this country should destroy itself – it is seething with bloody fools.' This criticism was one sided. Fuller never entirely recognized the Nazi regime for what it was. Consequently, his intellectual consistency became wrapped up – sometimes unconsciously – in defending or glossing over the evils of a regime for which he had expressed admiration some years earlier.[9]

There is another factor to be taken into account. General

Trythall rightly suggests that, notwithstanding Fuller's fascist bias, his views on the Second World War 'have come to represent today the balance of informed Western judgement'. This kind of praise however raises some difficulties. The debate over the conduct of the Second World War has become enmeshed in the controversy over the origins of the Cold War. Fuller was an incisive contributor to the Cold War debate; as ever, his histories had an underlying didactic purpose. The language of the Cold War provided Fuller with plentiful retrospective justification for his earlier warnings, but this language had a specific and highly polemical intent. It is therefore a dangerous guide when attempting to assess the validity of his prognosis. The Second World War must be treated on its own terms. The shibboleths or slogans of the Cold War no longer provide their own justification.[10]

The issue lying at the heart of Fuller's criticism of the breakdown between the vital connection linking grand strategy and grand tactics was the announcement at the Casablanca Conference in 1943 that the Allies would seek nothing less than the unconditional surrender of the Axis Powers. This policy failed to fill the gap between the conduct of military operations and the overall, rather idealistic aims the Allies had set themselves. Fuller claimed, in 1943, that 'though our aims must be fixed, as they are in the Atlantic Charter, our means of attaining them must be as flexible as possible'. Thus as 'circumstances are always changing, our means must fit them as they change, and our means are all the methods we employ in defeating the enemy – military, economic, political, moral, etc'. But unconditional surrender was a rigid doctrine which undercut the psychological factor, stimulated resistance and increased the amount of fighting required to defeat the enemy. As Fuller claimed, 'though the laws . . . of war recognize the unconditional surrender of armies and fortresses, they do not contemplate or legislate for the unconditional surrender of an entire nation'.[11]

Fuller considered that policy should be creative and not destructive in intention. 'Purely destructive wars', he wrote in 1943, 'have no real aim outside destroying the enemy, and such a climax is not necessarily synonymous to winning the war.' Indeed a year later he held that 'today the foundations of World War III are being inevitably laid'. In subsequent years Fuller developed this theme. With one eye on the ensuing Soviet domination of Eastern Europe, Fuller pointed out in 1948 that in order to substantiate

the somewhat nebulous hopes that had been invested in the
Atlantic Charter of 1941, the Allies should have taken the
opportunity after the Axis defeat in North Africa and Stalingrad to
'elaborate its clauses into terms of peace profitable to the Allied
Powers'. This moment had been bungled and, as 'no great power
could with dignity and honour to itself' comply with the demands
of unconditional surrender, the war had to be fought to the
finish, becoming almost religious in intensity. Once German
power was destroyed, Fuller concluded, the Soviet Union was left
as 'the greatest military power in Europe, and, therefore, would
dominate Europe . . . the replacement of Nazi tyranny by an even
more barbarous despotism'.[12]

Fuller's outspoken denunciation of unconditional surrender
formed part of a general (and largely right wing) revisionist view
of the war, as exemplified by Hanson W. Baldwin's *Great Mistakes
of the War* (1950) and Chester Wilmot's *The Struggle for Europe*
(1952). Fuller argued forcefully that, by refusing to discriminate
between Nazis and anti-Nazis, 'unconditional surrender crippled
opposition to Hitler within Germany and, like a blood transfusion,
gave two years of further life to the war'. Unconditional surrender
rested on the questionable assumption that there was no
reasonable alternative to the Nazi Party as the government of
Germany. Both Roosevelt and Churchill habitually referred to the
German General Staff as inveterate warmongers, interchangeable
with the Nazis, subscribing to the commonplace of the time that
Nazism was merely a reflection of Prussian 'militarism'. At
Casablanca Roosevelt and Churchill revealed themselves as victims
of their own propaganda. Both Allied leaders continued to display
ignorance of the anti-Nazi resistance. Whether any firm political
agreement with the resistance was possible is debatable, but the
effort was worth pursuing. The military dimension of German
resistance was wholly neglected: encouragement would have
promoted a military revolt which, whether successful or not,
could have convulsed Germany's 'inner front' and enfeebled
her resistance. Fuller's criticisms that the Allied leaders revealed little psychological insight, on this score, seem well
founded.[13]

Fuller and other revisionists are vulnerable themselves to
criticism because they too readily assume that the war was
obviously won by 1943. It did not seem that way to contemporaries
who lacked their benefit of hindsight. The Battle of the Atlantic

had still to be won and the tremendous problems involved in planning and executing a series of complex amphibious operations had yet to be surmounted. Thus defenders of unconditional surrender claim with some justice that the policy fitted the short-term needs of the Grand Alliance, papered over differences and allowed its members to concentrate on winning the war. On the other hand, treating 'the war' as a thing in itself, and the refusal to offer the Germans terms, increased the amount of fighting the Alliance had to undertake. Whatever the effect of the policy on the German people, and views on this question diverge, the resuscitation of the German war effort after Stalingrad was not inevitable. The German people had not shown any great enthusiasm for the war in 1939 and they were not charmed out of their indifference by the great victories of 1939–41. An opportunity was presented to launch a psychological offensive at the end of 1942 but the German resistance, left to its own devices, was crushed after the ill-fated July Plot of 1944.[14]

Despite these points the issue was by no means as clear as Fuller would have us believe. His account of both the Italian and Japanese surrenders is too dogmatic and tendentious to carry complete conviction. The same may also be said of the other dimension of Fuller's attack on the unremunerative, expanding scope of war, his indictment of strategic bombing, especially the doctrine of 'area bombing' of German cities. In his opinion this not only wasted finite resources but had little appreciable effect on German war production, which reached its peak as the bombing reached a crescendo in 1944. He also argued that strategic bombing did not truly become strategic until March 1944, when the French railways became primary bombing targets, as their destruction interrupted German military movements. These claims can be qualified. The dispersal of German factories prevented them from reaping the full fruits of economies of scale, reduced their efficiency and led to a shortage of skilled labour. In addition, a major proportion of military resources was diverted into anti-aircraft defence. It is possible to suggest that the cessation of strategic bombing would have allowed the Germans to field a more powerful army and rendered the Battle of Normandy more costly.[15]

This argument can be turned on its head. If the vastly superior resources of the Allies had been poured into the creation of even larger armies, a wide measure of superiority would have been assured. Further, there was no direct link between the size of German war production and the efficiency of its armies. In 1944–5 their resources were so dissipated that new produciton was only sufficient to replace losses in the field. An overweening faith in strategic bombing introduced an inflexibility into Allied planning, but critics of such bombing did not demand complete cessation, only the readjustment of its objectives. Communications and sources of energy rather than the bombed out suburbs of German cities should have become prime targets. As Fuller wrote, 'the economic attack only became a true strategic operation of war when it was directed against the sources of industrial and military energy and the means of distribution'. This conclusion has been upheld by recent historians. Fuller asserted instead the true strategic value – complementary to land power – of sea power as the true key to victory, and down-played air power.[16]

Strategic bombing without reference to the grand strategic aim contributed to a drastic decline in ethical values. 'In sheer barbarity we can advance no further, Fuller wrote in 1946, 'unless in the next World War the inhabitants of entire countries are exterminated.' Fuller perhaps downplayed the desperation that sprang from Nazi ruthlessness; it takes both sides to limit a war, and it was, after all, the democracies that faced extermination in 1940. In such circumstances total war demands the subordination of politics, economics and ethics to the fulfilment of strategy. Nevertheless the means must justify the end in the sense that they must have a connection with the object of the war, that they should not negate it, and the strategic utility of the means must warrant the massive investment. None of these conditions was met by strategic bombing. The emotional desire to bomb anything rather than nothing, though understandable, was a fragile basis on which to found policy, as were the development of Bomber Command into virtually a private army and the intellectual arrogance displayed by its leaders.[17]

The increasing scale of the Bomber Offensive was the product of an adjustment of initially limited ends to fit an expanding means and new weapons. Consequently, little effort was made to fill a gap in Bomber Command thinking; it never realized that incessant bombing, far from provoking a collapse of the inner front, actually tended to reinforce it and strengthened the hand of the Nazi Party in rallying support for the war. Strategic bombing neither contributed to an economic grand strategy nor, because it stimulated rather than broke down resistance, to a sound grand tactics.[18]

This pattern of an expanding destructive scope at the strategic level, coupled with an uneconomic grand tactics, was found increasingly also in the war on land. Sluggish grand tactics emerged during the Italian campaign. Fuller showed that tactical bombing in the mountains was of little value because it destroyed vital communications and hampered movement; when towns and villages were entered the troops 'had to spend hours clearing away the rubble in order to continue the advance. Our own bombing was piling up obstacles in the way of the advance of our ground forces.' 'Colossal cracks' – a combination of artillery fire and aerial bombing – simply transferred 'the psychology of strategic bombing from the enemy's cities to the battlefield.' The Allies did not draw the important conclusion that defenders could not be stunned by firepower alone. Thus in 1944, though the strategic conception and execution of Operation 'Overlord' were brilliant, 'the insistence on attempting to achieve tactical mobility by means of "colossal cracks" was asinine'.[19]

Though these criticisms are on the whole well founded, it should also be recognized that Fuller himself was partly to blame for a drift of thought which tended to denigrate the need for massed artillery bombardments. Montgomery had reinstated these as an important prelude to the advance. His action however does not excuse clumsy tactics that hampered the pursuit. Although Montgomery's defenders are prepared to admit that 'the resultant mass of debris took hours, if not days to clear in order to drive a way through. Therefore any prospect of rapidly exploiting the situation was out of the question', they still argued that 'colossal cracks' were justified on the grounds that they boosted infantry morale. These arguments do not justify the exception as a rule; tactics should never follow a 'routine'. Montgomery's chief of staff did have severe doubts about a policy that took 'a sledgehammer to crack a nut', believing that the destruction caused was excessive and indiscriminate.[20]

The evidence therefore supports Fuller's case in principle for supposing that new weapons rather than increased weight of fire could reinstate mobility. Novelty could have been provided, in Fuller's view, by Canal Defence Lights (CDLs), armoured vehicles capable of blinding the enemy with flickering light produced by an automatic movement of a shutter across an aperture of light.

'Why this novel and powerful weapon was never used is a mystery', he complained in *The Second World War*, '. . . it would have solved the tactical problem, which was never efficiently and seldom effectively solved by "colossal cracks", and thereby have shortened the war by months.' Fuller had been involved with CDLs since August 1933, urging them on a not unsympathetic CIGS, Field Marshal Sir Cyril Deverell, in 1937. By the summer of 1939 a special CDL turret had been developed and a training school set up. In *Lectures on FSR III*, Fuller, like Clausewitz, underlined the practical difficulties of night operations. Experience in both the Boer and the First World Wars had taught him than any night operation was 'a somewhat tricky undertaking'; he pointed out that 'in 1914–18 tanks were helpless in the dark', and thus it was rather unfair of Liddell Hart to suggest that he had neglected night operations. 'A large-scale night attack over open country is all very well; but try one in Surrey without a moon. The darker the night the better with CDLs.'[21]

In *The Second World War* Fuller denounced the 'conservatism of the military mind' and bemoaned the difficulties of getting revolutionary new weapons adopted in wartime – hardly a new theme in his writing. He was convinced that CDLs could have brought the Battle of Normandy to a decisive conclusion during the closing of the Falaise Gap in August 1944. They 'enabled the *blitz* attack to be carried out at night-time and in conditions far more favourable to the attacker than could possibly be found in daylight'. He also came to the conclusion that Montgomery had aimed to break out during Operations 'Goodwood' and 'Epsom' in July 1944, which he later claimed were simply holding operations while the Americans broke out on the right flank, 'and I think he could have,' added Fuller, 'had he used CDL tanks'.[22]

This is the case for the prosecution. Fuller's charge that 'blimpish' blockheadedness prevented any use of this weapon is exaggerated. The overwhelming impression gained from post-war evidence is that senior officers viewed CDLs sympathetically. 'I thought the idea promising, encouraged their use, but they never seemed to take on', recalled Alan Brooke. Alexander also favoured them, though he noted their weaknesses, especially a limited capacity for movement across open country. Lieutenant General Sir Archibald Nye, formerly VCIGs, underlined the administrative difficulties: as the amount 'which we could land daily [in Normandy] was very limited; and every ton was required for vital maintenance, . . . this factor alone must have put CDLs a long way back in the programme'. General Anderson summed up for the defence: 'The invention theatrically had great possibilities but practically was disappointing.' When the lights were switched on 'Deep shadow was cast by very small inequalities of the ground and in some cases these provided very effective help to a man in a trench . . . [the] light itself was not really completely blinding until it came close up – say 100 yards.'[23]

Anderson may have exaggerated these difficulties, but it may be doubted whether CDLs could have provided success on the scale claimed by Fuller. The case for using them remains unproven. It was true that Montgomery 'had no use for CDLs' but it is only fair to add that Hobart, an early tank pioneer, grew sceptical about their value also. Fuller may have had some grounds for criticizing Montgomery's caution in Normandy. Operation 'Totalize', mounted by Lieutenant General Symonds's 2nd Canadian Corps in July 1944, showed that the fundamental principles of the CDL night attack using artificial light were sound (though they were not used), and that the resulting confusion permitted the Canadians to breach the German defensive system. This point must be balanced however by knowledge that CDLs were wholly dependent on gaining surprise, and 'its value will be considerably reduced in view of the comparatively simple counter-measures necessary to neutralize its effects'. If Anderson was right and CDLs could only be used once, then subsequent operations courted considerable risk. If an enemy retaliated with searchlights of his own, or even smokescreens, then CDL effectiveness was greatly reduced. The only other evidence available of the military use of bright light at night underlines this element of risk. In 1945 the Russians used 140 searchlights in their final attack on Berlin. General Chuikov, responsible for the assault, thought them 'an actual nuisance'. The beam of light could not penetrate dust and smoke which reflected glare and silhouetted the attacking infantry. Confusion was heightened when the lights were switched off and then, because of conflicting orders, switched on again; the alternation of blinding light and complete darkness left the troops night blind. Such methods were just as capable of creating panic and confusion among the attackers as of hurling the defenders into disarray.[24]

Fuller's arguments on the need to reinstate mobility through the introduction of new weapons brought to the fore once more the persistent tension in his thinking between his notion of economy of force and velocity. Many of his strictures seem justified. The conduct of the Battle of Normandy on the British side was frequently lacking in imagination, flat-footed, with an excessive adherence, as in the First World War, to 'phase lines', which bore little connection to tactical conditions prevailing on the ground. Too many conferences hamstrung movement; British forces, as two historians have argued, 'always tended to organize their movements according to the text-books and official manuals'. Fuller pointed out in 1940 that the Germans realized that 'velocity demands the *preservation* of communications', therefore they cleared the roads with machine gun fire and not bombs. 'Even should technical superiority be so overwhelming that by bludgeon alone an enemy can be rendered insensible, unless warfare is to become purely ironmongering, the artist is still necessary.'[25]

The special conditions and limited resources of 1939–41 upheld this generalization, but the escalation of the war after 1942 rendered it a rather more dubious proposition. The experience of the CDL confirms *in principle* that new weapons might reduce the tension between economy of force and velocity, but whether CDLs could have destroyed the German Army totally in one battle is mere speculation. The better trained the Germans, the more difficult it was to mount successful envelopments. They fought with fanaticism in 1944–5 and manoeuvre lacked the moral effect achieved four years earlier. The only antidote the Allies found to German fanaticism was firepower, though they probably deployed this with excessive zeal and insufficient tactical subtlety. Fuller also claimed that a more efficient use of air power would have enhanced mobility. *'That, once superiority in the air is assured, the primary military purpose of aircraft in war lies in the logistical and not in the tactical sphere.'* The foolishness of the Allies in not thinking through their grand strategical and grand tactical problems was never more strikingly evident. As an aircraft 'is the ideal supply transporter when cost does not enter into the question', if fewer bombers had been built and more supply aircraft, then the pursuit could have been sustained after the Battle of Normandy, 'and its flanks could have been protected by aircraft, as Patton's right flank had been in his advance on Paris'.[26]

This is an attractive line of argument, though it typifies Fuller's sometimes cavalier attitude to logistical problems. He never seems to have understood that demands of the mass production economy curtailed strategical opportunism and that sudden changes in requirements could dislocate production. In any event Fuller had failed to take into account that air supply had important implications which cast some doubt on the efficacy of strategic paralysis. Troops supplied from the air, for instance, were less prone to be paralysed by deep penetrations; enveloped troops could co-operate efficiently with reserves to seal off the kind of penetration favoured by Fuller. Technological change was just as likely to undermine as to promote the cherished assumptions of the classical school. At the tactical level, why should Montgomery have courted defeat by fielding CDLs when he could save men's lives – less efficiently perhaps, but save them all the same – with high explosives? Similarly, at the strategic level, though there are strong grounds for questioning the wisdom of Eisenhower's preferred strategy of a 'broad front' advance into Germany in 1944, Fuller's complaint that it was a faulty, overly cautious strategem which violated the classical principles of war, missed one important point: these principles may be disregarded (though not with impunity, as the riposte delivered by the Germans at the Battle of the Ardennes in December 1944 showed) if the material resources of one belligerent so overwhelm those of the other as to justify the risk. This is another feature of Fuller's pre-war thinking which was not completely reconciled by his post-war adjustments.[27]

Fuller's view of the breakdown in grand strategical and grand tactical relationships remained his main preoccupation for the rest of his life. 'War to be a sane political instrument demands a sane political end, and to be attainable that end must be strategically possible.' This central assumption that strategy must be subordinated to policy, combining practicality with restraint, marks Fuller out as a leading contributor to the so-called 'realist' school. Including American theorists like George F. Kennan, the ideas of this group gained wide currency in the 1950s. In his first post-war book, *Armament and History* (1946), Fuller was forced to adapt his 'realist' thinking to the dropping of the atomic bomb. This he accomplished with ease. He demonstrated that nuclear weapons were in line with his prediction that weapon development involved the removal of the human element, 'intellect alone remaining'. Hence it reversed the law of military development as now war was the 'environment to which civilization must be adapted in order to survive'. Military research had now expanded to such an extent that 'not only will progress in armament be stupendous, but its influence on civil industry will be equally so'. Thus 'as technology advances, militarism advances too'. Future wars would become even more destructive because intense weapon development by the superpowers diminished the decisiveness of new weapons, as striking advances would soon be imitated. For this reason Fuller predicted that the Japanese attack on Pearl Harbor was 'likely to become the classic example of the declaration of future wars'.[28]

Armament and History expanded on the themes first rehearsed in *The Dragon's Teeth* and which received their fullest treatment in *The Decisive Battles of the Western World*. Fuller here argued with great breadth of vision that war had been 'the greatest catalytic in history' and 'the inventiveness which has always been stimulated by war has gone far to foster culture'. The brilliance of Fuller's historical writing has led some writers to suggest that 'Fuller the historian has influenced Fuller the theorist of war.' This is not the case. Fuller's historical writing was undertaken to support his military theories and not *vice versa*. He worked hard on *The Decisive Battles of the Western World*. As he informed Starr, it was 'really a military history of the Western World from beginning to end and the American edition . . . bears this title . . . it has taken me years longer than I calculated for.' Yet as the third volume concluded in bleak and sombre pessimism, Fuller's purpose became evident. With the arrival of the Red Army on the Elbe after the defeat of Nazi Germany in 1945, one thousand years of European history had been rolled back. The follies of 'total war' were laid bare. What Kitson Clark says of Macaulay seems apposite of Fuller: 'he was eclectic, undiscriminating and at times inaccurate in his use of evidence, and his prejudices are obvious'.[29]

It was central to the realist critique of the conduct of total war in the twentieth century that democratic statesmen had neglected the opportunities presented by the political, economic and psychological attack. In the future Fuller anticipated that these weapons would acquire an even greater value; therefore their true import must be understood. As smaller countries like Scandinavia and the Low Countries were tempted into neutrality, the Soviet Union would absorb into its sphere of influence the Baltic States and the Balkans,

not only to add to the strength of the Soviets, but to deprive

Europe as a whole of strength to wage war against the Soviets. Thus it comes about that it is not so much unattackable frontiers which the greater powers are now seeking to establish, as ever-increasing armament resources – mines, oil wells, coal-fields, etc.

Another problem that soldiers would have to tackle, a product of the political and psychological factors, would be terrorism.

Instead of the human world blowing up like one immense volcano, it will be shaken to pieces by an unending series of disruptive social earthquakes, in which knuckle-dusters, tommy guns, razor blades and coshes will prove more practical though less immediately destructive than atom bombs.[30]

These points were more fully explored in *The Conduct of War, 1789–1961*. Fuller was inclined to regard this book as the most important he had written. It is indeed a remarkable *tour de force* for a man well over eighty years of age, clearly organized, economical and superbly written; it offers an invigorating and exciting experience for all new readers. Fuller modestly claimed that the book 'is little more than a *balon d'essai*; the idea underlying it is, I think, vital; the execution sketchy – a series of brief essays rather than a book'. He intended to discuss 'the impact of the changes in civilization on human conflict, and to examine these changes and trace their influence on the conduct of war'; this was a neglected area of military history 'and it is one so vast and so intricate that my study of it can be no other than an imperfect and a tentative one'. Time was hardly on Fuller's side. 'At my age I can't set out to write another *Decisive Battles* and if the book was to be of any value it had to come out now.' Laudable though the book's historical analysis undoubtedly was – the study of war not from the military vantage point but 'instead from that of the pressure of political, economic and social developments upon it' – this only lent weight to Fuller's final valedictory conclusions on the nature of war and policy.[31]

The main theme of *The Conduct of War* was that forces unleashed by the French, Industrial and Russian Revolutions had transformed the character of war so profoundly that it had become 'total'. In developing this thesis Fuller touched upon an unsettling paradox: if the democracies were so peace-loving why were they so warlike?

His answer was that their formation had coincided with the rise of nationalism. 'The motive force of democracy is not love of others, it is the hate of all outside the tribe, faction, party or nation. The "general will" predicates total war, and hate is the most puissant of recruiters.' As the introduction of unlimited war reduced its utility, Fuller believed that the only way that harmony could again be restored to the relationship between grand strategy and grand tactics would be the development of Clausewitz's concept of limited war. Thus 'directly the political factor is introduced . . . the destructive means employed to achieve a profitable end must be limited'.[32]

In *On War* Clausewitz had looked forward to a time when war would be more limited, and decried attempts by statesmen to out-do one another in violence as 'means would cease to be commensurate with ends'; thus a leader in war should use 'no greater force, and setting himself no greater military aim than would be sufficient for the achievement of his political purpose'. So, in Fuller's opinion, 'Clausewitz's outstanding contribution to military theory is his insistence on the relationship of war and policy.' Any analysis of the political aim should be made from the point of view of *policy* and not from that of the soldier, administrator or politician. Conscious of the ignorance of Clausewitz shown by British and American leaders in the Second World War, Fuller condensed his chapter on him in *The Conduct of War* into 'some five or six thousand words. If statesmen and generals cannot digest that much, they had better pack up'.[33]

Fuller was one of the few military thinkers of his generation to develop constructively and appreciatively the ideas of Clausewitz. Much of his earlier commentary had been strikingly ambivalent; after 1945 Fuller was an admirer. In *The Second World War* Fuller had taught, following Clausewitz, that grand tactics was linked to grand strategy by the line of operations, 'the direction of the plan of war which links the plan to the centre of gravity of the war'. In *The Conduct of War* Fuller convincingly showed, notwithstanding personal animus towards Churchill and occasional Cold War polemics, that the democratic leaders had failed to appreciate this relationship. Churchill was emotional and capricious; Roosevelt 'looked upon war as a lethal game rather than an instrument of policy'. During the war, Fuller contended that battles had lost their political significance which was invested insisted in the wartime conferences. Roosevelt especially overlooked the need to fashion a practicable political formula to bridge the gap between his vague, idealistic, distant aims and his military means. The mechanics of his war policy were therefore gravely at fault and quite artificially compartmentalized. Stalin on the other hand, was 'a statesman who never fell into the error of looking upon war as anything other than an instrument of policy'.[34]

Fuller's indictment of democratic methods was influenced unduly by special pleading. Allied leaders were guilty of neglecting long-term considerations for short-term expedients. There was indeed an unhealthy fascination with slogans which lessened an emphatic need to think clearly about the results of Allied military policy. Policy was distorted by sentimental attachments, such as the preposterous expectations that the United States entertained of the warmaking potential of China. Yet despite all this, Fuller failed to provide convincing evidence that dictatorships freed themselves of these eminently human failings. He had to assume that Hitler was a rational statesman whose clear-cut aims could have been reasonably satisfied. This was an egregious misreading, not only of the evidence but of the spirit of the times through which he had lived – a warning of the dangers facing an isolated intellectual deceived by his own cleverness.[35]

As for the Soviet Union, though one may be impressed by the prescience and consistency of his warnings throughout the years 1939–45 that the Soviet Union would become the strongest power in Europe, and that Stalinism would replace Hitlerism, the implementation of Fuller's remedies would have required almost superhuman qualities of foresight. 'What mattered', he quite sensibly pointed out, 'was not whether Hitler was more evil than Stalin, . . . but which of their aims was the more dangerous to the democratic way of life.' Yet this variable factor could not have been employed as a constant in British policy because Fuller had all the benefits of hindsight and could indicate when a change of side was required. And Fuller's conclusion – that Communism represented a greater danger than Nazism – so typical of realist modes of thought – occluded the issue with a hollow value judgement. As a former fascist this view could hardly carry conviction as unprejudiced. Western statesmen simply did not have the freedom of manoeuvre required to embroil Nazi Germany and Soviet Russia in a war and stand on the sidelines: 'Should Russia then be winning, Hitler would be discredited, and support could be given to Germany, and should the reverse be the case,

Germany could be invaded from the west under favourable conditions.'[36]

All these comments contributed to the widespread error of supposing that dictatorships fight wars more efficiently than democracies. Actually the opposite is the case. Great Britain and the United States mobilized their resources more fully and with a greater degree of technological and intellectual sophistication than any other belligerent. If the Soviet Union could match their commitment she could not match their sophistication. Of course, Fuller had anticipated this need to conduct war more 'scientifically', but unlike Clausewitz, whose great work had as its undertow the 'friction' inherent in war, Fuller's more disparate and, on the whole, less well integrated writings were inclined to assume that technological improvement and the co-ordination of intelligence would affect an unprecedented mental control over the forces unleashed by war. This is only partly true. 'Overlord' and the Battle of Normandy showed that such control was not beyond the bounds of reason but the political dividends flowing from this campaign were disappointingly meagre, as Fuller was at pains to point out. He forgot that in the planning of modern battles a multiplicity of factors had to be co-ordinated. Therefore the chances of something going wrong were correspondingly greater. If the increasing scale and technological sophistication of war tightened man's ability to control the course of military operations, it simultaneously loosened his grip on their outcome.[37]

War is much more resistant to the designs of the human will than Fuller was prone to believe. Tension between the military and political factors is endemic in the character of warfare. In the twentieth century the military factor has been uppermost in the thoughts of military leaders, often to the exclusion of all else. Writing of the First World War, Fuller criticized its statesmanship because, if this conflict was

> to be profitable to the victor, then it was incumbent on the members of each alliance to decide on a common policy which would direct them towards that end. Were this not done, the war must inevitably be a chaotic one, and the peace which followed it none the less so.

He was not mistaken. Yet beyond demonstrating Clausewitz's general argument, Fuller offered no advice as to how statesmen should forge such a common policy and harmonize their diverse and conflicting interests. Apart from a passionate wish to see the warmaking process imbued with more rationality and less muddle, Fuller believed that the most sensible course would follow from a realistic assessment of the various choices in accordance with each state's interest. He did not answer the question left begging by Clausewitz, namely, how could this act of realism be reconciled with alliance differences? He assumed that power was an instrument of achievement measured by reference to a set of rational aims that could be clearly set out before a war was initiated. The achievements of statesmen could be assessed by their capacity to employ power to fulfil the stated ends.[38]

It is on this score that Fuller's development of Clausewitz's theory of limited war can be shown to be sometimes wanting. In theory he was right in his prescription that 'once you have knocked your enemy out, it is wise to set him on his feet again, because the chances are that you will need his assistance in the next conflict'. That has been the burden of experience in the twentieth century; but in practice it is much more difficult to execute such a disengagement. A gap emerged in Fuller's thinking: though he was prepared to contemplate the total mobilization of a nation's resources for warmaking in peacetime – total strategy – he refused to think through the consequences of that deployment in wartime. Likewise he enthused over the beneficial consequences of a *tactical* annihilation of an enemy, but he lamented its logical conclusion, *strategical* annihilation. Prolonged attrition is implicit in Fuller's thinking, as much of *The First of the League Wars* showed; but though he could foresee the return of tactical stalemate he was less able to understand its results, not only a reduction in the velocity of war, but a reduction in its decisiveness and the foreclosing of strategical options.[39]

His resultant analysis of the Second World War, though often acute and wise, is also frequently capricious and unfair. *The Conduct of War* painted an alluring picture of Bismarck's wars, no doubt the product of Fuller's imagination, in which war aims were politically limited without ideological or economic complications. Fuller forgot to point out that the pressure of public opinion was hardly absent from these wars once the pace of operations had slowed down and the Prussians were forced to besiege Paris. Once the tactical knife loses its cutting edge, it is not always possible to keep war aims clear cut and limited.

Clausewitz's idea of an absolute war has a distinct relevance here. The tension between the military and political factors returns and the former tends to cast distorting shadows over the latter.[40]

It is perhaps too soon to come to any definite conclusions about the value of Fuller's writings on the Second World War. They do contain some effective criticisms which should not be disregarded lightly. He was perfectly correct to state categorically that 'the crux in every war centres in policy and not strategy'. His thesis that, as the technological sophistication of warmaking advances, the quality of rational thinking about its *political* nature and aims declines, is thought provoking and valuable. His corollary that it is the grand tactical link between the fighting of battles and the enforcement of the political means which is the most important in war, carries weight. If his argument that mobility should be at least commensurate with weapon-power sometimes overlooks practical difficulties, it is, on the whole, convincing. Fuller also eventually came to realize that 'manpower will be required as well as machine-power' in any future war. Throughout the Second World War and the years immediately after, he had striven to be impartial; perhaps he had tried too hard. 'War, like diseases, takes many forms', he once wrote, 'and its surgeons and physicians must apply their remedies accordingly. . . . Quackery is not only the most universal of all pestilences but also the most common that afflicts mankind.' Fuller had made a forthright and honest attempt to resist quackery.[41]

Conclusion

... no people has ever despised and distrusted the intellect and the intellectual more than the British.

Leonard Woolf. 'G. E. Moore', *Encounter*, XII (1959) p. 68

The best books, he [Winston Smith] perceived are those that tell you what you know already.

George Orwell, *Nineteen Eighty-Four* (Harmondsworth: Penguin, 1971 edn) p. 161

I am a student of war and a military critic. 'Prophet?' always amuses me. After World War I I adopted as my slogan 'Half an inch of steel will keep out half an ounce of lead'. . . . To insist that a bullet will not penetrate a bullet-proof steel plate seems to me a poor kind of prophesy.

Fuller to Sloan, 18 April 1962, FP IV/6/23i

Fuller's last years were largely devoted to the study of military history. His main achievements, *The Decisive Battles of the Western World* (3 vols, 1954–6), *The Generalship of Alexander the Great* (1958) and *Julius Caesar: Man, Soldier and Tyrant* (1965) display a maturity of judgement sometimes lacking in his earlier historical works. A deepening interest in the study of history led him at one stage to contemplate applying for the Chichele Chair in the History of War at Oxford, though he later dropped the idea. For all their quality, Fuller's historical works tend to lack the vigour and novelty of his earlier books, when he came to terms with new ideas and worked out their implications in sweeping strokes.[1]

The diversity and range of Fuller's literary output was so vast that it might assist the reader if the general drift of his thought was summarized before any general conclusions are drawn. Major General J. F. C. Fuller's significance may largely be sought in his calculation of the influence of the Industrial Revolution, in all its changing phases, on the conduct of war. In this estimate his conclusions about the character of the First World War came to play a crucial part. Tracing back the origins of the developments

217

which resulted in the stalemate of 1914–18 brought Fuller to the conclusion that war must be studied *in toto* as a branch of the social sciences. His researches reinforced the conclusions of Sir Norman Angell and I. S. Bloch: that war had lost its political utility, as 'war between the great powers is nothing more than suicide'. The scale of war had increased in proportion with the resources that industrialized states could mobilize for warmaking, and changes in tactics reflected deeper structural and social changes. Decision in battle had become more difficult and the expense of war had accordingly increased. The result was an 'increasing probability of war being brought to an end by attrition and revolution in place of by force of arms'. In this process the mobilization of public opinion and its consequent detrimental influence on the ethical decline evident during the First World War played an important part.[2]

Fuller thus confronted directly the central dilemma facing the nation state during the twentieth century – the destructiveness of war. Where Fuller parted company with Bloch was in his profound belief that an alternative existed whereby the spiral of weapon development, social change and increased destructiveness and political dislocation could be avoided – by restoring movement to the battlefield; 'for until one or both sides could move there was no possibility of a decision by arms – famine alone must be the arbiter'. The tank, gas and aircraft were indications that weapons could restore movement to the battlefield and influence the character of war. If weapon-power was substituted for manpower then the size of armies could be reduced and, as nations were transformed from rural to industrial societies at varying speeds, the instrument of relations between them – 'war itself – must change with them'. Increasingly as armies came to depend on science and technology so would they become ever more highly mechanized. Hence Fuller's expectation that greater control could be exerted over warfare (especially in its opening phase) thanks to the detailed preparation of highly skilled staffs; subtlety and manoeuvre would be restored to the battlefield and the political object of war attained economically.[3]

Such in brief was Fuller's standpoint on war. He was absolutely right to point out that the British Army lacked experience and theoretical knowledge of how to conduct a war on a national scale, and that unless institutions were created to profit from the trial and error of 1914–18 that experience would be thrown away.

In the next great war, which Fuller thought inevitable, it was likely that the lessons of the Great War would have to be relearned. Hence the stress he placed on the need for a coherent grand strategical outlook in his earliest writings on mechanized warfare. The fear lurking behind these was that once other powers began to mechanize, Britain would not have the time, as she had in 1914–16, to mobilize her resources for war. 'Unpreparedness for war is a greater incentive to its outbreak than over-preparation.' The frequency of war between the great powers would be in inverse proportion to investment in weapon development.[4]

Fuller understood that the twentieth century was a period of drastic and rapid change. The next war would change its character as dramatically as did the Great War. Even when allowance is made for his mistakes and miscalculations, Fuller nonetheless predicted accurately the character of much (though not all) of the Second World War. This conflict did witness a high level of technological development and increased mobility. The scope of these changes however was not as dramatic as Fuller had predicted, though he was justified in arguing that mechanization would completely change the relationship between military velocity, force and space. Even during the last stages of the Second World War (when attrition had set in), the Allies were able to make enormous advances and destroy vast numbers of enemy troops: El Alamein to Tunis, Kursk to Minsk, Minsk to Bucharest. Mobility did have the strategical significance attached to it by Fuller, but its tactical importance was much less clear cut. Some writers have argued that the Second World War was but a repeat performance of the First. There are certain similarities, but the determinist thesis – that the lightning victories of 1939–41 were an aberration in a general movement back towards attrition does not completely convince for the reason that a return to attrition was by no means inevitable. The British Army had been committed to two theatres which favoured mobile operations – France and Flanders and North Africa. In both these it faced catastrophic defeat and, but for good fortune and the benefits of geography (like the proximity of the Channel or the strength of the El Alamein position), might well have been destroyed in the field.[5]

The years 1939–45 *did* witness a revival in the decisiveness of battle. Mechanized forces, though they confirmed Fuller's faith in the amount of ground they could cover, were not however *grand tactically* decisive as the enemy's collapse did not inevitably follow a catastrophic defeat in the field. The strategical advantages conferred by mechanization worked against any such possibility unless the geographical conditions favoured the attacker. With the possibility of great advances being made in short periods of time military operations moved away from the centre of gravity of the war. With the exception of the Fall of France in 1940 where strategical, tactical, psychological and geographical conditions worked in such a way as to provide an optimum example of the fulfilment of Fuller's theories, defeat however disastrous could be absorbed by industrialized nation states (and Britain survived France's collapse). The Second World War did not see another Poltava among the great powers: El Alamein and Stalingrad were indeed only the 'end of the beginning'.[6]

There are, of course certain areas where Fuller can be criticized legitimately as a false prophet. New weapons did not have the overwhelming moral effect claimed by Fuller. Neither was it impossible for an inferior equipped force to defeat a better equipped one, if it was handled with determination, as Auchinleck showed before Tobruk. Mechanization did not displace men fighting on their feet – even in the 1980s. Fuller exaggerated the extent to which the human element could be removed from the battlefield. The instincts of the conservatives here (in the short term) were surer. 'Ultimately it is the man who counts, it is the man who secures victory', wrote Cavan. Armies are still built around men fighting on their feet and this is unlikely to be changed unless at some future date a great war is decided by the exchange of intercontinental projectiles.[7]

The major error in Fuller's calculations was in supposing that mechanization would reduce the size of armies. It did not lead to the formation of small, highly professional mechanized armies but the contrary – the mobilization of infantry masses. Mechanization required constant re-investment of capital to keep armoured forces up to date, but his claim in 1943 that the Germans could have been defeated in 1940 if only Britain had fielded six armoured divisions, which 'would have required some 2000 tanks' and cost 'about £40 000 000 or three days war expenses', omits however to mention the cost that would have been involved in keeping this force up to date. Tactically Fuller was right, such a stroke may well have defeated the Germans in France and in the long run preparation for war necessarily economizes on the cost of fighting a war, though it involves a degree of investment which even the richest nations find difficult to sustain in peacetime.[8]

Fuller was attracted to mechanization not only because of his experience on the tactical level in the First World War, but also because he identified himself with a school of ideas which saw the tank as an admirable means towards fulfilling a more general strategical end. Fuller was a synthetic thinker, a *synthesizer* – a typical product of an intellectual current which reached its highest pitch before 1914 – and viewed the world as governed by laws and principles. He plucked from out of the air ideas that were current at the time and welded them into something quite novel. It has been said of Francis Bacon that he 'elevated into a coherent intellectual system what had hitherto been the only partially spoken assumptions of practical men'. The same may be said of Fuller. His intellectual framework was largely taken from the work of other thinkers. His thesis that armies resembled the organs of the human body, for example, was not in itself very new. He did not invent the principles of war but he codified them in a most cogent and stimulating manner. He was not present during the birth pangs of the tank – and other minds initially more adventurous than his, not least Swinton and Martel, were more radical in formulating the earliest tank tactics. And the conclusions that Fuller drew from his study of the potential of mechanization – that new weapons would 'humanize' war – had been made, though in a cruder form, by German writers before 1914. Yet Fuller moulded from these disparate sources an eclectic and original methodology which allowed him to develop afresh classical ideas.[9]

Fuller's work transcended the empirical impressionism of earlier writers (and even of his peers like Liddell Hart) and sought to get at the heart of the matter – the 'foundations' – by seeking out a method of universal application. It could be suggested that Fuller was the prisoner of his methodology; that his passion for seeing a system in all things was limiting and forced him to construct artificial barriers and raise non-existing compartments; that method blurred reality. False arguments are hardly absent from Fuller's books. *The Foundations of the Science of War* was littered with metaphysical fancies dignified as profound, self-evident truths. Nevertheless within the context of his development as a thinker, and especially in the difficult transition from a major premise to the working out of tactical detail in the speculative field, consistent methodology was a strength rather than a weakness. The clarity of tactical commentaries like *Lectures on FSR II* and *Lectures on FSR III* is impressive because both books are the product of clear thinking and a firm intellectual base. Method accounts too for the 'invigorating' experience which so many readers comment upon – of encountering ideas advanced cogently from a perspective not previously considered. Method endowed Fuller's books with vitality. An idea is probed systematically in terms of cause and effect, and he worked hard at this process. 'I have never claimed the wisdom of Minerva, my ideas do not spring full armed from my head, how could they?' he once asked. In a lighter vein he joked, 'when I get down to a new idea I am rather like a man in bed with a pretty girl – I do not like being disturbed'. Fuller's real difficulty was that he was profligate with ideas. His powers of discrimination were sometimes less than sharp. The result was a series of hastily written books. 'I am in no doubt', he wrote to Liddell Hart, 'that you are right in saying I write books too quickly; but I can't linger over them, otherwise I never finish them at all. Besides moving about from pillar to post with a suit-case library makes things difficult'. All of his books are padded out with polemical matter. One of his best organized books, *The First of the League Wars*, was also one of his worst. His passion for presenting logical arguments had the unexpected result that his works, though they may be logical and reasoned, can hardly be described as objective; nor were they scientific.[10]

The modern reader suspects that there is something pretentious about the label that both Fuller and Liddell Hart gave to their works – 'scientific'. Any such suspicions are largely unfounded. Both men were typical of the intellectual aspirations of their age and were not unusual in believing that if only enough study could be devoted to a subject, then a student could emerge as 'scientific' and detached. Fuller was a man of pronounced personality with strong views expressed in vigorous language. In the course of things it was never likely that he would remain on the margins of controversy, expressing balanced appreciations which gave full weight to all points of view, though he sometimes deluded himself into thinking that he managed to do just that. His achievement lay in precisely the opposite direction. Fuller was, as it were, a 'stirrer' – a stirrer of debate. The range and penetration of his work was bound to attract a rain of controversy down upon his head. His perspective was clear. If readiness for war was reflected in the depth and quality of the discussion that had preceded 1914, then intellectual attitudes must be galvanized before the next war. Of the restrictions against which he chaffed at the Staff College in 1913–14, Fuller found many to condemn and few to commend. He disliked what Henry James called 'people stuffing their heads with a lot of empty catchwords', and tried to give substance to British military thinking. By comparison with the years before 1914, the debate sparked off by Fuller's ideas after 1918 (as opposed to precise recommendations) was wide, open-minded and, on the whole, fruitful. Virtually single-handed Fuller forced the General Staff to consider the place of the tank in battle. That his writings do contain errors is clear; these alone are not sufficient for doubting the overall value of his work or for underrating his stature as a thinker. Fuller will be read in the future precisely because he was prepared to take risks, was frequently outlandish in expression and rarely expressed a conventional view when there was an unconventional alternative.[11]

Fuller was eager to take such risks because he had never been taught the necessity to exert intellectual self-discipline. He enjoyed shocking soldiers of the more conventional caste. He certainly had no doubts about the extent of his ability. The First World War had taught him 'that not one man out of every thousand has any brains at all'. Lord Bryce was reputed to boast on one occasion that he had learnt how to think before he had learnt anything, and Fuller prided himself on the same attribute. He resembled Havelock Ellis: a supreme example of the late Victorian autodidact, a polymath, following in the tradition of Darwin, Spencer and Frazer, who assumed that they could take the field of all knowledge as their rightful domain. Fuller believed that he could take all knowledge about war as his domain. As a professional soldier he held that ideas should directly influence action. 'Well, why should not battles be won in the study; are not most great and worthwhile things conceived in an armchair?' Geoffrey Best stresses that this was an eighteenth-century idea, and applies the term 'publicists' to what he calls 'those learned philosophers with a practical bent' who preached to an international audience, and Fuller (and Liddell Hart) were much more than journalists in the modern sense of that term. Fuller was a guru who stimulated thought. He should not therefore be criticized on the grounds that he failed to provide exact and tidy blueprints for future action. He was a provoker of thought; a mental stimulant. In a mischievous moment Fuller once likened himself to the Spanish fly, centharides, once used as an aphrodisiac and powerful antidote to impotence.[12]

Though Fuller's methodology may be justified in broadly intellectual terms, its strictly military application must be assessed within the historical framework he set up. It was true, as Liddell Hart pointed out, that Fuller's historical knowledge was patchy and he was prone to make historical generalizations which occasionally send a shudder down the spine of the more cautious professional historian who might not share his assumptions. In 1962 he claimed that he had too much imagination to be a really good historian, and he was aware that his broad approach was hardly 'free from error'. 'The method of tackling the whole subject of war in the round is a new one, and consequently, everything I say cannot be correct.' Still, Fuller taught us to think of war in the round as a subject more than worthy of study on its own terms and in relation to other subjects. If the details of his efforts are no longer satisfying, the *general idea* is frequently sound and, moreover, conducive to further development and study. Fuller's views on the American Civil War, for example, are now received wisdom in the United States; this alone is outstanding testimony to his ability as a historian. Whatever doubts may now be aroused by Fuller's methodology, it was stimulating and thought-provoking. Though it may not be the truth, at least it provided an avenue along which truth might be sought. Havelock Ellis once said of Freud that if he 'sometimes selects a very thin thread [in tying together his ideas], he seldom fails to string pearls on it, and these have their value whether the thread snaps or not'.[13]

If considered in these terms the comparison with Freud is apt. The development of Fuller's ideas about war and society were the result of his desire to extend a tactical justification for mechanization on to a more impressive historical and philosophical plane. With this effort Fuller laid the foundations for all thinking about mechanization. For instance, the discussion of weapons within their social context was framed and discussed in terms laid down by Fuller, and with a vocabulary largely coined by him: the phrase 'line of least resistance' was popularized by him. Lindsay and Hobart accepted that Fuller had made the pioneering contribution; but Liddell Hart was more reluctant to acknowledge Fuller's greater originality – except in the most general terms.[14]

It is likely that future historians will link the names of Fuller and Liddell Hart closely together as their aims and outlook were similar – though by no means identical. Their relative merits as thinkers should thus be examined. Fuller was the more profound and original. His exploration of a given theme was more probing and systematic. Many of Liddell Hart's books were collections of previously published articles, and little effort was made to integrate them; the result is often patchy though readable, and soldiers found it easier to read a short essay rather than a longer book. Though Fuller incorporated previously published material, each of his books was a finished product despite the rush entailed in its composition. Thus while in the *Remaking of Modern Armies*, Liddell Hart referred vaguely to 'cycles' of war, he never explained or clarified what he meant. Fuller did, linking these to social and technological change and introducing the idea of the constant tactical factor. The experience of war seems to justify his line of reasoning irrespective of the method he chose to advance the argument. Liddell Hart employed Fuller's methods for his own purposes. The similarity in the approach, content and style of Fuller's *The Reformation of War* and Liddell Hart's *Paris, or the Future of War* is striking though rarely remarked upon. Similarly, *The Ghost of Napoleon*, though an individual piece of work, is patently influenced by the methodology advanced in *The Dragon's Teeth*, which Liddell Hart studied carefully.[15]

Fuller was the most original thinker who tackled the subject of mechanization; Liddell Hart was its most assiduous and persuasive advocate. Liddell Hart was also interested in mechanization because it illustrated how a certain strategical formula – the indirect approach – could be fulfilled. His view of future mechanized operations was much less detailed than Fuller's. Also Fuller's thinking became increasingly abstract. There were no 'indirect approaches' or 'British Ways in Warfare' in his writing and few attempts to develop ideas about specific policies. Eventually Fuller lost touch with mechanization and admitted in 1943 that his 'knowledge of present day details is very limited'. His practical experience had been constrained by the technological limitations of early tanks. 'In 1917–18 tank tactics were practically a ceremonial parade – Cambrai certainly was – now movement rather than drill dominates.' Finally both Fuller and Liddell Hart admired eighteenth-century classical strategists. 'Our artists scoff at Saxe and others. But logically what do we fight for? To win! And if we win with lowest casualties so much the better.' But

Fuller placed more emphasis on the need 'To destroy the enemy's strength' on the battlefield. Consequently he was more firmly in the classical mainstream of thought by upholding the importance of battle.[16]

What remains of value in Fuller's work? Why should contemporary students of war read his books? The importance of Fuller's legacy is that he expounded the central elements that compose the art of war. In any estimate of his contemporary 'relevance', the historian of ideas should at all costs avoid what was once termed the 'smugness of contemporaneity': that all that is right and good should be judged by the preoccupations of the present. Nevertheless the military historian must approach this problem because military ideas have to be applied on the battlefield and here bullets speak louder than typewriters. Given the hazardous world in which we live, Fuller's writing does give a well reasoned discussion of the problems arising from the use of increasingly destructive weapons within the international environment. Though uninterested in nuclear questions, his work has assumed a new importance with the revival of interest in conventional war. In the 1950s it was believed that classical principles of war were obsolete; or such use as they had was confined to surrogates' wars – for example, between Israel and the Arabs. The ever burgeoning presence of nuclear weapons would involve automatically their use if a war with the Soviet Union broke out on the NATO Central Front. Such calculations are now by no means so certain. Technological changes – especially the improved guidance and accuracy of a category of projectile weapons called 'precision-guided munitions' (PGMs) – has reinforced the belief that any war with the Warsaw Pact could be confined to conventional defence. It is here that Fuller's detailed analysis of likely future battles becomes useful in drawing out the implications of possible operational concepts.

Fuller's corpus embodies a sustained exploration of the basic themes involved in a study of conventional warfare, whether they be organizational, operational, or concerning training and morale. Within his work can be found a clear, if contentious, discussion of conceptual problems, involving manoeuvre, penetration, the defensive–offensive, and counter-stroke. Fuller emphasises the connection between technology, doctrine and the principles of war and suggests the correct relationship between them. It is not that Fuller's work provides all the answers to these complex questions, to suggest as much would be ridiculous, but he does enhance our understanding of them. His work has an authority which we neglect at our peril. Fuller's efforts at working out a universal method – to reduce war to a system – though flawed, now appear to have secured a vindication because the basic elements of his analysis still have utility even though the controversies in which he was once engaged are redundant.[17]

The science of war evolved by Fuller was the reflection of a general philosophical standpoint which viewed all aspects of life as part of an indivisible whole. It can only be adequately understood if related to the intellectual climate of the time. Fuller extended into the study of war the view that any division between 'art' and 'science' was artificial; war was an art, he agreed, but the methods of science could profitably be applied to it. In Fuller's case his originality is not impaired by discussing the broader aspects of the intellectual history between the wars. The military journals show conclusively that conscientious students read him and not *vice versa*. The real difficulty lies in the tools Fuller chose for his dissection of war. They appear to be already dated by 1918. Closer examination reveals this to be a superficial judgement. A stream of thought cannot be compartmentalized rigidly like a salmon ladder according to dates and historical events. The ideas which found the young Fuller so responsive before 1914 persisted strongly after 1918. Social thought in Britain between the wars was dominated by the assumptions of the 1880s and 1890s. It was no coincidence that Fuller's *The Foundations of the Science of War* was followed three years later by Julian Huxley's ambitious book, *The Science of Life*. Fuller's faith in 'science' and 'planning' reflected, in his own dogged and singular way, the preoccupations of writers in other diverse spheres.[18]

It has been observed that the inter-war years in Britain saw a wide cleavage in many professions between younger reformers and the 'old guard' – a 'generation gap' in the arts, medicine, politics and so forth, a divergence accentuated by the Great War. Fuller's example reflected these tensions within the Army. In his case they were exacerbated by anti-intellectualism. This took two main forms. The first was the damage wreaked by Fuller's reputation as a 'troublemaker'. The main objection appears to be against the kind of intellectual that he personified. Nobody would now question the veracity of Fuller's motives in resigning command of the Experimental Brigade in 1927 – though many

might question his good sense. However much his folly may be
remarked upon, the resignation was done in such a way as to
play into the hands of those who attacked certain 'junior officers
who are anxious to get on', who 'ran down' everything British in
the Army. Bonham-Carter thought Fuller's action 'utterly disloyal;
his opinion [of him]', wrote Liddell Hart, 'had dropped to zero
. . . If he [Bonham-Carter] had been CIGS he would have kicked
Fuller straight out.' Moderate progressives felt the same. The
prejudice against clever officers was mainly directed against those
who were 'too clever by half' – usually those colonels who
presumed to lecture their seniors. This problem was exacerbated
by the acute financial problems that senior officers faced, which
Fuller, consumed with enthusiasm for new ideas, overlooked. In
1919 he proposed the formation of a tank volunteer force to serve
in Russia. General Harington commented: 'Colonel Fuller's
schemes for "thinking ahead" are always interesting but he is not
faced with the problem with which we are faced, viz, to get the
best out of a very limited sum of money.' Bright ideas inevitably
lose their lustre when they lack the polish of ready money.[19]

Another objection related to Fuller's savage criticisms of British
generalship in the First World War – an example of 'disloyalty' *par
excellence*. He had no patience with the British command system
as it 'still [is] what it was thirty years ago, all intelligence,
imagination and criticism are squeezed out of it'. Critics felt that he
was just being churlish. Lord Cavan wrote, after reading *Generalship:
Its Diseases and Their Cure*, 'Your writings always deserve attention,
in fact demand it. They are provocative, which is what you want.'
Cavan however felt constrained to defend the Army against
Fuller's attacks rather than to praise his recommendations for the
future. His denunciations were at times unfair, and they diverted
and annoyed.[20]

The substance of Fuller's charges was nonetheless valid. It is
simply not enough to put British defeats before 1942 down to
material deficiencies. The real problem was one of mental outlook
and training. The Germans and the Japanese owed their initial
victories not to *materiel* but 'to a command of military skills and
virtues which the British and British-led forces opposing them
simply did not, at that stage of the war, possess to a comparable
degree'. British forces were immobile, excessively road-bound and
lacking in initiative, and Fuller had given shrill and ample warning
of these weaknesses. He can be criticized for neglecting, or at any

rate, underrating the difficulties that rapid movement would entail for the supply of modern armies. If his main point, that tracked vehicles supported by road vehicles introduced a disharmony in movement because tanks became dependent on roads, ignored some practical problems, it is theoretically sound, and suggests that not enough thought had been devoted to the character of the pursuit in the planning of operations in the Second World War and indeed after.[21]

If his analysis of the weaknesses of British forces was sound enough, it must still be recognized that his efforts at reform were self-defeating. Fuller's achievements are difficult to gauge because a fundamental unresolved problem blocked their fulfilment. There existed an unbridgeable gap between the aims he set himself and the methods he employed within *the military context*. Had Fuller been content to state the problem in the abstract in a treatise considering the influence of force on policy, his difficulties might not have been so acute; but he was not an academic and he desired to forge a link between military ideas and military action, and seemed to think that the coherence of a given body of ideas would be sufficient on their own terms as a standard bearer of reform. 'It amuses me to state what I believe to be true, but whether my audience understands me or not I do not much care, because in the end truth wins through.' *The Foundations of the Science of War* was doomed to fail because of this combination of fatalism and arrogance. Much of this book did provide a clear sighted basis for developing a general doctrine for the Army. Yet his attempt to seek out a universal method whereby to secure it seems a hopeless miscalculation. He failed to employ a language suitable for his purpose. 'Every pioneer is somewhat of a martyr, and every martyr somewhat of a firebrand who kills with ridicule as well as with reason.' Fuller never seemed to realize that 'killing' was not enough: that his acerbic manner caused resentment, while his philosophical prognostications, in the eyes of his critics, substituted nothing positive for his sarcasm; indeed they were prone to view them as a riot of conceit and self-advertisement. That Fuller realized in later life that his methods were at fault is borne out by his admission that his attempt to universalize the principles of war had been an error.[22]

It was not simply a question of philosophy as this was but a symptom of a mental posture that eschewed prudence. His writings show little understanding of the political dimension of reform, and his later efforts at political activity were little short of disastrous. There was great merit in Fuller's stimulating approach, but he never grasped that, though a statement might be challenging in its implications, his language must be guarded. Certainly the fears aroused by his tactless comments that the Tank Corps might 'swallow' the Army, obscured, for example, the great value of Fuller's concept of the defensive–offensive. The main weakness of British tactics in North Africa was the inability to grasp the relationship between mobility and protection which lay at the core of his thinking. As he summed up in his old age: 'Should the offensive have a fair chance of succeeding, I would back it; otherwise I would put my money on the defensive, and if possible on the defensive–offensive – Clausewitz's stronger form.'[23]

These difficulties aside, it should be recognized that Fuller's work is comparable with that of Clausewitz in range, ingenuity and the imagination with which he attempted to tackle the problem of war in the round, but Fuller was not, as suggested by Liddell Hart, greater than Clausewitz. His methodology has dated more quickly and his deductions have proved more transient, too hasty and of less universal application. Fuller's writings were much more hastily conceived than Clausewitz's – though nonetheless the fruit of deep thought. Fuller never had much leisure during his most productive years. His books were often written under peculiar and vexing circumstances. In 1932 Liddell Hart observed that somehow their speedy production did not do him justice. He recommended that Fuller devote 'six months, or better a year, to produce one really great book that would be worthy of you'. Fuller was too restless to accept this wise advice. Once he had retired from the Army he had to cope with a journalist's hectic schedule and pressure for hasty amendments and posturing for effect – in which Fuller indulged himself more readily than he cared to admit.[24]

Even allowing for the fact that Fuller wrote too much too quickly, he still failed to achieve the level of philosophical detachment attained by Clausewitz in *On War*. Fuller's theoretical works are too opinionated, too polemical and controversial. *The Foundations of the Science of War* was perhaps an exception, for Fuller did not clutter up the argument by scoring debating points in favour of mechanization. But even this book includes a solid dose of polemic despite its 'scientific' pretensions. Neither do Fuller's leading ideas have the same general relevance as those of Clausewitz. They were different kinds of thinkers. Fuller surmised that once the drift of technological change had been gauged, future trends in warfare could be predicted. Clausewitz made no such effort, and Fuller's prescriptions were inevitably more polemical and his conclusions, over the long run, more tentative than Clausewitz's. The prime thesis of 'Plan 1919' on which so much of his later work was founded, that an enemy's command could be psychologically dislocated, was an original and daring insight. It must also be recognized, however, that it cannot carry conviction under every circumstance that may face a commander.

'In my opinion', Fuller wrote in old age, 'Clausewitz's level is that of Copernicus, Newton and Darwin – all were cosmic geniuses who upset the world.' Though a most significant figure, Fuller does not reach that level. His genius was fissured. If a comparison is to be risked, then Fuller's work stands in relation to that of Clausewitz as Herbert Spencer's does to that of Darwin. Fuller, like Spencer, followed in the footsteps of a great master, sometimes claiming that he was an ardent disciple developing his ideas, sometimes quite misunderstanding them. He also resembled Spencer in that he was self-educated, and their prolific writings lack the essential discipline of both Darwin and Clausewitz. Fuller's overriding concern was to find ways of restoring military action as the primary instrument for bringing wars to a successful conclusion. Thus his main achievements lay in the *tactical* sphere. Other aspects of his work, such as improvements in training methods and the education of officers are worthy of the highest praise. But Fuller's treatment of tactics was so broad that he was forced to study everything else as well, and again like Spencer, an initial treatment of a narrow theme brought him to contemplate a protean one, the social aspect of man's condition. Hence his understanding of what Correlli Barnett calls 'total strategy', that thinking, planning and conduct of war should percolate every department of state and influence the lives of every individual. Fuller, certainly more than Liddell Hart, bore in mind that 'War is not merely a matter of rational disputes which can be settled legally.'

Certainly there are some, but it is so wrapped up with the

irrational – instincts, emotions, deep down life forces and death forces, that its legal control is a hopeless path to follow. . . . In my opinion restriction is the right course.

Fuller rendered a great service to military thought in drawing out the implications of the relationship between mobility, weapon-power and carrying power and the place of attrition in wars between industrialized states, though he failed to grasp the scale of future conflict. His exposition of the principles of war and such concepts as economy of force must always by qualified. It was only after 1945 that he realized the true implications of scale on the industrialization of war. These only served to reinforce the urgency of his earlier warnings, as 'a decreasing moral sense has steadily kept pace with the growth in armament, for as explosives have gone up, morality has gone down'. Richard Crossman did not exaggerate when he suggested that Fuller 'displays original and valuable insight' into the problems facing modern states and 'expounds the central problem of our time with brutal relish. In many ways he is a latter day Hobbes'.[25]

In sum Fuller was a frustrated, indeed rather cantankerous, idealist who sincerely set out to use his not inconsiderable mental gifts to better the lot of mankind. He was fundamentally a wayward spirit who defied categorization. In 1926 he wrote to Liddell Hart: 'My dear Basil the Prudent. . . . The way to enjoy life is to be an intellectual tramp.' The result of Fuller's mental wanderings was that he brought war into the mainstream of intellectual life in Britain. He laid the groundwork – the foundations – for the study of war in the modern world. Wellington once described his great adversary and Fuller's namesake, Napoleon ('Boney'), as the 'Grand Disturber'. Fuller disturbed the tranquil, if not stagnant, waters of British military thought with grand style. When his sharp and penetrating eyes closed for the last time in February 1966, less than a year after the publication of his forty-sixth book, *Julius Caesar*, Fuller's most enduring legacy was bequeathing to us the very tools with which we can dissect his life work.[26]

Notes and References

Introduction

1. J. Terraine, 'The RAF in World War II: Lessons for Today?', RUSI *Journal*, 130 (1985) p. 10.
2. Tacitus, *The Annals of Imperial Rome* (Harmondsworth: Penguin, 1980), III, p. 17.
3. J. Keegan, 'The Inter-War Years', in R. Higham (ed.) *A Guide to the Sources of British Military History* (London: Routledge & Kegan Paul, 1972) p. 461.
4. Liddell Hart to Fuller, 11 March 1928, Liddell Hart Papers 1/302/128 (hereafter LHP).
5. G. Mattingly, *Catherine of Aragon* (London: Jonathan Cape, 1942) p. 11.
6. J. F. C. Fuller, *Empire Unity and Defence* (Bristol: Arrowsmith, 1934) p. 166. Hereafter all books and articles are by Fuller unless otherwise stated.
7. J. Harrison, *The Reactionaries* (London: Gollancz, 1967).
8. B. Crick, *George Orwell* (London: Secker & Warburg, 1980) pp. xxii, xxv.
9. A. Horne, *The Fall of Paris* (London: Macmillan, 1965) p. xi.
10. Liddell Hart to Fuller, 11 March 1928, LHP 1/302/128.

1. The Evolution of a Mind, 1878–1914

1. *Memoirs of an Unconventional Soldier* (London: Ivor Nicholson, 1936) pp. 1–4; A. J. Trythall, *'Boney' Fuller* (London: Cassell, 1977) pp. 1–4; Liddell Hart, *Memoirs* (London: Cassell, 1965) I, pp. 4–5; Fuller Papers IV/2/5–6 (hereafter FP).
2. *Memoirs*, pp. 6–7.
3. P. Clark, *Liberals and Social Democrats* (Cambridge: Cambridge University Press, 1978) p. 13. See also H. S. Hughes, *Consciousness and Society* (London: Macgibbon Kee, 1959).
4. *Memoirs*, p. 459; Fuller to Mrs Fuller, 17 October 1897, FP IV/3/2; IV/3/4.
5. Fuller to Mrs Fuller, 31 March 1899, FP IV/3/18.
6. A. Fairbanks, *The First Philosophers of Greece* (London: English & Foreign Philosophical Library, 1898) pp. 22–63; Books Read 1899, FP IV/4/1; Fuller to Meredith Starr, 13 July 1961, Starr Papers.
7. Letter of Alison Starr to the author, 2 February 1978; Fuller to Mrs Fuller, 1 May 1902, FP IV/3/103; *The Last of the Gentlemen's Wars* (London: Faber & Faber, 1937) pp. 25, 265.
8. Books Read 1898, 1899. Fuller to Mrs Fuller, 14 May 1901, FP IV/4/1, IV/3/60.

9. Books Read 1900, 1901, FP IV/4/1; Fuller to Mrs Fuller, 17 January, 15 February 1901, *ibid.*, IV/3/46/51.
10. Fuller to Mrs Fuller, 20 December 1900, 20 July 1901, FP IV/3/46/71; MS Diary, 25 January 1902; Books Read 1900, *ibid.*, IV/4/8/1.
11. Fuller to Mrs Fuller, 6 February 1900, 7 May 1901, FP IV/3/26/59.
12. Fuller to Mr Fuller, 7 May 1901, 24 January 1902, 27 July 1902, FP IV/3/59/91/110; MS Diary, 8 January 1902, *ibid.*, IV/4/8; *Last of the Gentlemen's Wars*, p. 268.
13. Fuller to Grandfather, 24 December 1903, FP IV/3/115a. On the 'Law of Three', 'three forces [which] enter into every manifestation, into every phenomenon and every event', see P. D. Ouspensky, *The Fourth Way* (London: Routledge & Kegan Paul, 1960) p. 16; *Memoirs*, pp. 17–18.
14. General Sir Beauvoir de Lisle, *Reminiscences of Sport and War* (London: Eyre & Spottiswoode, 1939), pp. 45, 271; De Lisle is identified in Fuller to Mrs Fuller, 17 August 1905, FP IV/3/134; General Sir Wyndham Childs, *Episodes and Reflections* (London: Cassell, 1930) pp. 30–6.
15. Books Read 1903, FP IV/4/1; Fuller to Mrs Fuller, 28 January 1904, 21 September 1905; Fuller to Mrs Fuller, 5, 20 April 1905; Fuller to Grandfather, 24 December 1903, FP IV/3/111b/137/121/127/115a.
16. '666 Biblioteca Crowleyana. . . .' Introduction by Major General J. F. C. Fuller, FP IV/16; Fuller to Mrs Fuller, 3 May 1907, IV/3/139c; *The Confessions of Aleister Crowley* (eds.) J. Symonds and K. Grant (London: Jonathan Cape, 1969) pp. 39–41; R. Ellman, *Yeats: The Man and the Mask* (London: Faber, 1948, 1961) pp. 91–2.
17. C. R. Cammell, *Aleister Crowley* (London: Richards, 1951) p. x; J. Symonds, *The Great Beast* (London: Rider, 1951) p. 94; *The Star in the West* (London: Walter Scott, 1907, 1978) p. 280; 'The Way of the Tao', 39, Crowley Papers AC MS 37; Fuller to Starr, 30 October 1928, Starr Papers.
18. Crowley to Fuller, 16 October 1906, FP IV/12/5; Cammell, *Crowley*, p. 34.
19. *The Reformation of War* (London: Hutchinson, 1923) p. 267; Trythall, *Fuller*, p. 21; MS Diary, 15 June 1907; Letter of Alison Starr to the author, 2 February 1978; the mystical state described here is that of *Dhyâna*.
20. Interview with Mrs Alison Starr, 16 March 1978; *Memoirs*, pp. 20–1; Fuller to Grandfather, 24 December 1903, FP IV/3/115a.
21. Crowley to Fuller, n.d. (?1907), 3 February, 23 May 1908, 17 November 1909, FP IV/12/16/35/42/47; MS Diary of Norman Mudd 1909, entry no. 4, p. 83, Crowley Papers; J. Overton Fuller, *The Magical World of Victor Neuburg* (London: W. H. Allen, 1965) p. 127; Fuller to Mrs Fuller, 21 September 1905, FP IV/3/137; H. Spencer, *First Principles* (London: Williams & Norgate, 5th edn, 1893) pp. 24, 60–1, 66–9, 84–5, 107; P. D. Ouspensky, *In Search of the Miraculous* (London: Routledge & Kegan Paul, 1950) pp. 77–81.
22. J. White, 'Andrew Carnegie and Herbert Spencer', *Journal of American*

Studies, XXI (1979) p. 61; J. Dewey, *Characters and Events* (ed.) J. Ratner (London: George Allen & Unwin, 1929) pp. 46, 50.

23. A. Powell, *To Keep the Ball Rolling* (London: Heinemann, 1976), I, p. 49; MS Diary 1907, entry 7 January, FP IV/4/10; *The Equinox*, I (1909) pp. 145, 296. Crowley's annotated copies of this journal are in the Crowley Papers. Fuller's biography of Crowley was later to form the basis of *Yoga: A Study of the Mystical Philosophy of the Brahmins and Buddhists* (London: Rider, 1925); Tacitus, *Annals*. IV, p. 56.

24. The Mystical Diary of W. H. Chesson, Starr Papers. Chesson was a minor poet and friend of Meredith Starr. Fuller was fond of quoting from William James, *Varieties of Religious Experience* (New York: Longmans, 1902); *Equinox*, I, pp. 146–7.

25. W. M. Simon, *European Positivism in the Nineteenth Century* (Cornell: Cornell University Press, 1963) pp. 5–6, 177, 199, 217–18, 227, n.76, 264, who stresses the importance of Henry Maudsley in popularizing Comte's methods in England; Samuel Hynes, *The Edwardian Turn of Mind* (Princeton: Princeton University Press, 1968) pp. 94–6.

26. Fuller to Crowley, 2 May 1911, FP IV/12/73; Trythall, *Fuller*, pp. 20–1, 24; Fuller, *Neuburg*, pp. 94–6, 152, 162, 18; F. King, *The Magical World of Aleister Crowley* (London: Weidenfeld & Nicolson, 1977) pp. 62–8; 'Magic and War', *The Occult Review*, LXIX (1942) p. 53.

27. Crowley, *Confessions*, p. 544; Crowley to Fuller, 3 February 1909, FP IV/12/35; Fuller to Liddell Hart, 21 December 1927, LHP 1/302/122; Books Read 1901, FP IV/4/1; A. J. P. Taylor, *Europe: Grandeur and Decline* (Harmondsworth: Penguin, 1967) p. 15; J. M. Thompson (ed.) *Napoleon's Letters* (London: Dent, 1954) pp. 203, 216; J. Luvaas, 'Napoleon on the Art of Command', *Parameters*, XV (1985) pp. 30–6.

28. R. S. Quimby, *The Background to Napoleonic Warfare* (New York: Columbia University Press, 1956) p. 336; D. G. Chandler, *The Campaigns of Napoleon* (London: Weidenfeld & Nicolson, 1967) pp. 180, 196, 146.

29. Napoleon au roi de Naples, 28 juillet 1806, *Correspondance de Napoleon Ier* (Paris, 1863) XIII, p. 13; A. F. Becke, *Napoleon and Waterloo* (London: Kegan Paul, 1914, 1936) I, p. 257.

30. Lt. Col. F. N. Maude, *The Leipzig Campaign 1813* (London: George Allen, 1908); *idem.*, *The Ulm Campaign 1805* (London: George Allen, 1912) pp. 41–3, 263; *idem.*, *The Jena Campaign 1806* (London: George Allen, 1909) pp. xvi, 9 (Maude's italics).

31. Lt. Col. A. Pollock, 'A Military Education', *Fortnightly Review*, LXXXI (1907) pp. 337–45; Fuller to Starr, 19 December 1955, Starr Papers; 'The Mobilization of a Territorial Infantry Battalion', *The Army Review*, V (1913) p. 186; *ibid.*, p. 300.

32. *Hints on Training Territorial Infantry* (London: Gale & Polden, 1913) pp. 40–2, 51, 56–7, 61, 67, 73 (hereafter, *Hints*); 'The Three Flag System of Instructing Infantry Fire Tactics', *AR*, VI (1914) p. 121; *Memoirs*, pp. 458–60.

33. *Hints*, pp. 97–102, 111.

34. *Training Soldiers for War* (London: Hugh Rees, 1914) pp. v–vi, 2–5, 8–9; 'Notes on the Entrainment of Troops', *AR*, VIII (1914) p. 213.
35. Hynes, *Edwardian Turn of Mind*, pp. 138–9; A. R. Skelley, *The Victorian Army at Home* (London: Croom Helm, 1977) pp. 137, 169 n.36; *Training Soldiers for War*, pp. 10–13; J. Joll, *Europe Since 1870* (London: Weidenfeld & Nicolson, 1973) p. 132.
36. *Training Soldiers for War*, pp. 14–23.
37. Fuller to Mrs Fuller, 14 May 1901, FP IV/3/60/36; *Training Soldiers for War*, pp. 21–6, 30–9, 41–6, 60–1, 119.
38. *Ibid.*, pp. 34, 47–54, 119; D. Porch, 'The French Army and the Spirit of the Offensive', in B. Bond and Ian Roy (eds.) *War and Society* (London: Croom Helm, 1976) I, p. 133.
39. Fuller to Starr, 7 January 1913, Starr Papers; Fuller to Mrs Fuller, 19 August 1913, FP IV/3/140b for a complete list of his examination marks; *Memoirs*, pp. 23–4; Trythall, *Fuller*, pp. 26, 28.
40. Fuller to Liddell Hart, 16 August 1926, LHP 1/302/96; *Memoirs*, pp. 24–5.
41. *Training Soldiers for War*, pp. viii, 42–3, 61, 69, 120; *Memoirs*, pp. 27–8; Liddell Hart's Notes on Fuller's *Memoirs*, LHP 1/302/262; Fuller to Tuker, 2 July 1960, Tuker Papers 71/21/16.
42. B. Bond, *The Victorian Army and the Staff College, 1854–1914* (London: Eyre Methuen, 1972) pp. 290–2; Fuller to Mrs Fuller, 29 August 1916, FP IV/3/200; *Memoirs*, p. 460.
43. Bond, *Staff College*, p. 290; Trythall, *Fuller*, pp. 137–9.

2. The Genesis of Armoured Warfare, 1914–18

1. 'The Procedure of the Infantry Attack', RUSI *Journal*, LVIII (1914), pp. 63–4, 65–6, 70, 73–4.
2. *Memoirs*, pp. 31–48; MS Diary 1914, entry 18 August, FP IV/4/11; 'The Training of the New Armies, 1803–1805', RUSI *Journal*, LXI (1916), pp. 779–90; the book was later published in 1925 in two volumes; Fuller to Mr Fuller, 4 July 1915, FP IV/3/148.
3. 'The Tactics of Penetration', RUSI *Journal*, LIX (1914), pp. 378–9, 384; T. H. E. Travers, 'The Offensive and the Problem of Innovation in Military Thought, 1870–1915', *Journal of Contemporary History*, XIII (1978), p. 543.
4. Travers, p. 546; G. C. Wynne, *If Germany Attacks* (London: Faber & Faber, 1940) pp. 147–58, 161.
5. Fuller to Mr Fuller, 18 August, 28 August, 11 November 1915, FP IV/3/155/156/167; MS Diary 1915, entry 28 July, *ibid.*, IV/4/11; Fuller to Mrs Fuller, 6 August 1915, *ibid.*, IV/3/153; Fuller to Mr Fuller, 28 August 1915, *ibid.*, IV/3/155.
6. Fuller to Mr Fuller, 7 May 1916, *ibid.*, IV/3/190; Spencer, *First Principles*, pp. 226, 239, 273, 514; 'The Principles of War, With Reference to the Campaigns of 1914–15', RUSI *Journal*, LXI (1916), pp. 2, 5.

7. *Ibid.*, pp. 2, 4, 6.
8. *Ibid.*, pp. 10, 22–4, 25–8, 39; Gen. Sir W. Robertson to Kiggell, 5 July 1916, Kiggell Papers IV/3.
9. Wynne, pp. 20–9, 42; J. E. Edmonds, *Military Operations, France and Belgium, 1915* (London: HMSO, 1928), II, pp. 9–10, 11, 20–1, 56–7, 94, 154, 157, 186–7, 212; *The Private Papers of Douglas Haig, 1914–1919*, (ed.) R. Blake (London: Eyre & Spottiswoode, 1952) p. 84.
10. 'Principles of War', pp. 33–5.
11. Edmonds, *1915*, II, pp. 56–7, 312–14; Travers, p. 543; Fuller to Mr Fuller, 18 March 1916, FP IV/3/186.
12. Fuller to Mr Fuller, 7 May 1916, *ibid.*; MS Diary 1915, entry 2 November, *ibid.*, IV/3/190, IV/4/11; *Memoirs*, pp. 63–9; H. Essame, *The Battle for Europe, 1918* (London: Batsford, 1972) p. 15.
13. S. Foot, *Three Lives* (London: Heinemann, 1934) pp. 158–9; *Extracts . . . Ward Jackson to his Wife*, 6 November 1918, p. 368 (Imperial War Museum); *Memoirs*, p. 79; Fuller to Mrs Fuller, 23 July 1916, FP IV/3/199.
14. B. H. Liddell Hart, *The Tanks* (London: Cassell, 1959) I, p. 92; E. K. G. Sixsmith, *Douglas Haig* (London: Weidenfeld & Nicolson, 1976) p. 165; the Official History agrees, see *France and Belgium, 1916*, II, pp. 176, 292–3.
15. Talk with Fuller, 29 March 1929, LHP 9/28/59; Letter of Brig. I. M. Stewart to the author, 19 June 1977.
16. Training Note No. 16, FP I/9 Tank Strategy and Tactics 1916/6 (hereafter TN16).
17. *Ibid.*; Sir Ernest Swinton, *Eyewitness* (London: Hodder & Stoughton, 1932) pp. 198–214.
18. TN16, FP I/9/TS/6.
19. *The Generalship of Alexander the Great* (London: Eyre & Spottiswoode, 1958) p. 5; TN16, FP I/9/TS/6.
20. HQ Tank Corps Reports, Recovery of Tanks Damaged in Action, 20 July 1917; Report on Action of Tanks, 31 July 1917, PRO WO95/92.
21. Projected Bases for Tactical Employment of Tanks in 1918, July 1917, FPI/3/TS/29; Wynne, pp. 147–58, 197, 245, 249–50, 277.
22. Projected Bases for Tactical Employment of Tanks, 11 June 1917, FP I/3/TS/16; Tactical Exercises, Tanks and Infantry, 15 May 1917, PRO WO95/92; *Memoirs*, pp. 153–4.
23. Fuller to Mr Fuller, 4 February 1917, FP IV/3/207.
24. Project for the Capture of St Quentin by a Coup de Main, 3 August 1917; Tank Raids, August 1917, FP I/45 Battle of Cambrai (hereafter BC); Assembly of Tanks, n.d., PRO WO95/91.
25. The Battle of Cambrai (note for lecture, n.d.) FP I/BC/1; Fuller to Mrs Fuller, 20 November 1917, 20 January 1918, FP IV/3/222/224.
26. Instructions on Tanks Operating with Fascines, June 1917, PRO WO95/91; Conference on Tank Training, 13 November 1917; Notes on Tank Operations, April–October 1917; Notes on Infantry and Tank Operations, n.d., *ibid.*, WO95/93; Outline of Tank Operations, 20–30 November 1917, Pt III, Results and Deductions, FP I/16/BC/1; Tank Operations, n.d. FP I/TS/40.

27. Liddell Hart, *The Tanks*, I, p. 54; Robertson to Haig, 1 November 1916, Kiggell Papers IV/4/122.
28. Fuller to Mrs Fuller, n.d., FP IV/3/225; Fuller to Liddell Hart, 22 September 1922, LHP I/302/20; for an example of staff demoralization see *War Letters of General Monash* (Sydney: Angus & Robertson, 1935) p. 227.
29. Fuller learned of the Medium D's potential at a Tank Corps Committee Meeting, 28 April 1918, see Medium D and Related Developments (Unpub. Memo by R. M. Ogorkiewicz, April 1964), LHP 9/28/120. The original version of 'Plan 1919', 'The Tactics of the Attack as Affected by the Speed and Circuit of the Medium "D" Tank (Paper given to [Gen. Sir] H. W[ilson] and Winston [Churchill] in June 1918)', is in FP I/208/TS/50. Churchill later claimed that the idea was his. Lord Moran, *Churchill: The Struggle for Survival* (London: Constable, 1966) p. 260.
30. Tactics of the Attack etc., FP I/208/TS/50. Martel only likened tanks to ships like 'destroyers', not to naval warfare as a whole. See A Tank Army, November 1916, Martel Papers P240/GQM/6/2a.
31. Tactics of the Attack etc., FP I/208/TS/50; Becke, *Napoleon and Waterloo*, I, p. 216; Clausewitz, *On War*, (eds.) M. Howard and P. Paret, (Princeton: Princeton University Press, 1976), III, 12, p. 206.
32. Tactics of the Attack etc., FP I/208/TS/50, an idea possibly taken from Clausewitz: 'most men would rather believe bad news than good, and rather tend to exaggerate the bad news'. *On War*, I, 6, p. 117.
33. R. M. Hatton, *Charles XII* (London: Weidenfeld & Nicolson, 1968) pp. 266–7; Arrian, *Anabasis of Alexander* (London: Loeb, 1929 edn) I, iii, 13, 2–6, p. 267; Fuller to Jay Luvaas, 8 July 1963, Luvaas Papers.
34. S. Bidwell, *Gunners at War* (London: Arms and Armour Press, 1970) p. 63.
35. B. Pitt, *1918: The Last Act* (London: Macmillan paperback edn, 1985) pp. 205–6.
36. E. Ludendorff, *My War Memories* (London: Hutchinson 2nd edn, 1920) II, pp. 680, 683, 700, 740, 745; Liddell Hart, *The Tanks*, I, p. 92; C. Barnett, *The Swordbearers* (London: Eyre & Spottiswoode, 1963) p. 274.
37. J. E. Edmonds, *France and Belgium 1918* (London: HMSO, 1947) IV, pp. 8, 242 n.2, 45–6, 85, 114, 156–7; G. Le Q. Martel, *In the Wake of the Tank* (London: Sifton Praed, 1931) pp. 23–4, 30, 33–5, 70; J. Terraine, *To Win a War* (London: Sidgwick & Jackson, 1978) pp. 110–11, 117, 189–90; C. N. Barclay, *Armistice 1918* (London: Dent, 1969) p. 90.
38. R. M. Ogorkiewicz, *Design and Development of Armoured Fighting Vehicles* (London: Macdonald, 1968) p. 29; Martel, p. 74; Edmonds, *1918*, IV, p. 53; Essame, pp. 136, 122.
39. Edmonds, *1918*, IV, pp. 154–7, 514; Liddell Hart, *The Tanks*, I, p. 183.
40. *Memoirs*, p. 349; Martel, p. 74; Col. P. Johnson, 'Major General J. F. C. Fuller'; Johnson to Fuller, 8 June 1918, Johnson's Papers are now part of the Liddell Hart Collection, LHP 9/28/104/119; evidence of Fuller's

practical grasp: Fuller to Maj. Gen. J. E. Capper, 29 March 1918, PRO
WO95/93.

41. Martel, pp. 34, 79; Johnson warned Fuller of the 'unsatisfactory state'
of Medium D design in a memorandum, 29 March 1919, LHP
9/28/104; there were no radios to co-ordinate the tanks, for example.

42. Fuller to Liddell Hart, 26 July 1929, LHP 1/302/177; Reorganization on
the Battlefield; Characteristics and Tactics of the Mark V, n.d., FP
I/36/TS/203/257.

3. The Reformation of War, 1919–23

1. Tactics of the Attack etc, FP I/208/TS/50; Liddell Hart, *The Tanks*, I,
p. 201.
2. *Ibid*.
3. 'The Application of Recent Developments in Mechanics and Other
Scientific Knowledge to Preparation and Training for Future War on
Land', RUSI *Journal*, LXV (1920) p. 239 (hereafter 'Applications').
4. *Memoirs*, p. 9; *The Reformation of War* (London: Hutchinson, 1923)
pp. 67–8, 85, 87–8, 134 (hereafter *Reformation*).
5. 'Applications', p. 243; B. Semmel, *Imperialism and Social Reform*
(London: George Allen & Unwin, 1960) pp. 63, 74; H. Mackinder,
Democratic Ideals and Reality (New York: Holt, 1942 edn) pp. 15, 23.
6. B. Bond, *British Military Policy Between the Two World Wars* (Oxford:
Clarendon Press, 1980) p. 36; on the generally complacent attitudes
to the 'lessons' of the First World War, see David French, ' "Official
but not History"? Sir James Edmonds and the Official History of the
Great War', RUSI *Journal*, CXXXI (1986) pp. 58–63; Fuller to Sir
Eustace D'Eyncourt, 7 May 1920, D'Eyncourt Papers DEY 22.
7. 'Applications', pp. 249, 254; Essame, p. 136; Liddell Hart, Notes on
Fuller's *Memoirs*, LHP 1/302/262.
8. 'Applications', pp. 249, 254.
9. 'The Development of Sea Warfare on Land', *RUSI Journal*, LXV (1920)
pp. 289, 291; C. Barnett, *The Desert Generals* (London: Kimber, 1960;
rev. edn 1984) p. 81; D. Young, *Rommel* (London: Collins, 1950, 1972)
p. 123, points out that Gen. Cruwell was shot down on the eve of the
Battle of Gazala.
10. *Tanks in the Great War* (London: John Murray, 1920) p. 313; 'The
Problems of Mechanical Warfare', *Army Quarterly*, III (1920) p. 290
(hereafter *AQ*); Fuller to Liddell Hart, 25 August 1920, LHP 1/302/7;
Michael Carver, *The Apostles of Mobility* (London: Weidenfeld &
Nicolson, 1979) p. 40.
11. *The Rommel Papers* (ed.) Capt. B. H. Liddell Hart (London: Collins,
1953) p. 52; W. G. F. Jackson, *The North African Campaign* (London:
Batsford, 1975) pp. 238–41; 'Sea Warfare on Land', p. 288.
12. *Tanks in the Great War*, pp. 309–10; Barry A. Leach, *German Strategy
Against Russia* (Oxford: Clarendon Press, 1973) p. 121; Winkelried
was probably an apocryphal figure, a Swiss hero who, with reckless

courage, threw himself on the Austrian lances at the Battle of Sempach (1386) to open a gap in their formation.

13. *Tanks in the Great War*, p. 310; Fuller to Liddell Hart, 10 June 1920, LHP 1/302/2.

14. Fuller to Mrs Fuller, 2 March 1921, FP IV/3/238; Fuller to Liddell Hart, 12 April 1922, LHP 1/302/15; 'The Purpose and Nature of a Fleet', *The Nineteenth Century and After*, XC (1921), pp. 703, 709–10; 'Tanks in Future Warfare', *ibid.*, p. 104.

15. W. G. F. Jackson, *'Overlord': Normandy 1944* (London: Davis Poynter, 1978) pp. 14–15.

16. Fuller to Liddell Hart, 15 September, 25 August, 26 October, 31 October, 17 November 1922, LHP 1/302/19/18/23/24/26.

17. Fuller to Liddell Hart, 27 March 1923, *ibid.*, 1/302/37; Carver, *Apostles of Mobility*, p. 34; *Reformation*, p. xii; Liddell Hart to J. M. Scammell, 22 February 1923, LHP 1/622.

18. Chandler, *Campaigns of Napoleon*, p. 180; P. Mackesy, 'Wellington: The General', in Michael Howard (ed.) *Wellingtonian Studies* (Aldershot: Wellington College, 1959) p. 32; R. Lewin, *Slim* (London: Leo Cooper, 1976) p. 224.

19. Fuller to Starr, 15 June 1920, Starr Papers; 'What Changes are Suggested in Naval Construction and Tactics as a Result of (a) The Experience of the War (b) The Development of Submarines and Aerial Warfare', *Naval Review*, 10 (1922) p. 78; *Reformation*, p. 27.

20. *Reformation*, p. 75; J. M. Keynes, *The Economic Consequences of the Peace* (London: Macmillan, 1919); T. H. E. Travers, 'Technology, Tactics and Morale', *Journal of Modern History*, 51 (1979) p. 265; J. D. Y. Peel, *Herbert Spencer* (London: Heinemann, 1971) p. 101.

21. *Tanks in the Great War*, pp. 318–20; 'Applications', pp. 246–7.

22. Clausewitz, *On War*, I, 1, p. 76; VIII, 3, p. 593; *ibid.*, (ed.) J. J. Graham (London: n.d.) III 'Guide to Tactics or Theory of Combat', pp. 250–1; *Reformation*, p. 100.

23. *Reformation*, pp. 64–7, 100, 105, 108–10; W. James, 'The Moral Equivalent of War', *Memories and Studies* (London: Longmans, 1911) p. 288; Fuller to Liddell Hart, 27 March 1923, LHP 1/302/37,

24. E. Longford, *Wellington: The Years of the Sword* (London: Weidenfeld & Nicolson, 1969) p. 472; Fuller to Liddell Hart, 5 November 1948, LHP 1/302/362.

25. B. Bond, *Liddell Hart* (London: Cassell, 1977) p. 43; *Reformation*, p. 150; B. D. Powers, *Strategy Without Slide-Rule* (London: Croom Helm, 1976) pp. 108–9.

26. Powers, p. 204; U. Bialer, *The Shadow of the Bomber* (London: Royal Historical Society, 1980) pp. 151–60.

27. Powers, pp. 14, 16, 22, 62, 108–9, 121–3. Fuller was to use precisely these arguments against strategic bombing after 1939.

28. This question is assessed more fully in Brian Holden Reid, 'Gas Warfare: The Perils of Prediction', in D. Carlton and C. Schaerf (eds) *Reassessing Arms Control* (London: Macmillan, 1985) pp. 143–58.

29. *Reformation*, pp. 47, 114–18, 159; Fuller to Liddell Hart, 10 June 1920, LHP 1/302/2.

30. Clausewitz, *On War*, IV, 12, p. 267; III, 12, p. 206; V, 4, pp. 285–9; *Reformation*, pp. 159–60.
31. Fuller to Liddell Hart, 10 June 1920, LHP 1/302/2; *Reformation*, p. 163; Clausewitz, *On War*, VII, 18, p. 547.
32. Fuller to Liddell Hart, 8 February 1922, LHP 1/302/14; J. Keegan, *The Face of Battle* (London: Cape, 1976) pp. 161–2; J. Weller, *Wellington at Waterloo* (London: Longmans, 1968) pp. 147–51.
33. 'Problems of Mechanical Warfare', p. 285; *Reformation*, pp. 161–4.
34. *Reformation*, pp. 163, 167–8.
35. *Ibid.*, pp. 161, 163; Cavan to Maurice, 6 February 1924, Maurice Papers 3/5/150; Tanks in Future Warfare', pp. 97, 107; Fuller to Liddell Hart, 29 May 1922, LHP 1/302/16.
36. *Reformation*, p. 163; C. Barnett, *Britain and her Army* (London: Allen Lane, 1970) p. 471.
37. Cavan to Maurice, 14 January 1924, Maurice Papers 3/5/149; Fuller to Liddell Hart, 8 February 1924, LHP 1/302/14.

4. 'The Dawn of a New Era in Military Thought'? 1924–8

1. Paget to Fuller, 7 December 1923, Fuller Papers (Rutgers University); Fuller to Liddell Hart, 6 April 1923, 21 February 1925, LHP 1/302/38/71; Paget to Fuller, 14 January 1920, FP (Rutgers University); Review in *AQ*, XII (1926) p. 165 (the reviewer was Brig Gen. (later Sir) J. E. Edmonds: Liddell Hart MS Diary, 1927, entry 17 March, LHP 11/1927/1); the RUSI *Journal* did not review it. 'When he [Fuller], was appointed to the Staff College, Ironside [the Commandant] received at least 20 letters saying . . . that Fuller was a dangerous man, who would instil wrong ideas into the students', Historical Note dictated by Maj Gen. G. M. Lindsay, Lindsay Papers; Brian Holden Reid, 'Colonel J. F. C. Fuller and the Revival of Classical Military Thinking in Britain, 1918–26', *Military Affairs*, XLVIV (1985), pp. 192–7.
2. R. Wilkinson, *The Prefects* (London: Oxford University Press, 1964) pp. 64–75; e.g. Wavell to Liddell Hart, 30 October 1931, LHP 1/733/16; Chandler, *Campaigns of Napoleon*, pp. xxxviii–xxxix; Clausewitz, *On War*, II, i, p. 141; II, 6, p. 192.
3. Interview with Mrs Alison Starr, 10 March 1978; *Memoirs*, pp. 417–18; Fuller to Liddell Hart, 3 September 1926, LHP 1/302/99.
4. *The Foundations of the Science of War* (London: Hutchinson, 1926) pp. 324–6 (hereafter *Foundations*); M. Howard, 'Jomini and the Classical Tradition in Military Thought', in M. Howard (ed.) *The Theory and Practice of War* (London: Cassell, 1965) p. 16; Clausewitz, *On War*, I, 7, p. 120; II, 4, p. 151; III, 16, p. 217.
5. G. Gore, *The New Scientific System of Morality* (London: Watts, 1906), pp. 7, 38–9, 40, 90–1, a book frequently quoted in *Foundations*. P. Paret, *Clausewitz and the State* (New York: Oxford University Press, 1976) p. 92; *Foundations*, p. 51.
6. Fuller to Liddell Hart, 22 May 1924, LHP 1/302/60; *The Dragon's Teeth* (London: Constable, 1932) p. 120; J. Luvaas, *Education of an Army*,

242

42 Notes and References

p. 351–2; Trythall, *Fuller*, pp. 111–12; quoted in Reid, 'Fuller and the Revival of Classical Military Thinking', p. 197 n.13.

7. *Foundations*, pp. 27–8, 54–61.
8. *Ibid.*, pp. 82–4.
9. *Ibid.*, pp. 84–5.
10. Liddell Hart to Fuller, 11 April 1923, LHP 1/302/41; Liddell Hart to Fuller, 25 December 1923, 5 February 1926, 21 February 1925, *ibid.*, 1/302/57/87/71; Wilkinson to Liddell Hart, 3 March 1928, *ibid.*, 1/748/6b.
11. Montgomery-Massingberd to Liddell Hart, 20 April, 27 April, 23 June, *ibid.*, 1/520; Paget to Fuller, 14 January 1920, FP (Rutgers University); Liddell Hart MS Diary 1927, entry 8 June, LHP 11/1927/1; Trythall, *Fuller*, p. 111.
12. Fuller to Liddell Hart, 2 March, 12 November, 15 November, 4 April 1923, LHP 1/302/32/54/55/44; Paget to Fuller, 7 December 1923, FP Rutgers University); Trythall, *Fuller*, p. 119.
13. Fuller to Liddell Hart, 26 July 1926, LHP 1/302/95; Trythall, *Fuller*, pp. 118, 135–44.
14. Montgomery-Massingberd to Liddell Hart, 3 May 1926, LHP 1/520; F. N. Maude, *The Science of Organisation and the Art of War* (Organisation Society, 1912), pp. 1–2; H. H. R. Bailes, 'The Influence of Continental Examples and Colonial Warfare Upon the Reform of the Late Victorian Army' (Unpublished Ph.D. Thesis, University of London, 1980), pp. 16–17.
15. Maj. Gen. Sir F. B. Maurice, *British Strategy* (London: Constable, 1929) pp. 1–2; *Foundations*, pp. 208–9, 238–9; Milne to Maurice, n.d., Maurice Papers 3/5/182; Maurice's book was less ambitious than Fuller's, 'a sort of Child's Guide to FSR and it does not pretend to be more than that' (Maurice to Liddell Hart, 21 November 1929, LHP 1/498). Fuller's annotation on Liddell Hart to Fuller, 5 March 1923 with a comment (n.d.) by Liddell Hart; Fuller to Liddell Hart, 7 March 1923, *Ibid.*, 1/302/34/35; Clausewitz, *On War*, II, 1, p. 141.
16. 'The Secrets of Napoleon', *National Review*, 77 (1921) pp. 416–18; W. James, *Pragmatism* (London: Longmans, 1907) pp. 43–81, 170, 181; *Foundations*, pp. 37, 40, 101, 324.
17. *British Strategy*, pp. 24–5; V. W. Germains, *The 'Mechanization' of War* (London: Sifton Praed, 1927) pp. 98–9, 103; *idem*, '"Science and War": Some Comments', *Fighting Forces*, V (1928), pp. 389–94 (hereafter FF); *Foundations*, pp. 17, 38, 98; 'Scientific Soldiership', *Royal Engineers Journal*, XLII (1928), p. 199; Viscount Montgomery, *Memoirs* (London: Collins, 1958) p. 86.
18. 'Applications', p. 251; *Reformation*, p. 168; Philip M. Morse and George F. Kimball, *Methods of Operations Research* (New York: Wiley, 1952) pp. 8–9, 59, 129; R. Lewin, *Ultra Goes to War* (London: Hutchinson, 1978) pp. 111–14.
19. Lewin, *Montgomery as Military Commander* (London: Batsford, 1971) p. 172; W. Murray, 'The German Response to Victory in Poland', *Armed Forces and Society*, XII (1981), pp. 285–98, provides evidence of German scientific evaluation; *Foundations*, p. 46; S. Zuckerman, *Scientists and War* (London: Hamish Hamilton, 1966) pp. 101, 115–16;

R. Bennett, *Ultra in the West* (London: Hutchinson, 1979) pp. 33, 38, 87.

20. *Foundations*, pp. 17, 48; K. Pearson, *The Grammar of Science* (London: A. & C. Black, 3rd edn, 1911), pp. 77, 81–5, 99–100; Quoted in M. I. F. P. Nallétamby, 'An Analysis of Karl Pearson's *The Grammar of Science*' (Unpublished M.A. Thesis, University of London, 1955) p. 80; see Fuller's 'The Third Cycle in Tactics', 17 December 1925, Martel Papers P240/GQM/6/2c.

21. Fuller to Liddell Hart, 13 January 1922, 7 March, 1923, LHP 1/302/10a/35/37; *Reformation*, pp. 29–46; *Foundations*, pp. 13–16.

22. Fuller to Liddell Hart, 3 June, 25 June 1924, LHP 1/302/61/63.

23. Germains, pp. 99, 105–7, 135, 206–9; Maurice, *British Strategy*, p. 215.

24. Clausewitz, *On War*, III, 18, p. 221, e.g. 'Dynamic Law in War' postulating, like Fuller dynamism and inertia in warfare; *Ibid.*, IV, 7, p. 241; IV, 29, p. 500; Fuller to Liddell Hart, 12 April 1924, LHP 1/302/59. The destruction of the enemy's forces combined with the protection of one's own, 'always go together: they interact', *On War*, I, 2, p. 98.

25. Trythall, *Fuller*, p. 114; Montgomery, *Memoirs*, p. 348; M. Howard, *The Mediterranean Strategy in the Second World War* (London: Weidenfeld & Nicolson, 1968) pp. 62–3.

26. *Foundations*, pp. 73–6, 105–10, 314.

27. Reid, 'Fuller and the Revival of Classical Military Thinking', p. 195.

28. *Foundations*, pp. 250, 252–3, 321, 265, 288.

29. *Ibid.*, pp. 155, 181, 259, 288; quoted in Chandler, *Campaigns of Napoleon*, pp. 163–9, 298, 467.

30. *Foundations*, pp. 299, 319; Clausewitz, *On War*, VI, 5, p. 370; Reid, 'Fuller and the Revival of Classical Military Thinking', p. 195.

31. *Ibid.*, p. 196.

32. Maurice, *British Strategy*, p. 87; Germains, pp. 207, 212–14; 'The Foundations of the Science of War', *AQ*, I (1920) pp. 91, 111; *Foundations*, pp. 276–7, 261.

33. *Ibid.*, pp. 284, 218–24, 125; on the lack of initiative shown by British soldiers 1914–18, see D. Winter, *Death's Men* (London: Allen Lane, 1977) pp. 39–41, 46; *Sir John Moore's System of Training* (London: Hutchinson, 1925) (hereafter *Moore's System of Training*); *British Light Infantry in the Eighteenth Century* (London: Hutchinson, 1925). Fuller invariably spelt morale as 'moral'.

34. 'Two Private Letters from Major General Sir John Moore, KB', *Journal of the Society for Army Historical Research*, X (1930), pp. 162–7, 171; C. Oman, *Sir John Moore* (London: Hodder & Stoughton, 1953) pp. 73–9, 233, 238, 265; *Moore's System of Training*, pp. 215–7; Fuller to Liddell Hart, 13 November 1924, LHP 1/302/66; 'Progress in the Mechanicalization of Modern Armies', *RUSI Journal*, LXX (1925), pp. 86–7; Liddell Hart, *Memoirs*, I, p. 112, implied that the idea was his.

35. *British Light Infantry in the Eighteenth Century*, p. 243; *Foundations*, pp. 133–40, 143.

36. *Moore's System of Training*, p. 138; *British Light Infantry in the Eighteenth Century*, pp. 79–86; Oman, *Moore*, pp. 26, 29.
37. *Moore's System of Training*, pp. 72, 86, 107, 144; Winter, *Death's Men*, pp. 38, 45–9.
38. *Moore's System of Training*, pp. 89–91, 95, 124–5; 'Moral, Instruction and Leadership', RUSI *Journal*, LXV (1920), pp. 661–3.
39. Sir E. Wood, *From Midshipman to Field Marshal* (London: Methuen, 3rd edn 1906) II, p. 259; Montgomery, *Memoirs*, p. 85; R. H. Ahrenfeldt, *A History of Psychiatry in the British Army in the Second World War* (London: Routledge & Kegan Paul, 1958) pp. 35–6, 103–8.
40. Fuller to Liddell Hart, 7 December 1925, 23 January 1926; Liddell Hart to Fuller, 11 March 1928, LHP 1/302/81/88; Capt. A. S. Wilson, 'The Scientific Method of Reasoning', *Royal Engineers Journal*, LI (1937) p. 231.
41. Fuller to Luvaas, 8 July 1963, Luvaas Papers; Fuller to Liddell Hart, 25 March 1923, 28 February 1935, LHP 1/302/37/256.

5. Student of Generalship, 1929–33

1. *Foundations*, pp. 329–34; *On War*, II, 1, p. 141; Paret, 'The Genesis of *On War*', pp. 8–13.
2. Brian Holden Reid, 'British Military Intellectuals and the American Civil War: F. B. Maurice, J. F. C. Fuller and B. H. Liddell Hart', *Warfare, Diplomacy and Politics: Essays in Honour of A. J. P. Taylor* (London: Hamish Hamilton, 1986) pp. 42–57; J. Luvaas, *The Military Legacy of the Civil War* (Chicago: Chicago University Press, 1959) p. 209; *Foundations*, pp. 328–9.
3. Fuller to Luvaas, 25 September 1950, Luvaas Papers; Ironside to Liddell Hart, 17 December 1929, LHP 1/401.
4. *The Generalship of Ulysses S. Grant* (London: John Murray, 1929) pp. 3–4, 8–9, 19, 76, 189 (hereafter *Grant*); M. Howard, *The Franco-Prussian War* (London: Hart Davis, 1961) pp. 83–5; Barnett, *Swordbearers*, pp. 60–1.
5. *Grant*, pp. ix, 186–7, 203.
6. *Ibid.*, pp. ix–x, 5.
7. *Ibid.*; Fuller's dislike of Lee was due to his fastidious professionalism; as a cadet he had been 'the "blue-eyed boy" of the [West Point] Academy', *Grant and Lee* (London: Eyre & Spottiswoode, 1933), p. 101; Review of *Grant* in *AQ* XX (1930) pp. 170–1 (The reviewer was Maj. Gen. Sir W. D. Bird, see Swinton to Liddell Hart, 1 January 1930, LHP 1/670/33); *Grant*, pp. 79, 82, 96, 417; M. Cunliffe, *Soldiers and Civilians* (London: Eyre & Spottiswoode, 1969) pp. 17, 68; S. E. Ambrose, *Duty, Honor, Country* (Baltimore: Johns Hopkins University Press, 1966) pp. 89, 98, 100, 136–8; T. H. Williams, *Lincoln and his Generals* (New York: Alfred A. Knopf, 1952) p. 311.
8. *Grant*, p. 20; *The Army in My Time* (London: Rich & Cowan, 1935) pp. 122–3; *Foundations*, p. 328; Montgomery-Massingberd to Liddell Hart, 25 August 1926, LHP 1/520. According to him (27 April 1926);

'Henderson forgot more [military history] than Fuller ever knew.' Bidwell, *Gunners at War*, pp. 65–6.

9. *Grant*, p. 26; *Grant and Lee*, p. 258; 'natural history' was a common generic term denoting the interaction of social, political and biological phenomena, P. Grosskurth, *Havelock Ellis* (London: Allen Lane, 1980) pp. 115, 207.

10. *Grant*, p. 28; *Grant and Lee*, pp. 17–56; M. Howard, *The Causes of Wars* (London: Temple Smith, 1983) p. 103.

11. *Grant*, pp. 26–8, 56, 62–6, 200, 256.

12. *Grant*, pp. 357–8; J. Buechler, '"Give 'em the Bayonet" – A Note on Civil War Mythology', *Civil War History*, VII (1961) pp. 129–31 (hereafter *CWH*); L. Lewis, *Sherman* (New York: Harcourt Brace, 1932, 1958) p. 386.

13. *Grant*, pp. 155, 260, 277–8; E. Hagerman, 'From Jomini to Dennis Hart Mahan', *CWH*, XII (1967) p. 217; R. F. Weigley, *History of the United States Army* (London: Macmillan, 1968) p. 237.

14. G. F. R. Henderson, *The Science of War* (London: Longman, 1916) pp. 268, 308, 310, 332–3; Luvaas, p. 214.

15. *Grant*, pp. 7, 209–13, 275, 359–63.

16. Fuller to Liddell Hart, 6 June, 14 June 1929, LHP 1/302/170/172; *Grant and Lee*, p. 369.

17. Fuller to Liddell Hart, 22 October 1932, LHP 1/302/231; Fuller to Liddell Hart, 19 April, 11 May 1929, *ibid.*, 1/302/165/166.

18. Liddell Hart to Fuller, 20 May 1929, 9 July 1929, *ibid.*, 1/302/169/175.

19. Fuller to Liddell Hart, 14 June, 4 December 1929, *ibid.*, 1/302/169/189.

20. D. Wecter, *The Hero in America* (New York: Scribners, 1941, 1973) pp. 330, 339; Liddell Hart to Fuller, 20 May 1929, LHP 1/302/169; F. B. Maurice, *Robert R. Lee: The Soldier* (London: Constable, 1925), p. 224; A. Badeau, *The Military History of U. S. Grant* (New York: Appleton, 1882) 3 vols.

21. *Grant*, pp. 122, 142, 194, 224, 235, 240, 244, 265, 295; Liddell Hart to Fuller, 20 May 1929, LHP 1/302/169; Liddell Hart's review, *The Daily Telegraph*, LHP 10/1929/137. Swinton claimed (1 January 1930): 'I should have reviewed it more severely . . . . Everything is not so damned simple as F[uller] makes out, and he is far too cock sure and dogmatic', LHP 1/670/33.

22. A. H. Burne, *Lee, Grant and Sherman* (London: Gale & Polden, 1938) pp. 66–7, 72, 173; L. H. Johnson, 'Civil War Military History', *CWH*, XVII (1971) pp. 122–4.

23. Liddell Hart to Fuller, 9 July 1929, LHP 1/302/175; B. F. Butler, *Butler's Book* (Boston, Thayer, 1892) pp. 582–3.

24. *Grant*, pp. 212, 216–18; Grant, *Personal Memoirs* (New York: Webster, 1886) II, p. 129; Williams, 'Military Leadership North and South', David Donald (ed.) *Why the North Won the Civil War* (New York: Collier, 1962 paperback) p. 51.

25. *Grant*, pp. 231, 235; E. Steere, *The Wilderness Campaign* (Harrisburg: Stackpole, 1960) pp. 19–24, 57–9, 259–62, 284, 301–2.

26. *Grant*, p. 195; Liddell Hart, *Sherman* (London: Eyre & Spottiswoode, 1930) pp. viii, 370; *Memoirs*, p. 139.

27. *Grant*, p. 216; *Lectures on FSR II* (London: Sifton Praed, 1931) pp. 55–6; D. S. Freeman, *R. E. Lee* (New York: Scribners, 1934–5) IV, pp. 58–85; *Grant and Lee*, pp. 240, 252, 264–6.
28. Fuller to Liddell Hart, 8 February 1923; Liddell Hart to Fuller, 19 February 1923, 12 July 1929, LHP 1/302/30/31/175/176; Reid, 'British Military Intellectuals and the American Civil War', pp. 46, 51; the second edition of both books was published by Indiana University Press.
29. Fuller to Liddell Hart, 9 January 1932, LHP 1/302/215; *Generalship: Its Diseases and their Cure* (London: Faber & Faber, 1933) pp. 7–8.
30. Review of *Generalship* in *TLS* (23 February 1933) p. 117.
31. *Foundations*, p. 88; Brooke before Dunkirk thought it 'quite maddening' being continually 'drawn into minor details', Bryant, *Turn of the Tide*, p. 85; *Generalship*, p. 13.
32. Montgomery, *Memoirs*, pp. 81–2, 166–8.
33. *Generalship*, pp. 57–9; G. Lefebvre, *Napoleon 1799–1807* (London: Routledge & Kegan Paul, 1969) pp. 219–20; D. G. Chandler, *Marlborough as Military Commander* (London: Batsford, 1973) p. 326; Montgomery, *Memoirs*, pp. 36, 89; *The Patton Papers* (ed.) M. Blumenson (Boston: Houghton Mifflin, 1974) II, pp. 423–4.
34. *Generalship*, pp. 71–2; J. E. Edmonds, 'The Diseases of Generalship', MS in Edmonds Papers V/4/1/13, *The Army, Navy and Air Force Gazette*, LXXIV (1933) pp. 442–4.
35. Fuller to Liddell Hart, 6 May 1930, LHP 1/302/246; R. R. James, *Gallipoli* (London: Batsford, 1965) p. 240; Ellis, *Victory in the West* (London: HMSO, 1968) I, p. 32; A. P. Wavell, *Generals and Generalship* (New York: Macmillan, 1941 edn) p. 6; H. Essame, *Patton the Commander* (London: Batsford, 1973) p. 33.
36. Oman, *Moore*, p. 592; Freeman, *Lee's Lieutenants* (New York: Scribners, 1944) III, p. 32; Wavell, *Generals and Generalship*, p. 15; leading from 'the front' cost the Afrika Korps five commanders per division annually, *Rommel Papers*, p. 270; Reid, 'British Military Intellectuals and the American Civil War', pp. 46–7.
37. *Grant and Lee*, p. 12.
38. Maj. Gen. I. S. Vesey to Edmonds, 17 July 1933; Montgomery-Massingberd to Edmonds, 17 July 1933, Edmonds Papers II/2; Liddell Hart, *Memoirs*, I, p. 172, implied wrongly that it was his *Sherman* that caused the stir and he is also mistaken in thinking that the course was closed down; Fuller to Liddell Hart, 6 April 1931, LHP 1/302/199.

6. 'The Natural History of War', 1930–2

1. Fuller to Liddell Hart, 12 November 1929, 9 June 1931, LHP 1/302/183/191; Ironside to Liddell Hart, 17 December 1929, *ibid.*, 1/401.
2. Fuller to Liddell Hart, 21 December 1927. 'Thus visualized . . . war becomes a story (or human story) not a collection of boxes'. Fuller to Liddell Hart, 8 March 1928, LHP 1/302/122/127.
3. *The Dragon's Teeth* (London: Constable, 1932) pp. v–vii, 7, 10 (hereafter

DT); *Imperial Defence, 1588–1914* (London: Sifton Praed, 1926) pp. 93–9; Fuller to Liddell Hart, 31 December 1931, 4, 16 October 1932, LHP 1/302/214/228/229.

4. *DT*, pp. 66–8, 77; *Foundations*, pp. 61, 64–7; A. J. P. Taylor, *The Struggle for Mastery in Europe, 1848–1918* (Oxford: Clarendon Press, 1954) pp. 69, 166, 361; F. H. Hinsley, *Power and the Pursuit of Peace* (Cambridge: Cambridge University Press, 1963) pp. 49–50.

5. *DT*, pp. 77–82; Fuller to Liddell Hart, 9 July 1931, LHP 1/302/207; Taylor, *Struggle for Mastery in Europe*, p. 138; Joll, *Europe Since 1870*, pp. 527–8.

6. *DT*, pp. 77–97, 198; Fuller to Starr, 7 August 1930, Starr Papers.

7. *India in Revolt* (London: Eyre & Spottiswoode, 1931) pp. 60–1, 125–6, a phrase borrowed from Keynes, *Economic Consequences of the Peace*, p. 3; Fuller to Starr, 13 December 1931, Starr Papers; *War and Western Civilization, 1832–1932* (London: Duckworth, 1932) pp. 261, 265, 268 (hereafter *WWC*).

8. P. Kennedy, *The Rise of the Anglo-German Antagonism* (London: George Allen & Unwin, 1980) pp. 58, 262–3, 305–26, 464; S. Newman, *March 1939* (Oxford: Clarendon Press, 1976); W. Murray, *The Change in European Balance of Power, 1938–39* (Princeton, N.J.: Princeton University Press, 1984) is a provocative analysis.

9. *WWC*, p. 224; *DT*, pp. 107–9; Semmel, pp. 167–9; H. Mackinder, *Democratic Ideals and Reality*, pp. 28–39; H. Mackinder, *Britain and the British Seas* (Oxford: Clarendon Press, 1930 edn) pp. 96–7; Fuller to Liddell Hart, 27 March 1923, LHP 1/302/37.

10. Hinsley, p. 51; H. Nicolson, *Diplomacy* (London: Thornton & Butterworth, 1939) is a traditional liberal view (see especially p. 52); *WWC*, p. 190; P. M. Kennedy, *The Rise and Fall of British Naval Mastery* (London: Allen Lane, 1976) p. 70.

11. *DT*, pp. 36–8, 119, 128, 207; *WWC*, pp. 256–7; G. Blainey, *The Causes of War* (London: Macmillan, 1973) pp. 70–1.

12. *DT*, pp. 133–5.

13. Fuller to Liddell Hart, 16 July 1926. A month later he reported that he was still struggling through Spengler – 'A Frenchman would have put the lot into ¼ of the space'. Fuller to Liddell Hart, 16 August 1927, LHP 1/302/95/96; S. Hynes, *The Auden Generation* (London: Bodley Head, 1976) pp. 83, 193.

14. *DT*, pp. 137–9.

15. *Ibid.*, pp. 53, 146–62, 250–1; Fuller to Starr, 3 January 1930, Starr Papers.

16. *DT*, pp. 133–5.

17. 'The Influence of Tanks on Cavalry Tactics', *Cavalry Journal*, X (1920) Pt 1, p. 110; *India in Revolt*, pp. 33–4; Fuller to Liddell Hart, 25 October 1931, LHP 1/302/212.

18. *DT*, pp. 204–5; Peel, *Spencer*, p. 137.

19. *DT*, pp. 212–13; Fuller does not use the term 'differential tactical factor' but it is consistent with his Darwinist terminology.

20. *DT*, p. 213; W. James, *The Varieties of Religious Experience* (New York: Longmans 1902) pp. 261–2.

21. *DT*, pp. 227–8.
22. Lt. Col. R. G. H. Howard-Vyse, 'A Defence of the Arme Blanche', *Cavalry Journal*, X (1920) p. 325. Howard-Vyse was later the British representative at General Gamelin's HQ during the Fall of France.
23. A. G. Baird Smith, 'The Sublimation of War', *The Nineteenth Century and After*, CIV (1928), pp. 771–5.
24. *DT*, pp. 230–1.
25. *Ibid.*, pp. 236–7, 238–40.
26. *Ibid.*, pp. 243–4, 262–8.
27. D. G. Macrae, 'Darwinism and the Social Sciences', S. A. Barrett (ed.), *A Century of Darwin* (London: Heinemann, 1958) p. 304; J. Beeler, *Warfare in England, 1066–1189* (Ithaca: Cornell University Press, 1966) p. 115; L. H. Addington, *The Blitzkrieg Era and the German General Staff, 1865–1941* (New Brunswick, N.J.: Rutgers University Press, 1971) pp. 68, 95.
28. M. Ginsberg, 'Social Evolution', M. Banton (ed.), *Darwinism and the Study of Society* (London: Tavistock, 1961) p. 126; J. D. Bernal, *Science and History* (London: C. A. Watts, 1969) III p. 833; W. W. Tarn, *Hellenistic Military and Naval Developments* (Cambridge: Cambridge University Press, 1930) p. 101.
29. Quoted in R. D. Milns, *Alexander the Great* (London: Robert Hale, 1968) p. 45; *DT*, p. 212; *WWC*, p. 252; P. Green, *Alexander of Macedon* (Harmondsworth: Penguin, 1974) pp. 483–6.
30. Lindsay to Broad, 15 February 1930, Lindsay Papers; K. Macksey, *Guderian* (London: Macdonald, 1975) p. 66; W. W. Tarn, *Alexander the Great* (Cambridge: Cambridge University Press, 1948, 1977) I, pp. 25, 47.
31. Clausewitz, *On War*, II, 5, p. 173; II, 8, p. 195; V, 3, p. 282; *DT*, p. 214.
32. F. Braudel, *Capitalism and Material Life, 1400–1800* (London: Weidenfeld & Nicolson, 1973) p. 55.
33. *DT*, pp. 63, 272–3, 290.
34. *Ibid.*, p. 252; *WWC*, pp. 26, 32–3, 50–2, 61–2, 75, 83, 100–10, 150, 190–5, 240; P. M. Kennedy, *The Realities Behind Diplomacy* (London: Fontana, 1981 paperback edn) pp. 56–7.
35. *WWC*, pp. 147, 157, 230, 248, 258–9; E. H. Carr, *The Twenty Years Crisis* (London: Macmillan, 1939) pp. 69, 134–5.
36. *WWC*, pp. 140, 252–3; Liddell Hart, 'Aggression and the Problem of Weapons', *English Review*, LIV (1932) pp. 601–5; Fuller to Liddell Hart, 20 July 1932, LHP 1/302/223a–b; S. W. Roskill, *Naval Policy Between the Wars* (London: Collins, 1968) I, pp. 326, 330, 332.
37. *DT*, pp. 24, 275, 296–9.
38. Fuller to Liddell Hart, 21 December 1928, 22 October 1932, LHP 1/302/158/231.

7. The Mechanization of War, 1928–32

1. Brian Holden Reid, 'J. F. C. Fuller's Theory of Mechanized Warfare', *The Journal of Strategic Studies*, I (1978) pp. 295–312; Luvaas, *Education*

of an Army, p. 359; Military Inventions: Their Antiquity and Influence on War', *AQ*, XXV (1933) p. 233.

2. Hobart to Lindsay, 27 February 1925, Lindsay Papers; Swinton to Liddell Hart, 9 December 1929, LHP 1/601/31; Hotblack to Lindsay, 24 December 1929, Lindsay Papers. Earlier (22 November) Hotblack wrote: 'Boney was even more indiscreet than usual in his references to the uselessness of other arms.' Fuller to Lindsay, 26 February 1930, *ibid.*; Fuller to Liddell Hart, 26 July, 17 September 1929, 26 February 1933, LHP 1/302/177/179/239; *Lectures on FSR III* (London: Sifton Praed, 1932) p. ix; Fuller to Liddell Hart, 9 June 1931, 13 December 1929, LHP 1/302/201/155.

3. *Lectures on FSR II*, p. 112 (hereafter *LFSR II*); *Lectures on FSR III*, pp. 3, 77 (hereafter *LFSR III*).

4. Fuller to Liddell Hart, 3 April 1928, LHP 1/302/133; B. H. Liddell Hart, *The Remaking of Modern Armies* (London: John Murray, 1927), p. 92; *LFSR II*, pp. 2, 10, 34; 'Military Inventions', p. 236.

5. 'The Progress of War', *The Nineteenth Century and After*, C (1926), p. 492; *LFSR III*, p. 7.

6. Reid, 'Fuller's Theory of Mechanized Warfare', pp. 298–9; see Brig. Sir H. Wake, 'Mechanization and War', *AQ*, XIX (1930) p. 360.

7. Fuller to Lindsay, 9 July 1926, Lindsay Papers; Fuller to Liddell Hart, 26 April 1948, LHP 1/302/336; see the second edition of *LFSR III*, *Armoured Warfare* (London: Eyre & Spottiswoode, 1943) p. 6.

8. *LFSR II*, p. 60; *LFSR III*, p. 41; 'The Mechanization of War', in *What Would be the Character of a New War?* (London: Gollancz, 1932) p. 53; *Grant and Lee*, p. 215.

9. *LFSR III*, pp. 9–10, 43–4, 45, 48–9, 59; *Rommel Papers*, p. 179; on the prevalence of oral orders, see N. Hamilton, *Monty* (London: Hamish Hamilton, 1981) I, pp. 670, 812; M. Carver, *Tobruk* (London: Batsford, 1964) pp. 41–2.

10. *On Future Warfare* (London: Sifton Praed, 1928) pp. 168, 171, 173; Sir Edward Spears, *Assignment to Catastrophe* (London: Heinemann, 1954) I, p. 162; *ibid.*, II, pp. 44, 194; Lord Ismay, *Memoirs* (London: Heinemann, 1960) p. 119; *Armoured Warfare*, p. 13 n.4.

11. *LFSR III*, p. 54; 'Mechanization of War', pp. 70–1.

12. Bryant, *Turn of the Tide*, pp. 108, 127–8.

13. W. G. F. Jackson, *The North African Campaign*, quoted in Reid, 'Fuller's Theory of Mechanized Warfare', pp. 301–2; Gort kept his head in 1940 and several French generals offered to serve under him, B. Bond, *France and Belgium 1940* (London: Davis Poynter, 1975) p. 128.

14. *Armoured Warfare*, p. 6; *LFSR II*, p. viii.

15. *Machine Warfare* (London: Hutchinson, 1943) p. 57; Spears, II, p. 45; *LFSR III*, pp. 4, 17–18; J. Erickson, *The Road to Stalingrad* (London: Weidenfeld & Nicolson, 1975) pp. 240–8; Trythall, *Fuller*, p. 166; I. S. O. Playfair, *The Mediterranean and the Middle East* (London: HMSO, 1960) III, pp. 216–17, 219, 294.

16. Fuller to Liddell Hart, 19 June 1929, LHP 1/302/173; Liddell Hart, *Memoirs*, I, p. 91; Fuller argued that 'objectives should not be far

distant from each other so that forces may frequently rally and reorganize', *LFSR III*, p. 86. Notes on Fuller's *Lectures on FSR III*, LHP 11/1932/49; Fuller to Lt. Col. F. E. G. Skey, 2 March 1923, LHP 1/302/36b.

17. *Memoirs*, I, p. 90; R. Higham, *Military Intellectuals in Britain* (New Brunswick N.J.: Rutgers University Press, 1966) pp. 85–6; J. Wheldon, *Machine Age Armies* (London: Abelard-Schuman, 1968) pp. 37–8; C. Messenger, *The Art of Blitzkreig* (London: Ian Allan, 1976) pp. 42–4; Liddell Hart's series of articles on infantry tactics in *The National Review* and 'The Development of the "New Model Army"', *AQ*, V (1924) pp. 37–50 (which was actually written in 1922) were completed *before* his recognition of the potential of armoured forces.

18. *LFSR III*, p. 64; *On Future Warfare*, pp. 224, 340; 'The Ancestors of the Tank', *Cavalry Journal*, XVIII (1928) p. 244.

19. *LFSR III*, pp. 14, 16, 39; 'Tank Lessons of the Great War', *FF*, III (1926) p. 199; *Rommel Papers*, pp. 196–7.

20. V. W. Germains, '"Armoured Warfare": A Plea for Common Sense', *AQ*, XVI (1928) p. 371; *"Mechanization" of War*, p. 69. See 'Why Prod? The Infantry Muddle and a Solution', *FF*, VIII (1931) pp. 190–1; 'The Last 800 Yards', *Army, Navy and Air Force Gazette*, LXX (1929) p. 893; Fuller to Liddell Hart, 6 January 1934, LHP 1/302/241.

21. Fuller to Liddell Hart, 8 September 1928, *Ibid.*, 1/302/241; L. H. Addington, *The Blitzkreig Era and the German General Staff, 1865–1941* (New Brunswick, N.J.: Rutgers University Press, 1971) pp. 122–3; *LFSR III*, pp. 47, 93, 127; 'Triumph of the Tank Idea', *FF*, VII (1930), p. 203; Fuller to Liddell Hart, n.d. 1929, LHP 1/302/180.

22. *LFSR III*, pp. 90–2; 'One Hundred Problems on Mechanization, Part 1', *AQ*, XIX (1929) p. 18; *On Future Warfare*, pp. 148, 151, 373–90; *LFSR III*, p. 93; Armoured Force Training Report 1928, PRO WO32/2838.

23. Liddell Hart, *Great Captains Unveiled* (London: Blackwood, 1927) p. 32; *The Remaking of Modern Armies*, pp. 8–9; 15, 50–1; *When Britain Goes to War* (London: Faber & Faber, 1935) pp. 192, 261.

24. *The Future of Infantry* (London: Faber & Faber, 1933) pp. 35–7, 45–6; Reid, 'Fuller's Theory of Mechanized Warfare', p. 307.

25. Spears, I, p. 142; A. F. Upton, *Finland 1940* (London: Davis Poynter, 1974) pp. 64–5; A. Seaton, *The Russo-German War, 1941–1945* (London: Barker, 1971) p. 542; Bidwell, *Gunners at War*, p. 157; Auchinleck to Churchill, 12 January 1942, Alanbrooke Papers 6/D/4a/H.

26. 'The Supremacy of Air Power', *Royal Air Force Quarterly*, I (1930) p. 242; J. A. I. Hamilton, *The Sidi Rezegh Battles* (Cape Town: Oxford University Press, 1957) p. 16.

27. *LFSR III*, pp. 91, 101–2, 126, 155–6, 64–5.

28. *Ibid.*, pp. 34, 88, 42–4; Bond, *France and Belgium 1940*, p. 44.

29. Leach, *German Strategy Against Russia*, p. 47; J. Lukacs, *The Last European War* (London: Routledge & Kegan Paul, 1977) pp. 239–45; Auchinleck to Ismay, 6 November 1941, Ismay Papers IV/Con/1/1c.

30. Lukacs, pp. 239–40.

31. *LFSR III*, pp. 34, 96, 132; Erickson, pp. 249–50.

32. *LFSR III*, pp. 30, 73, 129–31.
33. *Ibid.*, pp. 73–6, 89, 115, 121–3, 124–8; *Armoured Warfare*, p. 79 n.6; *Rommel Papers*, p. 194; Montgomery of Alamein, *El Alamein to the River Sangro* (London: Hutchinson, n.d.) p. 12; E. Belfield and H. Essame, *The Battle for Normandy* (London: Batsford, 1965) p. 144.
34. *LFSR III*, pp. 89, 124; Spears, I, p. 244; Reid, 'Fuller's Theory of Mechanized Warfare', pp. 299, 308–9; G. A. Sheppard, *The Italian Campaign, 1943–1945* (London: Barker, 1968) pp. 238–9; Ellis, *Victory in the West*, I, p. 251; *Armoured Warfare*, p. 6, quoted in Reid, p. 299.
35. Quoted in Liddell Hart, *The Tanks*, II, p. 400; Reid, 'Fuller's Theory of Mechanized Warfare', pp. 298–9.
36. Note on *Armoured Warfare*, 27 November 1943, LHP 11/1943/92; *LFSR III*, pp. 23–4; 'One Hundred Problems on Mechanization, Part 2', *AQ*, XX (1930) p. 258; *LFSR III*, pp. vii, 24, 51, 53–4, 91, 95, 104, 133, 145; Ellis, *Victory in the West*, I, p. 310.
37. A. Horne, *To Lose a Battle* (London: Macmillan, 1968) pp. 200, 258–60; *LFSR III*, p. 33; W. G. F. Jackson, *Alexander of Tunis as Military Commander* (London: Batsford, 1971) p. 253; R. H. S. Stolfi, 'Chance in History', *History*, 65 (1980) pp. 214–18; M. Howard, *War in European History* (Oxford: Oxford University Press, 1976) pp. 132–3.

8. Military Critic as Fascist, 1934–9

1. Lindsay to Fuller, 11 September 1930, Lindsay Papers; Ironside to Liddell Hart, 7 December 1931, 2 January, 25 September 1933, LHP 1/401.
2. *Grant and Lee*, p. 312 n.10; *Memoirs*, pp. 447–8; Trythall, *Fuller*, pp. 178–9; Note on Fuller being 'Put on the Shelf', LHP 11/1933/33; Ironside to Liddell Hart, 25 September 1933, *ibid.*, 1/401.
3. Mosley Interview, 25 August 1977; *March to Sanity* (Greater Britain Publications, 1937); R. Griffiths, *Fellow Travellers of the Right* (Oxford: Clarendon Press, 1980); W. F. Mandle, 'The Leadership of the British Union of Fascists', *Australian Journal of Politics and History*, XII (1966) pp. 362–3, 368.
4. *Empire Unity and Defence* (Bristol: Arrowsmith, 1934) pp. 9, 19–20, 58, 148, 169, 200, 228–30, 250–4; FP IV/4/62; 'Higher Direction for War' (1933), Alanbrooke Papers 4/9/1.
5. *Empire Unity and Defence*, pp. 8–9, 25–30, 187–214, 215–18; 'Higher Direction for War', p. 7; 'Imperial Defence', *Nineteenth Century and After*, CXVII (1935) p. 136; A. J. P. Taylor, *Beaverbrook* (London: Hamish Hamilton, 1972) pp. xiv, 22, 263–4, 294.
6. *Memoirs*, p. 267; J. Russell Kennedy was Editor of the *Army, Navy and Air Force Gazette*; Fuller to Starr, 14 July 1936, Starr Papers.
7. Swinton to Liddell Hart, 16 March 1935; Fuller to Liddell Hart, 28 February 1935; Liddell Hart to Fuller, 7 April 1935; Observations on the Severity of Fuller's Criticisms, LHP 1/670/302/256/258; 11/1936/264.
8. *The Army in My Time* (London: Rich and Cowan, 1935) pp. 16, 53–4, 69–70, 73, 83, 99, 117, 125, 129, 164.

9. *Memoirs*, pp. 6–7.

10. *Ibid.*, pp. 21, 28–9.

11. *Ibid.*, pp. 114–15.

12. *Ibid.*, pp. 72–3.

13. *Ibid.*, pp. 371–2, 420. Cavan had also personally censored a lecture given by Fuller at the RUSI in 1924. Fuller to Liddell Hart, LHP 1/302/65/66. Actually officers of this generation enjoyed much *more* freedom of expression than they do now. See Brian Bond, 'Outsiders Influence on British Defence Policy in the 1930s', RUSI *Journal*, 127 (1982) p. 10.

14. Ismay, *Memoirs*, p. 68; A. G. Baird Smith, 'The Army from Outside', *AQ*, XXIII (1936) pp. 147–53. As Fuller put it, 'Where does the fault lie? Is it in the individual or in the system?' *Empire Unity and Defence*, p. 254.

15. Letter to the author, 21 December 1976; Pearson, *Grammar of Science*, p. 55; J. Lees-Milne, *Harold Nicolson* (London: Chatto & Windus, 1980), I, p. 155; Leach, *German Strategy Against Russia*, pp. 88, 90.

16. Fuller to Liddell Hart, 7 November 1936, LHP 1/302/267; R. Skidelsky, *Oswald Mosley* (London: Macmillan, 1975) p. 320; 'The Supremacy of Air Power', p. 240; G. Best, *Humanity in Warfare* (London: Weidenfeld & Nicolson, 1980) pp. 263–83; M. S. Smith, *British Air Strategy Between the Wars* (Oxford: Clarendon Press, 1984) pp. 66–70.

17. Roskill, *Naval Policy Between the Wars*, I, pp. 115, 123–7, 222–3, 417, 534; A. R. Wells, 'Staff Training in the Royal Navy, 1918–1939', in Bond and Roy (eds.) *War and Society* (London: Croom Helm, 1977) II, pp. 86–106.

18. Fuller to Liddell Hart, 27 August 1937, 6 May 1937, LHP 1/302/151/281; Bond, *Military Policy*, pp. 176–7, 180; Memorandum on the Substitution of Armoured Vehicles for Cavalry, 31 October 1927, PRO WO32/2846.

19. *Memoirs*, p. 447; J. Keegan, 'Regimental Ideology', in G. Best and W. Wheatcroft (eds.) *War, Economy and the Military Mind* (London: Croom Helm, 1976) pp. 3–18; J. Baynes, *Morale* (London: Cassell, 1967) p. 29; B. Fergusson, *Wavell* (London: Collins, 1967) p. 18; Gen. Sir F. Pile, *Ack-Ack* (London: Panther, 1956 paperback edn) p. 22; 'Applications', p. 260; 'Tank and Anti-Tank Weapons', *FF*, XIV (1937) p. 45; Belfield and Essame, p. 90.

20. Brooke MS Diary 1940/1942, entries for 8 October/3 March, Alanbrooke Papers 5/4/5; North to Fuller, 17, 26 June 1936, North Papers IV/4c/55/56; Bond, *Military Policy*, p. 68.

21. Liddell Hart to Scammell, 22 February 1923, LHP 1/622; Review of *Memoirs* in *TLS*, 18 April 1936, p. 326; 'Boney Fuller' (*c.* 1937) *ibid.*, 1/302/668/669a–d.

22. Swinton to Liddell Hart, 2 November 1936; Jerrold to Liddell Hart, 15 October 1936, LHP 1/302/245/1; Fuller to Starr, 14 August 1934, Starr Papers; Review of *The First of the League Wars* in *British Union Quarterly*, I (1937) p. 110.

23. Fuller to Starr, 3 January 1930, Starr Papers; *The First of the League Wars* (London: Eyre & Spottiswoode, 1936) pp. viii, 145 (hereafter *FLW*); L. Mumford, *Technics and Civilization* (London: Routledge &

Kegan Paul, 1932, 1946 edn) pp. 371, 399, 410, 417, 426–7; 'Dictatorship and Generalship', *AQ*, XXXV (1937) pp. 56–67; Skidelsky, pp. 311–15.

24. *FLW*, pp. 165–73; *Empire Unity and Defence*, pp. 111, 89; Kennedy, *The Rise and Fall of British Naval Mastery*, pp. 253–5.

25. *Towards Armageddon* (London: Lovat Dickson, 1937) p. 55; *FLW*, p. 174; see E. Robertson, *Hitler's Pre-War Policy and Plans* (London: Longman, 1963) pp. 88–9.

26. *Empire Unity and Defence*, pp. 257, 284; 'Our Higher Direction for War', pp. 6–7; *FLW*, p. 198; *Towards Armageddon*, pp. 76, 223, 217; Skidelsky, pp. 299, 315; 'Our Recruiting Problem and a Solution', *AQ*, XXXIII (1937) pp. 222–33; P. Dennis, *Decision By Default* (London: Routledge & Kegan Paul, 1972) p. 147.

27. 'Is War More Horrible?' *AQ*, XXXI (1936) pp. 239, 242–5; *FLW*, pp. 201, 208–9; T. Harrisson, *Living Through the Blitz* (London: Collins, 1976) pp. 55, 135–6, 251.

28. Fuller owed this to Ironside who had interceded with the CIGS on his behalf. Talk with General Ironside, 6 May 1937, LHP 1/401; Report by Maj. Gen. J. F. C. Fuller of Visit to General Franco's Army in Spain, 31 March 1937, PRO WO106/1578; Report on a Visit to Spain, 28 October 1937, *ibid.*, WO106/1579; Report on a Visit to Spain, 27 April 1938, *ibid.*, WO106/1585; Harrisson, p. 38.

29. *FLW*, pp. 218–20; *Towards Armageddon*, pp. 196, 204–5, 208; R. H. Spector, *Eagle Against the Sun* (Harmondsworth: Viking, 1985) p. 84.

30. Pile to Liddell Hart, 25 October 1935, LHP 1/575/21a; *FLW*, p. 215. Infantry warfare was based on 'the cultivation of offensive power, that of mechanized warfare will be the opposite'. Report on a Visit to Spain, 27 April 1938, PRO WO106/1585; Fuller to Liddell Hart, 9 April 1937; *Decisive Battles* (London: Eyre & Spottiswoode, 1939–1940), II, p. 1029.

31. *FLW*, p. 85; *Towards Armageddon*, p. 162.

32. Reflections on Fascist Sympathisers, 26 April 1937, LHP 11/1937/31; Liddell Hart to Fuller, 25 January 1937, *ibid.*, 1/302/271; Notes in *Towards Armageddon*, p. 125, *ibid.*, 1/302/278; Fuller to Liddell Hart, 25 November 1937; Liddell Hart to Fuller, 6 May 1937, *ibid.*, 1/302/280/282.

33. North to Fuller, 25 November 1936, North Papers IV/4c/57a; *Towards Armageddon*, p. 76.

9. 'A Watcher of War': Critic of the Second World War, 1939–66

1. *Decisive Battles*, I, pp. 82, 180, 192, 199; Skidelsky, p. 449; Trythall, *Fuller*, pp. 216–17; *The London Observer* (ed.) J. Leutze (Boston: Little, Brown, 1971) pp. 282–3; Brooke MS Diary 1941, entry 20 November, Alanbrooke Papers 5/5; 'The Cancer of Europe', *Fascist Quarterly*, I (1934) pp. 66–86; R. E. Herzstein, *The War that Hitler Won* (London: Hamish Hamilton, 1979) pp. 333–4.

2. *The Decisive Battles of the United States* (London: Hutchinson, 1942); Liddell Hart to Fuller, 12 April 1942; Fuller to Liddell Hart 28

April 1943, LHP 1/302/293/295; *Machine Warfare* (London: Hutchinson, 1942) p. 7.

3. Dedication in Liddell Hart's copy of *Thunderbolts* (London: Skeffington, 1946); *Machine Warfare*, pp. 21–2, 65–5, 83, 14–15.

4. *Ibid.*, pp. 19, 67, 174; Arnold Lunn, *Come What May* (London, 1940), quoted in Fuller to Luvaas, 8 July 1963, Luvaas Papers.

5. *Watchwords* (London: Skeffington, 1944) pp. 66, 70–1, 125; *Thunderbolts*, pp. 37, 50, 54–5.

6. Liddell Hart MS Diary 1942, entry 12 June; Talk with Fuller, 12 June 1942, LHP 11/1942/1b/44; Fuller to Liddell Hart, 20 July 1942; Talk with Beaverbrook, 19 March 1942, LHP 11/1942/1b/44/15, 1/302/285.

7. Fuller to Liddell Hart, 12 March 1949, 20 July, 6 September, 8 October 1942, *ibid.*, 1/302/328/285/289/290.

8. *Memoirs*, pp. 222–6, 240, 360–1, 373–4; *Towards Armageddon*, p. 86. There had been past friction. Fuller recalled how in 1936 over dinner 'Winston had rudely interrupted him and told him to stop talking until he (Winston) had finished – that was characteristic of the man's desire to hold the floor.' Talk with Fuller, 12 June 1942, LHP 11/1942/44. Fuller to Martel, 24 August 1946, Martel Papers P 243/GQM/8a–b; Fuller to Liddell Hart, 7 September 1949, LHP 1/302/418; Suetonius, *The Twelve Caesars* (Harmondsworth: Penguin, 1957) p. 240.

9. Fuller to Starr, 20 May 1947, Starr Papers; Dwight D. Eisenhower, *Crusade in Europe* (New York: Doubleday, 1947) p. 4; Fuller to Liddell Hart, 26 August 1948, LHP 1/302/351; *The Second World War* (London: Eyre & Spottiswoode, 1948) pp. 23–31, 83–6, 116.

10. Trythall, *Fuller*, p. 239.

11. *Watchwords*, pp. 95–6.

12. Fuller to Liddell Hart, 12 August 1943, 22 June 1944, LHP 1/302/305/316; *Second World War*, pp. 258–9.

13. *Second World War*, p. 275; A. Armstrong, *Unconditional Surrender* (New Brunswick N.J.: Rutgers University Press, 1961) p. 22–7, 30, 251; Watt, *Too Serious a Business* (London: Temple Smith, 1975) pp. 144–8; Roosevelt to Hull, 1 April 1944, *The Roosevelt Letters* (London: George Allen & Unwin, 1950), III, p. 492.

14. J. L. Chase, 'Unconditional Surrender Reconsidered', *Political Science Quarterly*, LXX (1955) pp. 258–79; J. Ehrman, *Grand Strategy* (London: HMSO, 1956), VI, p. 5; S. E. Ambrose, *The Supreme Commander* (London: George Allen & Unwin, 1968) p. 388; H. Graml, *The German Resistance to Hitler* (London: Batsford, 1970) pp. 50–2; A. E. Campbell, 'Unconditional Surrender Reconsidered', in Richard Langhorne (ed.) *Diplomacy and Intelligence in the Second World War* (Cambridge: Cambridge University Press, 1986) is a steadfast defence of the policy.

15. M. Howard, *Grand Strategy* (London: HMSO, 1972) IV, pp. 522–9, 534–5; B. Paskins and M. L. Dockrill, *The Ethics of War* (London: Duckworth, 1980) pp. 56–7; *Second World War*, pp. 220–31, 314–16, 391–2; R. J. Overy, *The Air War, 1939–1945* (London: Europa Publications, 1980) pp. 122–5.

16. K. Greenfield, *American Strategy in World War II* (Baltimore: Johns

Hopkins University Press, 1963) p. 6; *Second World War*, pp. 250, 316; Overy, *Air War*, p. 208; S. W. Roskill, *Churchill and the Admirals* (London: Collins, 1977) p. 206; Fuller to Liddell Hart, 20 July 1942, LHP 1/302/285; Exterior and Interior Lines – a Note, FP IV/4/63.

17. *Thunderbolts*, p. 34; N. Frankland, *The Bombing Offensive Against Germany* (London: Faber & Faber, 1965) p. 103; S. Zuckerman, *From Apes to Warlords* (London: Hamish Hamilton, 1978) pp. 218–19, 223–7, 252–3, 270.
18. Paskins and Dockrill, pp. 36–7. Though this is *not* to suggest that strategic bombing strengthened German civilian morale.
19. *Second World War*, pp. 263, 266, 268–9, 297, 303–4.
20. *LFSR III*, pp. 91–5; Maj. Gen. Sir F. Guingand, *Operation Victory* (London: Hodder & Stoughton, 1947) pp. 309–10; J. Ellis, *The Sharp End of War* (London: David & Charles, 1978) pp. 60, 77.
21. Fuller to Alanbrooke, 30 April 1946, FP II/4; Clausewitz, *On War*, IV, 14, p. 275; *LFSR III*, pp. 139–40; Fuller to Liddell Hart, 15 June 1948, LHP 1/302/348.
22. *Second World War*, pp. 413–15.
23. Brian Holden Reid, 'The Attack by Illumination: The Strange Case of Canal Defence Lights', RUSI *Journal*, 128 (December 1983) pp. 44–6 and the sources cited there.
24. *Ibid.*, pp. 47–9.
25. Belfield and Essame, *The Battle for Normandy* (London: Batsford, 1965) p. 116; C. D'Este, *Decision in Normandy* (London: Collins, 1984); *Second World War*, pp. 80, 164, 250.
26. *Ibid.*, pp. 333, 362; S. Bidwell and D. Graham, *Fire-Power: British Army Weapons and Theories of War* (London: George Allen & Unwin, 1982, 1985 paperback) pp. 289–91.
27. Bidwell and Graham, *Fire-Power*, pp. 211–12; *Second World War*, pp. 348–9; Ellis, *Victory in the West*, II, p. 353.
28. *Second World War*, p. 398; *Armament and History* (London: Eyre & Spottiswoode, 1946) pp. 83, 163–4, 172–4, 189, 193.
29. *Ibid.*, pp. 27–9; *The Decisive Battles of the Western World* (London: Eyre & Spottiswoode, 1954–6), I, pp. xi, 1–3; D. H. Zook, 'John Frederick Charles Fuller Military Historian', *Military Affairs*, XXIII (1964) p. 192; Fuller to Starr, 10 September 1954, Starr Papers; G. Kitson Clark, *The Critical Historian* (London: Heinemann, 1967) p. 33.
30. *Armament and History*, pp. 171, 197; for a brilliant prediction of future nuclear rivalry, see pp. 194–5.
31. Sloane to Fuller, 9 February 1961, FP IV/6/9; Fuller to Luvaas, 28 July 1963, Luvaas Papers; Fuller to Liddell Hart, 27 October 1961, LHP 1/302/553; *The Conduct of War, 1789–1961* (London: Eyre & Spottiswoode, 1961) p. 12.
32. *Conduct of War*, pp. 27–9, 33, 37–8, 41, 313–15; see G. F. Kennan, *American Diplomacy* (London: Secker & Warburg, 1950) p. 61.
33. *Conduct of War*, pp. 13, 63–4; Clausewitz, *On War*, VIII, 3, p. 585; Fuller to Sloane, 3 February 1961, FP IV/6/6.
34. *DT*, pp. 210–11, 255–6; *Thunderbolts*, p. 62; *Second World War*, pp. 90–1, 253–4, 273.

35. See Christopher Thorne, *Allies of a Kind* (London: Hamish Hamilton, 1978) pp. 173, 275–81.
36. *Conduct of War*, pp. 249, 264; Kennan agreed: 'there is no more dangerous delusion . . . than the concept of total victory' (*American Diplomacy*, p. 102).
37. Clausewitz, *On War*, I, 1, p. 85; *Second World War*, p. 55.
38. Paskins and Dockrill, p. 109; M. Howard, 'The Influence of Clausewitz', pp. 30–5; Taylor, *Struggle for Mastery in Europe*, pp. 535, 567; J. Gooch, 'British War Aims', in B. Hunt and A. Preston (eds.) *War Aims and Strategic Policy in the Great War* (London: Croom Helm, 1977) pp. 21–38.
39. *Conduct of War*, p. 13; *LFSR III*, p. 37.
40. *Conduct of War*, pp. 116–17.
41. Fuller to Liddell Hart, 14 September 1964, LHP 1/302/622; Fuller to Martel, 15 July 1950, Martel Papers P242/GQM/6/3b.

Conclusion

1. Fuller to Liddell Hart, 9 December 1957, 29 January 1964, LHP 1/302/493/606; North to Fuller, 11 August 1938, North Papers; Swinton to Liddell Hart, 8 March 1946, LHP 1/670; Luvaas, *Education of an Army*, p. 371.
2. *Armament and History*, p. 201; *WWC*, pp. 162, 164, 180, 186.
3. *Reformation*, p. 201; *WWC*, pp. 161, 164, 180, 186; *Armament and History*, p. 32.
4. *Reformation*, pp. 246–8.
5. Ellis, *Sharp End of War*, pp. 31–8, 41–2, 72–4.
6. Bidwell and Graham, *Fire-Power*, pp. 207–10.
7. See Cavan's speech, n.d. (1924), Cavan Papers WO79/66.
8. *Reformation*, pp. 140–1.
9. Christopher Hill, *The Intellectual Origins of the English Revolution* (London: Panther paperback edn, 1972) p. 87; Best, *Humanity in Warfare*, pp. 154–6, 160.
10. Luvaas, *Education of an Army*, pp. 351–2; Fuller to Liddell Hart, 3 April, 17 April 1928, 22 October 1932, LHP 1/302/133/135/231.
11. And praise was given to his series of articles, 'The Influence of Tanks on Cavalry Tactics', *Cavalry Journal*, X (1920) pp. 109, 526–8, 531; Martel, *In the Wake of the Tank*, pp. 7, 16; 'Ponocrates', '"On Future Warfare": Two Reviews', *RUSI Journal*, LXXIII (1928) p. 783.
12. Fuller to Mrs Fuller, 8 July 1918, FP IV/4/232; Grosskurth, *Ellis*, p. 217; Fuller to Liddell Hart, 2 May 1943, LHP 1/302/298; Best, *Humanity in Warfare*, p. 34; Fuller to Luvaas, 8 July 1963, Luvaas Papers.
13. Fuller to Sloane, 18 April 1962, FP IV/6/23; Fuller to Liddell Hart, 21 December 1927, LHP 1/302/122; quoted in F. J. Salloway, *Freud* (New York: Harcourt Brace, 1979) p. 502.
14. Liddell Hart, *Memoirs*, I, pp. 86–91, greatly underplays his influence.
15. Bond, *Liddell Hart*, pp. 53, 90, 173; a good estimate of the inconsistencies of Fuller's style can be found in Bird's review of

Grant, AQ, XX (1930) pp. 170–1; Liddell Hart, *Remaking of Modern Armies,* p. 49; *Ghost of Napoleon* (London: Faber & Faber, 1933) pp. 16, 30, 66, 101, 168–77.

16. Fuller to Hobart, 15 January, 4 February 1943, Hobart Papers; Fuller to Liddell Hart, 8 September 1928, LHP 1/302/153; M. Kitchen, *A Military History of Germany* (London: Weidenfeld & Nicolson, 1975) p. 23.
17. The best recent study which combines historical analysis with a contemporary perspective is John J. Mearsheimer, *Conventional Deterrence* (Ithaca: Cornell University Press, 1983).
18. Fuller to Starr, 16 November 1946, 28 July 1947, Starr Papers; A. J. P. Taylor, *English History 1914–1945* (Oxford: Clarendon Press, 1965) p. 299.
19. Montgomery-Massinberd to Liddell Hart, 27 April 1927, LHP 1/520; Montgomery-Massingberd to Maj. Gen. A. R. Cameron, 22 March 1926, Report of the DSD's Committee on the Proposals for the Reorganization of the Staff College, PRO WO32/4840; Liddell Hart MS Diary 1927, entry for 1 June, LHP 11/1927/1; Employment of Tanks Against Bolshevists in Russia, 8 April 1919, PRO WO32/5865.
20. 'Passchendaele', *FF,* XI (1934) p. 430; Cavan to Fuller, 14 February 1933, Cavan Papers WO79/69.
21. M. Howard, *The Continental Commitment* (Harmondsworth: Penguin, 1974) p. 144; M. Van Creveld, *Supplying War* (Cambridge: Cambridge University Press, 1977) p. 215; *Watchwords,* pp. 46, 116.
22. Fuller to Liddell Hart, 27 March 1923, LHP 1/302/37; *Reformation,* p. xii; Fuller to Luvaas, 28 July 1963, Luvaas Papers. On hearing that Montgomery-Massingberd had turned 'red' on reading one of his articles, Fuller was delighted and predicted that he would turn 'blue' and then 'purple' after reading the next two. Fuller to Liddell Hart, 16 August 1926, LHP 1/302/96.
23. A Note by J. F. C. Fuller, 4 November 1960, LHP 1/302/541a.
24. Liddell Hart, *The Tanks,* I, P. 221, this generous claim nevertheless had the advantage of not requiring a detailed assessment of his influence; Liddell Hart to Fuller, 19 October 1932, LHP 1/302/230; Fuller to Liddell Hart, 26 July 1926, 9 January 1935, LHP 1/302/95/231/250.
25. Fuller to Sloane, 3 February 1961, FP IV/6/6; Bond, *Liddell Hart,* p. 275; C. Barnett, *Strategy and Society* (Manchester: Manchester University Press, 1975) p. 8; Fuller to Starr, 7 December 1946, Starr Papers; *Armament and History,* p. 176; R. Crossman, *The Charm of Politics* (London: Hamish Hamilton, 1958) pp. 209–11.
26. Fuller to Liddell Hart, [?] November 1926, LHP 1/302/102. Fuller was only idealistic when it came to ideas not people. Long reflection on his life and work has convinced me of the sagacity of Lady Mosley's observation that 'I think . . . his greatest fault was that he sincerely despised the human race.' Letter of Lady Mosley to the author, 16 May 1980.

Bibliography

This bibliography is divided into five parts: a listing of all primary materials consulted; a bibliography of Fuller's writings; an accompanying list of the most important of Liddell Hart's writings; a critical discussion of the most valuable recent writing on Fuller; and a select bibliography of modern war.

PRIMARY MATERIAL

Unpublished

Official Documents and Reports in the Public Record Office, London

WO32   Miscellaneous Files on Mechanization and the Reorganization of the Army
WO79   Cavan Papers
WO95   HQ Reports, Tank Corps 1917–18
WO106 Reports of Major General J. F. C. Fuller on visits to Spain, 1937–8
WO161 Master General of the Ordnance – Papers on the Reorganization of the Infantry

Private Correspondence

Liddell Hart Centre for Military Archives King's College, London
The papers of the following were consulted:
Field Marshal Viscount Alanbrooke
Brigadier General Sir James Edmonds
Major General J. F. C. Fuller
Captain Sir Basil Liddell Hart
Major General Sir Percy Hobart
General Lord Ismay
Lieutenant General Sir Lancelot Kiggell
Major General G. M. Lindsay
Field Marshal Sir A. A. Montgomery-Massingberd
Major General Sir Frederick Maurice
Major John North

Senate House Library, University of London
Harry Price Occult Collection

Warburg Institute, London
Gerald Yorke Collection of Crowley Papers

Imperial War Museum, London
The papers of the following were consulted:

Lieutenant General Sir Giffard Martel
Lieutenant General Sir Francis Tuker
Extracts of Letters written in France during the Great War by Major
   C. L. A. Ward-Jackson (unpublished typescript)

House of Lords Record Office
Beaverbrook Papers

Royal Naval College, Greenwich
Sir Eustace d'Eyncourt Papers

Archibald Stevens Alexander Library, Rutgers University, New Jersey, USA
Sloane Collection of Fuller Papers

In Private Hands
Luvaas Papers (Professor Jay Luvaas, US Army War College, Carlisle
   Barracks, Pennsylvania, USA)
Starr Papers (Gordon Grey Esq., Cheltenham, England)

Oral Sources

Interviews with:
Sir Oswald Mosley
Colonel R. Macleod
Mrs Alison Starr

WRITINGS BY MAJOR GENERAL J. F. C. FULLER

This is not intended as a complete Fuller Bibliography which is itself a
subject for an entire volume: it lists Fuller's most important writings and
omits, for example, his journalism.

Books

The Star in the West: A Critical Essay upon the Works of Aleister Crowley
   (London and Felling-on-Tyne: Walter Scott, 1907; reprinted 1974
   Gordon Press).
Hints on Training Territorial Infantry (London: Gale & Polden, 1913).
Training Soldiers for War (London: Hugh Rees, 1914).
Tanks in the Great War (London: John Murray, 1920; New York: Dutton).
The Reformation of War (London: Hutchinson, 1923; New York: Dutton).
Sir John Moore's System of Training (London: Hutchinson, 1925).
British Light Infantry in the Eighteenth Century (London: Hutchinson, 1925).
Atlantis, or America and the Future (London: Kegan Paul, 1925).
Yoga: A Study of the Mystical Philosophy of the Brahmins and Buddhists
   (London: Rider, 1925; reprinted 1978).
The Foundations of the Science of War (London: Hutchinson, 1926).
Imperial Defence, 1588–1914 (London: Sifton Praed, 1926).
Pegasus, or Problems of Transportation (London: Kegan Paul, 1926).

260

Bibliography

On Future Warfare (London: Sifton Praed, 1928).

The Generalship of Ulysses S. Grant (London: John Murray; New York: Dodd Mead, 1929; 2nd edn, Bloomington: Indiana University Press, 1958).

India in Revolt (London: Eyre & Spottiswoode, 1931).

Lectures on FSR II (London: Sifton Praed, 1931).

Lectures on FSR III (London: Sifton Praed, 1932).

The Dragon's Teeth: A Study of War and Peace (London: Constable, 1932).

General Grant: A Biography for Young Americans (New York: Dodd Mead, 1932).

War and Western Civilization, 1832–1932: A Study of War as a Political Instrument and the Expression of Mass Democracy (London: Duckworth, 1932; New York, Libraries Press, 1969).

Grant and Lee: A Study in Personality and Generalship (London: Eyre & Spottiswoode, 1933; New York: Scribners; 2nd edn, Bloomington: Indiana University Press, 1957).

Generalship: Its Diseases and their Cure; A Study of the Personal Factor in Command (London: Faber & Faber, 1933; Harrisburg, Pa.: Military Service Publishing, 1936).

Empire Unity and Defence (Bristol: Arrowsmith, 1934).

The Army in My Time (London: Rich & Cowan, 1935).

The First of the League Wars: Its Lessons and Omens (London: Eyre & Spottiswoode, 1936).

Memoirs of an Unconventional Soldier (London: Ivor Nicholson, 1936).

Towards Armageddon: The Defence Problem and its Solution (London: Lovat Dickson, 1937).

The Last of the Gentlemen's Wars: A Subaltern's Journal of the War in South Africa, 1899–1902 (London: Faber & Faber, 1937).

The Secret Wisdom of the Qabalah (London: Rider, 1937).

Decisive Battles: Their Influence Upon History and Civilization (London: Eyre & Spottiswoode, 1939–1940; New York: Scribners), 2 vols.

Machine Warfare: An Enquiry into the Influence of Mechanics on the Art of War (London: Hutchinson, 1942).

The Decisive Battles of the United States (London: Hutchinson, 1942; New York: Harper; reprinted 1953, Beechhurst Press).

Armoured Warfare: An Annotated Edition of Fifteen Lectures on Operations Between Mechanized Forces (London: Eyre & Spottiswoode, 1943).

Warfare Today: How Modern Battles are Planned and Fought on Land, at Sea and in the Air (London: Odhams, 1944) (with Admiral Sir R. Bacon and Air Marshal Sir P. Playfair).

Watchwords (London: Skeffington, 1944).

Thunderbolts (London: Skeffington, 1946).

Armament and History: A Study of the Influence of Armaments on History from the Dawn of Warfare to the Second World War (London: Eyre & Spottiswoode, 1946; New York: Scribners).

The Second World War, 1939–1945: A Strategical and Tactical History (London: Eyre & Spottiswoode, 1948; New York: Duell, Sloane & Pearce; reprinted 1968, Meredith Press).

How to Defeat Russia (London: Eyre & Spottiswoode, 1951).

The Decisive Battles of the Western World and their Influence Upon History
(London: Eyre & Spottiswoode, 1954–56; abridged edition edited by
John Terraine, St Albans: Granada (Paladin, 1970 and successive
reprints); New York: Funk and Wagnalls, published as *A Military
History of the Western World*; 1967 reprinted Minerva Press).
The Generalship of Alexander the Great (London: Eyre & Spottiswoode, 1958;
New Brunswick, NJ: Rutgers University Press, 1960; reprinted Minerva
Press, 1968).
*The Conduct of War, 1789–1961: A Study of the Impact of the French, Industrial
and Russian Revolutions on War and its Conduct* (London: Eyre &
Spottiswoode, 1961; Eyre Methuen paperback edition, 1972 and
successive reprints; New Brunswick, N.J.: Rutgers University Press;
reprinted 1968, Minerva Press).
Julius Caesar: Man, Soldier and Tyrant (London: Eyre & Spottiswoode,
1965; New Brunswick, N.J.: Rutgers University Press; reprinted 1969,
Minerva Press).

Books with Introductions by Fuller

Supply in Modern Warfare [Colonel G. C. Shaw] (London: Faber & Faber,
1938).
The Stilwell Papers (New York and London: Macdonald, 1949).
The Living Thoughts of Clausewitz (ed.) J. I. Greene (London: The Living
Thoughts Library, 1943).
In Flanders Fields [Leon Wolff] (New York and London: Longmans, 1958).

Articles in Journals

'The Temple of Solomon the King', 4 Parts, *The Equinox*, I (1909–11).
'The Eyes of St Ljnbor', *The Equinox*, I (1913).
'The Mobilization of a Territorial Infantry Battalion', *The Army Review*, V
(1913).
'The Three Flag System of Instructing Infantry Fire Tactics', *The Army
Review*, VI (1914).
'Notes on the Entrainment of Troops to and from Manoeuvres', *The Army
Review*, VII (1914).
'The Procedure of the Infantry Attack', *Journal of the Royal United Services
Institution*, LVIII (1914).
'The Tactics of Penetration', *Journal of the Royal United Services Institution*,
LIX (1914).
'The Training of the New Armies 1803–1805', *Journal of the Royal United
Services Institution*, LXI (1916).
'The Principles of War, with Reference to the Campaigns of 1914–15',
Journal of the Royal United Services Institution, LXI (1916).
'The Influence of Tanks on Cavalry Tactics', *Cavalry Journal*, X (1920), 3
Parts.
'The Application of Recent Developments in Mechanics and Other
Scientific Knowledge to Preparation and Training for Future War on

Land' (Gold Medal [Military] Prize Essay for 1919), *Journal of the Royal United Services Institution*, LXV (1920).

'The Foundations of the Science of War', *The Army Quarterly*, I (1920).

'The Development of Sea Warfare on Land and its Influence on Future Naval Operations', *Journal of the Royal United Services Institution*, LXV (1920).

'Moral Instruction and Leadership', *Journal of the Royal United Services Institution*, LXV (1920).

'The Introduction of Mechanical Warfare on Land and its Possibilities in the Near Future', *Royal Engineers Journal*, XXXVI (1921).

'The Secrets of Napoleon', *The National Review*, 77 (1921).

'Tanks in Future Warfare', *The Nineteenth Century and After*, XC (1921).

'The Problems of Mechanical Warfare', *The Army Quarterly*, III (1922).

'What Changes are Suggested in Naval Construction and Tactics as a Result of (a) The Experience of the War (b) The Development of Submarines and Aerial Warfare in the Future?' (RUSI First Naval Prize Essay for 1920), *Naval Review*, X (1922).

'The Influence of Aircraft on Imperial Defence', *Naval Review*, XI (1923).

'Progress in the Mechanisation of Modern Armies', *Journal of the Royal United Services Institution*, LXX (1925).

'The Discipline of Robert Jackson', *The Army Quarterly*, X (1925).

'The Americans', *The National Review*, 84 (1925).

'The Canadians', *The National Review*, 85 (1925).

'The Battle of the Iron Horse', *The National Review*, 86 (1925).

'Tanks in Rear Guard Operations', *Journal of the Royal Artillery*, LII (1925–26).

'The English Spirit', *The National Review*, 88 (1926).

'Tank Lessons of The Great War', *The Fighting Forces*, III (1926).

'Major General Henry Lloyd: Adventurer and Military Philosopher', *The Army Quarterly*, XII (1926).

'The Tactics of Penetration', *Journal of the Royal Artillery*, LIII (1926–27).

'The Ideal Army of the Artillery Cycle', *Journal of the Royal Artillery*, LIII (1926–27).

'The Progress of War', *The Nineteenth Century and After*, C (1926).

'Tactics and Mechanization', *The Fighting Forces*, IV (1927).

'The Influence of Armour from Alexander to Joan of Arc', *The Army Quarterly*, XVI (1927).

'The Problems of Air Warfare', *Journal of the Royal Artillery*, LIV (1927–28).

'The Reign of the Bullet', *The Fighting Forces*, IV (1927).

'The Changing Conditions of War', *The Nineteenth Century and After*, CI (1927).

'The Foundations of War Control', *Journal of the Royal Artillery*, LIV (1927–28).

'The Days of Electrical Battles', *Radio Times*, 6 July 1928.

'A Greater than Scipio Africanus', *The Army Quarterly*, XV (1928).

'The Ancestors of the Tank', *Cavalry Journal*, XVIII (1928).

'Science and War', *The Nineteenth Century and After*, CIII (1928).

'Scientific Soldiership', *The Royal Engineers Journal*, XLII.

'The Elimination of War', *The Nineteenth Century and After*, CIII (1928).

'The Future of Military Engineering', *The Royal Engineers Journal*, XLII (1928).

'Economics and Modern Warfare', *Journal of the Royal Artillery*, LV (1928–29).

'The Importance of Military Inventions', *Army, Navy and Air Force Gazette*, LXX (1929).

'One Hundred Problems on Mechanization, Part 1', *The Army Quarterly*, XIX (1929).

'The Last 800 Yards', *Army, Navy and Air Force Gazette*, LXX (1929).

'The Natural History of War', *Journal of the Royal Artillery*, LVI (1929–30).

'The Supremacy of Air Power', *The Royal Air Force Quarterly*, I (1930).

'One Hundred Problems on Mechanization, Part 2', *The Army Quarterly*, XX (1930).

'The Rise of the Artillery Cycle and Certain Speculations', *Army, Navy and Air Force Gazette*, LXXI (1930), 3 Parts.

'Two Private Letters from Major General Sir John Moore', *Journal of the Society for Army Historical Research*, X (1930).

'The Triumph of the Tank Idea', *The Fighting Forces*, VII (1930).

'The Influence of the Constant Tactical Factor in the Development of War', *Journal of the Royal Artillery*, LVII (1930–31).

'Tactics 1450–1740: An Introduction to the Study of Marlborough's Campaigns', *The Army Quarterly*, XXII (1931).

'Co-ordination of the Attack', *The Fighting Forces*, VII (1931).

'Why Prod? The Infantry Muddle and a Solution', *The Fighting Forces*, VIII (1931).

'Tank versus Tank (24 April 1918)', *The Royal Engineers Journal*, LXV (1931).

'Gandhi – Saint or Sinner?', *The Nineteenth Century and After*, CX (1931).

'The Artillery of the Carthaginians, Greeks and Romans', *Journal of the Royal Artillery*, LVIII (1931–32).

'Ironclad Field Artillery', *Army Ordnance*, XIII (1932).

'Artillery in the Classical Age', *Army Ordnance*, XIV (1933).

'Military Inventions: Their Antiquity and Influence on War', *The Army Quarterly*, XXV (1933).

'The Place of the American Civil War in the Evolution of War', *The Army Quarterly*, XXVI (1933).

'Sir John Moore: A Lecture on British Discipline', *Journal of the Royal Artillery*, LX (1933–34).

'War and Peace', *The English Review*, LVIII (1934).

'Our Artillery Racket', *Army, Navy and Air Force Gazette*, LXXV (1934).

'The World as a Dead-End', *The Fighting Forces*, X (1934).

'Summary of Tank Operations, 1916–1918', *Royal Tank Corps Journal* (1934).

'The Foundations of a European Order', *The Fighting Forces*, XI (1934).

'Robert E. Lee', *Army, Navy and Air Force Gazette*, LXXV (1934).

'War and Western Civilization', *The Nineteenth Century and After*, CXV (1934).

'Passchendaele', *The Fighting Forces*, X (1934).

'Germany – As I See It', *The English Review*, LX (1935).

'A Study of Mobility in the American Civil War', *The Army Quarterly*, XXIX (1935).
'Imperial Defence', *The Nineteenth Century and After*, CXVII (1935).
'The Cancer of Europe', *Fascist Quarterly*, I (1935).
'Fascism and War', *Fascist Quarterly*, I (1935).
'Our Military Jungle', *The Nineteenth Century and After*, CXVII (1936).
'Our Defence Problem', *Fascist Quarterly*, II (1936).
'Is War More Horrible?', *The Army Quarterly*, XXXI (1936).
'Totalitarian War', *Army Ordnance*, XVII (1936).
'The Development of Totalitarian Warfare. A Lecture delivered at the Royal Artillery Institution', *Journal of the Royal Artillery*, CXIII (1936–37).
'The War in Spain', *The British Union Quarterly*, I (1937).
'Dictatorship and Generalship', *The Army Quarterly*, XXXV (1937).
'The Problem of Tank and Anti-Tank Weapons', *The Fighting Forces*, XIV (1937).
'Our Recruiting Problem and a Solution', *The Army Quarterly*, XXXV (1937).
'Propaganda and War', *Journal of the Royal Artillery*, LXIV (1937–38).
'The Soviet–Spanish War to September 1938', *The Army Quarterly*, XXXVII (1939).
'The War in Europe', *The War* (1940).
'The Soldier and the Journalist', *The New English Weekly* (1940).
'The War in Europe', *Army Ordnance*, XX (1940).
'Magic and War', *Occult Review*, LXIX (1942).
'The Attack by Magic', *Occult Review*, LXIX (1942).
'The City and the Bomb', *Occult Review*, LXXI (1944).
'Das Problem Europa', (Berlin, 1944).
'The Artillery Rocket', *New English Review*, XV (1947).
'Science and the General Staff', *New English Review*, XVII (1948).
'The European Problem', *Fellowship* (1949).
'Unstrategic Bombing and World Ruin', *Army Ordnance*, XXIX (1949).
'Sir John Moore's Light Infantry Instructions of 1798–99', *Journal of the Society for Army Historical Research*, XXX (1952).
'How to Block Russia', *US News and World Report* (1952).
'Warfare and the Future', *Armor*, LXII (1953).
'The Changing Face of War', *Ordnance* (1957).
'The Military Situation', *Ordnance* (1958).

Articles in Books

'The Mechanization of War', in *What Would be the Character of a New War?* (London: Gollancz, 1932).
'A Soldier-Journalist in Abyssinia: My Outlook on the Approaching War', Ladislas Farago (ed.), *Abyssinian Stop Press* (London: Robert Hale, 1936).

WRITINGS BY CAPTAIN SIR BASIL LIDDELL HART

Books

This is not a complete list; books irrelevant to this study have been excluded.

Paris, or the Future of War (London: Kegan Paul, 1925).
A Greater than Napoleon: Scipio Africanus (London: Blackwood, 1926).
The Remaking of Modern Armies (London: John Murray, 1927).
Great Captains Unveiled (London: Blackwood, 1927).
Reputations: Ten Years After (London: John Murray, 1928).
The Decisive Wars of History (London: Bell, 1929).
Sherman: The Genius of the Civil War (London: Eyre & Spottiswoode, 1930).
The Real War (London: Faber & Faber, 1930).
Foch: The Man of Orleans (London: Eyre & Spottiswoode, 1931).
The British Way in Warfare (London: Faber & Faber, 1932); enlarged edition, *When Britain Goes to War* (London: 1935).
The Future of Infantry (London: Faber & Faber, 1933).
The Ghost of Napoleon (London: Faber & Faber, 1933).
'T. E. Lawrence' in Arabia and After (London: Jonathan Cape, 1934).
The War in Outline, 1914–1918 (London, Faber & Faber, 1936).
Europe in Arms (London: Faber & Faber, 1937).
Through the Fog of War (London: Faber & Faber, 1938).
The Defence of Britain (London: Faber & Faber, 1939).
Dynamic Defence (London: Faber & Faber, 1940).
The Strategy of Indirect Approach (London: Faber & Faber, 1941).
The Current of War (London: Hutchinson, 1941).
This Expanding War (London: Faber & Faber, 1942).
Thoughts on War (London: Faber & Faber, 1944).
Why Don't We Learn from History? (London: George Allen & Unwin, 1944).
The Revolution in Warfare (London: Faber & Faber, 1946).
The Other Side of the Hill (London: Cassell, 1948); enlarged edition 1951.
Defence of the West (London: Cassell, 1956).
The Tanks (London: Cassell, 1959), 2 vols.
Deterrent or Defence (London: Stevens, 1960).
Memoirs (London: Cassell, 1965), 2 vols.
History of the Second World War (London: Cassell, 1970).

Books Edited by Liddell Hart

The Letters of Private Wheeler, 1808–1828 (London: Michael Joseph, 1951).
The Rommel Papers (London: Collins, 1953).
The Soviet Army (London: Weidenfeld & Nicolson, 1956).

Articles

'Are Infantry Doomed?' *The National Review*, LXXIX (1922).
'Infantry – "The New Model"', *The National Review*, LXXIX (1922).

'The Future Development of Infantry', *The National Review*, LXXX (1922).
'The Development of the "New Model" Army', *The Army Quarterly*, V (1924).
'The Value and Originality of "The Foundations of the Science of War"', *The Army Quarterly*, XII (1926).
'Hannibal and Rome', *The Atlantic Monthly*, 142 (1928).
'The New Romulus and the New Rome', *The Atlantic Monthly*, 142 (1928).
'Behind the German Front', *The Atlantic Monthly*, 144 (1929).
'Armament and its Future Use', *The Yale Review*, XIX (1930).
'The Inner Story of the Aisne', *The Fortnightly Review*, DCCLXX (1931).
'The Tale of the Tank', *The Nineteenth Century and After*, CXII (1932).
'The March Retreat', *The English Review*, LIV (1932).
'The Problem of Weapons', *The English Review*, LV (1932).
'Foch and the Fate of Britain', *The Fortnightly Review*, DCCCII (1933).
'Lord Milne and the Army', *The English Review*, LVI (1933).
'The Psychology of a Commander', *The Army Quarterly*, XXX (1935).
'Future Warfare', *The Atlantic Monthly*, 158 (1936).
'The Strategic Future of the Mediterranean', *The Yale Review*, XXVI (1937).
'Lessons of the Spanish War', *The National Review*, 109 (1937).
'From Tortoise to Tank', *World Review* (1940).
'From Clausewitz to Hitler', *World Review* (1940).
'War, Limited', *Harper's Magazine* (1946).
'Defence of the West', *The World Review* (1949).
'The Objective in War – Battle or Indirect Action?' *Brassey's Annual* (1950).
'The Outlook for NATO', *Blackwood's Magazine*, 292 (1962).

WRITINGS ABOUT MAJOR GENERAL J. F. C. FULLER

Virtually all histories of mechanization include generalized references to Fuller, such as J. Wheldon's *Machine Age Armies* (London: Abelard Schuman, 1968). Many of these are narrow in scope, have made no use of primary source material and show little understanding of the broader implications of Fuller's thought. The works of Richard Ogorkiewicz are outstanding (see Bibliography), especially for their technical grasp, while Colonel Harold R. Winton places him in the broader context in his estimate of 'The Evolution of British Mechanized and Armoured Doctrine, 1919–38', RUSI *Journal*, 130 (1985). The best short account of Fuller's thought is the chapter in Jay Luvaas, *The Education of an Army* (London: Cassell, 1965). The more one reads this chapter, the more one admires it. The fullest account of Fuller's life is Major General A. J. Trythall, *'Boney' Fuller: The Intellectual General* (London: Cassell, 1977), which also has the advantage that the author enjoys an intimate knowledge of the workings and eccentricities of the British Army.

The most detailed assessment of Fuller's views on armoured warfare is B. H. Reid, 'J. F. C. Fuller's Theory of Mechanized Warfare', *Journal of Strategic Studies*, I (1978) and 'The Attack By Illumination: The Strange Case of Canal Defence Lights', RUSI *Journal*, 128 (1983); the latter includes comment on Fuller's post-1939 views on developments in mechanization.

R. H. Larson, *The British Army and the Theory of Armoured Warfare, 1918–1940* (Newark: University of Delaware Press, 1984), though ambitious, adds little to our knowledge of Fuller's writing, though it does indicate the strong interest in him in the United States, as exemplified not only in D. H. Zook, 'John Frederick Charles Fuller Military Historian', *Military Affairs*, XXII (1964), which is now rather dated and inaccurate in detail, but also in Colonel M. D. Wyly, 'J. F. C. Fuller: Soldier and Historian', *Marine Corps Gazette*, 68 (1984). Fuller's interest in the United States is examined in B. H. Reid, 'British Military Intellectuals and the American Civil War: F. B. Maurice, J. F. C. Fuller and B. H. Liddell Hart', *Warfare, Politics and Diplomacy: Essays in Honour of A. J. P. Taylor* (London: Hamish Hamilton, 1986).

For the Soviet reaction to his writing, see P. H. Vigor, 'The Soviet View of Fuller and Liddell Hart', *RUSI Journal*, 123 (1978). For an analysis of his views on chemical warfare which have continuing relevance, see B. H. Reid, 'Gas Warfare: The Perils of Prediction', in David Carlton and Carlo Schaerf (eds.), *Reassessing Arms Control* (London: Macmillan, 1985). The same author has explored the wider intellectual background and influences on the inter-war military thinkers in 'T. E. Lawrence and Liddell Hart', *History*, 70 (1985) and 'Colonel J. F. C. Fuller and the Revival of Classical Military Thinking in Britain, 1918–1926', *Military Affairs*, XLIX (1985). On his friendship with Liddell Hart and the cross fertilization of ideas, see Brian Bond, *Liddell Hart* (London: Cassell, 1977), which is an object lesson in lucid and balanced scholarship.

SELECT BIBLIOGRAPHY OF MODERN WAR

This bibliography is not intended as a comprehensive list of all works consulted in the writing of this book, which would be enormous. It is intended as a general pointer to those works found most valuable and as a guide to further reading. Particular points (including areas in the history of ideas) will be found supported in the footnotes by specific works, many of specialist or even esoteric interest. Neither is this bibliography intended to supply detailed guidance on specialist topics (like, for example, the massive literature on the two World Wars or the American Civil War), but rather to provide a sign-post to the range of issues posed by Fuller's writing.

Books

Aron, R., *Clausewitz: Philosopher of War* (London: Routledge & Kegan Paul, 1983).

Addington, L. H., *The Blitzkrieg Era and the German General Staff, 1865–1941* (New Brunswick, N.J.: Rutgers University Press, 1971).

——, *The Pattern of War* (Bloomington: Indiana University Press, 1985).

Ahrenfeldt, R. H., *A History of Psychiatry in the British Army in the Second World War* (London: Routledge & Kegan Paul, 1958).

Ambrose, S. E., *Duty, Honor, Country* (Baltimore: Johns Hopkins University Press, 1966).
——, *Eisenhower* (London: George Allen & Unwin, 1984), 2 vols.
Badeau, A., *The Military History of U.S. Grant* (New York: Appleton, 1882), 3 vols.
Barclay, Brig. C. N., *Armistice 1918* (London: Dent, 1969).
Barnett, C., *The Desert Generals* (Kimber, 1960; 2nd edn, George Allen & Unwin, 1984).
——, *The Swordbearers* (London: Eyre & Spottiswoode, 1963).
——, *Britain and her Army* (London: Allen Lane, 1970).
——, *The Collapse of British Power* (London, Allen Lane, 1973; paperback edition, Gloucester: Alan Sutton, 1984).
——, *Strategy and Society* (Manchester: Manchester University Press, 1975).
Baynes, J., *Morale* (London: Cassell, 1967).
Beckett, I. F. W. and Simpson, K. (eds.), *A Nation in Arms* (Manchester: Manchester University Press, 1985).
Belfield, E. and Essame, H., *The Battle for Normandy* (London: Batsford, 1965).
Bennett, R., *Ultra in the West* (London: Hutchinson, 1979).
Best, G., *Humanity in Warfare* (London: Weidenfeld & Nicolson, 1980).
—— and Wheatcroft, A. (eds.), *War, Economy and the Military Mind* (London: Croom Helm, 1976).
Bialer, U., *The Shadow of the Bomber* (London: Royal Historical Society, 1980).
Bidwell, Brig. S., *Gunners at War* (London: Arms and Armour Press, 1970).
——, *Modern Warfare* (London: Allen Lane, 1973).
—— and Graham, D., *Fire-Power* (London: George Allen & Unwin, 1982; paperback edn, 1985).
Blainey, G., *The Causes of War* (London: Macmillan, 1973).
Bond, B., *The Victorian Army and the Staff College, 1854–1914* (London: Eyre & Spottiswoode, 1972).
——, *France and Belgium 1939–1940* (London: Davis Poynter, 1975).
——, *Liddell Hart* (London: Cassell, 1977).
——, *British Military Policy Between the Two World Wars* (Oxford: Clarendon Press, 1980).
——, *War and Society in Europe, 1870–1970* (Leicester: Leicester University Press; Fontana paperback, 1984).
—— and Roy, I. (eds.), *War and Society* (London: Croom Helm, 1976–78), 2 vols.
Bryant, A., *The Turn of the Tide* (London: Collins, 1957).
——, *Triumph in the West* (London: Collins, 1959).
Burne, Lt. Col. A. H., *Lee, Grant and Sherman* (London: Gale & Polden, 1938).
Carr, E. H., *The Twenty Years Crisis* (London: Macmillan, 1939).
Carver, Field Marshal Lord, *Tobruk* (London: Batsford, 1964).
——, *The Apostles of Mobility* (London: Weidenfeld & Nicolson, 1979).
Chandler, David G., *The Campaigns of Napoleon* (London: Weidenfeld & Nicolson, 1967).

——, *Marlborough as Military Commander* (London: Batsford, 1973).

——, *The Art of War in the Age of Marlborough* (London: Batsford, 1976).

Childs, J., *Armies and Warfare in Europe, 1648–1789* (Manchester: Manchester University Press, 1982).

Childs, Gen. Sir W., *Episodes and Reflections* (London: Cassell, 1930).

Clausewitz, Gen. Karl von, *On War* (eds.) Michael Howard and Peter Paret (Princeton: Princeton University Press, 1976).

Creveld, M. van, *Supplying War* (Cambridge: Cambridge University Press, 1977).

——, *Command in War* (Harvard: Harvard University Press, 1985).

Cunliffe, M., *George Washington: Man and Monument* (London: Collins, 1958).

——, *Soldiers and Civilians* (London: Eyre & Spottiswoode, 1969).

——, *The Age of Expansion, 1848–1917* (London: Weidenfeld & Nicolson, 1974).

Dennis, P., *Decision By Default* (London: Routledge & Kegan Paul, 1972).

D'Este, C., *Decision in Normandy* (London: Collins, 1983).

Donald, D. (ed.), *Why the North Won the Civil War* (New York: Collier, 1962).

Edmonds, Brig. Gen. Sir J. E., *et al.*, *Military Operations, France and Belgium* (London: HMSO, 1922–47).

Ellis, J., *The Sharp End of War* (London: David and Charles, 1980).

Ellis, Major L. F., *Victory in the West* (London: HMSO, 1962–8), 2 vols.

Erickson, J., *The Road to Stalingrad* (London: Weidenfeld & Nicolson, 1975).

——, *The Road to Berlin* (London: Weidenfeld & Nicolson, 1983).

Essame, H., *The Battle for Europe, 1918* (London: Batsford, 1972).

——, *Patton the Commander* (London: Batsford, 1973).

Frankland, N., *The Bombing Offensive Against Germany* (London: Faber, 1965).

Freeman, D. S., *R. E. Lee* (New York: Scribners, 1934–35), 4 vols.

——, *Lee's Lieutenants* (New York: Scribners, 1944), 3 vols.

French, D., *British Economic and Strategic Planning, 1905–1915* (London: George Allen & Unwin, 1980).

Fussel, P., *The Great War and Modern Memory* (New York: Oxford University Press, 1975).

Germains, V. W., *The 'Mechanization' of War* (London: Sifton Praed, 1927).

Gooch, J., *Armies in Europe* (London: Routledge & Kegan Paul, 1980).

Graham, D and Bidwell Brig. S., *Tug of War* (London: Hodder & Stoughton, 1986).

Grant, General U. S., *Personal Memoirs* (New York: Webster, 1886), 2 vols.

Hamilton, N., *Monty* (London: Hamish Hamilton, 1981–6), 3 vols.

Harrisson, T., *Living Through the Blitz* (London: Collins, 1976).

Haig, Field Marshal Earl, *The Private Papers of Douglas Haig, 1914–1919*, (ed.) R. Blake (London: Eyre & Spottiswoode, 1952).

Henderson, G. F. R., *Stonewall Jackson* (London: Longman, 1911 edn).

——, *The Science of War* (ed.) Neil Malcolm (London: Longman, 1916).

Higham, R. (ed.), *A Guide to the Sources of British Military History* (London: Routledge & Kegan Paul, 1972).

——, *The Military Intellectuals in Britain* (New Brunswick, NJ: Rutgers University Press, 1966).

Hinsley, F. H., *Power and the Pursuit of Peace* (Cambridge: Cambridge University Press, 1963).

Holmes, R., *Firing Line* (London: Jonathan Cape, 1985).

Horne, A., *The Price of Glory* (London: Macmillan, 1962).

——, *The Fall of Paris* (London: Macmillan, 1965).

——, *To Lose a Battle* (London: Macmillan, 1968).

Howard, M., *The Franco-Prussian War* (London: Hart Davis, 1961).

—— (ed.), *The Theory and Practice of War* (London: Cassell, 1965).

——, *The Mediterranean Strategy in the Second World War* (London: Weidenfeld & Nicolson, 1968).

——, *Grand Strategy*, IV (London: HMSO, 1972).

——, *The Continental Commitment* (Harmondsworth: Penguin, 1974).

——, *War in European History* (Oxford: Oxford University Press, 1976).

——, *War and the Liberal Conscience* (London: Temple Smith, 1978).

—— (ed.), *Restraints on War* (Oxford: Clarendon Press, 1979).

——, *The Causes of Wars* (London: Temple Smith, 1983).

——, *Clausewitz* (Oxford: Oxford University Press, 1983).

Ismay, Lord, *Memoirs* (London: Heinemann, 1960).

Jackson, Gen. Sir W. G. F., *Alexander of Tunis as Military Commander* (London: Batsford, 1971).

——, *The North African Campaign, 1940–1943* (London: Batsford, 1975).

——, *'Overlord': Normandy 1944* (London: Davis Poynter, 1978).

James, R. R., *Gallipoli* (London: Batsford, 1965).

Jeffery, K., *The British Army and the Crisis of Empire, 1918–1922* (Manchester: Manchester University Press, 1984).

—— (ed.), *The Military Correspondence of Field Marshal Sir Henry Wilson, 1918–1922* (London: Bodley Head, 1985).

Joll, J., *Europe Since 1870* (London: Weidenfeld & Nicolson, 1973, revised edn, 1983).

——, *The Origins of the First World War* (London: Longmans, 1984).

Keegan, J., *The Face of Battle* (London: Jonathan Cape, 1976).

——, *Six Armies in Normandy* (London: Jonathan Cape, 1982).

Kennedy, P. M., *The Rise and Fall of British Naval Mastery* (London: Allen Lane, 1976).

——, *The Rise of the Anglo-German Antagonism* (London: George Allen and Unwin, 1980).

——, *The Realities Behind Diplomacy* (London: Fontana, 1981 paperback edn).

——, *Strategy and Diplomacy* (London: Fontana, 1984).

Keynes, J. M., *The Economic Consequences of the Peace* (London: Macmillan, 1919).

Kitchen, M., *A Military History of Germany* (London: Weidenfeld & Nicolson, 1975).

——, *The Silent Dictatorship* (London: Croom Helm, 1976).

Langhorne, R. (ed.), *Diplomacy and Intelligence in the Second World War* (Cambridge: Cambridge University Press, 1985).

Leach, B. A. *German Strategy Against Russia* (Oxford: Clarendon Press, 1973).

Lefebvre, G., *Napoleon 1799–1807* (London: Routledge & Kegan Paul, 1969).

Lewin, R., *Montgomery as Military Commander* (London: Batsford, 1971).

——, *Hitler's Mistakes* (London: Leo Cooper, 1984).

Lewis, L., *Sherman* (New York: Harcourt Brace, 1932, 1958).

Lisle, Gen. Sir B. de, *Reminiscences of Sport and War* (London: Eyre & Spottiswoode, 1939).

Longford, E., *Wellington: The Years of the Sword* (London: Weidenfeld and Nicolson, 1969).

Ludendorff, Gen. E., *My War Memories* (London: Hutchinson, 1920 edn), 2 vols.

Lukacs, J., *The Last European War* (London: Routledge & Kegan Paul, 1977).

Luvaas, J., *The Military Legacy of the Civil War* (Chicago: Chicago University Press, 1959).

Mackinder, Sir H., *Democratic Ideals and Reality* (New York: Holt, 1942 edn).

——, *Britain and the British Seas* (Oxford: Clarendon Press, 1930 edn).

Macksey, Maj. K., *Guderian* (London: Macdonald, 1975).

McFeely, W., *Grant* (New York: Norton, 1981).

McNeil, W. H., *The Pursuit of Power* (Oxford: Blackwell, 1983).

Martel, Lt. Gen. Sir G., *In the Wake of the Tank* (London: Sifton Praed, 1931).

Maurice, Maj. Gen. Sir F., *Robert E. Lee: The Soldier* (London: Constable, 1925).

——, *Governments and War* (London: Heinemann, 1926).

——, *British Strategy* (London: Constable, 1929).

Milward, A. S., *War, Economy and Society, 1939–1945* (London: Allen Lane, 1977).

Montgomery, Field Marshal Viscount, *Memoirs* (London: Collins, 1958).

Moran, Lord, *Churchill: The Struggle for Survival* (London: Constable, 1966).

Morse, P. M., and Kimball, G. F., *Methods of Operations Research* (New York: Wiley, 1952).

Murray, W., *The Change in the European Balance of Power, 1938–1939* (Princeton: Princeton University Press, 1984).

Nickerson, H., *The Armed Horde, 1793–1939* (New York: Putnam, 1940).

Ogorkiewicz, R. M., *Armoured Forces* (London: Arms and Armoured Press, 1970 edn).

——, *Design and Development of Armoured Fighting Vehicles* (London: Macdonald, 1968).

Oman, Carola, *Sir John Moore* (London: Hodder & Stoughton, 1953).

Overy, R. J., *The Air War, 1939–1945* (London: Europa, 1980).

Packenham, T., *The Boer War* (London: Weidenfeld & Nicolson, 1979).

Paret, P., *Clausewitz and the State* (New York: Oxford University Press, 1976).

Parish, P. J., *The American Civil War* (London: Eyre Methuen, 1975).

Paskins, B. and Dockrill, M., *The Ethics of War* (London: Duckworth, 1980).

Patton, Gen. G. S., *The Patton Papers* (ed.) M. Blumenson (Boston: Houghton Mifflin, 1974), 2 vols.

Pearton, M., *The Knowledgeable State* (London: Burnett, 1982).

Pile, Gen. Sir F., *Ack-Ack* (London: Panther, paperback edn, 1956).

Pitt, B., *1918: The Last Act* (London: Macmillan, paperback edn, 1985).

Porch, D., *The March to the Marne* (Cambridge: Cambridge University Press, 1976).

Powers, B. D., *Strategy Without Slide-Rule* (London: Croom Helm, 1976).

Quimby, R. S., *The Background to Napoleonic Warfare* (New York: Columbia University Press, 1956).

Roskill, S. W., *Naval Policy Between the Wars* (London: Collins, 1968–76), 2 vols.

——, *Churchill and the Admirals* (London: Collins, 1977).

Seaton, A., *The Russo-German War* (London: Barker, 1971).

Semmel, B., *Imperialism and Social Reform* (London: George Allen & Unwin, 1960).

——, *Marxism and War* (London: Oxford University Press, 1981).

Sheppard, G. A., *The Italian Campaign, 1943–1945* (London: Barker, 1968).

Skelley, A. R., *The Victorian Army at Home* (London: Croom Helm, 1977).

Smith, M. S., *British Air Strategy Between the Wars* (Oxford: Clarendon Press, 1984).

Spears, Sir E., *Assignment to Catastrophe* (London: Heinemann, 1954), 2 vols.

Spector, R. H., *Eagle Against the Sun* (Harmondsworth: Viking, 1985).

Spiers, E. M., *Chemical Warfare* (London: Macmillan, 1986).

Strachan, H., *European Armies and the Conduct of War* (London: George Allen & Unwin, 1983).

Stone, N., *The Eastern Front, 1914–1917* (London: Hodder & Stoughton, 1975).

Taylor, A. J. P., *The Struggle for Mastery in Europe, 1848–1918* (Oxford: Clarendon Press, 1954).

——, *English History 1914–1945* (Oxford: Clarendon Press, 1965).

——, *Beaverbrook* (London: Hamish Hamilton, 1972).

——, *The Second World War* (London: Hamish Hamilton, 1975).

Terraine, J., *Douglas Haig* (London: Hutchinson, 1963).

——, *To Win a War* (London: Sidgwick & Jackson, 1978).

——, *The Right of the Line* (London: Hodder & Stoughton, 1985).

Thorne, C., *Allies of a Kind* (London: Hamish Hamilton, 1978).

Watt, D. C., *Too Serious a Business* (London: Temple Smith, 1975).

Wavell, Field Marshal Lord, *Generals and Generalship* (New York: Macmillan, 1941 edn).

Weigley, R. F., *History of the United States Army* (London: Batsford, 1968).

——, *The American Way of War* (Bloomington: Indiana University Press, paperback edn, 1977).

——, *Eisenhower's Lieutenants* (London: Sidgwick & Jackson, 1981).

Weller, J., *Wellington at Waterloo* (London: Longmans, 1968).

Winter, D., *Death's Men* (London: Allen Lane, 1977).

Wynne, G. C., *If Germany Attacks* (London: Faber & Faber, 1940).
Zuckerman, Lord, *Scientists and War* (London: Hamish Hamilton, 1966).
——, *From Apes to Warlords* (London: Hamish Hamilton, 1978).

Articles

Barnett, C., 'The Impact of Surprise and Initiative in War', RUSI *Journal*, 129 (1984).
Beuchler, J., '"Give 'em the Bayonet" – A Note on Civil War Mythology', *Civil War History*, VII (1961).
Bond, B., 'Outsiders' Influence on British Defence Policy in the 1930s', RUSI *Journal*, 127 (1982).
French, D., '"Official But Not History": Sir James Edmonds and the Official History of the Great War', RUSI *Journal*, 131 (1986).
Hagerman, E., 'From Jomini to Dennis Hart Mahan', *Civil War History*, XII (1967).
Luvaas, J., 'Napoleon on the Art of Command', *Parameters*, XV (1985).
Murray, W., 'The German Response to Victory in Poland', *Armed Forces and Society*, XII (1981).
Reid, B. H., 'A Survey of the Militia in 18th Century America', *The Army Quarterly and Defence Journal*, CX (1980).
——, 'The Civil War Between the Services', *Military History*, January 1984.
——, and White J., '"A Mob of Stragglers and Cowards": Desertion from the Union and Confederate Armies, 1861–1865', *The Journal of Strategic Studies*, VIII (1985).
Stolfi, R. H. S., 'Equipment for Victory: France in 1940', *History*, 52 (1970).
——, 'Chance in History', *History*, 65 (1981).
Travers, T. H. E., 'The Offensive and the Problem of Innovation in British Military Thought, 1870–1915', *Journal of Contemporary History*, 13 (1978).
——, 'Technology, Tactics and Morale', *Journal of Modern History*, 51 (1979).
——, 'The Hidden Army: Structural Problems in the British Officer Corps', *Journal of Contemporary History*, 17 (1982).

Index